Sandra Wot.
5753

S0-BFD-291

THE TEACHINGS OF
MAIMONIDES

THE TEACHINGS OF
MAIMONIDES

JACOB S. MINKIN

Introduction by
ARTHUR HERTZBERG

JASON ARONSON INC.
Northvale, New Jersey
London

First Jason Aronson Inc. Softcover Edition – 1993

Copyright © 1987 by Jason Aronson Inc.

Copyright © 1957 by Thomas Yoseloff, Inc.

10 9 8 7 6 5 4 3 2 1

All rights reserved. Printed in the United States of America. No part of this book may be used or reproduced in any manner whatsoever without written permission from Jason Aronson Inc. except in the case of brief quotations in reviews for inclusion in a magazine, newspaper, or broadcast.

Introduction by Arthur Hertzberg reprinted with permission from *The New York Review of Books*. Copyright © 1986 by Nyrev, Inc.

ISBN 0-87668-953-5 (hb)
ISBN 1-56821-039-6 (pb)

Library of Congress Catalog Number 87-70737

Manufactured in the United States of America. Jason Aronson Inc. offers books and cassettes. For information and catalog write to Jason Aronson Inc., 230 Livingston Street, Northvale, New Jersey 07647.

INTRODUCTION

THE HEADQUARTERS of UNESCO in Paris was an improbable place at which to celebrate, in mid-December of 1985, the eight-hundred-fiftieth anniversary of the birth of Maimonides. The United States had formally withdrawn from UNESCO the year before, after charging the organization with being a center of anti-Western propaganda, of support for "guided democracy," and, especially, of a "third world"-style controlled press. Just a few days before the Maimonides conference was to convene, Great Britain had announced its decision to withdraw from UNESCO, for reasons almost identical to those given by the Americans. Both governments had attacked Amadou Mahtar M'Bow, the director general of UNESCO, for his third world proclivities and extravagant budgets. Several people in Paris suggested to me that he might be helped by the appearance of fairness and reasonableness that this conference would give him.

It did not turn out that way. The staff of UNESCO was on strike against the director general that week. It sat downstairs in the lobby, in protest against personnel cuts that M'Bow had announced to compensate for the revenue, one fourth of the total, that was lost with the departure of the United States. It seemed clear that M'Bow's politics were seen to be the enemy of much of the UNESCO bureaucracy, of their jobs and of their programs. No late nod to the Jews could now make a difference to his survival, especially since it was being whispered in the corridors that the Russians had abandoned him.

The idea for the conference on Maimonides had come from the World Jewish Congress in 1983. This international Jewish group did not back away, even

i

after the Americans and British departed from UNESCO, largely because the Israelis had chosen to support the conference despite their own grievances against the organization for repeatedly condemning Israel's archeological efforts in Jerusalem as attacks on Islam. The Maimonides anniversary would serve to reduce Israel's isolation, and turn attention at UNESCO to a Jewish topic for the first time in at least a decade. A strange assortment of countries, none of which had normal relations with Israel, were cosponsors of the conference: Pakistan, India, Cuba, Spain, and the Soviet Union. (Spain and Israel later announced, in January 1986, their intention to exchange ambassadors.) The scholars who came to the meeting were an even more surprising assortment. They came from Algeria, Morocco, Senegal, and Nigeria—as well as from Saudi Arabia, Kuwait, and Iran.

When, European-style, the assembled scholars elected a presidium to conduct the sessions, three of the four vice-presidents were chosen from countries that do not have diplomatic relations with Israel: Souleymane Bachir Diagne, from Senegal; Mohammed Arkoun, a Moroccan who lives in Paris; and Vitaly Naumkin, of the Academy of Sciences of the USSR. The fourth was M. H. Zafrani, a North African Jew who teaches in Paris. The officers were elected quickly by consensus, and no one seemed to have any problem with designating me, an American and a Jew, as president of the body. M'Bow not only gave a reception for the visiting scholars on the first evening of the conference, but he opened the meeting that morning, with a speech summarizing Maimonides' biography which seemed to come straight out of an encyclopedia. This flat performance by a nonscholar nevertheless raised a series of basic issues: Why is Maimonides the only religious figure since the biblical prophets about whom such an international conference could have been convened? Why are there, and have there been, so many diverse, and often clashing, schools of thought claiming sole possession of Maimonides as their true ancestor?

The answer to the first question was given in M'Bow's opening remarks, and was soon echoed by the scholar Vitaly Naumkin of the USSR. Maimonides stood at the confluence of four cultures: Arab, Christian, Greek, and Jewish. More than anyone else, this single mind carried the main intellectual currents of his time.

Moses, the son of Maimon, was born in 1135 in Córdoba, which had been the intellectual center of Muslim Spain for more than two centuries. There were Christians as well as Jews in the city, and they were not sealed off from one another. In this milieu Jews were even writing war poems and drinking songs in Hebrew that were based on Arab models. The young Maimonides preferred philosophy to poetry. He composed his first work, a treatise on logic, when he was perhaps no older than sixteen. The manner of its writing suggested that Maimonides regarded himself as capable of thinking about philosophy as a rationalist among rationalists. It is striking that the young author made not a single reference to a Jewish source.

Maimonides and his family did not live long in Córdoba; they were forced to leave by a fanatical sect of Muslims, the Almohads, who conquered the city in 1148. The next dozen years in Maimonides' life are obscure. We do not know exactly how long the family remained in Córdoba after the arrival of the Almohads, or where they went after they left the city. By 1160, however, when Maimonides was twenty-five, he had arrived in Fez, where he spent the next five years. The family then took to wandering again. After a brief stay in the Holy Land, Maimonides established his permanent residence in Fustat, a suburb of Cairo. For the first eight years he was supported by his brother, David, who traded with India.

When David drowned on one of his voyages, Maimonides had to earn a living. He became a physician in the court of al-Fadhil, the vizier of Egypt under Saladin. Maimonides also served as head of the Jewish community, receiving people at the end of the day when he returned from his medical duties. He also conducted a large correspondence. Questions of law and policy were sent to him from throughout the Jewish world, but most especially from Arabic-speaking Jews; he almost invariably replied, sometimes at length, and with an overt passion that was absent from his more formal writing. We know the details of his daily schedule from a letter that he wrote to Samuel ibn-Tibbon, the translator of the *Guide of the Perplexed* from Arabic to Hebrew. Ibn-Tibbon wanted to visit him in Egypt; Maimonides was discouraging because he was afraid that his excessively crowded days would allow no time for any intellectual encounter.

Most of Maimonides' literary work was devoted to Jewish law. He had been bred to the subject because his father was a *dayyan*, a Jewish religious judge, who saw to it that his son learned the whole of rabbinic literature. Maimonides turned his genius in this subject first to an interpretation of the Mishnah, which is the core text of the Talmud. The six volumes of the Mishnah are a code of Jewish law based on thousands of rabbinic interpretations of the Bible, and other rabbinic traditions. It was composed in the second century in Palestine by Rabbi Judah, "the Prince," who was then the acknowledged head of Jewry. During the next nine centuries, in Babylonia and Palestine, the Mishnah was studied and interpreted by scholars who often disagreed among themselves. The discussions that took place in the major Jewish centers during the earlier three centuries were recorded in two collections, the Babylonian Talmud and the Palestinian Talmud. For the next six centuries scholars and religious judges studied these enormous commentaries, especially the Babylonian Talmud, and added to them.

By the time of Maimonides, this legal corpus had grown so large that only scholars could find their way through its labyrinths. The original meaning of the core text, the Mishnah, had thus been obscured by generations of interpretation. Maimonides wrote his commentary on the Mishnah in Arabic, and he consciously tried to recover the meaning as it was intended by Rabbi Judah.

Maimonides' interpretations for the most part tended to follow the explanations of the Mishnah that were recorded in the Babylonian Talmud. Occasionally he infuriated the traditionalists by interpreting passages of the Mishnah by his own lights, independent of earlier authorities. Thus, one of his first comments on the Tractate Sanhedrin, which deals with the judiciary, boldly contradicted what was written in the Babylonian Talmud. It was held there that an "expert," who was authorized to sit as the sole judge in civil cases, was to be defined as someone whom the public had accepted or who had been authorized to act as judge by the exilarch, the lay head of Babylonian Jewry. Maimonides is emphatic in insisting that such an "expert" could exist only if he were ordained in the Holy Land by a Jewish religious court.

This dissent from the Babylonian Talmud's interpretation of the Mishnah was part of a continuing quarrel that Maimonides had with the lay and rabbinic leaders of Babylonian Jewry. He refused to accept their authority. Even though Maimonides had remained only briefly in the land of Israel, the ordained religious leaders in the Holy Land were the only people who, in his view, had any claim to ultimate authority in Judaism. Maimonides did not doubt for a moment that his own reason, and his own learning, were superior to what could be gleaned from the religious rulings of the Babylonians, the rabbis (they were called *geonim*) of his day and of the recent past.

The commentary on the Mishnah foreshadowed Maimonides' majestic summation and reworking of all rabbinic literature in the book which he boldly called *Mishneh Torah*. (I think that this title is best translated as "The Teachings of the Tradition"), thus inviting comparison to the second-century Mishnah itself. In this long work, Maimonides codified all of Jewish law in fourteen major sections, each with many subsections. He announced his purpose in the introduction: he intended a book that laymen could consult; it would no longer be necessary for anyone, except the occasional scholar, to study rabbinic literature, or to have recourse to the scholarly keepers of its mysteries. Maimonides opened his code not with ritual or civil rules but with a statement of what theological doctrines Jews must believe. He was particularly insistent that God was incorporeal and that all biblical references to Him as a person were concessions to human speech. This assertion enraged his literalist critics. Many of them were even angrier that one man, even though one of acknowledged genius, was setting himself up as the supreme arbiter of Jewish law.

The *Mishneh Torah* was the only major book that Maimonides wrote in Hebrew. It was, and remains, in addition to its legal importance, a classic composition in the sacred language. Nonetheless, this most Jewish and rabbinic of Maimonides' works was not so self-contained as it appeared. It owed a deep debt to Islamic models. Islam, like Judaism, is a religion of commandment and of law. In the earliest centuries after the Koran was composed precepts and decisions in every aspect of human life, from religious ritual to political conduct, were derived from its text, or from authoritative accounts of the life of the Prophet. During the ninth century two major collections of such traditions — called *hadith* — were published by the Islamic scholars al-Bukhari and al-Hajjaj (called "Muslim"). Such codes continued to be composed for the next three centuries and some were produced during Maimonides' lifetime. These works contained not only rules about ritual, and civil and political conduct; they also set down, firmly, what a Muslim had to believe. Maimonides' approach to codifying Jewish law was thus in keeping with the "spirit of the age." Even though he nowhere mentions any of the Muslim codifiers, the structure and organization of the *Mishneh Torah* showed that Maimonides was more than aware of Islamic models.

Indeed, one of the greatest Arabists of this century, Franz Rosenthal, insisted that aside from Maimonides' comments in the opening section of the *Mishneh Torah* on relations with non-Jews, the rest of the introductory "Book of Knowledge" was a "summary in miniature" of the supreme philosophical-legal work of his older Muslim contemporary al-Ghazzali, the Ihya'. Rosenthal writes that "Maimonides possessed an original and extremely fertile mind" and that "he did not have to have recourse to any conscious imitation of any model. However, it is obvious that his 'Book of Knowledge,' occurring as it does at the beginning of the *Law Code*, owes its title, its being, and its place to the attitude of Muslim civilization toward 'knowledge.'"[1]

Maimonides was also the supreme theologian of medieval Jewry. In his theological work he was much more openly influenced by philosophical work that was current in Islam. His magnum opus, *The Guide of the Perplexed*, which he completed in Egypt in 1200, was an attempt to reconcile reason and revelation. It was cast in the form of an address to Joseph ibn Aknin, his favorite student and disciple. Ibn Aknin was representative of many Jews who had difficulty, especially, with the anthropomorphisms in the Bible, for their conception of God had been fashioned in the Aristotelian philosophical tradition. Maimonides boldly explained away all the anthropomorphic passages extraneous to the central religious meaning of the Bible.

Maimonides' fundamental observation about theology, both in the *Mishneh Torah* and *The Guide of the Perplexed*, is that, contrary to Aristotle, the world has not always existed; it was created by God. So he begins his code with the assertion that "the basic principle of all basic principles and the pillar of all sciences is to realize that there is a First Being who brought every existing thing into being." Since God created the world, He is totally other from all His creations: "His real essence is unlike that of any of them." Therefore, Maimonides asserts again and again in the many passages in both his major works devoted to anthropomorphism, all anthropomorphic expressions

> are adapted to the mental capacity of the majority of mankind who have a physical perception of bodies only. The Torah speaks in the language of men. All these phrases are metaphorical, like the sentence "If I whet my glittering sword" (Deut. 32:41). Has God then a sword and does He slay with a sword? The term is used allegorically, and all these phrases are to be understood in a similar sense . . . . But God's essence as it really is, the human mind does not understand and is incapable of grasping or investigating."
> [This passage, too, is from his code; the *Mishneh Torah*, the "Book of Knowledge."]

Maimonides repeated in *The Guide of the Perplexed* what he had ruled earlier in his legal works, that he who believed in the plain text of the Bible held false doctrine.

---

[1]Franz Rosenthal, *Knowledge Triumphant* (Leiden: E. J. Brill, 1970), p. 96.

The Guide of the Perplexed was written in Arabic, but it was soon translated into Hebrew and widely disseminated throughout the Jewish world. It created an immediate and continuing storm in Europe, where philosophical speculation barely existed among Jews. Some European rabbis refused to believe that the great Talmudist, Maimonides, could have written so heretical a book; they insisted that *The Guide of the Perplexed* was a forgery. Others, especially after Maimonides' death, simply excommunicated the book; they distinguished between Maimonides the Talmudist, whom the Orthodox revered, and Maimonides the philosopher, whom they abhorred.

There was reason for their fury, even though Maimonides was not the first Jew to attempt to harmonize revelation with reason. Maimonides hardly refers to any of his Jewish predecessors, not even to a very famous scholar, Saadya, who had written a book in Arabic entitled *Faith and Reason* two and a half centuries earlier. For Maimonides the important philosophers were a group of Arab interpreters of Aristotle, and especially al-Farabi, who died less than three decades before the birth of Maimonides. Al-Farabit had taught that reason was superior to revelation and that the true teachings of divine revelation could be reached, and thus confirmed, by philosophical speculation. At least on the surface of the texts in *The Guide of the Perplexed*, Maimonides refused to go that far; he insisted that revelation was superior to reason and that revelation taught truths which God had left mysterious, their reasons unknowable, to be accepted on faith.

Whether Maimonides really meant this, or whether he wrote cryptograms beneath the surface of his text to suggest to the close reader that he was, like al-Farabi, more philosopher than believer, has been the subject of argument from his day to the present. That controversy has been the subject, in the past year, of a series of exchanges in *The New York Review*. In a review of the work of Leo Strauss, M. F. Burnyeat (May 30, 1985) reminded us that Strauss argued repeatedly that Maimonides is the lineal ancestor of Spinoza's philosophical universalism, and that this was the "hidden teaching" of his work. Against this view a distinguished Conservative rabbi, Robert Gordis, has insisted that Maimonides was a rationalist rabbi, and that his life's work was devoted to proving that there is no contradiction between faith and reason. The notion that there is only one Maimonides, who is preeminently a rabbi, has been argued in recent books by Isadore Twersky of Harvard, and by David Hartman of the Hebrew University in Jerusalem, both of whom are Orthodox rabbis of the "enlightened" kind.

A passage in Gordis's second letter to *The New York Review* (April 24, 1986) speaks for their viewpoint:

> *He was not a closet philosopher for whom self-expression was the ultimate goal. Maimonides was an active leader of the Jewish community, deeply involved in their problems and concerns. He was strongly committed to propagating the truth as he saw it, even among the broad sectors of the people.*

Gordis argues that there is no hidden meaning to *The Guide of the Perplexed*. Maimonides' statements in the introduction that the contradictions in his text were intended to lead the attentive reader to meanings that were not immediately apparent were, according to Gordis, mere pedagogical devices. To this Burnyeat has most recently replied that Maimonides, beyond any reasonable doubt, indicated, to those capable of understanding his intentions, that his text had an esoteric meaning; the only question that can be argued, in Burnyeat's view, is what the nature of that meaning is.

Burnyeat is not a specialist on Maimonides (nor for that matter is Gordis, who is mainly a Bible scholar) but his view is similar to that of Shlomo Pines, professor emeritus at the Hebrew University, the author of the most important contemporary translation of *The Guide of the Perplexed*, to which, not incidentally, Leo Strauss wrote a brilliant introduction. Pines was the star at the conference in Paris. His presence gave the meeting an intellectual and political distinction that it would not otherwise have had.

In his lecture to the conference, Pines repeated his view that Maimonides' philosophical theology worked on at least two levels of meaning. One striking example of his point was that Maimonides explicitly insisted that the doctrine of the resurrection of the dead is a central religious dogma; nonetheless, in the text of *The Guide of the Perplexed*, he dissented from one of his Arab sources, the philosopher Avicenna, and agreed with ibn Bajja, the founder of Aristotelean philosophy in Spain, that "not even the soul remains after death" (*Guide*, Part I, chapter 74). Maimonides was not hesitant to say that the permanent existence of souls "is a thing of which it has been indubitably demonstrated that it is false."

Why then did Maimonides follow the twelfth-century Muslim thinker Averroës—both of them drawing on Aristotle—in requiring all members of a community to hold some religious beliefs in common? Pines argued:

> *Maimonides had very strong convictions concerning the utility and even necessity of an official system of religious beliefs for the preservation of communal obedience to the*

*law. What is more, he lived up to his convictions by formulating in his commentary on
the Mishnah the thirteen principal dogmas of Judaism.*

In the very next sentence, however, Pines wrote that "many of these dogmas
ran counter to philosophical truth."[2] Pines made it clear that in saying this he
was not putting forward his own analytical judgment but stating something
he believed Maimonides knew very well. The drift of Pines's argument is to
make the link between Maimonides the philosopher and Maimonides the supreme codifier of the law, a matter not of faith but of politics: Maimonides, in
Pines's view, felt compelled to insist on beliefs and practices that kept the Jewish community alive as a discrete entity, even as he "knew" that men were divided only by their specific histories – and thus that Jewish religious practices
were not the ultimate content of revelation.

I doubt that such assertions about Maimonides led themselves to proof either
way. They have a familiar ring to someone like myself who spent his earliest
years in scholarship attempting to understand the development of modern Zionist thought. The supreme admirer of Maimonides among Zionist ideo-
logues was Ahad ha-Am, a turn-of-the-century Russian Jewish intellectual
who was the founder of "cultural Zionism." Even as he followed Darwin and
Spencer in becoming an agnostic – and thus asserted that there was no special
religious revelation to the Jews – Ahad ha-Am insisted with great passion on
the uniqueness of Jewish historical experience and on the need for it to continue in the form of cultural nationalism. For Ahad ha-Am, religious practices were not ultimately a problem of the belief in revelation; they were a tool
of national survival. In the modern era, religious observances could and had
to be replaced by the Zionist emphasis on land and language.

Shlomo Pines has depicted a Maimonides who saw Jewishness as an affirmation of community and who argued passionately that Judaism, as a faith for
the masses, is superior to its competitors, Christianity and Islam, even though
no particular religion is to be equated with philosophical truth; for such truth
is available to men of intellect, of whatever origin. In entering a wider intellectual world, Maimonides and Ahad ha-Am, seven centuries apart, both sur-
rendered much of their intellectual particularism, and yet remained Jews. I
take this to be the "faith" of the Israeli universities today. They are secular and

---

[2]Moses Maimonides, *The Guide of the Perplexed*, translated with an introduction by Shlomo Pines
(University of Chicago Press, 1963), p. cxviii.

universalist in their scholarship and yet strongly nationalist. Shlomo Pines is a major figure in Israeli intellectual life not only for his superb scholarship but for the ways he has helped to formulate his position.

Rabbinic intellectuals, such as Twersky, Hartman, and Gordis, have a different problem. To be consistent, they need to maintain that university scholarship and the Talmud academy are not incompatible and that, indeed, these two cultures are one. They need an intellectual ancestor who united these two worlds in himself and even "proved" that, correctly understood, there is no tension between them—and so it is not at all surprising that their Maimonides is an uncontradictory figure, a majestic unifier of faith and reason.

Isadore Twersky, who is generally acknowledged to be the premiere authority on Maimonides in the United States, is well aware of the history of Maimonides' other life and work and of the contradictory interpretations of both that have emerged. A "second posthumous Maimonides," Twersky writes, "has been continuously recreated and refashioned in successive generations." Through the ages he has been admired, and sometimes attacked, by a variety of opinions. Fundamentalist Jews have hated him, and some mystics have tried to make this rationalist philosopher into one of their own. Twersky knows that the main problem is whether Maimonides is to be interpreted as "a multifaceted but essentially an harmonious personality" or whether he was "tense and complex," riddled, whether consciously or unconsciously, with paradox and inconsistency." Some pages later in the essay from which I am quoting, Twersky does not hesitate to endorse the first view: Maimonides "wanted to unify mood and medium, to integrate the thought of eternity with the life of temporality, to combine religious tradition with philosophical doctrine." The legalist and the philosopher are one, so Twersky insists, as he "warns against the widespread misleading tendency on the part of students to fragmentize Maimonides' works."[3] These "students" include Leo Strauss and clearly also Schlomo Pines.

---

[3]These quotations are from the preface and introductory essay by Twersky to his *A Maimonides Reader*; see especially page xiv and page 26. It was revealing that later, in 1980, in his magnum opus on Maimonides as a legalist, entitled *Introduction to the Code of Maimonides*, Twersky twice denies that Maimonides was very much influenced by Arabic models. But he also admits (pages 77 and 259) that even Maimonides "was generally aware of the surrounding tendencies" in the Islamic world to write codes of law, and that this could have provided a stimulus for him. It is intriguing that in a long and definitive volume on the *Mishneh Torah*, the subject of Islamic models is dismissed in a few lines, with the assertion, in the second passage, that the subject cannot really be investigated.

Twersky was invited to Paris but was unable to come. His absence was regrettable for, without him, there was no counterweight to the tendency to see Maimonides as a fragmented thinker. As I have said, such views came primarily from Arab scholars, but apart from Pines, who had given a paper about the esoteric meanings in *The Guide of the Perplexed*, the Arabs were joined by one of the Jewish scholars, M.H. Zafrani, who, as I noted above, is a Sephardi who was born in North Africa. Zafrani's Maimonides came very close to being a supreme intellectual within the mode of Arab culture, having followed "the same intellectual itinerary" as the leading Arab philosophers. What divided him from that culture was the "attitude of independence which Judaism preserved, in its contact with Islam, on the fundamental question of religion."

The discussion of Zafrani's paper was the occasion for the most heated debate—it was very nearly an outburst—of the conference. Abderrahmane Badawi, a scholar from Kuwait, had earlier, in his own paper, gone much further than Zafrani. He had discussed a murky period in Maimonides early life. After the fanatical Almohads conquered his native Córdoba in 1148, Maimonides remained in the city for some years. Two medieval Arabic authors asserted that Maimonides, when trapped in Córdoba, had converted to Islam. Jewish scholars have generally denied that this was possible, since, they have argued, Maimonides was never attacked by his opponents for conversion.

Badawi made a reasonable case for the contrary view. He argued that Maimonides could not have survived under the Almohads for even a day without conversion, and that he was not criticized for this by his enemies because such conversion to save your life until you could revert to Judaism was not unusual in those terrible times. During the discussion that followed, Badawi went farther still, arguing that Maimonides' supposed forced conversion was not entirely insincere. Badawi had looked through the text of *The Guide of the Perplexed*, he said, and he had not found a single uncomplimentary reference to Mohammed. At this point Shlomo Pines intervened, with more than a bit of sarcasm, to remind Badawi that there were many dozens of references to "the prophet" and that in every one of them Maimonides had made clear his distaste for the teaching of the Koran.

The dispute became more tense after Zafrani gave his paper. Badawi wanted to claim Maimonides for the Mediterranean world and to take him away from the bellicose Ashkenazim, the Westernized politicians and intellectuals whom he saw as the leaders of contemporary Jewry. The Sephardim, the

Jews who were in the tradition of Maimonides, he argued, had always lived comfortably in Islamic culture; the ferociously particularist Ashkenazim had no right to claim Maimonides for themselves.

Badawi's insistence on the glories of Jewish-Muslim cooperation evoked from Roland Goetschel of Strasbourg University an angry reminder that Maimonides had been persecuted for his faith. I reminded Badawi that his fundamental thesis about the present was wrong. Every analysis of the Jewish world, and especially of Israel, has shown that Sephardim, the Arabic-speaking Jews of today, take a much harder line in their politics than the Ashkenazim. The very Jews whom Badawi liked the least, the Ashkenazi intelligentsia, were the ones who largely made up the moderate political forces in Israel or supported them.

This quarrel was the most vocal of the conference, but it was ultimately less important than the Arab-Jewish discussion provoked by the paper of Hassan Hanafi, a professor of philosophy at Cairo University, now on leave at the United Nations University in Tokyo. Hanafi has an excellent, and deserved, reputation as a leading exponent in contemporary Islam of the reconciliation between faith and reason. His doctoral dissertation for a French university was an attempt to reinterpret orthodox principles of Islamic jurisprudence in the terminology of modern Western philosophy. At the very beginning of his career, Hanafi has undertaken to show how a believing Muslim could live in some balance with twentieth-century intellectual developments. He could be seen as the contemporary equivalent in Islam of the enlightened traditionalism that Twersky, Hartman, and Gordis argue for in modern Judaism. Like them, he supported those who see no contradiction between Maimonides the believer and Maimonides the philosopher.

As it drew to a close, his learned paper reached a political conclusion. Hanafi had argued, convincingly, that as philosophers, medieval Muslims, Jews, and Christians shared the same philosophical premises, which ultimately derived from Aristotle. Without any further discussion of political and social issues in the twelfth century, Hanafi asserted:

> *Mankind can be unified through universalism not ethnocentrism, sectarianism, parochialism, and chauvinism. Universalism, longtime-defended by the prophets since Noah, Abraham, and Moses, reaffirmed by Christ in the name of the new covenant and realized in Islam, in the Andalusian model of Spain, is a permanent virtue in a Pal-*

estinian model in which Jews, Christians, and Muslims can live again and under its protection.

For the first time, I suspect, the "posthumous Maimonides" was enlisted as an ancestor of the Palestinian National Covenant.

Hanafi was, of course, challenged. A state of Palestine that would supersede Israel based on a Muslim majority, with the promise of fairness for Jews and Christians, is an impossible fantasy. It could come about only at the end of some horrible, probably nuclear, war, which would leave few Arabs, Jews, and Christians to create such a Palestine. Still, in spite of the politics of this paragraph, there was something fundamentally hopeful in Hanafi's tone, and in his general approach. Hanafi told a number of us later that he was giving a seminar in contemporary Islam at the United Nations University in Tokyo, and that he would be eager to have one of the Jewish scholars join him in discussions on the relationship between Judaism and Islam.

Another hopeful moment was the report by Vitaly Naumkin on the study of Maimonides in the Soviet Union. It was somewhat startling to hear that Igor Medvedev, an associate in the Institute of Oriental Studies of the Academy of Sciences in Russia, was working on a translation into Russian of parts of Maimonides' legal code, and that he was giving considerable attention to the rabbinic commentaries on this work, and even to the sources of Maimonides in the seldom-studied Talmud of Jerusalem. Still, this news had to be interpreted with some caution. Even during Stalin's murderous persecution of Yiddish culture during the 1950s, several scholars of classic Jewish texts, and even of modern Hebrew, continued to work in major libraries, and especially in the library in Leningrad, which houses the great Guinzberg collection of Jewish books and manuscripts.

The most unexpected participant among those who spoke during the conference was Huseyin Atay, a Turk by nationality, who is a professor at the University of Petroleum and Minerals in Dahram, Saudi Arabia. Of all the Arab states, the Saudis have been among the most careful through the years to avoid all contact with Israel and with Judaism. Atay's presence suggested that something had changed. Atay is the editor of a critical edition of the Arabic text of *The Guide of the Perplexed*. In his remarks he took issue with Pines's translation of the *Guide* into English on a number of specific points. Pines answered in detail—and the result was a learned discussion about the meaning of medieval Arabic philosophical terms conducted by two scholars whose countries have remained at war since 1948.

The least likely of all the participants was Professor Pourjawadi, of the department of philosophy of the University of Teheran. Pourjawadi said not a word in the public discussion, and he read no paper, but he did not miss a single minute of the sessions. Pourjawadi is reputed to be a senior advisor of the Iranian government. Nonetheless, he had come, and he could not help but take back with him the dominant mood of the conference: elation that such a meeting had taken place and that the discussions had, on the whole, been so civil.

As I have reread the papers and thought back on the discussions, I have found myself, if anything, a bit further away from the historical Maimonides than closer to him. I left Paris with the feeling, which has only deepened afterward, that Maimonides would have been amused by the sight of an intellectual victory over the Islamic fanatics who had chased him out of his native land in Córdoba and over the Jewish fundamentalists who had so often excommunicated him. Indeed, I suspect that my own reactions to the conference have something to do with my own life as a Jew who grew up in the Hitler era and whose religious commitments are not those of the ultra-Orthodox. Distinguishing between what we learn from Maimonides as he would have wanted us to learn from him, and what we make of him because that is what we want to hear, remains an insoluble problem. So it is with the Bible, and with all other great texts. Polite but intense intellectual conflicts took place in Paris, but, even as some of us were inventing some new Maimonides for ourselves, we were united by a reverence for the texts and for the man who wrote them, mainly in Arabic, at a high point in the history of the relations between Islamic and Hebrew cultures.

ARTHUR HERTZBERG

PREFACE

Moses maimonides is one of the most widely written about Jewish scholars in the world. His was by far the most comprehensive mind the Jews produced, in fame and influence, unconditioned by space and time. He is one of the few Jewish men of learning whose spiritual physiognomy is well marked among men outside his own race and faith. A representative Jewish scholar and an authoritative expounder of Judaism, he was also one of the advanced spirits of his time. The keenest minds in Western Europe paid him the tribute of their admiration. They were great devotees of his teachings, and their works abound in references to *Rabi Moyses Judaeus*.

A prolific and brilliant writer himself, the literature inspired by the Cordova-Fostat Sage is rich in volume and content and is written in almost all the cultured languages of the world. He wrote most of his works in the Arabic language, the idiom of his time and country, but an early Latin translation from the Hebrew version of *The Guide for the Perplexed* spread his fame throughout the non-Jewish European world. And as to *Mishneh Torah*, his great rabbinic Code, Alexander Marx wrote of a bibliography of Hebrew commentaries, compiled by Adolf Jellinek, numbering no fewer than 220 entries. That was in 1893, sixty-four years ago; since that time many more volumes have been added to the list.

The passing years have not lessened the interest nor marred the influence of Moses Maimonides. Serenely, his high and gentle spirit

5

walks the earth across the centuries with thousands eager to pay him the tribute of their love and admiration.

The octocentennial of his birth and the 750th anniversary of his death were observed by the Jews of the world with the devotion and dignity befitting his commanding figure. In Israel a Maimonides Year was proclaimed on the anniversary of his death, and wherever Jews lived it served as an occasion for contemplating his life and disseminating his teachings.

England was a fertile field of the modern Maimonides revival. The signal was given in 1881 by Michael Friedländer's English translation of *The Guide for the Perplexed* from the original Arabic. Since then, culminating in the Maimonides Anniversary, any number of learned tomes, popular biographies, scholarly monographs, and commemorative volumes appeared, covering almost every phase of Maimonides' philosophical, theological, juridical, scientific, and literary activity.

The Jews of the United States have more than kept pace with their English coreligionists in their dedication to the "Great Eagle" and the dissemination of his teachings. Besides impressive cultural meetings, the Maimonides Anniversary was marked by the more enduring tribute of a number of literary and scientific contributions not unworthy of the great Sage and Teacher.

This volume is the result and outgrowth of a long-time dedication to the work and personality of the man almost universally regarded as the greatest of Jews since Bible times. On the occasion of the 750th anniversary of Maimonides' death, this writer published a number of articles. They were intended, as well as one could in a popular publication, to present the general features of the life and work of the man who, loved and admired by his contemporaries, continues to cast the light of his genius upon our time. These articles are greatly amplified, gaps filled, new material introduced, and, wherever possible, Maimonides is made to speak for himself.

Based on scattered passages throughout his writings, the reader will find in the second part of the book a carefully arranged selection of Maimonides' religious, philosophical, and ethical teachings. Since this book is primarily designed for the general reader rather than for the specialized scholar, technical discussions, which only too often obscure rather than clarify a subject, were purposely omitted. Students who wish to pursue the subject further will find ample material in the accompanying Bibliography.

In a time when "to the making of books there is no end," especially on so appealing a subject as Moses Maimonides, it is almost impossible to remember and acknowledge one's indebtedness to every book and scrap of material which were helpful in the composition of this volume. Named or unnamed, the writer's gratitude goes out to them all in unbounded measure. The author is particularly thankful to the editors, translators, and publishers of Maimonides' several works for their gracious permission to use their material. Special mention must be made of books and authors who were of invaluable service in the composition of the present volume. They are: *The Guide for the Perplexed* (English), by M. Friedländer; *Sefer ha-Madda* (English), by Moses Hyamson; *The Code of Maimonides* (Yale Judaica Series); *A Treasury of Jewish Letters,* edited by Franz Kobler; *A History of Medieval Jewish Philosophy,* by Isaac Husik. *Kobez,* occurring frequently in the notes, refers to *Kobez Teshubot ha-Rambam* (Leipzig, 1859).

It is a pleasure to record the writer's deep-felt gratitude to the libraries of the Jewish Theological Seminary of America and the Hebrew Union College-Jewish Institute of Religion and their staffs for their never-failing courtesy and patience.

Due acknowledgment for the care and devotion she bestowed on the making of this book must be made to my dear wife. Without her interest and encouragement at every step the task would have been much more difficult and taxing than it was. Patiently she read and re-read the proofsheets, made corrections, suggested changes, and supervised the final form of the book. Let this be a modest tribute to her labor of love.

JACOB S. MINKIN

CONTENTS

1. YEARS OF WANDERING

IN THE HISTORY of civilization, there are men whose importance increases with the flight of time; their influence is revealed more clearly with the passing centuries. There are few men in Jewish history of whom this may be maintained with greater truth than of Moses Maimonides, familiar in learned Jewish circles as the *Rambam* —the anagrammatic abbreviation of Moses ben Maimon.

To thousands of Jews he is the "Great Eagle," the incomparable sage and master of Jewish learning whose works they study, whose thoughts they ponder, and with whose Thirteen Articles of Faith they conclude their morning devotions. Indeed, so great is their love and reverence for this twelfth-century sage and teacher that he is the only man in history whose birth and death are to this day commemorated throughout the Jewish world as national anniversaries.

Maimonides was the last—and the foremost—figure of the "Golden Age" of Jewish learning in Spain. His was the most comprehensive mind of medieval Jewry; he was, after the masters of the Talmud, the greatest Jewish personality to emerge. He reached the loftiest heights possible for his time and, indeed, for centuries after his time. He strove to build up the spiritual ramparts of Judaism so as to make them impervious to attack. Almost singlehanded, he brought about a revival of Jewish learning and culture at a time when they seemed to be dying. Jews have paid no greater tribute to any man than they did to Moses ben Maimon when they compared him to Moses ben Amram, "The man of God."

His literary activity was incredible, his range of scholarship ency-

13

clopedic. He was the most prolific of Jewish writers. He explored
almost all knowledge and mastered nearly every science known to
his age. He gave to the world not one *magnum opus* but several. His
scholarship encompassed the Bible and the Talmud, mathematics,
astronomy, jurisprudence, ethics, philosophy, and medicine; and in
everything to which he gave his mind he attained outstanding results.
He intruded himself into posterity. Today, more than seven hundred
and fifty years after his death, his achievements in Jewish thought
and learning are still a vital force in the scholarly life of thousands
of Jews.

His appeal is universal. The only Jewish scholar whose prestige
and influence extend far beyond the confines of his own people,
Christian and Moslem theologians recognized—and disputed with—
him. It is impossible to read the works of the medieval schoolmen
without finding approval or disagreement with Maimonides' teachings dominating their pages. He had the merit—a merit he shared
with the greatest of his age—of imposing his convictions. He fought
against resistance; he battled against ignorance, bigotry, and superstition. The kindest and most humble of men, his personality was
combative and aggressive. He excited violent animosity; he was the
victim of calumny and misrepresentation, but there was a quality in
him which could not be ignored or set aside. He never suffered final
defeat.

Although he is among the most contemporary of Jewish scholars,
much of his philosophy is outdated. His theology was bitterly fought
against during his own lifetime. The perplexities which the "Doctor
Perplexorum" had set out to resolve have since been increased and
multiplied by perplexities he could not have foreseen. But the ideal
for which he stood and the challenge which rings forth from his
pages are still alive and new. He believed in science and education,
in freedom of thought and utterance, in the acquisition of correct
ideas and ideals rather than the acquisition of wealth and the material
things of life. He was tolerant in an age that was seething with intolerance. He set a good part of the Jewish world ablaze against him
by holding a pagan philosopher a little lower than the Prophets. A
deeply pious Jew who believed in the divine origin of the Torah and
carried out punctiliously all its laws and precepts, he was nevertheless tolerant of other faiths, and he recognized Christianity and
Mohammedanism as stepping-stones to the true worship of God.

It was Mohammedan Spain, the only land of freedom the Jews knew in the nearly thousand years of their dispersion, which made the genius of Moses Maimonides possible. There is nothing in history so strange and striking as the contrast between Christian Europe and Mohammedan Spain in the treatment of their Jews. "By their very religion," writes Milton Steinberg (1903–1950), "Moslems were enjoined to intolerance. Nonetheless, as a general rule, the Mohammedans treated the Jews with liberality, generosity and tolerance. In the Christian world, on the other hand, conduct was inferior to theory. The very heart and essence of Christian doctrine was ostensibly love and tolerance. In practice, however, no Christian love was wasted on Jews." [1]

When there was oppression and persecution of Jews in Christian Europe, forcing them to hide from the light of day, there was a gleam of light and freedom for their coreligionists on the Iberian Peninsula. While, during the Crusades, the armored Knights of the Cross spread death and devastation in the Jewish communities of the countries through which they passed, Jews were safe under the sign of the Crescent. They were not only safe in life and possessions but were given the opportunity to live their own lives and develop a culture so unique and striking that it went down in history as the "Golden Age."

The Moors, the Mohammedan conquerors of Spain in 711, were not religious fanatics. They were too young to be intolerant and too busy and ambitious to be bigoted. They were strong in their faith but generous with regard to the religious convictions of others. Their hearts were set on conquest and not on conversion. When, therefore, the Jews and Moors had met on the banks of the Guadalquivir, they met as friends and not as enemies. The Moors had long since forgotten their old grievance against the Jews. They forgot the Prophet's chagrin that, in the early days of his ministry, the Jews had rejected his blandishments, would not accept his faith, and even made fun of his revelations. What the Moors remembered was that the Jews and Arabs were racial cousins that, through Ishmael, they traced their origin back to the common ancestry of Abraham. The Moors were flattered by the kinship, and they showed their appreciation by a friendly relationship with the Jews which lasted for nearly five hundred years.

The Jews were said to have assisted the Moors in their invasion and conquest of Spain. The charge has not been substantiated; but if they did, who could blame them? The Visigoths had oppressed and persecuted the Jews, the Moors freed them; the former bound them mind and body, the latter struck off their shackles so that they could breathe again. The Visigoth Bishop of Cordova forbade Christian intercourse with Jews on pain of excommunication, the Moors invited them as welcome partners in the work of civilization. With the Moslem conquest of Spain, the country turned over a new leaf. The intellectual blight of centuries was gone, and a fresh start was made in the pursuits of the spirit which were long banned under Visigoth domination.

The Moors had not only come, seen, and conquered, but they laid the foundation for a civilization which was unique and striking for its rapid strides in the arts and sciences. Out of that civilization, at the height of its splendor in the ninth and tenth centuries, sprang up a culture which more than rivaled the best born in Europe under Christian rule. The Renaissance of Art in Italy, says George A. Dorsey,[2] has blinded us to the Renaissance of Science in Spain, which fostered science, promoted culture, encouraged learning, and set a premium on intellectual pursuits, no matter whether the intellect was Moslem, Christian, or Jew. Not since the days of Greece had the world known such thirst for knowledge, such passion for learning, such craving for the higher things of the spirit shared by prince and courtier alike.

The Jews more than kept pace with the liberating forces of Moorish civilization. With amazing speed, they recovered from the centuries of serfdom which the Visigoth rulers had imposed upon them and became the harbingers of a culture which has not lost its savor; indeed, to which we pay homage to this day. The flickering light of Jewish learning and culture which sputtered in Christian Europe and was near extinction burned brightly in Mohammedan Spain. With an eagerness and swiftness typical of the Jewish genius, they paid their tribute to their new-found freedom by engaging energetically and enthusiastically in the social, economic, and political development of the country without, at the same time, neglecting the more enduring values of the spirit. The arts were cultivated, the sciences were studied, philosophy had its devotees, and statecraft, not fostered by Jews for close to a thousand years, was actively practiced by them. Samuel Ibn Nagdela (993–1055) was part-time scholar and part-time statesman. When, as Prime Minister of Granada, he was not busy guiding the affairs of the State, he was writing Hebrew poetry and delivering lectures on the Talmud. Hasdai Ibn Shaprut (915–990), Minister to 'Abd el-Rahman, was both a brilliant diplomat who carried out important diplomatic missions for his royal master and one of the most accomplished linguists of his time, with a thorough command of the Hebrew, Arabic, Greek, and Latin languages.

Cordova, Granada, Toledo, Seville, Lucena evoke historic recollections in the Jewish mind of the poets, scholars, philosophers, and scientists who lived and labored there and cast over them an aura of splendor and greatness which time has not dispelled. Unlike their brethren of other lands and later times, the alien influence had not affected the inner substance of the Spanish Jews. They spoke and wrote in the language of the Koran, but Judaism remained at the core of their being. They knew they were the favored sons of destiny, and they bore their responsibility in a historic manner. The rigid, binding, and unrelenting ties of the Talmud were not relaxed but the scholars widened and deepened its study by their philosophical and philological researches. The Hebrew language, which had been all but dead for centuries or had survived as an archaic relic of the past, with little left of its former grace and beauty, was revived in the ecstatic lines of Solomon Ibn Gabirol (1021–1058), in the matchless poetry of R. Judah Halevi (1085–1140), and in the melancholy verses of Moses Ibn Ezra (1070–1138) to mention but a few.

A tense, almost feverish, intellectual and spiritual activity took hold of the Jews of Islamic Spain, as though they sensed that their day was short. They packed into a little more than two hundred years religious and cultural achievements which, ordinarily, might have taken many more centuries. They tackled tasks, they mastered fields of knowledge which, because of the depression of the other Jewries in the world, were left undone by them. Thanks to the intensive study, energy, and devotion, and the benevolent rule of the enlightened Caliphs, the Jews of Moslem Spain soon came to occupy a position of Jewish cultural leadership which was formerly held by the Babylonian academies of Sura and Pumpedita. What was wanted, what was indeed the crying need of the time, was the emergence of a man of superb moral and intellectual genius who could synthesize the varied intellectual and spiritual activities of his people into one integrated whole and give them enduring, authoritative expression.

17

That such a man—one who towered far above his contemporaries and the generations which preceded him—emerged in the person of Moses Maimonides was one of the greatest events in Spanish Jewish history and at the same time an event which marked the opening of a great era in the exile-life of the Jewish people.

It was in such atmosphere of learning and culture that Moses Maimonides was born in Cordova at one o'clock in the afternoon on the eve of Passover 4895, corresponding to March 30, 1135. His is the only instance of a Jewish scholar whose exact day and hour of birth was faithfully recorded, signifying the importance history attached to the event. He hailed from a long line of distinguished rabbis and scholars who traced their ancestry back through Rabbi Judah the Patriarch (135–220), compiler of the Mishnah, to the royal house of King David. At the conclusion of his *Mishnah Commentary*, Maimonides describes himself as "Moses, son of Maimon the *dayyan*, son of Rabbi Joseph the Sage, son of Isaac the *dayyan*, son of Joseph the *dayyan*, son of Obadiah the *dayyan*, son of Solomon, son of Obadiah *the dayyan*." His father, a member of the rabbinical college of Cordova, was a thoroughly cultured man, well versed in the sources of Judaism and in the sciences and literature of the Mohammedans.

We know practically nothing of the mother who gave birth to this man. Whereas Maimonides occasionally refers to his father, he never mentions the woman who brought him into life. But legend has it that his father was commanded in a dream to marry the daughter of a butcher. He obeyed the command, and from that union Moses was born. This fable probably is to be taken no more seriously than the report that the father of Saadiah Gaon (882–942) was successively or simultaneously a butcher, a barber, a leech, and a muezzin, a Moslem priest who calls the faithful to prayer.[3]

Probably equally legendary is the story, reported by some of his biographers, that in his childhood Maimonides showed little taste for study, and that the disappointed father packed "the butcher boy" off to Rabbi Joseph Ibn Migash (1077–1141), hoping that his conduct would improve under his influence. This, however, is highly improbable, for the works produced by him in his early manhood show that their author could not possibly have spent his youth in idleness.

Maimonides was endowed from his youth with great energy, remarkable talents, and an unusual receptive mental faculty. His mind matured early under the tutelage of his father, who instructed him in the Bible and Talmud, and the tuition of Arabic scholars who initiated him in what branches of secular learning they knew. Diligence and native genius united in the youthful student, so that at a young age he was already recognized as a scholar prepared for his future learned career.

Not much is known of Maimonides' childhood, if he had a childhood in the ordinary sense of the word. It is not likely that, in view of the time in which he lived and the rigid discipline he imposed on himself, he had much time for the joys and freedom which go with normal childhood. Yet his childhood cannot have been a joyless one, and his mind could not have been over-freighted by his encyclopedic education. He was a precocious child who learned easily and forgot little, probably not an exception among the gifted children of his age. Did not Solomon Ibn Gabirol, Maimonides' predecessor by more than a hundred years, sing: "Though I am but sixteen, I have the wisdom of a man of eighty?"

Although more is known about the life of Moses Maimonides than about many another medieval Jewish scholar, we are in complete ignorance of his early scientific training beyond that already indicated. And this is unfortunate, for we are concerned with a new era in the history of Jewish scholarship, and we should like to know the steps in the mental development of the man who was responsible for inaugurating the new epoch. The best that can be assumed, is that the Bible and the Talmud formed the basis of Maimonides' early education, but that these, in conformity with the spirit and outlook of his time, were regarded by him not as an end in themselves but as part of the spiritual whole he set out to acquire. As though conscious of his mission, his overpowering thirst for knowledge led him to explore every field and master every science.

Those were happy years for young Moses Maimonides. He knew that he was born to be a scholar and he wished for nothing better. To prepare himself for the task, to be worthy and deserving of it, became his sole and highest ambition. Providentially, Cordova supplied him with every opportunity he needed for his career. In Cordova, Moorish civilization reached the height of its brilliance. Gleaming cupolas, gilded minarets, magnificent squares and parks made the city one of the most splendid capitals in Europe, if not in the world. But what gave the city her greatest distinction, was her open spirit and intellectual atmosphere. The Marovides were the political masters of Andalusia, and they loved learning and cultivated the arts and sciences. Cordova was a city of schools and libraries, a focus of Jewish and general learning to which students streamed from many parts of Europe in order to sit at the feet of famous masters.

Soon, however, the night descended upon "the choicest pearl" of the western Arabian empire, and the darkness that fell over her set at nought all the dreams and hopes the Jews placed on this, their hoped-for center of Judaism. The solitary gleam of light the Jews enjoyed in a world of almost universal darkness was snuffed out, and with it went the peace and serenity the young scholar had needed for the maturing of his genius and the working out of his destiny. It was a cruel awakening and a sharp disappointment which he later phrased in pathetic, painful words. At the age of thirteen, he witnessed what he never thought he would experience—the destruction of his native city and the ruin of its Jewish population.

The blow came from the Almohades, a fanatical Mohammedan tribe in North Africa which, rigorous in its belief, branded the slightest deviation from the Koranic rule as heresy. The Almohades had no use for education, no taste for culture, no feeling for poetry, and they shunned the philosophical involvements of their Moorish brethren. Abdallah Ibn Tumart, a frustrated fanatic with mystical tendencies, raised the new sect to power and violence by attacking the luxurious life of the Andalusians and demanding a return to simplicity of the Moslem life and creed. He found willing followers among the barbarous tribes of the Atlas range, who flocked to him and proclaimed him a *Mahdi,* or reincarnation of the Prophet. It was a tragic day for the pride and banner of the Arab empire when the eyes of the power-drunk Almohades turned on Andalusia.

When Cordova fell in 1148, the civilizing work of centuries, in which Jews and Moors had cooperated, came to an abrupt end. Her cultured life was destroyed, her high noon turned to darkness; Jews and Christians, no less than Moslems, were wrapped in mourning. There was no limit to the destructive frenzy of the conquerors. The Crusades had taught them the fallacy of showing clemency to the Jews, who suffered irretrievable losses. The beautiful Cordova synagogue, built with the piety, devotion, and the refined taste of the Andalusian Jews, was destroyed, and an end was put to the historic labors of Hasdai Ibn Shaprut and Samuel ha-Nagid. Those who had not fled before the marauding hordes were offered the alternative of apostasy or exile. Many Jews chose exile; many others, loath to leave their native land and the burial places of their ancestors, paid lip-service to the Mohammedan formula of conversion while in their hearts and in the privacy of their homes they carried out the religious precepts of their inherited faith. Maimon and his family belonged to the more conscientious of the Cordova Jews and, scorning the sub-terfuges of the double life they would have to live, left their home and possessions and went into exile.

They endured the hardships of their bitter exile as best they could. For ten years they lived a life of roving nomads, wandering in southern Spain from place to place in the hope that conditions would change and they could return to their native land. Young Moses was made to experience his people's historic homeless lot. Together with some other exile Jews, the Maimons stayed for a while in Port Al-meira, a Christian Spanish state, where they were magnanimously welcomed and were allowed to rest from their weary march. But their respite was brief, for soon Port Almeira, too, fell to the Almo-hades' conquering sword, and once again the refugees had to move on.

There is no historical record as to what happened to the Maimon family during the years of their exile. Their fortune, if they had one, was gone, their property was confiscated; they could carry nothing away with them but their courage and their indomitable faith in God. What little material sustenance they needed to keep them alive they eked out of the small jewelry trade which was carried on by the head of the family and his younger son, David. Moses, who had little talent for business, was allowed to follow his scholarly pursuits and to devote himself to his books. Unfortunately, these were too few, and he must have looked back longingly to the great library which lined the walls of his father's study in Cordova, all of which had been left behind in their hasty flight. Luckily, however, the young scholar was endowed with such a memory that, having read a book once, he retained its contents without the loss of a word or thought. "Unlike many other people," Maimonides wrote in later years to a friend, "I never suffered in my youth from forgetfulness."

It was a precarious existence in which Moses Maimonides spent his youth, but his experience did not embitter him. It even broadened and deepened his range of thought and vision. He came to realize his people's unique position—a homeless people in a seemingly bound-less world. He was driven by the desire to build up his people's inner shrines, to widen their spiritual frontiers—and that not by invent-ing fresh talmudic subtleties or new delicate points of their religious life. His thoughts moved on a higher plane. His mind was set on channeling his intellectual activity in an entirely different direction.

He early realized that the influences of the Jewish-Arabic culture in which he was brought up were by no means universal in every respect, that while the culture produced many great men and ex-traordinary activity in almost every sphere of Jewish cultural life, the great masses of Jews were steeped in ignorance and overburdened with superstition. Without higher knowledge and correct ideas, they discharged their religious requirements in a perfunctory mechanical manner, unconscious of their inner spiritual meaning. They were ignorant of the Bible, which they could no longer read in the lan-guage in which it was written, and there was even greater innocence of the traditional sources of Judaism on the part of the so-called professionally learned Jews. He remembered the statement of Rabbi Joseph Ibn Migash, his father's and his own early teacher, that most of the *dayyanim* were so little versed in rabbinic literature that they could hardly comprehend a simple talmudic passage.

On the other hand, the Jewish intellectuals who knew their religion and were acquainted with its literature regarded Judaism as an an-tiquated creed to which they paid formal respect but did not really take to their hearts. The Greco-Arabic philosophy, which was the fashion of the day, had a decided attraction for them; they knew lit-tle and cared little how much of it was alien and even dangerous to the spirit and teachings of their ancient faith. They lived in an at-mosphere, says Josef Kastein, in which the spirit was no longer sup-pressed and muzzled but free, and it began to feel its wings. The period fostered science and rational thought and was impatient of unenlightened dogmatic creeds. Maimonides was in sympathy with this spirit, "and he wished his people to enjoy its advantages without suffering any loss of faith, or rather with their faith confirmed and strengthened." [4] It was to this purpose that, while still in his adoles-cent years, Maimonides' future lifework stood clearly mapped out in his mind. He was to teach and expound Judaism—the whole of Judaism, biblical and talmudic, its laws and precepts, its rites and

22

ceremonials, so that the people might realize their value and be guided by its light.

He began his literary career, as was the convention of Jewish scholars of the time, by writing commentaries on the Talmud. The Talmud, the most authoritative source of Judaism, second only to the Bible and in some cases even superseding it, had no sooner appeared, in about 500 A.D., than, because of its difficulty of style and content, it became the subject of almost endless commentaries. Maimonides had barely emerged from his childhood when he composed commentaries on several tractates of the Babylonian Talmud as well as a book on the laws of the Palestinian Talmud which, although he occasionally refers to them in his writings, had been lost. At the age variously given as sixteen and twenty-three, he showed his proficiency in astronomy and philosophy by writing two short treatises, *Ma'mar ha-Ibbur,* on the Jewish calendar, and *Millot Higgayon,* on logic, both probably composed in Arabic, the latter translated into Hebrew with a commentary by Moses Mendelssohn (1729–1786).

When, laden with years and weary of his nomadic life, Maimon took his two sons and daughter and sailed for the Maghreb, "the Land of the West," he took the most inexplicable step in his family's dramatic life. There was a settlement of Jews in Morocco dating back to great antiquity (legend has it since the days of King Solomon), and they resembled the native population in language, dress, and customs. They saw Romans, Christians, and Mohammedans overrun and dominate the country. After the dissolution of the Jewish State in the year 70 A.D., Jews had already inhabited a considerable part of Mauritania—later known as Morocco—and engaged in agriculture, cattle-raising and trade. When, under Christian rule, the Jews were persecuted, they pretended never to have heard of Jesus of Nazareth and could not therefore be held guilty of the crime imputed to their ancestors.

Under Islamic control the Jews were well treated, and, as in Spain, they rose to high positions. Talmudic schools and a high degree of cultural activity made Morocco one of the flourishing Jewish communities in the Moslem world. Isaac Alfassi (1013–1103), who in later years emigrated to Spain, was one of the celebrities of North African Jewry. But when the Maimons took flight to Fez, the sky had darkened over Morocco, and under the fanatical Almohades, the Jews went through a period of considerable suffering Neither Jew nor

Christian was tolerated. Synagogues were destroyed, churches were razed to the ground, exile or conversion to the dominant faith of the country was decreed against both the followers of Judaism or Christianity.

In these circumstances, the flight of the Maimon family to Fez, the capital of Morocco, is one of the unresolved mysteries of history. The Almohades were the masters of both Spain and Morocco, and for Jews strong in their faith changing one insecure abode for the other was like turning willingly to destruction. Castile was a Christian country friendly to Jews, and the Maimon family, had they chosen, might have found there an amicable reception, as did other refugees from the Almohade persecution.

Conjectures were made by scholars to account for the strange and unexplained motive of the Maimons in choosing Fez for their place of refuge, the most unlikely being that, not regarding Mohammedanism as an idolatrous religion, they made some slight concession to the Islamic faith on entering the bigotry-infested Moroccan capital. The charge "is refuted," says Israel Friedlaender (1877–1922), a profound student of Maimonides, "by the mere consideration that in the extremely vehement polemics which broke out after his death and centered around his person, none of his opponents ever made mention of his alleged conversion, which would surely have proved an effective weapon in the hands of his enemies to discredit his lifework." [5]

The five years (1160–1165) Moses Maimonides spent in Fez were years of comparative peace and security. He relaxed from the hardships of his long odyssey, resumed his studies, and took time out of his work to cultivate the friendship of Jewish and Mohammedan scholars. He found in Judah ha-Kohen Ibn Shoshan, who, because of his long residence in Morocco, was not molested, a man of learning and saintly character, like himself deeply interested in the scientific study of rabbinic literature. And among the Moslem literati he met with a high regard for the pursuit of culture and enlightenment. Young and a stranger in the city though Maimonides was, they readily recognized his extraordinary talents and admitted him into their company.

Did the Moslem scholars suspect that the gifted young man with the long name—'Imran Musa Ibn Abd Allah—who was walking in their midst and whose wit and wisdom they admired, was a Jew and, according to the tenets of their faith, an unbeliever? It did not seem

24

to matter much whether they did or not, for in the intellectual brotherhood to which they belonged race and religion did not count provided one proved his mettle in the battle of wits.

It was, however, out of keeping with the high character and moral responsibility of Moses Maimonides that he should enjoy the freedom and security of his exceptional position as a scholar while thousands of his brethren were exposed to the insufferable lot of oppression and persecution. Like his namesake before him, Moses the son of Maimon "went out to his brethren" and what he saw made a shocking impression on his fine and sensitive mind. He felt at every turn the tragedy and hopeless condition of his people. What in his childhood he experienced in Spain, he saw repeated on a still larger and more cruel scale in Morocco. A fresh wave of religious fanaticism broke out which threatened the destruction of the African Jewish communities and the dissolution of Judaism. Judaism had to hide from the light of day, its laws and precepts practiced in secret, its adherents facing expulsion and even martyrdom. As in Spain, only the strongest-minded could continue long under the mask of the religion that was forced on them while inwardly remaining Jews. Many others, gradually becoming accustomed to the situation, yielded to the oppressor and forswore their religion.

It was in the overwhelming despair which overtook the Jews of North Africa that Maimon ben Joseph, the father of the philosopher (who deserves a much larger niche in the story of his famous son than was accorded him), wrote in 1160 his *Letter of Consolation* "to one of his brethren that it might serve as a source of consolation for himself, and of delight for many souls which were perplexed on account of the sorrows of captivity." The *Letter* was particularly appropriate to the condition in which his afflicted coreligionists lived. It was both an exhortation and a magnificent vision of Israel's future which the writer held up before his heavy-laden people, all the more encouraging since it came from so high an authority as the erstwhile *dayyan* of Cordova.

To those who feared that God had abandoned them, Maimon wrote:

Know, then, that it is clearly and distinctly laid down in the writings of the Prophets and the comments of the Rabbis that God is true, that the messages He has sent us are true, and that which generation after generation

25

*has handed down to us is true. In these there is no doubt, no flaw, no decep-
tion. God does not desire a thing and then contemn it; He does not favor
and then reject. It is only man from whom the knowledge of the future is
hidden, who desires a thing and then, when something happens which he did
not anticipate, scorns it. But how can He, whose knowledge of every event
precedes its happening, and who brings to pass every event in accordance
with His will, how can He wish a thing and then hate it? How can He distinguish a people and then reject them? . . . It is necessary that we should
rely upon God, and believe in Him, and not doubt His promises, just as we
do not doubt His existence. Nor should we fear that He will cast us off
when He has promised that He will draw us near unto Him. Nor should
the prosperity of the nations terrify us. . . . And in spite of their victory
over us, and their rage against us, and our subjection to them, and the re-
newal of our calamities we confide in God and put our faith in His promises. . . .*

Maimon exhorted the victims of persecution to lay hold of the cord
of the Law and not loosen their hand from it:

*For one in captivity is like one who is drowning. We are almost totally im-
mersed. . . . The waters are overwhelming us, but the cord of the ordinances
of God and His Law is suspended from heaven to earth, and whoever lays
hold of it, has hope. . . . But he who loosens his hand from the cord has no
union with God . . . and he dies. And according to the manner of his taking hold of the cord is his relief from the fear of drowning. He who clings
to it with all his hand has certainly more hope than he who clings to it with
but part of it; and he who clings to it with but the tips of his fingers has
more hope than he who lets it go altogether. So none are saved from the
toils of captivity except by occupying themselves with the Law and its commentaries, by obeying it, and cleaving to it, and by meditating thereon day
and night, in accordance with the words of David, "Unless Thy Law had
been my delight, I should then have perished in my affliction" [Ps. 119:92].*

Skilfully he wove into his *Letter* the emotional elements of Judaism. "And sentiment," say Yellin-Abrahams, "is perhaps the best
guide for an individual in such a case of conscience as presented itself
to the Jews of his day." [6] He urged the people to pray, in the Arabic
language if the Hebrew tongue was not familiar to them,

*. . . because prayer is permissible in any language. . . . And he who does not
know the whole prayer, should pray the abridged one at the appointed time,*

and not remain without prayer altogether, for those who do not join the practice of prayer and those who separate themselves from religion altogether are alike.

He enjoined his brethren not to be discouraged by the events of the passing hour, and he drew a masterly picture of the ideal religious Jew.

One who is devout [he said], does not set too much store by the events of this world. If all goes well with him, he is not elated, and if things do not go well with him, he is not depressed, for he is without understanding who desires this world with a desire which draws him away from God. . . . But he who is prudent looks to his Master, and strives by means of union with God to be happy, cleaving to God, being contented in this world with little when it is difficult to attain much, nay, being contented with a mere trifle.

Maimon concluded his *Letter of Consolation* with "The Prayer of Moses, the man of God" (Ps. 90) which, with deep feeling and exquisite fancy; he interpreted in terms of contemporary conditions. Carried away by an impassioned outburst, the writer cried out:

. . . when misfortunes overtake us, and there is no king to order our affairs, and no adviser to guide us, and no place of safety whither we can flee, and no army wherewith we may be protected, and no power even to speak, when we are deprived of every resource . . . and when every refuge is cut off and all our hopes are frustrated, there is no escape but to Thee. We call and Thou assistest, we cry and Thou answerest, for Thou art our refuge, as it is said, "O Lord, Thou hast been our refuge. . . ." [7]

Before the *Letter of Consolation* had time to accomplish its full healing effect, the Jewish communities of North Africa were stirred by an epistle by an unnamed writer who categorically declared that any man of the Jewish faith who so much as pronounced the Moslem confession, even without believing it in his heart, or entered a Mohammedan place of worship, even if he did not pray, could no longer be regarded as a Jew and a member of the Jewish community, although he privately carried out all the religious behests of the Torah. The pronouncement was in direct opposition to Maimon's *Letter of Consolation,* and it spread panic and consternation among the pseudo-Mohammedan Jews. Many of them, who were unequal

27

to the martyrdom demanded of them by the anonymous zealot but held on to their inherited religion with the "tips of their fingers," were ready to go over to the dominant religion altogether since, according to the writer, they could not hope for forgiveness and salvation. It was a crisis in Judaism and a crisis in the lives of thousands of Jews whose lacerated hearts were deprived of the last glimmer of hope to which they clung.

Moses Maimonides was but twenty-five years old when the issue was raised and his authority was not yet universally established, but, sensing the danger and realizing his responsibility, he wrote in Arabic his famous *Ma'amar Kiddush ha-Shem*, also known under the title *Iggeret ha-Shemad (Letter Concerning Apostasy)*.[8] The letters of father and son are as different from each other as were the writers. Whereas one appealed to history and sentiment, the other applied the basic principles of Judaism; Maimon soothed and comforted, holding up before the distraught people the certainty of the divine promises and their fulfilment; Maimonides met the adversary on his own ground and confounded him with authorities he dared not dispute.

The *Letter Concerning Apostasy* is one of the greatest documents in the epistolary literature of the Jews, and it shows Maimonides in all the qualities of his personality. Caustic, belligerent, argumentative, he was full of tenderness and compassion toward the wronged. Indeed, the *Letter* foreshadows the future "Eagle" in the learning, courage, and sagacity the writer displayed.

He [(the anonymous rabbi) Maimonides wrote] does not distinguish between those who sin under compulsion and those who do so from sheer wickedness. Such harsh judgment is untenable. It contradicts Scripture and the testimonies of the past. The Children of Israel before they left Egypt, with the exception of the tribe of Levi, were submerged in sin. And yet Moses himself was punished because he suspected the faithlessness of the people.[9] Elijah was blamed by the Lord because he inveighed against the apostasy of Israel.[10] In the days of Isaiah, many people became idolaters and evil-doers who despised God and religion, but Isaiah's accusation was atoned for only by his death at the hand of Manasseh.[11] If Israel's great men have been punished thus because they maligned Israel, how can an ordinary man dare to assail whole communities and their scholars? They have not strayed from the Law because of their evil passion, but because they were threatened by swords and blows, while they in their heart revere God and keep his ordinances.

It is erroneous to maintain that he who has entered a mosque without praying there, and later went home and prayed to God, would not find his prayer answered. Eglon, king of Moab, who oppressed the Israelites, was rewarded that his descendant Solomon [by his daughter Ruth] "sat on the throne of the Lord" because when Ehud said to him, "I have a message from God," he arose from his throne.[12] Of Ahab, king of Israel, who had denied God and worshiped idols but afterwards fasted and prayed to God, the Talmud says that his prayers were accepted and God had mercy upon him.[13] Even Nebuchadnezzar, who was guilty of the slaughter of number-less Jews and the destruction of the Temple, was allowed to reign as long as King Solomon because he honored the Lord on one occasion.[14]

With regard to the transgression of the Law under duress, Maimonides appealed to precedent and cited the example of Rabbi Meir and Rabbi Eleazar,[15] both great masters of the Talmud who, in a persecution, had saved their lives by feigning heathenism.

Whoever [he wrote], has yielded to coercion instead of suffering death has acted badly, but no punishment has been imposed upon such deed, and no Jewish court can intervene against him. [He then clinched his argument]: The present persecution differs from previous experiences. In former cases, Israelites have been called upon to transgress the Law in action. Now we are asked not to render active homage to heathenism but only to recite an empty formula which the Moslems themselves knew we utter insincerely in order to circumvent the bigot. . . . Indeed, any Jew who, after uttering the Moslem formula, wishes to observe the whole 613 precepts in the privacy of his home, may do so without hindrance. Nevertheless, if, even under these circumstances, a Jew surrenders his life for the sanctification of the name of God before men, he has done nobly and well, and his reward is great before the Lord. But if a man asks me, "Shall I be slain or utter the formula of Islam?" I answer, "Utter the formula and live. . . ." [He advised, however, that] we should go forth from these places, and go to a place where we can fulfil the Law without compulsion and without fear, and that we should even forsake our homes and our children, and all possessions. Divine Torah means more for the prudent than all ephemeral possessions; these will vanish, but she will remain.

While the *Letter* was a brilliant success among the guilt-conscious pseudo-Mohammedan Jews and saved many from renouncing their faith completely, it was quite natural that it did not advance Maimonides' popularity in the land of rabid religious fanaticism. The epistle, which was written in Arabic so that all Jews might read it, could not be kept a secret, and when its contents became known to the authorities, Maimonides was a marked man. Had he stayed on, he might not have fared any better than his friend and colleague Ibn Shoshan, who was attacked and hacked to death in the course of an aroused religious frenzy. Suspicion had already fallen on the writer of the *Letter* and it would have gone ill with him if it were not for a friend, a distinguished Moslem poet and theologian, who suggested to him that he leave the city before it was too late.

In the darkness of the night of April 18, 1165, Moses Maimonides and his family secretly slipped out of their home and boarded a waiting vessel bound for the Holy Land.

Their passage was long and perilously eventful. For six days their sailing was smooth and pleasant. The sea was kind and benevolent after what they had experienced on land. But on the seventh day a storm arose which made the frail boat reel from side to side, threatening at any moment to be swallowed up by the huge black waves. Dark clouds hid the sun from view, while all the time the ship was tossed high in the air like a rubber ball. The Maimons lay huddled in their cabin-hole without food and drink and not speaking a word, except words of prayer. Maimonides vowed that, if spared, he would spend every anniversary day of the storm in solitary contemplation as a fast day and offer charitable donations to the poor. All his life Moses Maimonides remained fearful of the sea and, when more than thirty years later, Samuel Ibn Tibbon (1150–1230) made plans to visit him on matters connected with his translation of *The Guide for the Perplexed*, Maimonides, with the suffering he experienced fresh in his mind, dissuaded him.

On Sunday night, the third of Sivan, Maimonides and his family, after a month's voyage, arrived safe and happy at Acco, the principal Palestine port, and he vowed to set aside the day of his arrival as an annual family holiday to be celebrated with distribution of gifts to the poor. "We left Acco on the fourth day of Marheshvan and reached Jerusalem after a perilous journey," Maimonides entered in his notebook. "I spent the entire day, as well as the following two days, praying at the remains [the Wailing Wall] of the ancient Temple. On Sunday, the ninth of Marheshvan, I left Jerusalem for Hebron, where I prayed at the graves of the Patriarchs in the cave of Macpelah. These three days, the sixth, seventh, and ninth of Marheshvan, I appointed as festivals for me and mine, which should be passed in prayer and feasting. May God help me and bring to fulfillment in me the words of the Psalmist, 'My vows I will pay unto the Lord.' " (66:13).

He found Palestine a waste and desolate land, without schools and scholars, without an intellectual environment or spiritual companionship on which one could rely to relax and sustain one's mind. What Jews there were in the country were few and scattered, most of them petty traders and workingmen. "What am I to say to you with regard to the country? Great is the solitude and great the waste, and to characterize it in short, the more sacred the places, the greater the desolation! Jerusalem is more desolate than the rest of the country; Judea more than Galilee. . . . There are no Jews. For, since the arrival of the Tartars, some fled, others died by the sword." [16] This letter on the condition of the Jews in the Holy Land was written to his son by Moses ben Nahman (1194–1270), famous Spanish scholar, mystic, and Bible commentator, in 1267, just about one hundred years after Maimonides' visit to the country. One may safely assume the country's still greater desolation at the time of Maimonides, when the Second Crusade was fought in Palestine with such savage fury and violence.

For the third time, then, in his comparatively young existence—he was thirty years old—Moses Maimonides found himself without a home and fixed station in life. His odyssey had led him through many places, but nowhere had he found a secure abode where he could continue the work which was stirring in his mind. He escaped forcible conversion in Spain; he evaded death by martyrdom in Fez, and Palestine, the land of his fondest dreams and hopes, he found bitterly disappointing. It was one of the most crucial moments in Moses Maimonides' life, and it depressed and discouraged him. His soul rebelled against making his home in the country whose soil was reeking with the blood of the slain of his people, and he knew of no other land where he might safely take up his abode. A wave of extreme religious fanaticism held sway over the world. In Christian countries the Jews lived on the brink of complete extermination, and in Mohammedan lands Judaism had to hide from the light of day and its adherents walk under the mask of a hypocritically adopted faith.

Egypt, strange to say, the land of painful memories, was the only oasis in the almost universal desert of religious bigotry and fanaticism. Under the mild and benevolent rule of the Fatimid dynasty, Jews were

31

not only tolerated but were accorded complete freedom to develop their own religious and cultural life. Rights and privileges Jews had not enjoyed in other countries of the world were granted them in the land of their old-time suffering. Their lives were safe, their possessions secure, their religious rites and customs were protected, and the Jews developed a community life that was rather rare in those days. They had their schools and scholars, and a *Nagid,* the Grand Signior of the Jews, who represented them at the court. It was indeed a striking contrast to what Maimonides knew of the relation of other Moslem countries to their Jews. It was destined that the country which knew its first Moses should become the home of the second Moses who, like his great namesake, was to lead his people from spiritual darkness to the light of the divine spirit.

2. VICISSITUDES AND TRIUMPHS

THE COLLAPSE of Jewish civilization in Spain contributed to the growth and development of the Jewish cultural center in Egypt. When, after his experience in Spain and Morocco, Moses Maimonides looked to the country of the Nile for a domicile, he carried with him the torch of Jewish learning and scholarship which for thousands of years had been of the most absorbing concern and interest to Jews.

The continuity of Jewish life in Egypt is one of the most remarkable features of Jewish history. All through history there was hardly a time when Jews and Egypt had not known each other. The ancient land of the Pharaohs boasted the oldest Jewish settlement in the world except Palestine. On the banks of the Nile stood the cradle of the Jewish nation. There its ancestors had slaved and suffered and built Pithom and Ramases. But there Moses was born, and the first round in Israel's struggle for independence was fought and won.

The Exodus from Egypt was not the last time the country had seen the Hebrews, and, according to the record, the Exodus was not universal. There were laggards and cowards who remained behind, and the Bible tells of men who found the "flesh pots" of Egypt more alluring than the years of wandering in the wilderness and slunk back to their old chains and servitude. There was commercial and political intercourse between Israel and Egypt almost all through early Jewish history. Notwithstanding the ancient vow never to return to the land of their first suffering, whenever there was hunger or distress in the kingdoms of Judah and Israel, the granary of the ancient world lay too conveniently close not to take advantage of its plenty and security.

Moses Maimonides overruled the Rabbis of the Talmud and reversed his own decision that "it is permitted to settle everywhere except in Egypt"[1] when he left Palestine for the peace and security he envisioned in the land of the Fatimids. He found in Egypt a widespread and solidly established Jewish community in all the principal cities of the country with nothing to disturb them in their religious and cultural life. The Fatimid dynasty, claiming direct descent from Fatima, the Prophet's favorite daughter, were enlightened and tolerant rulers, and they left the people in their dominion unmolested in the exercise of their religious rites and cultural aspirations.

There were a number of prominent and influential Jews in Fatimid Egypt who served their rulers as bankers, tax-farmers, courtiers, and physicians and often, because of their knowledge of languages, as diplomatic agents. As compared with their brethren in other countries, the Jews of the Nile Valley felt themselves free in almost every respect, even to the extent of enjoying a certain kind of autonomous government of their own. In their internal affairs they were ruled by a Nagid (Prince), who also represented them before the government, whose official Arabic title was *Rais al-Yahud*, Head of the Jews, counterpart of the Babylonian Exilarch. "The custom has been," writes Jacob Mann "that the Rais should be of the Rabbinic community to the exclusion of the other communities, though he sat in judgment over all the three sections, Rabbanite, Karaite, and Samaritan."[2] The Nagid would relegate some of his powers to lower or subordinate dignitaries, such as the *Roshe ha-Kahal*, community heads, whose authority, however, was more local than national.

It was, therefore, not a chaotic or disorganized community of Jews that Maimonides found when he arrived and settled in Egypt, but a well-knit and cohesive Jewry, knowing and responsive to its own needs and generous in meeting the needs of their less fortunate brethren in other lands. It was also a hospitable community of Jews which welcomed visitors with lavish hand and heart. When, not many years before Maimonides, Judah Halevi, the great Hebrew poet, had tarried for a while in a number of Jewish communities in Egypt on his way to the Holy Land, he was received with the utmost cordiality and friendship. Gratitude moved him to dedicate to his hosts some of his finest verses.

Alexandria, the city in which Maimonides settled with his family upon their arrival in Egypt, was in olden times as much the capital of Jews as was Jerusalem their religious and national capital. Alexandria was a city of a great historic past which at one time bade fair to rival the fame and glory which belonged to the Judean capital. The Jews kept pace with Alexandria's fluctuating fortunes, sharing through the centuries in all her trials and vicissitudes. Whether under Ptolemy, Roman, or Arab rule, the Jews formed an integral and at one time an important part of the city's population. The country's proximity to Palestine gave the Jews of Alexandria the advantage of sharing in her religious and cultural life. The Jews of Alexandria were generous in their support of Palestine's academies of learning and, in exchange, visitors from the Holy Land helped to keep their struggling light of Judaism alive by teaching and instructing them.

But it was a faint and fading light, without any strength and sustenance of its own; it had to be coaxed into life by outside hands. Despite their prosperity and numbers—Alexandria had a standing Jewish population of three thousand Jewish families—the Jews of the Nile Delta had not succeeded in developing schools and scholars but looked abroad for their cultural stimulation. Their masses were ignorant, their rabbis without real learning, their men of affairs without the mental and spiritual vision of Jewish leaders in other Islamic lands. Silly superstitions supplanted the knowledge of the Jewish religion, and borrowed Samaritan and Karaitic customs usurped the authentic teachings of Judaism. Indeed, it was, a far cry from what Maimonides remembered of the religious and cultural activity of his native Spain, her scholars, poets, and philosophers. Jewish literature and scholarship were little enriched by the politically undisturbed life of the Jews under the Fatimid dynasty. Time and again a Jewish scholar from a foreign country, who fought superstition and dispelled ignorance, would be attracted to the opulent shores of Alexandria, but at his death or departure there were few hands to carry on his work.

The reason for Maimonides' short stay in Alexandria—probably less than two years—and his decision to make his home in Fostat, the old Arabic capital of Egypt, has not been fully explained. Alexandria was one of the greatest cosmopolitan centers of the Fatimid empire, with a teeming population of Moslems, Jews, and Christians. Ships carrying the wealth of nations weighed anchor at her harbor. She was also a city famous for her schools and libraries and men of scientific attainments. The Fatimid rulers were liberal and generous monarchs who encouraged learning and were devoted to the sciences. Indeed, their more conservative brethren of the faith branded them heretics. They were indiscriminate in their favors, and there were high-placed Jews at their courts.

If, in their talmudic learning the Jews of Alexandria had not reached a high level, they were keenly alive to their less fortunate coreligionists' needs and neglected no opportunity of serving them. Among the treasures of the *Genizah* which Solomon Schechter brought to light are fragments of documents which testify to the public-spiritedness of the Alexandrian Jewish community. But Maimonides had his own personal reason for his change of domicile. He refused a public position, which the Jews of Alexandria would gladly have offered him. He disdained to derive material advantage from his knowledge of the Torah, and preferred to subsist on his small income from the family's business in precious stones, in which he owned a share. It would seem that Maimonides envisaged Fostat, a city in close proximity to Cairo with her royal court and nobility, as offering the more likely opportunities for the business in which he and his family were interested than did Alexandria.

Maimonides had not had time to relax from the weariness of his wandering years when, on coming to Fostat (described by him as "two Sabbath days' journey from Cairo"), he was confronted with a community of Jews torn by strife, offering him, as he saw it, little time for the work which lay all these years dormant in his mind. Because of the old family quarrel between the traditionalists and the Bible literalists (or, as they came to be known, the Rabbanites and Karaites), in Mohammedan and Christian countries the Jews presented to the world the spectacle of two armed camps, debating, arguing, anathematizing, and hurling at each other biblical and talmudic invectives.

The Babylonian Talmud was not more than 200 years old when rumblings of dissatisfaction with its minute rules and regulations made themselves heard on the part of Jews in the tolerant Mohammedan countries where men were free to live and believe as they chose. But it was not until about the middle of the eighth century that, through one Anan ben David, a learned Jew of high station in Babylonia, the tiny voice of dissent rose to a clamorous demand to get back to the basic truths of the "old-time religion of the Bible" without the interpretation of the Rabbis. The movement spread rapidly, and men, seeing their opportunity of escaping from what they called the taxing laws of the Talmud without at the same time altogether severing their old association with their faith and people, enthusiastically enlisted under its banner. The Rabbis of the time were weak and futile; they knew only the Talmud and could not offer effective opposition to the swelling tide of protest, with the result that, in the briefest time in Jewish history, a new sect, almost a new religion, calling itself Karaism, or the "Religion of the Bible," came into existence with adherents in Palestine, Persia, Syria, Babylon, and Egypt.

The opposition to what the followers of Anan considered the hardships of the talmudic law probably went far beyond what the founder of the movement had originally intended. The changes and innovations that were introduced into the religious life and practices of the Jews had not broadened or liberated Judaism but fettered and fossilized it. The free and flexible spirit of the Torah became frozen and hardened in the hands of the enthusiasts of the new faith. The "yoke" of the Law was not made easier but harder to bear. Rejecting the old interpretation of the Rabbis, they were drinking their own legal brew instead. The Sabbath ceased to be an *oneg,* a joyful day, and became a gloomy and dismal day; no light was permitted on Friday night; no warm food on the Sabbath; prisoner-like, one had to keep himself indoors all day long. Stern and rigorous was the law of the Karaites; feast-days were reduced, the number of fast-days was raised. Drastic changes were made in the synagogue ritual, in the calendar, in the marriage and divorce laws, etc., so that, in course of time, an insuperable wall was raised between the two sections of Jewry. "Thus, for the third time," writes the historian Graetz, "the Jewish race was divided into a battle camp. Like Israel and Judah in the first period, and the Pharisees and Sadducees in the time of the Second Temple, the Rabbanites and Karaites were now in opposition to each other. Jerusalem, the holy mother, which had witnessed so many wars between her children, again became the scene of a fratricidal struggle." [3]

When Moses Maimonides arrived at Fostat, the Rabbanites and Karaites were to all intents and purposes two separate and distinct communities. There was no religious accord between them, no social relations, not even trade or business dealings with each other. There was no intermarriage between members of the two groups; they would not circumcize each other's children; they would not eat at each other's tables; they would not bury each other's dead; there was no community of feeling between them, no sense of belonging, no recognition of the fact that, however fierce their antagonism, they were members of the same race, worshiped the same God, and revered the same Book. The Karaites were extremely active. While the Rabbanites denounced them and preached sermons from the pulpit, the disciples of Anan carried on a vigorous propaganda. They increased rapidly in numbers, wealth, and influence, and it was not long before they rivaled their opponents in the official recognition of the government. The Shiites, branded by the orthodox Moslems as heretics, had naturally a friendly feeling for the Karaites, who were likewise stigmatized by their brethren as unbelievers.

The expansion of Karaism had not added to the creative wealth of the Jewish spirit. It did not come as a natural growth and development of the genius of the Jewish people, but as a forced and arbitrary imposition from without which, if not opposed and checked, might have ended in destroying Judaism. Anan ben David, the founder of the Karaite movement, was neither a philosopher nor endowed with a keen historic sense. He did not reckon with the feelings and emotions of the people, with their deep-rooted religious longings and their centuries-old spiritual sentiments. He created a religion that was dull and stolid without an uplift of heart and soul. He was likewise without a sense of poetry and song, without a feeling for the quickening and inspiring influence of the synagogue hymns and melodies. He deprived worshipers of the spiritual influence which they found in the poetic compositions of the divine service and introduced in their place disconnected selections from the Bible, cold and dry and lifeless in his arrangement.

Healthier and brighter aspects were imputed to the Karaites. Rejecting the authority of the Talmud, they put their emphasis on the Bible. They were credited with having stimulated and disseminated Bible study which, it is maintained, became a fertile subject in their hands. "Search the Bible thoroughly," was Anan ben David's symbol and the slogan of the sect he had founded. But, strange to tell, the living breath of Bible study and its resultant Hebrew revival came not from the Karaites but from Saadia Gaon of Babylon and the Hebrew poets, grammarians, lexicographers, and philologists of Spain who remained loyal to the traditional Jewish faith. By the very essence of its faith and outlook, Karaism came into Jewish life not as a revival but as a retreat; it marked not a moving forward but a turning back. Its so-called return to the source of Judaism was neither orderly nor logical, for, unlike Talmudism, it did not further development but checked it. Wrote Abraham Geiger: "It is a remarkable phenomenon that just those who looked only to the letter and regarded only the Scriptures as their canonical book, who held to it to the exclusion of the later works, that those men yet achieved nothing important in explaining the Scriptures, and stand far behind the Rabbanites." [4]

For reasons suggested above, the Karaites made Egypt their favorite hunting-ground, occupying at times a dominant position in the Jewish communities of the country and displaying a fierce hostility to the Talmudists. In a Responsum, Maimonides expresses his chagrin at the discord and wrangling he found in Fostat among the two factions, the Karaites and Rabbanites: "The House of Israel that bears the name of Jacob and upholds the religion of Moses, our Teacher, must be one united community. Nothing whatever should create dissension. You are wise and understanding people, you must know how serious are the consequences of discord, and to what misfortune it might lead."

As champion of traditional Judaism and exponent of the teachings of the Rabbis, Maimonides could not but be hostile to the Karaite heresy and violently oppose its odious doctrines; but as a man of peace and goodwill, and thinking of the harm disunity would bring to Israel, he pleaded for tolerance toward the Karaites "who spring from the seed of Abraham, obey the Law of Moses, and acknowledge only one God." [5] While on the one hand he castigated the pretensions and arrogance of the Karaites toward their talmudic brethren, he succeeded, on the other hand, in healing their strained relations by his policy of conciliation and friendship. He thus describes in a letter of 1167 his early experience in Fostat and the task to which he had dedicated himself:

In times gone by, when storms raged and threatened us, we wandered from place to place. But, by the mercy of God, we have now been able to find a resting place in this city. Upon our arrival, we noticed to our great dismay that the learned were disunited, that none of them turned his attention on

39

what was going on in the congregation. We, therefore, felt it our duty to
undertake the task of guiding the holy flock, of reconciling the hearts of
the fathers to their children, and of correcting their corrupt ways. The mis-
chief is great, but we succeeded in effecting a cure and, in accordance with
the words of the Prophet: "I will seek the lost one, and that which has been
cast out, I will bring back, and the broken one I will heal."

Maimonides, who was, besides a scholar and a man of letters, an
active and energetic man took a hand in one of stormiest political
episodes of the Jews in Egypt, which for convenience's sake may be
put down as the "Affair Zuta," after the name of the chief villain
of the story. Maimonides had not been long in the country, when the
Jewish community of Egypt was scandalized by one Yahya-Zuta,
who gave himself the high-sounding title of *Sar-Shalom,* "Prince of
Peace," but whom his countrymen, because of his intrigues and dis-
turbing of the peace, called *Shor-Shalom* (a complete ox). Vainglori-
ous and with an itch for power, he denounced Samuel ben Hananya,
a man of learning and noble ancestry and Nagid of the Jews of
Egypt, for alleged irregularities in his office. Zuta had Hananya de-
posed from his position and himself appointed in his place. To complete the humiliation of the Nagid (now in his old age), Yahya even
succeeded in having him jailed on false charges for sixty-six days.
The so-called "Affair Zuta" outraged the Jews of Egypt; finally
public protestations of Samuel's innocence made to the government
resulted in clearing the aged Nagid's name and reinstating him in his
former office. Zuta was defeated in his ambition, although not until
after he served as short-term Nagid. But Maimonides never ceased
fearing the frustrated man's vengeance. It was with Yahya-Zuta in
mind that, in a letter to the Rabbi of Acco, Maimonides confided his
fear of informers against him. Maimonides had good reason for anxiety, for the slightest suspicion that he had not made himself known
as a Jew in Morocco and was now openly living as one in Egypt
would have cost him his freedom, if not his life.

Moses Maimonides was not a salaried official of his congregation and
community. He denounced nothing so severely as the commercializa-
tion of learning. He spoke out sharply and indignantly against ex-
ploiting the Torah for personal gain. Those who do so, he said, bring
shame upon themselves and dishonor to the word of God, which
should be taught free and without material reward. He held up as an

example the "Disciples of the Wise" who disdained to accept remuneration for their public service, but taught out of the purity of their hearts and the saintliness of their lives. The motto was, "Make not of the Torah a crown wherewith to aggrandize thyself, nor a spade wherewith to dig" (Ab: 4, 5).

With few exceptions, all the leading rabbinical authorities were working at some trade or occupation. The great Hillel was a woodcutter, his rival Shammai a carpenter, and among the celebrated Rabbis of aftertimes we find shoemakers, tailors, carpenters, sandlemakers, smiths, potters, builders, weavers, coal-burners, etc., in short, every variety of trade and occupation. Thus it is recorded that one of them was in the habit of discoursing to his students from the top of a cask of his own making, which he carried every day to the academy and that another was actually summoned from his trade of stone-cutting to the High Priestly Office.

We can scarcely wonder that, when some years later Maimonides' friend and favorite pupil, Joseph Ibn Aknin, consulted the master regarding a school of learning he contemplated establishing, Maimonides wrote him: "It is better for you to earn a drachma as wages for the work of a weaver, tailor or carpenter than to be dependent on the stipend of the Exilarch. . . . My opinion is that you should pay full attention to your trade and medical practice and at the same time continue the study of Torah." [6] Unfortunately, the combination of study with honest manual labor—the one to support the other —had not always been equally honored in Israel, and Maimonides was furious against the salaried rabbinical officials. He likewise turned sharply against those who, by erroniously interpreting older sources, "imposed regular dues upon individauls and communities and induced them to believe in their simplicity that it was their duty to support scholars, students, and all those who professionally pursued the career of learning." [7]

Maimonides exemplified in his own life the ideal he preached. What time he could spare from his studies, he devoted without compensation to the community in which he lived and to other Jewish communities. As already referred to, he derived a small income, sufficient for his needs, from the family business in precious stones in which he was a silent partner, and he asked for no more. His younger brother, David, carried on the active affairs of the family while he was left free to devote himself undisturbed to his studies and what duties he felt he owed his community.

A list of Maimonides' activities in almost every phase of Jewish life would seem almost fantastic in view of his prodigious scholarly work. His residence in Fostat had the effect of transforming the comparatively small and unimportant community into a nerve-center of Jewish life. In his mild and gentle manner, he succeeded in winning the trust and confidence of the Karaites and in bringing many of them back to the Jewish fold. He gathered about him a select group of students to whom he lectured on talmudic and philosophical subjects. He had no taste for honorific titles; he was not an officially appointed head of the Jews of his town or country, but the religious and mundane affairs of almost all Jewry were brought to him. He found the divine worship in the synagogue in a disorganized and chaotic condition, and he restored order and decorum. Eminent scholars from many countries turned to him, as the recognized rabbinic authority of his time, for decision in matters affecting the religious and secular life of their communities. The magnitude of his work in this field alone may be judged by the fact that the edition of his four hundred Responsa, or answers to questions that were addressed to him, far from exhausted his contribution to this special branch of rabbinic literature.

He took a hand and, indeed, played a leading part, in one of the most important welfare activities of the time—one to which the Jews of Egypt had devoted themselves unsparingly. It was the rescue of Jewish captives. On the basis of the *Genizah* fragments which Solomon Schechter had brought back with him from Cairo, Jacob Mann pieced together a story of one of the most depressing episodes of Jewish experience in Mohammedan countries. It seems that when piracy flourished, the boats that arrived at Egyptian harbors contained a goodly number of Jewish traders and merchants who were captured at sea. They were robbed of their possessions, were treated cruelly, and, when not quickly ransomed, they were in danger of being sold as slaves. The Cairo-Fostat-Alexandria communities were alive to the situation of their captive coreligionists, and when a boat arrived from Byzantine ports, local Jews never failed to be present to ascertain whether Jews were aboard. What with the number of captives and the high ransom demanded for their release, the burden on the local communities proved too taxing and appeals to share in the *mitzvah* of *pidyon shebuim* (ransom of captives) went out to other communities in the land. Maimonides had not only personally raised money for this purpose in his own country but had sent representatives to neighboring countries asking his coreligionists to emulate the generous example of Egyptian Jewry. Maimonides' original letter, writes Alexander Marx, was discovered by Solomon Schechter in the *Genizah* and is the property of the library of the Jewish Theological Seminary of America.[8]

Unfortunately, Maimonides' zest for work and his unflagging devotion to every manner of communal activity were suddenly interrupted by a succession of tragedies which deprived him of his peace of mind and impaired his never too-robust health. He had not been long installed in his new domicile when his father died. Moses Maimonides had deeply loved his father and was tenderly attached to him. He revered him as a father, and in his Introduction to *Zeraim* he paid tribute to him as his teacher. He mourned his loss, and, learning of his grief, both his Jewish and his Mohammedan friends shared in his sorrow.

Maimonides had hardly recovered from this bereavement when he was struck down by the blow of his brother David's death. It was a catastrophe which left him disconsolate for years; not only was David the youngest member of the family, whose teacher he was and whom he loved affectionately but, as the head of the family business, David was his own, his father's, and his sister's supporter. David was drowned in the Indian Ocean on a business trip, and with him went down what of the family fortune in cash and precious jewels he carried with him. For the philosopher who preached and taught the Sovereignty of Reason, his unrestrained lament over the death of his brother bears remarkable testimony to his deep-seated human feelings and emotions.

After eight years of mourning, Maimonides wrote to Japhet ben Iliahu, *dayyan* of Acco, who befriended him on his arrival in the Holy Land:

In Egypt I met with great and severe misfortunes. Illness and material losses came upon me. In addition, various informers plotted against my life. But the most terrible blow which befell me, a blow which caused me more grief than anything I have experienced in my life, was the death of the most perfect and righteous man, who was drowned while traveling in the Indian

43

Ocean, and with him was lost considerable money belonging to me, himself, and others. He left me his widow and a little daughter to take care of.

For nearly a year after I received the sad news, I lay on my bed struggling with fever and despair. Eight years have since passed, and still I mourn, for there is no consolation. What can console me? He grew up on my knees; he was my brother, my pupil. He was engaged in business and earned money that I might stay at home and continue my studies. He was learned in the Talmud and in the Bible and an accomplished grammarian. My one joy was to see him. Now my joy has been changed into darkness. He has gone to his eternal home, and has left me prostrated in a strange land. Whenever I come across his handwriting or one of his books, my heart grows faint within me and my grief reawakens. In short: "I will go down into the grave unto my son mourning." Were not the study of the Torah my delight, and did not the study of philosophy divert me from grief, "I should have succumbed in my affliction." [9]

Upon the death of David, Moses Maimonides was confronted with the very prosaic problem of providing for his own family and that of his brother. He continued his instruction to the group of young scholars and did not relax his activities in the religious and communal affairs of Fostat. To dispel the gloom of his personal misfortunes, he even took on the additional responsibility of acting as *Rosh Ab Bet-Din* (Presiding Judge of the Judicial Court). But neither of the activities in which he was engaged provided him and his dependents with the certainty of a livelihood. Proverbially, scholarship did not pay and, with his aversion to commercializing knowledge of the Torah, he would not attempt to make it pay. In the circumstances of the increasing demands of his dependents, he decided to put to practical use his knowledge of medicine—a theoretical science he had acquired as an aid to his talmudic studies, but until then had not practiced.

Although the story of Maimonides' medical career belongs to a somewhat later period of his life, and will be treated fully in its proper place, the observation may be volunteered here that in all likelihood his success as a physician was a slow achievement. The medical works of Hippocrates and Galen were popular in translation, in Egypt, as were the Arabic writings of Rhazes and Avicenna. Cairo, as the capital of the Egyptian empire, was a city of famous doctors. Maimonides suffered from the disadvantage of being both a Jew and a foreigner whose intrusion the local physicians resented.

There were Jewish physicians at Saladin's court, but it was not until some years later that Maimonides was accorded the honor of joining their company. This may account for the fact that when in 1167 Benjamin of Tudela visited Cairo in the course of his travels and left a record of the Jewish notables he had met, the name of the physician-philosopher was not among them.

Maimonides was immersed in his medical profession and in his self-imposed communal activity. He suffered from ill-health and lived in a position of perpetual insecurity because of the jealousy of his medical colleagues and the enemies he suspected of plotting his destruction.[10] Nevertheless, in spite of these acute pressures, Maimonides, at the age of thirty-three, in the year 1168 completed his monumental *Perush al ha-Mishnah*, his Commentary on the Mishnah, on which he had worked intermittently for ten years, through the stresses of his stormy life.

A work universally regarded as one of the most brilliant achievements of rabbinic learning, the *Commentary* was composed under unimaginable difficulties. In the conclusion of his Introduction, Maimonides described the hardships under which the first of his three masterpieces was produced. "I was troubled," the author wrote in the postscript, "by the suffering and exile which God had imposed on me, since I was driven from one end of the world to the other. . . . God knows that I have explained some chapters whilst on my wanderings, and others on board ships, in inns, on roadsides, and without any access to books. Besides, I have devoted myself to the study of the sciences." He continued with an appeal to the critics for leniency should they discover any errors in the work. Maimonides called the *Commentary*, which is written in Arabic, *Siraj* (the Luminary), because of the light it cast on the Mishnah.

But what is the Mishnah which Moses Maimonides devoted ten years of his life to explain and interpret? The word *Mishnah*, derived from the Hebrew verb *shanah*, "to repeat," is used to designate the Law which is transmitted orally, in contradistinction to *Mikra*, which is the Law of the written text of the Bible. Specifically, Mishnah connotes the collection of laws made by Rabbi Judah ha-Nasi (the Patriarch, 135–220) who, because of his singularly high moral and pure life, was named "holy" but was also known simply as "Rabbi." His collection includes the Oral Law accumulated from the earliest period to the compiler's own time. The Mishnah is therefore a digest of Jewish ritual and jurisprudence and forms the text on which both the Jerusalem and Babylonian Talmuds are based. In the Mishnah, "Rabbi" included large extracts from earlier collections, principally the Mishnah of Rabbi Akiba (50–132).

Although superficially the Mishnah may be considered a legal textbook for teachers and judges, a manual of information on ritual and religious practices, it is in reality much more than that. It is the first authoritative formulation of the rabbinic law and lore, an epoch-making work, based on Scripture and providing the material for later expansion and development, which became the spiritual rampart of the Jewish people for hundreds of years. Four hundred years of the religious and cultural activity of the Jews of Palestine went into its making. For the great majority of believing Jews, its laws and regulations, its rules and interpretations, carry the same sanctity and authority as the Written Law or the Pentateuch itself.

The Mishnah is indeed a unique work, as complex a literature as was the life of the people which created it. Religious laws and regulations, moral and ethical exhortations, are interspersed with discussions on criminal law, domestic relations laws, laws of agriculture, trade, commerce, hygiene, medicine, etc. Trivial matters with no recognizable religious or ethical significance, rules, customs, and usages which accumulated round Jewish life through the centuries, are treated with the same gravity and importance as the cardinal beliefs and practices of Judaism. Various rites and rituals of the past are placed on the same plane with the religious needs and requirements of the time in which the Mishnah came into existence. Codes of law, as a rule, are intended for the time and conditions of life they come to serve, yet approximately one third of the Mishnah deals with phases of legislation pertaining to the priesthood, sacrifices, and the Temple service which, with the destruction of the Sanctuary by Titus in 70, no longer had any practical bearing upon the religious life of the Jews.

Rabbi Judah the Patriarch performed a great historic task for the preservation of Judaism when he fashioned the uniform and methodically-arranged Mishnah of the traditions floating about among the people and the private collections of laws in the hands of teachers. Henceforth any man wishing to know the law on any particular matter was no longer exposed to the embarrassment of having to consult the various schools and choose (something he was not always able to do) between conflicting and contradictory views and opinions. The Patriarch's great love for the Hebrew language, which it was his ambition to revive, made him compose his Mishnah in the graceful language of the Bible, or rather neo-Hebrew (not, however, without occasional intrusion of Greek and Latin terms).

Briefly described, the Mishnah is divided into six principal sections, or *sedarim*, called *Shisha Sidre Mishnah* (six orders of the Mishnah) known under the abbreviation as *Shas*. Each section, or order, contains a number of treatises, which are divided into *perakim*, or chapters.

SECTION I, *which begins with a treatise on Prayers, treats of agricultural laws—the various tithes and donations to the Priests, the Levites, and the poor from the products of the land; the Sabbatical year; and the prohibited mixtures in plants, animals, and garments.*

SECTION II, Moed *(Festivals) contains twelve treatises dealing with the feasts and fasts of the year, the work prohibited, the ceremonies ordained, and the sacrifices offered on them. They are:* Sabbath; Erubin, *dealing with the means by which inconvenient regulations of the seventh day may be obviated;* Pessahim *(Passover);* Shekalim, *the half-shekel poll-tax for the Temple upkeep;* Yoma, *or* Yom ha-Kippurim *(the Day of Atonement);* Sukkah *(the Feast of Tabernacles);* Bezah *(egg), precepts observed on half-holidays;* Rosh ha-Shanah *(New Year);* Ta'anit, *rules concerning fast-days;* Megillah *(the Scroll of Esther), laws pertaining to Purim;* Moed Katan, *minor festivals;* Hagigah *(Festal Offering).*

SECTION III, Nashim *(Women), contains seven treatises:* Yebamot, *women subject to Levirate Marriage;* Ketubot *(marriage contracts);* Nedarim *(vows);* Nazir, *prescriptions regarding the Nazarite vows;* Gittin *(bills of divorce);* Sotah *(women suspected of infidelity);* Kiddushin *(betrothal).*

SECTION IV, Nezikin *(Injuries), contains ten treatises:* Baba Kamma *treats of injuries and compensation;* Baba Metzia *contains laws concerning sales, leases, usury, and found objects;* Baba Batra *deals with ownership of property and right of succession;* Sanhedrin, *with judicial procedure and criminal law;* Makkot *(blows), regulates the number of stripes as punishment by law;* Shebuot *(oaths), sets rules regarding different oaths;* Eduyot *(evidence);* Abodah Zarah, *defines regulations concerning idolatry and idolaters;* Abot, *or* Pirke Abot *(Chapters of the Fathers);* Horayot *(decisions), deals with religious and legal decisions made in error.*

47

SECTION V, Kodashim *(Hallowed Things)*, *contains legislation concerning animal offerings, meal offerings, animals killed for food, firstlings, vows and valuations, substituted offerings, etc. This section contains eleven treatises:* Zebahim *(sacrifices)*; Menahot *(meat-offerings)*; Hullin *(profane)*, *slaughtering of nonconsecrated animals*; Bekorot *(first-born)*, *laws concerning firstlings*; Arakin *(estimations)*, *regulations regarding ransom of dedicated things*; Temurah *(exchange)*, *exchange of dedicated animals*; Keriot *(extirpation)*, *punishment by excommunication*; Me'ilah *(trespass)*, *trespass in case of dedicated objects*; Tamid, *pertaining to daily morning and evening burnt-offerings*; Midot *(measures)*, *describing the apartments and furnishings of the Temple*; Kinnin *(birds' nests)*, *rules pertaining to offering of doves.*

SECTION VI, Tohorot *(purification)*, *contains twelve treatises:* Kellim *(utensils)*, *uncleanliness attached to vessels*; Oholot *(tents)*, *defilement occasioned by a corpse*; Negaim *(leprosy)*, *regulations concerning leprosy*; Parah *(red heifer)*, *purification by ashes obtained from the red heifer*; Tohotot *(purities)*, *minor defilements*; Mikvaot *(ritual baths)*; Niddah *(menstruation)*, *laws concerning defilement caused by menstruation*; Makshirin *(predisposings)*, *contact with things predisposed to defilement*; Zabin *(sufferers from discharge)*; Tebul Yom *(one who immersed himself that day)*, *according to Lev.15:5, a man in such case is regarded as unclean until sundown*; Yadaim *(hands)*, *defilement and cleansing of hands*; Ukzin *(stems)*, *relation of fruit to the stems, skin, and seeds with reference to defilement.*

With the completion of the Mishnah (about 1168), the civil and religious life of the Jews was definitely fixed. They now had not only the Bible to depend on for guidance in their religious and mundane affairs but also its authoritative interpretation to the last detail. The Jewish way of life in all its ramifications was unalterably formulated for generations. The Mishnah became a bond, a spiritual rampart, which was later strengthened and rendered all the more impregnable by the Talmud. It is characteristic of the high ethical level of the compiler that he did not limit his compendium to *halakic*, or legal decisions, but included in his collection the wealth of agadic, ethical sayings, and maxims which make up the *Chapters of the Fathers*, "a kind of rabbinic Book of Proverbs," George Foote Moore calls it, "wholly devoted to the moral and spiritual life . . . and for a knowledge of the ideals of rabbinic ethics and piety no other easily accessible source is equal to Abot." [11]

The Mishnah had no sooner made its appearance than, like the Bible, it became a kind of national possession of the Jews. It did not have to struggle for recognition; it supplanted the older Mishnaic collections and was universally accepted as the only authoritative lawbook. It gained its popularity among teachers and students alike not only because of its intrinsic excellence but, in a large measure, because it bore upon it the stamp of *Rabbenu ha-Kadosh*. It was maintained that not since Moses had there been any other man in whom Torah *u'gdulah* (learning and greatness) [12] were so perfectly united. Rabbi Judah's Mishnah became the classical textbook of the traditional law to an extent that, according to one teacher, its study was tantamount to offering sacrifices (Lev. R.7); according to Rabbi Joshua ben Levi, "The Mishnah is a firm iron pillar, and none may stray from it" (*Ibid.*, 21). Laws in possession of schools not presided over by the Patriarch which in his opinion were not vested with sufficient authority, or were useless repetitions of those he published, were called *Beraitot* (External). The *Tosefta* (Additions) comprises the larger part of excluded decisions. Though it is of considerably later time, it greatly resembles the Mishnah in language, style, divisions, and subdivisions.

Yet, notwithstanding the fact that the Mishnah served to preserve and consolidate the Jews and Judaism in one of the most critical periods of their history, when the aggressive power of Rome on the one hand and the Christian propaganda on the other threatened to disrupt if not destroy them, it had to wait close to a thousand years for a commentary. The Talmud, of course, is in a large sense an interpretation of the Mishnah, but it is less exegetical in nature than a means of expanding its legal material to wider application. Although there were some early comments on the Mishnah and complete commentaries on a few single tractates, Maimonides surpassed his predecessors in composing a systematic commentary on the whole Mishnah.

After the nearly thousand years of its composition, Maimonides saw the need of bringing the Mishnah to the level of the people. With the flight of centuries, the Patriarch's code became antiquated and not easily comprehended by great masses of Jews. Its style became difficult, its diction in many places foreign, and its subject matter was in need of explaining. What was needed was a clear and precise statement not only of its legal decisions but of beliefs and doctrines implied in them. This Maimonides undertook to do, and he did it superbly.

3. COMMENTATOR AND PHILOSOPHER

MAIMONIDES' COMMENTARY on the Mishnah was a pioneer work. Later commentators proved more popular for the study of the Mishnah because of their literal interpretation of the text, but Maimonides penetrated the subject in all its ramifications—ethical, theological, and philosophical. He brought to bear upon the Mishnah his qualities of insight, depth and acquaintance with sciences not usual with any of the other commentators. He approached the Mishnah as he was later to approach the Bible, exploring the inner meaning which lay behind its words.

Moses Maimonides was thus the great popularizer of the Mishnah. He set out to teach it to ever-widening circles in Israel, to make it accessible, as Rabbi Isaac Herzog put it "to the struggling trader or the toiling laborer . . . after a hard day's work." [1] It was his ambition to make the knowledge of the Oral Law understood and loved by all the Jews, not limited to the select few scholars. This is what led Maimonides to compose his *Commentary* in the Arabic vernacular rather than the language of the Bible or the Aramaic idiom of the Rabbis, which not many understood. Master of brevity and preciseness, he often summarized involved discussions in the Talmud of several folio pages in a few brief sentences, without sacrificing lucidity to brevity.

Maimonides is as much the literary historian of the Mishnah as he is its commentator. He was a pioneer in the scientific study of Judaism, and the credit for having been the founder of Jewish *Wissenschaft* may justly be accorded to him. At the time Maimonides began to write there was no Jewish history, least of all a history of the Oral Law. Maimonides supplied the need by providing the six divisions of the Mishnah with Introductions—the first of their kind —which were complete dissertations in themselves. These described the historical process and development of the Oral Law, as well as its unity and structure. To the student of rabbinic literature they are of immense importance, containing a wealth of instructive scholarly material. Maimonides aimed at deepening the knowledge and study of the Oral Law, to present the Mishnah not merely as a legal code but as a fountain of wisdom and moral and ethical instruction.

He thus devotes almost as much time and space to the speculative parts of his *Mishnah Commentary* as to its purely legal enactments and provisions, to man's social and ethical relations as to his religious obligations. To him, both were of equal importance. In fact, he regarded the moral principles of the Law as of higher importance than the fulfillment of its rites and rituals.

The Introductions are the distinctive feature of Maimonides' *Perush al ha-Mishnah*. They give the work its novelty and freshness. They also contain in elementary popular form the quintessence of the philosopher-commentator's system of religious thought and ideas. What he was later to develop at greater length and more precisely in the first section of his *Mishnah Torah* and in *The Guide for the Perplexed* is adumbrated in the prefatory dissertations with which he adorned the six "orders" of Rabbi Judah ha-Nasi's Mishnah. Indeed, one is tempted to believe that Maimonides was less concerned with commenting upon the Mishnah than with building up his conception of the religious beliefs and philosophy of Judaism. And he found the Mishnah a suitable and convenient vehicle for what he had in mind. For the rabbinic post-biblical code is not an ordinary record of legal rules and decisions but a treasure trove of ethical maxims and observations which lend themselves to the widest possible interpretation.

Maimonides' Introductions are not all of the same size or length. But whether they are of the proportion of complete monographs—as is the case of his prefaces to *Zeraim,* the first division of the Mishnah, the Chapters of the Fathers, *Hellek,* the first Mishnah of the tenth chapter of *Sanhedrin,* and *Tohorot,* the sixth section of the Mishnah —or the briefer prefatory remarks which the writer appended to whole divisions or individual segments of the Mishnah, they are all of equal importance and significance to the careful talmudic student.

One and all, they are luminous masterpieces of exposition, magnificent interpretations of often involved and difficult subjects, precise and polished renditions of obscure discussions and controversies.

Starting out from the premise that, for an intelligent comprehension of the Oral Law, one must know its origin, nature, and development, Maimonides presents the reader in his Introduction to *Zeraim* with what amounts to a complete history of Jewish tradition from its Sinaitic origin to the completion of the Mishnah. Holding firm to the traditional view that the law which the Jew is bound to follow is not confined to the Written Code, but includes the explanations, regulations and provisions of the Rabbis, which are of equal validity with the Written Law, he but restates the talmudic adage that anything which any student will teach at any future time was already communicated to Moses on Mount Sinai. To validate his contention of the unity and historic continuity of Jewish Tradition, he traces the steps by which the Tradition passed from the original Lawgiver to Joshua, the "Elders," the Prophets, the Men of the Great Assembly, and was then passed on from generation to generation to Rabbi Judah the Patriarch, the redactor of the Mishnah.

Maimonides established the historic process of Jewish Tradition and philosophized upon it. With great learning, skill and penetration, he detached the essential halakah from the great mass of talmudic debate which often obscured and complicated it. He made the Mishnah easy and comprehensible to students by the logic, simplicity, and brevity of his style and diction. He made clear the grammatical form of words and explained their derivation when they hailed from foreign sources. He was in his element when the text of the Code called for scientific exposition. Due to his well-organized mind, he looked for the organic unity of the Mishnah. Contrary to a statement in the Talmud that the Patriarch had not followed a logical plan in arranging the six divisions of the Mishnah, Maimonides shows the logical and coherent sequence in which the tractates follow each other.

The originality of Maimonides' *Mishnah Commentary* is all the more remarkable when one takes into account the paucity of material he had to work with. There was not as yet a commentary upon the entire Mishnah on which he could lean. He had, of course, the *Gemara* to depend on, but he was not always satisfied with its interpretations, and he not infrequently ventured explanations of his own. He was imbued with the profoundest reverence for the masters of the Talmud and he spoke in touching terms of their wisdom and saintliness. He ranked the Rabbis as the equals of the Prophets; in fact, he placed them even at a degree higher since the decision of the Law lies with them and not with the Prophets. Nevertheless, where the natural sense of the Mishnah required it, he did not hesitate to incorporate comments and explanations of his own without regard to the *Gemara*. It was with reference to the later commentators, on whom, to his regret, he sometimes leaned, that he wrote to Joseph Ibn Aknin that many errors in his Commentary were due to his adherence to his precursors. He excepted, however, the explanations he received from his father and from Joseph Ibn Migash, his father's teacher, of whom he spoke with great respect.

In his Introduction he anticipated the subject of Prophets and Prophecy, which he was to treat in *The Guide for the Perplexed* with great thoroughness and psychological insight. He held up Moses, the Man of God who heard the Voice of Sinai, as the greatest of prophets —not only by reason of his moral and intellectual attainments but because he received his communication directly from God. Maimonides startled his contemporaries by his declaration that what the Israelites heard at Sinai directly from God were only the first two commandments, and that, through the medium of an impersonal voice specially created for that purpose, the rest of the Decalogue and the entire Torah had been communicated to them by Moses. Maimonides drew a clear distinction between Moses and the other prophets, a distinction determined not by his greater wonders and miraculous deeds but by reason of the fact that he was always in possession of the Spirit. He was the "Man of God." He experienced God always. He was His chosen instrument, at once the Revealer of God, the Liberator and Lawgiver of His people.

Maimonides the philosopher and ethicist was in his elements when his Commentary reached *Abot* (Fathers), better known as *Pirke Abot* (Chapters of the Fathers), included in the fourth of the six divisions under which the Mishnah is arranged, where he could display the whole wealth of his thought on the moral and philosophical content of Judaism. What could have suited better the moral and ethical temperament of the man who always looked for the inner substance of Judaism than the pithy, sparkling sentences of the Chapters of the Rabbis which tersely sum up the ideals of Jewish life and conduct? "In the Mishnah," says Israel Abrahams in the annotated edition of the *Daily Prayer Book*, "there is, indeed, no distinction between the legal, the ritual, and the moral; all these ideas were regarded as indissolubly associated in the whole body of religious thought and practice. But *Abot* is more consistently *ethical* than the other tractates of the Mishnah, if we employ this adjective in the restricted sense now usually attached to it." So highly were these "Chapters" regarded by the Jews because of their elevated thoughts and magnificent phrasing, that already in Geonic times they were introduced into the prayer book for recital during the summer months of the year, a custom which persisted to this day.

There is no *Gemara* to the Chapters of the Fathers, but Maimonides supplied it with a commentary which goes beyond the explanation of words and uses it as a vehicle of his thoughts and ideas on a large variety of matters. In one place Maimonides wrote a long dissertation in the style of the English essayists on the subject of Speech and Silence; in another place he moralized on modesty and humility and was eloquent upon the baneful effects of pride and vanity; in connection with still another text (*Abot*, 1, 16), he launched a general assault against scholars who, not having acquired a gainful trade or profession, commercialize their knowledge of the Torah.

It is, however, the *Shemonah Perakim* (Eight Chapters), a small but attractive and highly significant ethical treatise with which Maimonides prefaced his commentary to the Chapters of the Fathers, which demonstrates best the protean genius of the author. In its small compass, the writer assumes many shapes and forms. He is moralist and philosopher, social scientist and religious teacher, curer of souls and healer of the body, both Rabbi and Hellene. Although its leading thought—the Golden Mean—comes by the way of Athens, it is presented in the mishnaic style of Jerusalem. In other words, whereas the motif of the little monograph is recognizably Aristotelian, its high moral and ethical tone and outlook are unmistakably Jewish, suffused with supporting evidence from the Prophets and the Sages of the Talmud.

Although one of Maimonides' earliest writings, the Eight Chapters is a model of the writer's simplicity of thought and style, which account for its popularity among all classes of readers. Maimonides' ethical pronouncements are scattered widely in all his works, in his legal, philosophical, and Responsa writings, but with his genius for crystallization, they are summarized most clearly and succinctly in the Eight Chapters, which may be designated more appropriately as the Book of the Soul. For it is with the uniqueness of the human soul that the writer is chiefly concerned, its functions and qualities, its capacities and potentialities, its powers for good and evil.

Briefly stated, Maimonides wrote that souls, like bodies, may be well or ill. A soul is well when it is rational, disposed to the performance of the normal good and proper things; on the other hand, the soul is sick when its inclination is toward the perverse and the wicked. Just as those who realize that they are sick of body consult a physician who tells them what they must do or refrain from doing so that they may be well again, so, too, those who suffer from soul-sickness, must repair to the Sage who is the physician of the soul (*rophe ha-ne-fesh*) who by his instruction to choose the good and shun evil will restore the soul to its natural well-being. It will, however, go ill with them who, being sick, are not aware of their illness, or being aware, spurn the doctor's instructions and refuse to be healed.

In the fourth, the crucial chapter of the tract, Maimonides discussed the cure of the sick soul. Our author believed that moral excellences and defects are not innate. Virtues or vices are implanted by country, parents, friends, and associates. They are, above all, the result of habits and practices over long periods of time. Now, these habits may be of two extreme kinds: excessively good or excessively bad. In neither extreme does virtue, or good conduct, lie. Thus, neither lavishness nor stinginess, neither recklessness nor cowardice, neither self-abasement nor haughtiness pave the way to the well-ordered, happy life. But there is the middle way, the *Golden Mean*, which holds the equilibrium between the two excesses. Thus, between spend-thriftness and parsimony is liberality; between recklessness and cowardice is bravery; between haughtiness and self-abasement is modesty. When, however, one has become so habituated in his excesses that he cannot easily be won over to the rule of moderation, it may be necessary to pass from the extreme evil to the extreme good until he maintains the proper balance. Thus, when one has become an addict to the vice of niggardliness, he should be made to practice extravagance till his moral reformation has been effected.

Maimonides defended the doctrine of the *Golden Mean* [1b] against the "pious ones," meaning the ascetics, who, to restore their souls' health, deviated from the equilibrium by keeping nightly vigils, refrained from eating meat and drinking wine, clothed themselves in rough woolen garments, and dwelt in mountain caves, never realizing that such things are contrary to the law of God and the dictates of reason. For God does not desire the destruction of the body and its legitimate desires and appetites but their sanctification. Indeed, the Rabbis teach that it is becoming that a scholar should have a pleasant dwelling, a beautiful wife, and domestic comforts.[2] Since, Maimonides asserted, the goal in life is to acquire wisdom and the knowledge of God, the body should be kept in a fit and healthy condition that it may provide him with the proper mood for the higher exercise of the soul.

In the concluding chapter of the treatise, Maimonides discussed the problem of Freedom of Will, a subject he was to treat in greater detail in his subsequent works, notably the *Guide,* and made short shrift of the contention of the astrologers who maintained that man's destiny, his actions and conduct, are influenced by the constellations under which he is born. Both the Bible and the philosophers, he said, agree that man acts under his own control, that he himself and no outside force is responsible for his virtues or vices. "Were a man compelled according to the dictates of predestination, then the commands and prohibitions of the Torah would become null and void, and the Law would be completely false, since man would have no freedom of choice in what he does."

Maimonides pursued the subject with all the vigor of logic, and it can best be stated in his own words:

Were not man master of his own life, it would be useless, in fact, absolutely in vain, for man to study, to instruct, for a man to learn an art, as it would be entirely impossible for him, on account of the external force compelling him . . . to gain certain knowledge, or to acquire a certain characteristic. Reward and punishment, too, would be pure injustice, both as regards man toward man, and as between God and man. . . . This theory is, therefore, positively unsound, contrary to reason and common sense, subversive of the fundamental principles of religion, and attributes injustice to God (far be it from Him). In reality, the undoubted truth of the matter is that man has full sway over all his actions. If he wishes to do a thing, he does it; if he does not wish to do it, he need not, for there is no external compulsion controlling him. There God very properly commanded man, saying, "See, I have set before thee this day life and the good, death and evil . . . therefore choose thou life."[3]

In conclusion, Maimonides touched upon the related metaphysical subject of God's Knowledge, for the full treatment of which the reader must again be referred to the *Guide*. Briefly, however, he said that it is erroneous to measure God's Knowledge by man's knowledge, for "God does not know by means of knowledge and does not live by means of life, so that He and His knowledge may be considered two different things in the same sense that this is true of man; for man is distinct from knowledge, and knowledge from man, in consequence of which they are two different things." He admitted, however, that "This conception is very hard to grasp, and thou shouldst not hope to understand it thoroughly by two or three lines in this treatise."

The *Eight Chapters*, which, according to Dr. Joseph I. Gorfinkle, was written sometime between 1158 and 1168 along with the rest of the commentary on the Mishnah and was made public in 1168, was translated into Hebrew by Samuel Ibn Tibbon in 1202, two years before Maimonides' death. It saw many editions and translations and appears, together with the author's commentary on *Abot*, in most editions of the *Talmud*. The latest modern critical edition and translation into English of the *Eight Chapters* is the work of Dr. Gorfinkle.[4]

By far the most important of Maimonides' Introductions is his essay on the opening words of the *Mishnah* in *Sanhedrin* (Chap. 10, 1), "All Israel have a portion in the World-to-Come," which tradition affixed to each of the six chapters of *Abot*. A world of thought and speculation, philosophical and theological reflection, were implied in the words "Israel" and "World-to-Come" to the man whose mind was busy with the interpretation, or reinterpretation of the Jewish faith and doctrine. For what, indeed, is an Israelite? By what can he be known or distinguished from the world about him, and what are the distinctive features of his faith and teachings? Maimonides was surrounded by a large number of Jews, some weak and faltering in their faith, others good and pious men who carried out the behests of the Law punctiliously, but entertained all kinds of silly notions and superstitions about Judaism. Were they ideal Israelites? And as to the "World-to-Come," what article of the Jewish faith has become so buried in extravagant beliefs, visionary hopes, and absurd fancies as this? Maimonides set himself to the task of correcting the popular errors which encrusted the belief in the World-to-Come, to examine and define what makes an "Israelite." In doing it, he wrote one of the most significant and enlightening sections of the *Mishnah Commentary*.

Maimonides was grieved by the false and fantastic ideas, nurtured by centuries of superstition men formed of the exalted spiritual ideal of the World-to-Come. He discussed the material views which credulous, misinformed people have taken of eternal bliss in the after-life and divided them into several groups. Some spell out the reward for their good and pious life in terms of sensual pleasures and satisfactions—scenes of beauty and elegance, palaces of gold and rubies, and rivers of flowing milk and spiced wines and ointments; conversely, Hell is a place of eternal agony and torment, where the sinners are writhing in the distress and pain of their wicked life. Others fancy their expected good to come in the Messianic Era when they shall be like angels, handsome, of gigantic stature, and very prolific. Their food and raiment will grow out of the earth without themselves having to toil and labor, but the godless will enjoy none of these things. A third class of misled visionaries look forward to Resurrection, when they shall be reunited with their friends and families, enjoy the pleasures of their law-abiding life, and never have to die again. The fourth group is made up of the people who mistakenly believe that the Messianic era will mark the termination of the suffering of the Jews, their restoration to the Holy Land, and domination over their oppressors. The fifth and last class—and they are by far in the majority—combine all the previous misleading ideals. They hold that after the Messiah will have come, the dead will be revived and they will be all translated to the Garden of Eden where, through eternity, they will eat and drink and know trouble and sorrow no more.

Maimonides was caustic in his censure of the supercilious notions the ignorant masses had formed of the pure and grand ideal that is implied in the conception of *Olam ha-Ba*. It irked him to see this high and lofty vision of the future state of life preached by the prophets and taught by the Rabbis of the Talmud mocked and degraded as a thing to be ashamed of. What would the nations of the earth think of such childish grotesque notions entertained by a people of which the Lawgiver said: "This great nation is a wise and understanding people?" [5] Would they not rather reverse their judgment and say, "Verily, this small nation is a foolish and ignorant people?" He blamed their teachers and reproached them in scornful words for misleading the people and encouraging them in such fantastic, credulous beliefs.

Maimonides was shocked to hear Jews all around him converse on such subjects as to how and in what manner the dead should arise. Would they, when quickened to life at the time of Resurrection, arise naked or clothed? Would they be attired in the embroidered shrouds in which they were interred or dressed in simple garments to cover their flesh? And with regard to the advent of the Messiah, no higher thought or ideal stirred their minds than to speculate whether there would be rich and poor, weak and strong. Now, wrote Maimonides, it is well enough for the prudent and understanding teacher to attract his youthful pupil by the promise of figs and honey and other such things a child likes in order to make him study and raise the reward for his diligence as time goes on and the pupil matures with age. But must grown, intelligent men be meted out the same treatment? Must they be bribed into goodness and the knowledge of God like the schoolboy who is unable to appreciate the value of knowledge for its own sake?

Living in a world brutally hostile to him, the Jew understandably yearned for greater bliss and happiness than this life gave him, and he sought and found it in the dream world of the Life-to-Come. Hungrily, he surrounded it with all the glamour and splendor which his miserable terrestrial existence had denied him. Thus, the prophets and poets of Israel, and especially the Sages of the Talmud, contrived with their tender pity and compassion to surround the future with an aura of hope and beauty. Rabban Gamaliel, a grandson of Hillel, in the first half of the second century, when the Jewish State and Temple lay in ruin and the Jews were in desperation over their fate, poetically visioned the future when the Palestine soil would produce cakes and silk dresses, the trees of the Holy Land would bear fruit continually, and the women would give birth to children every day [6] and still more extravagant fancies of the future in other parts of the Talmud.[7] References are not wanting in rabbinic literature to the materialistic rewards of the good and pious at "the end of days," banquets of the Leviathan [8] washed down by wines as old as the creation of the world.[9] What, however, the Rabbis intended to be taken metaphorically, as fanciful imaginings of men bent upon relieving the stress and tension of afflicted people, was taken literally by generations of Jews till it became almost part of their religious creed.

In formulating his own conception of the Hereafter, Maimonides was probably the first great authority to repudiate the naïve mythical notion associated with *Olam ha-Ba*. When, he said, the Rabbis vividly drew superb pictures of the celestial abode as a banquet hall for the righteous and purgatory of the wicked, they but expressed poetically the existence of a spiritual retribution without the physical or material interpretation which popular error associated with them. For the truly pious men are not children. Their life and their love of God are motivated not by threats and bribes but by pure overmastering yearning for Him. Although the materialistic conception of Heaven and Hell and Reward and Punishment, stimulated by the fantastic legends connected with them, became very popular, Maimonides staunchly insisted on their more exalted spiritual meaning, maintaining with Antigonos of Socho, "be not like servants who serve their master upon the condition of receiving reward, but be like servants who minister to their master without the condition or receiving reward," [10] and the still more pointed comment of Rabbi Eleazar on the verse, "In His commandments he delights exceedingly" [11]—"In His commandments, not in the rewards for them, he delights." [12]

The conventional belief in Resurrection is severely shaken in Maimonides' Introduction to *Hellek*. Whereas the philosopher spoke with great eloquence and conviction of Immortality, he was less enthusiastic about the bodily resurrection of the dead. Indeed, how could he who taught the spiritual conception of the Soul and the Hereafter join the multitude in the crude notions it associated with the quickening of the dead? Had he dared, he would have remained silent altogether on this delicate and sensitive subject. But how could he, when for centuries Jewish philosophy and theology remained under the influence of the traditional belief in the revival of the dead—when, indeed, each morning every Jew begins his day's devotions with the beautiful prayer, *Elohai Neshamah*, "O, my God, the soul which Thou gavest me," etc., and thrice daily he affirms his faith in *Tehiyat ha-Metim*, resurrection of the dead, in the "Eighteen Benedictions"?

Prophet and Sage alike were positive in their affirmation of the resurrection of the dead. In Isaiah we read: "Thy dead shall live; my dead bodies shall arise, awake and sing ye that dwell in the dust, for Thy dew is as the dew of light, and the earth shall bring to light the shades." [13] Rabbi Eleazar Hakappar was quite unambiguous in his declaration: "Those that are born are destined to die, and the dead to be brought to life again." [14] Maimonides, however, without specifically expressing himself on the form Resurrection was to take, asserted generally that not the wicked but the righteous only would be resurrected. When, some years later, he was challenged by Samuel bar Ali, Maimonides replied with his *Ma'amer al Tehiyat he-Metim*,[15] referred to elsewhere, in which he wrote: "The resurrection of the dead is a cardinal doctrine of the Law of Moses, peace be unto him, and he who does not believe in it is without religion and can claim no affiliation with the Jewish faith. But it is the reward of the righteous only, for how shall the evil-doers live after death, seeing, as it is maintained by the Sages, that they are dead even in life."

Unlike Resurrection, which appeared to Maimonides as being incapable of philosophic proof, he treated with special relish the subject of Immortality which, he maintains, expresses the real teaching of Judaism on life after death. But it was an intellectualized immortality that Maimonides taught, a life of disembodied spirits whose delights are spiritual, whose pleasures are unworldly, whose highest satisfaction is derived from the ability to contemplate and comprehend God. He dismissed as allegorical the exquisite stories of the Rabbis of the Talmud of the material delights awaiting the righteous in heaven and, instead, quoted fondly Rab's statement: "There is neither eating nor drinking nor any sensual pleasure nor strife in the World-to-Come but the righteous, with their crowns upon their heads, sit around the table of God delighting in the splendor of the Divine Presence." [16]

When the exalted state which is set up for the pious after death—their blissful enjoyment of God's majesty—is reached, there are no earthly joys or pleasures of the senses which can compare with it. Man, living in the material world with his physical faculties adjusted only to what he can see, feel, and experience, can as little comprehend the delights of the soul after it has disrobed itself of its earthly trappings as the blind can distinguish color or the ear deaf to sound can appreciate a musical melody. "No eye hath seen it, O God, beside Thee," said Isaiah.[17] This, one infers from Maimonides concerning Immortality, is the recurring message of the Prophets and the Sages of Israel, which in course of time, due to the adverse circumstances in which the Jews lived, became grossly materialized, its meaning changed, its truth distorted.

Maimonides revised the folklorish conception of the Messiah and the Messianic Age by maintaining with Samuel the Babylonian of the third century that "the Messianic Age will differ from the present in nothing, except that Israel will throw off the yoke of the nations and regain its political independence." [18] Dismissing the mystical speculations concerning the Messiah, his origin, activity, and the marvellous superhuman powers ascribed to him, Maimonides insisted that he must be regarded as a mortal human being, differing from his fellow-men only in the fact that he will be greater, wiser, and more resplendent than they. He must be a descendant of the House of David and, like him, occupy himself with the Study of the Torah and observance of its commandments. Although he must restore the Davidic dynasty and effect the political independence of the Jews so that they may devote themselves to the study of the Torah and the sciences, no extraordinary changes in the world, in the general run of the world, and in human life are to be expected of him. For then, as always, there will be rich and poor, strong and weak, wise and simple—the ready-made garments and baked bread produced by the earth which the Rabbis promise as incidental to the coming of the Messiah denoting only the ease with which man will acquire the necessities of life when freed from the trammels and hardships of life. Being mortal, the Messiah will suffer death and be succeeded by his descendants in whose hands the Messianic dynasty will remain forever.

After his comprehensive exposition of *Olam ha-Ba* and the problems of life after death connected with it, Maimonides proceeded to the much-contested formulations of the beliefs and teachings of Judaism incumbent upon a Jew to accept if he would have a share in the World-to-Come. It was a daring thing for a young man—Maimonides was then only thirty-three years old—to attempt to fix the principles of the Jewish faith when neither in the Bible nor in the Talmud was there the least warrant for it. The nearest approach to the denial of future bliss is in Mishnah (Sanhedrin, X, I), where the following are enumerated: he who denies the resurrection of the dead; he who says that the Torah—both the Written and the Oral Law— is not divinely revealed, and the epicurean who does not believe in the moral government of the world. But the Mishnah does not categorically cut one off from the Jewish community for denying these principles as would Maimonides for refusing to accept his system of belief.

It must be admitted that the time in which Moses Maimonides lived called for drastic action. The question of what to believe and how one was to act if one was to remain a Jew was not an abstract but an intensely practical matter. Wherever he went, in Spain, Morocco, and Egypt, he saw some of his coreligionists denying their faith; others, in fear of persecution, were concealing their Judaism, while still others adopted rites and symbols not of their religion. "What he [Maimonides] wished to remind his contemporaries," says Etienne Gilson, "was that Judaism is first of all a religion; that a religion is not based upon liberty of thought, but a free acceptance of a certain way of thinking, but that one is not free to repudiate it if one pretends to profess that religion.[19]

The "Thirteen Articles of Faith" (*Ikarim*) as they appear in prose in the prayer-book, and in poetic form, in *Yigdal* (likewise in the prayer-book), are an abbreviated rendition based on Maimonides' Introduction to *Abot*. They are: belief in the existence of a Creator; belief in His Unity; belief in His Incorporeality; belief in His Eternity; belief that all worship and adoration are due to Him alone; belief in Prophecy; belief that Moses was the greatest of all Prophets; belief in the Revelation of the Law through Moses at Sinai; belief in the unalterability of the Law; belief that God knows the thoughts and deeds of all men; belief in God's just reward and punishment; belief in the advent of the Messiah; belief in the resurrection of the dead.

As though anticipating the criticism with which his "Articles" would meet, Maimonides exhorted the reader in the Introduction: "Know these [words] and repeat them many times, and think them over in the proper way. God knows that thou wouldst be deceiving thyself if thou thinkest thou hast understood them by having read them once or even ten times. Be not, therefore, hasty in perusing them. I have not composed them without deep study and earnest reflection."

But the critics were not mollified. Some resented the dogmatizing of the faith of Israel altogether, regarding it as an imitation of the Christian and Mohammedan confessions of faith; some objected on the score, in the words of a modern Jewish theologian, that "Judaism lays all stress upon conduct, not confession; upon a hallowed life, not a hallowed creed," while Moses Mendelssohn expressed his dissent on the ground that it is the greatness and glory of Judaism that it has no dogmas or formal authority to enforce them. Jewish authorities through the ages after Maimonides found fault with the "Articles" not so much because of their doctrinal principles as because of their number and the emphasis the author places upon one Jewish *credo* rather than another. Don Isaac Abravanel (1437–1508), while on the whole defending Maimonides against his critics, was nevertheless of the opinion that it was a mistake to formulate dogmas of Judaism, since every word in the Torah must be considered as a dogma in itself.[20]

Nevertheless, notwithstanding the coldness with which the "Articles" were first received, "Maimonides," writes Dr. Solomon Schechter (1847–1915), "must indeed have filled a gap in Jewish theology, a gap, moreover, the existence of which was very generally perceived. A century had hardly elapsed before the Thirteen Articles had become a theme for the poets of the synagogue. And almost every country where Jews lived can show a poem or prayer founded on these Articles. Rabbi Jacob Molin (1420) of Germany speaks of metrical and rhymed songs in the German language, the burden of which was the Thirteen Articles, and which were read by the common people with great devotion." [21]

Whereas Maimonides' Introduction to *Zeraim* is in reality a general discourse on the history and composition of the Talmud and the evolution of the Oral Law, and his preface to the Chapters of the Fathers an essay on the ethical and theological teachings of Judaism, his Introduction and commentary to *Tohorot* (Cleanness), the sixth "order" of the Mishnah, is a masterpiece of talmudic scholarship. Indeed, competent students of rabbinic literature hailed it as an extraordinary mark of Maimonides' halakic genius, Zachariah Frankel [22] going so far as to maintain that if Maimonides had written nothing other than his Introduction and commentary on *Tohorot*, especially its subdivisions *Negaim* and *Ohalot*, he would deserve the eternal gratitude of scholars. For *Tohorot* is one of the most baffling and subtle of the mishnaic tractates, avoided even by the initiate. With the exception of *Niddah*, there is no Gemara to *Tohorot*, since at the time of the Amaraim "cleanness" and "uncleanness" was purely an academic matter because of the destruction of the Temple. Maimonides, however, who held that "every one of the six hundred and thirteen precepts serves to inculcate some truth, to remove some erroneous opinion, to establish proper relations in society, to diminish evil, to train in good manners, or to warn against bad habits," made no distinction between the moral and ceremonial laws of the Torah.

In the lack of Gemara to *Tohorot*, it was Maimonides' task to dig out from the stupendous mass of rabbinic material such scattered references as bear on the subject and make them as clear and coherent for the student as could be done. Maimonides describes the process of his work and its value for the student of the subject, using Herbert Danby's translation of the *Book of Cleanness* in the Yale Judaica Series:

For the principles prefixed to this Introduction are of great value: there is not one over which I have not expended great toil in order to formulate it clearly and to make it plain. And I have collected these principles "one from a city and two from a family" [23] *from all corners of the Talmud and the secret places in the Baraitas and Tosefta, so as to compile this Introduction, that it may serve as a key both to what I wish to expound in this Division and also to the many difficult rules [about cleanness and uncleanness] which occur [elsewhere] in the Talmud.* [24]

It is therefore not surprising that, in face of the extreme delicacy of the subject Maimonides should warn the student to be attentive to the principles he established for the understanding of the Mishnah, as he later pleaded with Joseph Ibn Aknin to be careful in his study of *The Guide for the Perplexed* (availing myself again of Herbert Danby's translation):

You must [warns Maimonides], from the beginning, keep in mind every one of these premises . . . and memorize them so well that they come off the tongue readily, without effort. . . . It is not enough just to read them over, for even if you read them a thousand times yet do not memorize them, it will do you no good: they must be as habitually in your mind as the Shema, *and you must master them in their entirety with your memory, understanding and intelligence, if you would comprehend the contents of this Division. For it treats of things most difficult in themselves, with much that is doubtful and extremely obscure.* [25]

4. THE LETTER TO YEMEN

ALTHOUGH the *Mishnah Commentary* was one of the greatest achievements of rabbinic learning, it did not meet with immediate universal recognition at the hands of Jewish scholars. Some rabbis remained indifferent to the work of the young Spanish scholar from motives of jealousy; some challenged the fundamental character of Maimonides' Thirteen Articles of Faith; others resented the introduction of what they called irrelevant controversial scientific material into purely talmudic subjects, while still others took exception to the writer's frequent departure from the talmudic interpretation of the Mishnah in favor of his own exposition. There was but the faintest understanding of Maimonides' great historic work in his own country, in Egypt, and the Franco-German scholars, never much given to philosophical involvements, had their own commentator in the revered Rashi (1040–1105) and were in no need of any other.

The language in which the Commentary was written may have had something to do with its slow progress among talmudic scholars. Students of the Torah were accustomed to see Jewish scholarship written in the national language of the Jews. Not to say the Geonim, but the schools of talmudic learning which followed them, had, with rare exceptions, composed their works in any other but the Hebrew language, albeit a far cry from the language of the Bible. Rashi wrote a beautiful, even poetic, Hebrew, which was the case of a good many other commentators of the Bible and the Talmud. Arabic was to the Jews the language of the descendants of Ishmael who enjoy a rather unenviable reputation in rabbinic literature. Although the Commentary was early translated into Hebrew, the style is heavy and often difficult to follow.

It was, however, not very long before the Commentary received the recognition that was due it. It appeared in most editions of the Talmud, it met with the accolade of scholars, and its lengthy excursions were widely hailed as having laid the foundation for talmudic scholarship on historic-scientific lines. Modern scholars have been unstinting in their praise of and admiration for his unprecedented stupendous work. "It (the Commentary) was the first scientific treatment of the Talmud, and only so clear and systematic a thinker as Maimonides could have originated it," says the historian Graetz. "He blazed a path not trodden by any other man before," writes Zachariah Frankel, and so high a non-Jewish authority as Hermann Strack pronounced the Commentary an indispensable guide to the study of the Mishnah.

Maimonides' genius was equalled only by his character. The man who delved into the deepest metaphysical problems was not a secluded scholar who lived in isolation from the world. He was profoundly concerned with the troubles and vicissitudes of the world, especially as they affected the fortunes of his troubled people. Intellectual aristocrat though he was, he was never more completely at home than when in the midst of the humblest of his coreligionists. Whereas the scholars admired him for his great learning, the great masses of Jews knew him as their unfailing guide and wise counselor. His life had no higher devotion than the touching dedication to his sorrow-stricken, suffering brethren. He knew from his own experience the "luxury" of being a Jew in a strange and hostile environment.

Moses Maimonides had not been long in Egypt and was busy on the final draft of his Commentary when the political affairs of the country took a sudden turn which resulted in the overthrow of the tottering Fatimid dynasty and its displacement, in 1171, by Saladin as the undisputed monarch of the Moslem world. It came at the end of a prolonged struggle for the possession of Egypt in which Amalric, the Christian Emperor of Jerusalem, and Nureddin, the Moslem Caliph of Syria and hero of the Second Crusade, were involved. The fortunes of war changed almost daily till Shirkuh and Saladin, uncle and nephew respectively, both military geniuses of the first order, and bound to Nureddin by long family friendship, took command of the forces. By rapid marches, Shirkuh and Saladin approached the Egyptian frontier, gave battle to the enemy, captured Cairo and, on January 18, 1169, Shirkuh was appointed Vizier, shortly afterwards upon the death of the ailing Fatimid Caliph, becoming Sultan of Egypt. His triumph, however, was short-lived, for Shirkuh himself had not long survived the legitimate Sultan's death, making room for his talented nephew, Saladin, destined to play his distinguished role in the drama of history.

The wars were fought not without frightful losses to Jews, not as combatants but as victims of the wild unchecked religious frenzy of the Crusaders. Hundreds, possibly thousands, were slain by the crusading armies, and those who managed to escape with their bare lives were sold as slaves. The slave markets of the world were gutted with Jewish war captives. Jewish communities had literally impoverished themselves by ransoming as many of their captive brethren as possible, *pidyon shebuim,* the delivery of captives, being regarded by the Rabbis as one of the greatest mandatory laws of the Torah. As soon as Moses Maimonides was apprised of the situation, he organized committees, collected funds, and used his great authority with his own and adjacent communities to rush to the rescue of their hapless brethren.

Maimonides had no sooner succeeded in the rescue of the Jewish war victims than he was confronted with the more formidable problem of the Jews of Yemen, buried for centuries from the eyes and knowledge of the world in the mist of myth and legend. A story unique and dramatic became revealed to the world when, about the year 1172, the oldest Jewish community in existence—save that of Jerusalem—appealed to Moses Maimonides in one of the periodic agonies of its strange and turbulent life.

For many hundreds of years the Jews of the world were little aware of the fact that in the dazzling suns and scorching sands of the most primitive of Arabian lands called Yemen, known to ancient historians as Arabia Felix, there lived a tribe of Jews so utterly remote and isolated from the world that for centuries they were all but erased from the memory of their fellow-Jews. Their lives were bitter, their outlook hopeless; they were oppressed and persecuted, slaves to masters whom they were the first to instruct in the rudiments of civilization. Attempts were made to convert them by Christian missionaries and Mohammedan Imams. But staunch and loyal to their faith, they withstood every lure and threat.

An aura of romance hovers about the Jews of Yemen. History is vague on the life and fortunes of the Yemenite Jews, but legend supplies the missing data. Thus, there is a tradition of an Israelite colony in the Arabian Peninsula at the time of King David, a story of the first arrival of Jews in Yemen who came in the entourage of the Queen of Sheba on her return from her romantic visit with King Solomon, of thousands of Judeans who crossed the Jordan and settled in the Arab land at the destruction of Jerusalem by Nebuchadnezzar. When on his return from the Babylonian captivity Ezra called upon the Jews of the Dispersion to come and help rebuild the Holy Temple, the Yemenite Jews are said to have refused, whereupon he predicted that they would never have any peace. For centuries, the story goes, the Arabian Jews preserved a feeling of guilt for having preferred to remain with their fields and fortunes in captivity rather than join their brethren in the land from which they had been exiled.

The misty traditions surrounding the Jews of Yemen for hundreds of years which hid them from the eyes of the world were slightly cleared up by the destruction of the Jewish State by the Romans and the catastrophic events that followed. In consequence of the loss of their State and Temple and the unsuccessful rebellions of the death-defying patriots, thousands of Jews fleeing the Roman sword passed in straggling bands into Arabia, either for refuge or to continue from there their struggle against the oppressor. Jews from other lands converged on southern Arabia, some refugees from persecution, some because they found the place good to live in, making the country one of the largest centers of Jewish immigration.

On the shores of Babylon the Jews sat down and wept. They hung up their harps upon the willows when their captors asked them for words of song. No such lament, however, is recorded of the Jewish arrivals in Yemen, not because they had forgotten Zion, but because they found the land good, the population friendly and the surroundings congenial. The Arabs treated the newcomers well, for they had no greater love for Rome than the Jews who fled her sword. They were given full freedom of the country; they were allowed to work and trade and to practice the behests of their religion without let or hindrance. The Jews and Arabs had much in common. They descended from the same Semitic race, and their languages bore a strong resemblance to each other. In course of time the two elements of the population became so completely identical that they differed only in their religious beliefs.

It was not long before their association with each other became close and intimate even in matters of religion. For the Jews had brought with them their Bible and the religious traditions of their people, which made such a powerful impression on the simple but sensitive minds of the idolatrous sons of the desert that many of them, without persuasion or propaganda, became converts to the Jewish religion. When a chieftain became a Jew, Graetz says, his whole clan at once followed him. It was, of course, a superficial conversion, for many of the proselytes continued in their native mythologies, but it prepared the way for one of the most striking episodes in the Arab-Jewish relations.

Benjamin of Tudela who visited Yemen (1160) and left notes of his exploration, describes the Yemenite Jews as "an independent tribe. The extent of their land is sixteen days' journey among the northern mountains. They have large and fortified cities, with the capital city of Tema. Their Nasi is Rabbi Nanan." He identifies them with the Rechabites of the Bible [1] (Jer. 35), an obscure ascetic sect which resisted settled city life and followed the nomadic ideal. "The Rechabites," Benjamin writes, "make marauding expeditions in distant lands with their allies, the Arabs, who live in the wilderness in tents. The neighboring countries fear the Jews, some of whom cultivate the land, raise cattle, and contribute tithes for the men learned in the Law, for the poor in Palestine, and for the mourners of Zion and Jerusalem, who, except on Sabbath and holy days, neither eat meat nor drink wine, and who dress in black and live in caves." [2]

It is one of the most singular, if not exciting, incidents in Jewish history that about five hundred years after the destruction of the Jewish State in Palestine there was a Jewish commonwealth in Yemen presided over by Dhu Nowas (520–530) with the adopted biblical name of Joseph, the fourth of Jewish monarchs of the new royal line. While his is the only royal Jewish house history records, the probabilities are that he was the last of a procession of Yemenite monarchs who proselytized to Judaism. Unfortunately, however, his reign was short, for, wreaking harsh vengeance on neighboring Christian states for their treatment of Jews, he was defeated in battle, his kingdom was destroyed, and Nowas himself, in order not to fall into the hands of his enemies, committed suicide by jumping with his horse into the sea from a high overlooking cliff. Isaac Marcus Jost (1793–1860), the historian, seems to be of the opinion that after the death of Dhu Nowas the majority of Jews of his kingdom were absorbed in the general population and that only a remnant remained Jews by custom and religion.

Hostile shadows fell over the Jews of Arabia with the death of Dhu Nowas and the disappearance of his kingdom. The Christian sword raged with the vengeance of fire and destruction in the land where but a short while ago the Jews had been masters. Thousands were massacred, and those who escaped death had their rights curtailed, their liberties forfeited, able to worship their God only in the most guarded secrecy. Desertions from Judaism followed; only the bravest and most heroic spirits held out under the pressure and remained loyal to their faith.

There was every reason for Mohammed to be grateful to the religion which did so much to feed and sustain his prophetic ambition. The Bible provided the background for his teachings, and the Jewish expectation of the Messiah led the Arabs to recognize in him the appointed messenger of God. He counterfeited the message of the Prophets; he adopted some of the rites and practices of Judaism; he paraphrased Israel's declaration of faith, "Hear, O Israel, the Lord our God, the Lord is One" into "There is no God save Allah, and Mohammed is his Prophet"; borrowed from the lofty principles of the Jewish faith, he taught the crude, heathenish Arabs a way of life and conduct that was high above the incalculable deities they feared and worshipped. He was flattering to Jews and was respectful to Judaism; he had hoped by his blandishments to win them for his faith.

He was successful in getting some Jews to follow him, but the great majority of them spurned his advances. How could they seriously consider the apostolic pretensions of one whose personal life was an open scandal, whose harem was crowded with ten wives and two concubines, an illiterate son of the desert who could neither read nor write, a prophet who employed a Jewish secretary to take down the messages as they came from angel Gabriel? When Mohammed became convinced that he could not have the Jews as friends, he treated them as enemies. He declared war on the "infidels"; he resolved to destroy them; he plundered their property and obliterated their cities; he inspired in his followers an implacable hatred of Jews which remained unresolved for centuries.

Mohammed's victory over the Jews was complete. Arabia was no longer safe for Jews, and Yemen was the pit of their deepest degradation. They had no rights; they could claim no protection; they were helpless victims in the hands of fanatical Imams. It was a miracle that they survived. Yet not only did they survive but they managed to preserve the faded scrolls of their ancient faith, the teachings of the Prophets, the lessons of the Sages, and the memories of their great historic past. They fought off death by remaining true to their religion, loyal to their traditions, and they even contributed their modest share to the development of Jewish culture. Unlike some others of their dispersed brethren, they had not lost contact with their people. In rare propitious times, they sent their merchant caravans to Palestine and Babylon which brought back in return the precious tomes of their sacred literature.

They remembered their past and they remembered the land of their past. The Holy Land was the lodestar of their life and hope. With unshaken faith they believed in their redemption. They did not abandon the struggle, but the greater their suffering the keener was their faith in their future. Everlastingly they reminded themselves that God had made a covenant with their people: "Jerusalem and the cities of Judah shall be rebuilt again." They turned their faces in prayer toward the Holy City and daily awaited the coming of the Messiah. They not only remembered Zion but their poets sang of her and draped her memory with the ancient visions of her prophetic splendor. In Egypt, the aged Jeremiah spoke the same language Ezekiel addressed to his people in Babylon: "Lo, the days come, saith the Lord, that I will cause my people to return to the land that I gave to their fathers. Therefore shall they come and sing in the height of Zion. Again I will build thee, and thou shalt be built, O Virgin of Israel, for I have loved thee with an everlasting love." [3]

The tragic fate of the Jews of Yemen reached its desperate climax about the year 1170, when a mad Shiite Mahdi emulated the example of the distant fanatical Almohades in demanding that the Jews become Mohammedans on pain of death. There was boundless terror among the Jews, but there was little they could do. Saladin was a just and gracious ruler, and considerate of the Jewish subjects of his realm, but the political and military conditions of the time kept him in other parts of his empire and the governance of Yemen was in the hands of local administrators unfriendly to his rule. They were the adherents and partisans of the overthrown Fatimid dynasty, regarded Saladin as a usurper, and would welcome an opportunity to rise in rebellion against him.

A scholarly apostate added to their anxiety by raising an agitation among the Jews that they submit to the Mahdi's order and accept the Islamic faith, at the same time endeavoring to prove that Mohammed was a divinely-ordained prophet alluded to in the Bible charged to bring about a union between the two religions. Some Jews, exhausted by the struggle, lent ear to the seducer, lost faith in the splendid promises of Jehovah, and joined the religion of the oppressor. Other Jews, however—and they were in the great majority—did not give up hope. Their suffering inspired them with the patience to wait. Their hearts were wrung and their life wretched, but they kept their souls as a kingdom for Jehovah when He would come and redeem them.

He did come, at least in the fevered imagination of a young deluded visionary who proclaimed himself as forerunner of the Messiah come to announce to the oppressed and persecuted the glorious hope of a triumphant future. He harangued the people to be ready for the Deliverance which, he said, was close at hand, to repent of their sins, to dispose of their property and distribute the money to the poor. He found the ground well prepared for him, and his coming created a great commotion. The flickering flame of messianic deliverance had never died among the pious. For more than a thousand years prophets and liturgists had set that hope ineradicably into the hearts of millions of Jews. Dreamer or impostor, thousands eagerly listened to his message.

The commotion of the messianic revival reached the ears of the government and it boded ill for the Jews. Memories of similar untoward events were too fresh in the minds of the people to disregard the suspicion of skeptics. To what other man would Jews turn for advice and counsel in their perplexity than to Moses Maimonides upon whom the eyes of Jewry in all the lands of their Dispersion were focused? It fell to the task of Jacob al Fayumi, a learned representative of the Yemenite Jews, to write to the Sage of Fostat, whose reputation had spread to distant Arabia. Unfortunately, the text of the letter is lost, but from Maimonides' celebrated response we are given a clear idea of its contents.

Iggeret Teman,[4] "Letter to the South," or *Petach Tikvah*, "Gate of Hope," which Maimonides addressed to the Jews of Yemen, is a striking instance of the writer's minor writings. It is a classic of medieval Jewish epistolary literature, and it reveals the man in all the greatness and nobility of his character. "The 'Letter to Yemen,'" writes Franz Kobler in his admirable *A Treasury of Jewish Letters*, "addressed to a community on the outer fringe of the Jewish world, has become a letter to the whole Jewish people, defining the task of the people and giving meaning to its suffering and destiny." The "Letter" was written in Arabic in a lucid and fluent style.

"The whole Jewish community of Egypt," Maimonides wrote, "shares your grief. . . . Our minds are bewildered; we feel unable to think calmly, so great is the alternative in which Israel has been placed on all sides, from the East to the West." He endeavored to revive the people's downcast spirit by telling them that the Jews were a unique and indestructible nation, and that while persecution would never cease, they could not be annihilated. Dust, he said, is trodden by all and still increases in volume; it is stamped upon by all, yet rises upon him who treads upon it. Israel has been assailed in diverse ways and by different methods: by the brutal power of Nebuchadnezzar and Titus, by the deceptive seductions of the Hellenes, and by the false pretensions of the Cross and the Crescent. These latter, Maimonides averred, were the greatest danger to which the Jews were exposed, for Christianity and Mohammedanism did not dispute the Sinaitic Revelation but claimed to have superseded it.

Be assured, my brethren [Maimonides called out], that our three opponents, namely, the system of coercion, that of sophistry, and that which seeks to impress a high origin to which it is not entitled, will vanish. They may continue to prosper for a certain time, but their glory shall shortly disappear.

Our brethren of the House of Israel, scattered to the remote regions of the globe, it is your duty to strengthen one another, the older the younger, the few the many. . . . My brethren, it behooves us to keep ever present before our minds the great day of Sinai, for the Lord has forbidden us ever to forget it. Rear your offspring in a thorough understanding of that all-important event. Explain before large assemblies the principles it involves. Show that it is a lucid mirror reflecting the truth, aye, the very pivot on which our religion turns. . . . Know, moreover, you who are born in this covenant and reared in this belief, that the stupendous occurrence, the truth of which is testified by the most trustworthy of witnesses, stand alone in the annals of mankind. For a whole people heard the word of God and saw the glory of Divinity. From this lasting memory we must draw our power to strengthen our faith even in periods of persecution.

He expressed himself contemptuously with regard to the apostate who claimed that Judaism had been superseded by Mohammedanism and was caustic in his reply to the renegade that the "Prophet" had been predicted in the Bible. The religious teachings of Mohammed, he said, as compared with those of the Torah were as a statue compared with a living being. "The apostates themselves laugh at the idea, but they wish to deceive the Gentiles by pretending that they believe." He derided the pretensions of the would-be Messiahs who, he said, were no doubt madmen, and those who profess faith in them misguided creatures who had not formed a correct idea of the true nature of the Messiah. Maimonides expressed surprise that his correspondent who possessed learning and was no doubt acquainted with the teaching of the Rabbis in reference to Messiah should even entertain doubts about the true identity of the impostor cloaked though he be in the guise of meekness and piety.

Not the least interesting part of Maimonides' "Letter" is the recital of the suffering which a number of bogus Messiahs had brought to the Jews in Islamic countries, notably Persia, Morocco, and Andalusia. "The prophets have predicted and instructed us," wrote Maimonides, "that pretenders and simulators will appear in great number at the time when the advent of the true Messiah will draw nigh, but they will not be able to make good their claim. They will perish with many of their partisans." As to the Yemenite "madman," Maimonides counseled that he be put away for a time and his insanity be circulated among the Gentiles. "In that manner the people will be saved from persecution and peace and harmony will be restored to the community."

He warned the Yemenite Rabbi against the danger of attempting to calculate the time of the Messiah's coming because of the distrust and desperation it might entail when proved wrong. "The precise date of the messianic advent cannot be known," wrote Maimonides, and the Rabbis had long ago pronounced a ban on such idle speculations. It is related in the Talmud that the Divine Presence departed from Jacob because he wished to reveal to his children "the time of the end" before his death.[5] There were, however, extenuating circumstances for R. Saadia's calculations, for the Jews of his time were perplexed and bewildered and would have given up hope altogether were it not for the certainty of redemption he held out to them. Nevertheless, in the same "Letter" Maimonides himself derives the exact date of the coming of the Messiah from Nu. 23:23. This is most strangely inconsistent with the advice given by him in his essay *Tehiyat ha-Metim* and in his remarks to the twelfth of the Thirteen Articles of Faith: "No date must be fixed for his [Messiah's] appearance, neither may the Scriptures be interpreted with the view of deducing the date of his advent."

As in his *Epistle Concerning Apostasy,* Maimonides counseled the Jews suffering from persecution to emigrate to other lands where they would be free to serve their God unmolested. "Should ever the necessity arise to flee for your lives to a wilderness and inhospitable regions—painful as it may be to sever oneself from dear associations, or to relinquish one's property—you should still endure all and be supported by the consoling thought that the Omnipresent Lord who reigns supreme can compensate you commensurately with your deserts in this world and in the World-to-Come. . . . It often happens that a man will part from kindred and friends and travel abroad because he finds his earnings inadequate to his wants. How much more readily ought one follow the same course when he stands in danger of being denied the means of supplying his spiritual necessities!"

In conclusion, Maimonides asked Jacob al-Fayum to send copies of his letter to every community in the cities and hamlets "in order to strengthen the people in their faith and put them on their feet. Read it at public gatherings and in private, and you will thus become a public benefactor." At the same time he warned him to take the greatest precaution that its contents be not divulged to the Gentiles by an evil person so that disaster might not befall him and them. "When I began writing this letter," Maimonides said, "I had some misgivings about it, but they were overruled by my conviction that the public welfare takes precedence over one's personal safety. . . . Our Sages, the successors of the Prophets, assured us that persons engaged in a religious mission will meet with no disaster. What greater religious mission is there than this?"

The "Letter" accomplished its purpose. As was requested by the writer, it was copied and dispatched to all Jewish communities and congregations in Yemen. It was read at public meetings and circulated privately. All men and women were made acquainted with it, and children had it read to them by their parents. As was predicted by Maimonides, the persecution did not last long. For with Saladin's enlightened, tolerant policy, order was restored when his elder brother Turin Shah wrested the reins of government from the hands of the local Shiite Mahdi.

Moses Maimonides was idolized by the Jews of Yemen, who hailed him as the hero of their deliverance. In their gratitude, they included his name in the first paragraph of the *Kaddish,* the prayer of sanctification, which was made to read, "May He establish His kingdom during your life and during your days, during the life of all the House of Israel, *and during the life of Moses, the son of Maimon,*" an honor theretofore reserved only for the Prince of Captivity on his accession to office.

5. A PATH THROUGH THE TALMUD

MOSES MAIMONIDES was one of the most energetic and industrious of Jewish scholars. Few others had equaled him in his ability and capacity for work. There was no room in his life for leisure. He employed every minute of his time profitably. A hunger for achievement and desire to be of service to his faith and people drove him on from one activity to the other. When he was not writing books, he wrote letters. Indeed, he may be said to have been the most prolific letter-writer of his time. It was said, and not without some justice, that his influence on the Jews of his day was due no less to his active correspondence with all parts of the Jewish world than to his strictly literary work. It was with his *Epistle Concerning Apostasy* that he had first introduced himself to the Jewish world and his *Letter to Yemen* made his name a household word among the Jews of that far-away Asian community.

He was in touch with nearly all the leading rabbis of his time whose correspondence he promptly answered in his own careful, ornate style. Like Alfasi, the great authority of the eleventh century, he wrote his responsa mostly in Arabic, the language of the Jews in Syria, Spain, North Africa, Yemen, and Egypt, but they were translated into Hebrew and circulated throughout Jewry. But laymen, too, wrote to him, sometimes on serious, sometimes on trivial matters, which he likewise answered with great care and courtesy. Moses Maimonides was not only the son of a *dayyan* but he was a *dayyan*—rabbi, judge and arbiter—himself, and his parish was as wide as Saladin's empire. He had the ear of Alfadhel, Saladin's trusted and influential Vizier, with whom he was on friendly terms, and he some-times interceded with him in behalf of co-religionists who entreated him for assistance.

He had no taste for titles, no liking for official positions, the pro-fessionalization of learning was abhorrent to him. He was the head of the Fostat community, but he held no appointive position; he was the greatest teacher of Oriental Jewry and spiritual leader of the Jews of Egypt, but he did not bear the title *Nagid* (Prince), official rep-resentative of the Jews at the court, although it seems probable that, had he wanted it, the honor would have been conferred upon him.

How with his exacting duties and interests Maimonides found the time to write his epoch-making works is one of the mysteries of his genius. For he had no sooner completed his *Mishnah Commentary* than, without rest or pause, he started on the codification of Jewish law. Any other man would have been satisfied to rest on his laurels with such work as the Commentary, for with this work alone he would have won for himself an enduring place in Jewish scholarship. But the Commentary was but a prelude to and not the consummation of his lifework. For just as Rabbi Judah Hanasi's Mishnah led to the creation of the Talmud, so Maimonides designed his *Mishnah Com-mentary* to serve as a sort of introduction to his more ambitious *Mishneh Torah (The Second Torah)*, a complete codification and summary of the biblical and rabbinical law, religion, and ethics.

It was a courageous task on which he had entered. Jewish legal literature as represented by the Talmud is an extremely difficult sub-ject. It is without order or system. The continuous ever-growing stream of oral doctrines, flowing and swelling over many centuries, staggers the capacity of the best-trained scholar. The laws of the Talmud are exasperatingly scattered; many a legal discussion is often interrupted by quite irrelevant dissertations. The Talmud arose from the collective labor of many successive generations. It includes utter-ances of sages who differed in training and outlook; hence the be-wildering contradictions one often finds in it. The creators of the Talmud were polyglots; they mastered other languages besides the Hebrew and Aramaic, which are the principal idioms of the Talmud. They spoke, or at least understood, the Latin, Greek, and Persian languages and introduced their technical legal terms.

The codification of the laws of the Talmud was beyond the capac-ity of a mere Talmudist. It required a combination of gifts and talents and an innate capacity for extraordinary clarity and precision. It required a keen, critical mind and an almost uncanny insight into the labyrinths of dialectical exercises in order to separate the kernel from the chaff, the essential from the accidental. It required unusual courage to decide between conflicting opinions of equally eminent authorities, and sometimes set aside authority and state his own view, as he did concerning witchcraft and demonology when he wrote: "These things are all false, and whoever believes that they are founded on fact is a mere fool."

It was the merit of Moses Maimonides that he possessed to a superlative degree all the necessary qualifications for the work he undertook. He had the widest acquaintance with the whole field of talmudic law; he possessed extraordinary intellectual powers; his logical faculties were sharpened by his philosophical studies. But before approaching the task of codifying the whole body of legal material contained in the talmudic, midrashic, geonic, and later authoritative sources, Maimonides found it necessary to catalogue the precepts of the Mosaic legislation which were fixed by tradition to amount to six hundred and thirteen—two hundred and forty-eight positive and three hundred and sixty-five negative commandments. This he did in *Sefer ha-Mitzvot*, the *Book of Precepts*,[1] in itself a highly valuable work which the writer later prefixed to the Mishneh Torah.

In the introduction to his Code Maimonides states clearly the reasons which moved him to launch on this project—one not undertaken before except, among less successful efforts, by Alfasi. He said:

In our time disasters continually follow one another. The need of the moment sets aside every other consideration. The wisdom of our wise men is lost, and the learning of our learned men is hidden. All the interpretations, codes, and responses which the Geonim composed, and which they thought were easy of understanding, have become unintelligible in our days, and there are but few who are able to comprehend them. As to the Talmuds themselves, both the Babylonian and Palestinian, and the other talmudic literature, I have no need to say that they require wide knowledge and great intelligence, and that it takes a long time before anyone can find out the right way concerning all the things permitted and forbidden, and concerning all the other commandments of the Law. Therefore, I, Moses, the son of Maimon, the Spaniard, have girded my loins and put my trust in the Lord, blessed be He, have studied all these works and made my mind to collect the results derived from them, and expounded them in precise language and concise manner, so that the entire Oral Law may be made accessible to everyone without any arguments or counterarguments, but in clear and unmistakable terms, in entire accord with the decisions which may be deduced from all the treatises and interpretations existing since the time of Rabbi Judah the Patriarch, compiler of the Mishnah, until the present day. In short, my intention is, that no man shall have any need to resort to any other book on any point of Jewish law. . . . For this reason I called the name of this work Mishneh Torah [*The Second Torah*], *for all that a man has to do, is to read first the Written Law* [*the Bible*] *and follow it up by this work, and he will know the entire Oral Law without the need of reading any other book between them.*

It is evident that Maimonides wrote the second of his great trilogy not with the Mishnah of Rabbi Judah in mind, but with the Torah of Moses, hence the name by which he called it, *Mishneh Torah*. It is, however, better known by its subtitle, *Yad ha-Hazakah (The Mighty Hand)*, an allusion to the last verse in Deuteronomy, or simply *Yad* (hand), having in Hebrew the numerical value of fourteen, into which number he divided his work. Firmly convinced that the Code would become an authoritative work for all Israel, whether living in Christian or Moslem lands, Maimonides composed it in the Hebrew language instead of the vernacular Arabic in which he wrote all his other books. Maimonides explained in his preface to the *Book of Precepts* the style he chose for the Code: "I have chosen not to compose it in the style of the prophetical books, for that language is not sufficient to express all the details of the laws, nor will I use the style and language of the Talmud, for only few will understand it on account of its construction and difficult words, but I will adopt the style and the language of the Mishnah so that the majority of our people may understand it." According to Maimonides' own statement, he devoted to the task ten long years, working day and night. But, "really," says Graetz, "time stands in no relation to the magnitude of the performance," [2] for it represents the greatest attempt ever made by any one man to bring order, clarity, and coherence into so titanic a confusion as is the Talmud. The artist and the scientist are fused together in the *Mishneh Torah;* the philosopher and the theologian join hands in its pages. Law-books are dry and dull, they do not make pleasant reading for the uninitiated. But Maimonides' Code is that rare thing, a book about law which the general reader with a sufficient knowledge of Hebrew can enjoy. It is a great work of rabbinic scholarship not only because of the width of its learning, its penetration, and integrity but for its stylistic beauty, clarity of thought, and diction. Moses Maimonides is the expositor of the whole Law. Nothing was to him superfluous, outgrown, or antiquated; everything was vital, alive, and functioning. The laws of priesthood, sacrifices and the Temple service were to him as integral a part of the Jewish religious consciousness as the laws in active practice today.

One must disagree with Graetz that by his Code, Maimonides created "a new Talmud." [3] The old Talmud is there; all its elements are there; not a law or precept has been omitted, except the superstitions which are offensive to reason. But such was Maimonides' literary and artistic craftsmanship that, in his hands, the old Talmud was made to look new. Where, in Maimonides, is the "thorny underbrush" which makes access to the Talmud forbidding? Where the eternal wrangling of schools and scholars which leaves one dizzy? Where, too, is the contradiction of opposing views and opinions when one wants to find the law on any given matter to discharge his religious duty? Israel Friedlaender gives the clearest distinction between Maimonides and the Rabbis of the Talmud. "The difference between his Code and the Talmud," he says, "is the same as between a warehouse of accumulated materials and a magnificent palace. The warehouse, no doubt, contains a vast amount of valuable stuff; one may find there silver and gold, and very often even jewels. But all these treasures make the proper impression only when arranged in order and co-ordinated with one another. The palace of Maimonides betrays the marvelous architect. The tremendous edifice is, as it were, of one cast. There is a ravishing harmony in all its parts." [4]

Mishneh Torah is the greatest contribution to Jewish jurisprudence not only by reason of its practical advantages but because of its systematic orderliness. The Hebraic genius is noted for many things—its insight, depth, and originality, but orderliness is not one of its virtues. "It probably never occurred to them (the Jews) that law and history should be written systematically," says H. S. Lewis.[5] In the Pentateuch, ceremonial laws and historical narratives are often thrown together seemingly at random, and of Rabbi Judah Hanasi's Mishnah, the best thought-out collection of tannaitic laws, the remark is often made in the Talmud that it is without logical order or system.

Besides its many other qualities, it is its logical and well-proportioned arrangement which gave Maimonides' compendium its greatest influence and distinction. It was only a critic like Abraham ben David of Posquieres, commonly known as *Rabad* (1125–1198), who was, after all, only a great Talmudist who saw nothing else beyond it, who scented danger in the unified system of religion, law, and philosophy, the average intelligent student realizes with wonder how talmudic jurisprudence became transformed in Maimonides' hands. In our author's Code, every chapter is a model of clarity, every paragraph and statement a lesson in brevity and precision. "If I had been able to put the whole of the Oral Law into one chapter I would not have used two," Maimonides once said.

He was terse in his style, careful of his diction; he was a writer of extraordinary skill and elegance. He placed great emphasis on the external form in which he expressed his ideas. In his *Mishneh Torah* the Hebrew language may be said to have had its second rebirth. Of his manner of writing, Maimonides said: "All our works are carefully sifted and cleansed. It is never our intention to swell the volume of our writings. . . . When we have to explain a topic, we only explain that which is absolutely in need of explanation. . . . Outside of this, we usually confine ourselves in our writings to a brief exposition of the subject." [6]

Maimonides loved the Hebrew language and he regarded it as the "Holy Tongue." He wrote all his other works, besides the *Mishneh Torah,* in Arabic because he wanted to give circulation to his ideas and teachings among classes of Jews who no longer understood the language of the Bible, but his greatest devotion was to the Hebrew idiom. Thus, he wrote to the Rabbis of Lunel: ". . . with regard to your request that I may translate the text [of the *Guide for the Perplexed*] into the holy tongue for you—I myself could wish that I were young enough to be able to fulfill your wish concerning this and the other works which I have composed in the language of Ishmael, and I should be very pleased thus to free their superior from their inferior elements and to give back the stolen goods to the rightful owner. But I must blame the unfavorable times for preventing me from doing this. I have not even time to work out and to improve my commentaries and other works produced in the rabbinic language, which contain various obscurities, in order to arrange new editions—to say nothing of making translations from one language into another." [7]

Some years before, in 1191, after his epoch-making *Mishneh Torah* appeared and one Joseph Ibn Gabir of Baghdad, who was deficient in the Hebrew language, asked Maimonides for a translation, he replied: "If you want to study my work, you will have to learn Hebrew little by little. It is not so difficult, as my book is written in an easy style, and if you master one part, you will soon be able to understand the whole work. I do not intend, however, to produce an Arabic edition, as you suggest; the work would lose its specific color. How could I do this when I should like to translate my Arabic writings into the holy language!" [8] Maimonides was deeply gratified at hearing from Samuel Ibn Tibbon that he was at work on a Hebrew translation of *The Guide for the Perplexed,* and, among highly interesting personal information, he gave him several rules on the art of translation.

Although the *Mishneh Torah,* soon after its appearance, was bitterly attacked, legend, which is sometimes a corrective of history, embellished Maimonides' gigantic lifework with the story that Moses had appeared to him in a dream, looked into his book, and bestowed his blessing upon him in the words, "You have done well by continuing my work. May you succeed and prosper."

The *Mishneh Torah,* which revolutionized rabbinic learning and influenced Jewish religious life for hundreds of years, grew out of a digest of the talmudic laws which Maimonides drew up for his own personal use. With his advancing years and the increased demands made on his time, Moses Maimonides made an abstract of the rabbinic legislation so that he would not have to wade through the whole "Sea of the Talmud" when he was in need of a legal decision on any occasion. He soon, however, realized that what applied to him was true in still greater measure of people who, when in need of a clear and decisive opinion on a question of a legal or religious character, could not cope with the enormous mass of talmudic material. It is thus that, for the rabbi in his study, for the student in his quest for the law, and the layman who had neither the time for nor the knowledge of the intricacies of the Talmud that the digest, originally designed for Maimonides' own private use, grew into the *Mishneh Torah,* with its fourteen books and one thousand chapters.

In a letter to Joseph Ibn Aknin in 1190, Maimonides told how the *Mishneh Torah* came to be written and the opposition to it he expected:

I want to tell you the following: First, I did not write this book [the Code of Law] to gain honor and glory among the Jews. God knows, I started the work for my own practical use that I should not be compelled to search all of talmudic literature for particular material. Then, as the years passed by, I decided to devote my labor to the Lord. I realized that the nation had no code of law presenting the decisions without controversy and errors. So I carried my plan for the sake of the honor of God.

Second, I was anticipating that the book would fall into the hands of spiteful fanatics who would run it down. The ignoramus, who cannot appreciate such a work, will find it of little use. The immature and confused beginner will stumble over passages the roots of which he does not know; or, he will be too slow of understanding to follow, with necessary exactness, the given details. Those who consider themselves wise and intelligent will criticize the book on religious grounds. These will be in the majority.

A few, however, will receive the book in fairness and justice and will understand what I was aiming at. You are one of them. Were you the only one at the present time, I would be satisfied. I have also received letters from the scholars of France and other countries; they are pleased with my work and desire to see the book completed. I am confident that at some future day, when envy and desire for power will vanish, the Jews will be ready to accept my work.

Kobez II, 30

The brevity and conciseness which Maimonides planned for his work is not always consistently carried out. Nor could it be expected of the man who, besides being a jurist, was a theologian, philosopher, and scientist. For, to Maimonides, the laws and ordinances of the Bible and the Talmud were not merely legal decisions or arbitrary commandments, but "judgments of righteousness flowing from the well of wisdom" containing deep moral and philosophical truths. Therefore he did not hesitate in obedience to a higher plan to introduce into his Code philosophical and scientific discussions which, in the opinion of his critics, have little relation to the formulation of the rabbinic law.

There was a lapse of nearly seven hundred years between the Talmud and Maimonides, and a still longer time between the Mishnah and the *Mishneh Torah*. There was no need for a philosophy or metaphysic of Judaism in the days of the Tannaim and Amoraim. The Jews lived by their own inner light and did not care for any other wisdom. They drew their religion, history, and ethics from their

Bible, and the Talmud crystallized for them everything a Jew should know or cared to know. Neither the Rabbis of the Mishnah nor of the Talmud felt the need of explaining God, proving His existence and spirituality. He was taken for granted, and men loved, adored, and worshiped Him from their inner necessity. The Mishnah, which is the groundwork of the Talmud, could therefore briefly launch out on the subject of prayer with the question, "From what time in the evening may the *Shema* be recited?" without discussing the metaphysical and theological problems involved in prayer. Not so Moses Maimonides, who lived at a time when the mode of living and believing of a large number of Jews no longer harmonized with their religion; when, indeed, the question was not when, but *why* the *Shema* should be recited. It was therefore necessary for Maimonides to reverse the process of his religious code and start out with *Sefer ha-Madda*, "The Book of Knowledge," which deals with the philosophy and theology of Judaism, before discussing its rites and rituals.

Although Maimonides' Code follows the general arrangement of the Mishnah, it goes considerably beyond it inasmuch as it includes a number of laws which were omitted by Rabbi Judah. The Patriarch did not deem it necessary to dwell upon the regulations pertaining to Hanukah or assign special tractates to such religious usages as those of phylacteries, fringes, and *mezuzah*, either because their laws were generally known or because their practice was widespread. Maimonides, however, conscious of the general ignorance of the Torah prevailing in his time and the neglect of its precepts, was anxious to put into the hands of his people a Code that contained the whole of the Written and Oral Law.

"The whole arrangement of the general subjects [of *Mishneh Torah*]," writes A. Marmorstein, "as well as the composition of the details, bears all the traces of the master's skill in logic and systematizing scholarly materials." [9]

Maimonides divided his Code into fourteen books. The first book, *Sefer ha-Madda*, the "Book of Knowledge," discusses the fundamental principles of the Jewish religion, such as the belief in the existence of God, His Unity, Incorporeality, Providence, Free Will, Prophecy, the laws relating to the Thirteen Articles of Faith, the composition of the physical and metaphysical world, the laws concerning the study of Torah, prohibition of idolatry, and the laws and method of Repentance.

Book II, called *Ahabah* (Love), discusses one's devotion to God through such religious acts and symbols as relating to the recital of *Shema*, prayer, phylacteries, *mezuzah*, circumcision, the blessings of the priests, the order of the synagogue ritual, and the laws connected with the writing of a *Sefer Torah* (Scroll of the Law).

Book III, called *Zemanim* (Seasons), includes the precepts concerning the major and minor feasts and fasts of the year, such as the Sabbath, Passover, Sukkoth, Purim, Rosh ha-Shanah, Yom Kippur, Tisha b'Ab, their ceremonies and observances.

Books IV and V, denominated *Nashim* and *Keddusha* (Women) and (Holiness), respectively, contain groups of laws regulating permitted and prohibited marriages, including *Yibbum*, Levirate Marriage, or marriage with a brother's widow. The fifth book contains laws concerning forbidden sexual relations, as well as forbidden foods. And since Israel is distinguished by these commandments from the other nations and was sanctified thereby, it bears the name "Holiness."

In Book VI the author takes up the subject of oaths and vows, and the prescriptions regarding the Nazarite, one who has made a vow of abstinence. And because his rule of life sets him apart from the regular conduct of life, this section is called *Haflaah* (Separation).

Book VII, which is called *Zeraim* (Seeds), sets forth the laws relating to agriculture as well as those pertaining to the Sabbatical year, and the tithes due to the priests and Levites serving in the Temple.

Books VIII, IX, and X, bearing the respective titles *Abodah* (*Divine Services* [in the Temple]), *Korbanot* (Sacrifices), and *Tohorot* (The Book of Cleanness), cover three groups of laws not applicable to Jewish life since the destruction of the Temple. Maimonides, however, who made no distinction between laws in force and laws not in force, included them in his Code as part of the revealed will of God, their temporary practicability or impracticability notwithstanding. Herbert Danby [10] quotes Maimonides' *Guide for the Perplexed* (III, chapter 31): "The truth is undoubtedly . . . that everyone of the six hundred and thirteen precepts serves to inculcate some truth, to remove some erroneous opinion, to establish proper relations to society, to diminish evil, to gain in good manners, or to warn against bad habits."

Book XI, *Nezikin* (The Book of Torts), in contrast to the ten previous books which deal chiefly with the symbolic and ritual observances of the Law, is concerned with civil and criminal law—damages or injuries derived from theft, robbery, and homicide. In other words, while almost all the preceding books are concerned with the relations between man and God, the Book of Torts deals with the more mundane relations between man and his fellowmen.

Book XII, called *Kinyan* (Acquisitions), discusses the laws governing sales and purchases, partnership, agency, and slavery, since in the Hebraic law slaves were regarded as real property.

Book XIII, *Mishpatim* (Judgments), belongs in point of subject matter to the two previous books. The subdivisions of the book consist of laws concerning hiring, borrowing and depositing, creditor and debtor, pleading and inheritance. A point of special interest, says Jacob J. Rabinowitz,[11] are the perorations in three of the five subdivisions of the book which reveal a depth of feeling and beauty of style quite rare in halakic literature.

Book XIV. While the concluding volume of Maimonides' Code bears the overall title *Sefer Shoftim* (The Book of Judges), and sets forth the laws governing the judiciary system, it is made up of the following component parts: *Sanhedrin* (the Judiciary), ranging all the way from the Supreme Court of seventy-one to a court of twenty-three, and even to a court of one qualified judge; "Evidence," the examination of witnesses and the grounds on which they may be disqualified from rendering testimony; "Rebels," those who rule contrary to the decision of the Supreme Court; "Mourning," ritual laws bearing on mourning over those who died a natural death and persons convicted and executed by court; "Kings and Wars;" royal prerogatives of monarchs, the authority vested in them by law, and the limitations of their powers. This section of the book also differentiates between mandatory and optional wars. The treatise concludes with two chapters on the Messianic Era with the consequences accruing from it to Israel and humankind.

Dr. Abraham M. Hershman, in his introduction to *The Book of Judges*,[12] calls attention to a highly interesting long passage in the early manuscripts and early printed editions of the book, not mutilated by the hand of the censor, concerning the founders of Christianity and Islam. To quote Dr. Hershman in part: "There is toward the end of Section 4, a long passage concerning the founder of Christianity, the contention that the commandments of Scripture have become obsolete, and the part which Christianity and Islam have played in the higher education of the human race, i.e., in the propagation of the God idea, the Messianic doctrine, etc." [13]

6. THE GREAT CONTROVERSY

ONE CANNOT read far in Maimonides' Code without sensing its high moral and ethical quality. A rare spirit of love of humanity dominates its pages. If a man's philosophy, his view of life, is the outgrowth of his character and personality, then the Code is the clearest revelation of the writer's essential sympathy, kindliness and warm-hearted attitude to the world and mankind. Everywhere in *Mishneh Torah* one is made to feel that it is not only the judge and legislator that speaks but the great humanitarian, the generous-souled son of the people which taught the world to look beyond the strict measure of the law.

The ethical vision of the Maimonidean Code is rooted deep in the tradition of the Bible and the Talmud. Although in his philosophy Moses Maimonides is abstract and intellectual, making knowledge, wisdom and understanding a condition of the good life, there is a glow of sympathy and tenderness in the Code which makes goodness and piety the rule of human perfection. The drama of human pain and suffering had often led the stern rationalist-philosopher to reverse himself. Thus, much as Maimonides hated every form of superstition and waged unrelenting war against it, he nevertheless permitted a person stung by a scoripon to have a spell whispered over the injured part so as to relieve the sick man's mind.

The kindness and compassion he demanded were extended to all men alike, irrespective of race or creed. He ordained that Jews conduct themselves mercifully toward the indigent non-Jews, that they feed their hungry, bury their dead and comfort their mourning, for

God's mercy, he said, extends to all His creatures. When his opinion was solicited with regard to the Gentiles, Maimonides wrote: "Know that the Lord desires the heart, and that the intention of the heart is the measure of all things. That is why the Sages say: 'The pious men among the Gentiles have a share in the World-to-Come.' " [1]

The individual stands high in the ethical philosophy of Moses Maimonides. He saw something unique and holy in every individual being, something not to be abased or violated. For man bears the image of God, the imprint of His character and personality, as it were. Morality is not a theory that thrives in a vacuum. The relation of man to his Maker is largely determined by his relation to his fellow beings. A human being is neither a tool nor a chattel; while we may have a right to his service or labor, his honor and dignity are supremely his own and must not be tampered with.

Slavery was to Maimonides an "accursed" institution on which the economy of the world he lived in depended, and he could do nothing about it except, in the spirit of the Bible and the Talmud, soften and restrain some of its hardships. While in the words of Juvenal, a Roman poet of the first century, the slave was "not really a human being" and thus could be hurt without redress, even killed without serious consequences to the slayer, he emerges from Maimonides' Code with a God-given personality which may be neither degraded nor violated. He must not be taunted or offended; he must not be made to suffer injury of word or hand. "Cruelty and effrontery," wrote Maimonides, "are not frequent except with the heathen. The children of our father Abraham, however, i.e., the Israelites, upon whom the Holy One, blessed be He, bestowed the favor of the Law, and laid upon them statutes and judgments, are merciful people who have mercy upon all." [2]

Maimonides' ethics vis-à-vis the individual included the right to his reputation. A man's reputation is his personality, and it should be sacredly regarded. All great religious teachers and moralists insist on this, and the Bible and the Talmud are rich in exhortations against the evils of venomous gossip. Thrice daily the Jew concludes the Eighteen Benedictions with the beautiful meditation, "O my God! Guard my tongue from evil and my lips from speaking guile." Maimonides castigated severely the spreading of damaging reports about one's neighbor and counted it among the sins for which one is punished in this world and forfeits his portion in the World-to-Come.

In several sections of the seventh book of the Code under the heading *Matnot Aniyim*, Maimonides occupied himself with the discussion of *zeddakah*, that most untranslatable word in the Hebrew vocabulary, denoting the whole gamut of human sympathy, kindness, tenderness, benevolence and social justice. The poor, he said, have a rightful claim on us for their maintenance, and only he who is distinguished for his charity may be regarded as a worthy descendant of Abraham, our father, as is said, "For I know him to the end that he commands his children and his household to keep the way of the Lord to do *zeddakah*." [3] Through *zeddakah*, Maimonides said, no man is impoverished, nor will any evil befall him because of it. He never heard of a Jewish community that did not possess a *kupah shel zeddakah* (charity chest). If not to their fellow Jews, Maimonides' plea rang forth, to whom shall our poor turn? Shall they turn to the nations of the earth who hate and despise us and rejoice in our misfortune? [3a]

Maimonides was not contented with merely urging the need of giving *zeddakah* but was deeply concerned with the manner of its execution. He regarded benevolence as a virtue, ennobling both the giver and the recipient, when it is practiced with a glad hand and joyous spirit. "Whoever gives alms to the poor," said Maimonides, "with bad grace and downcast look, though he bestow a thousand gold pieces, all the merit of his action is lost," [4] for, say the Rabbis, it is better to give nothing at all than to cause a blush to the recipient. [5] The story is told of Rabbi Yannai that he saw a person giving a *zuz*, a rather big coin, to a poor man in public, whereupon the Rabbi told the philanthropist: "It would be better that you do not give anything than give in such manner as to put the poor man to shame." [6] It is the kind word, the gentle reception, and sympathetic attitude that help to encourage the needy and humble even more than the giving of money. It is written, "Happy is he who *considereth* the poor," [7] and the Sages point out that the word used is "considereth," not giveth. [8] "Woe to the person who shames the poor," Maimonides cried out. "Be to him rather like a parent whether in compassion or in kindly words." [8a]

Notwithstanding Maimonides' high regard for the individual and the inviolable sacredness of his personality, his theory of life was social, his philosophy—the collective good. Man, said Maimonides, is naturally a social being; by virtue of his nature he seeks to form communities; he is different from other living beings that are not compelled to combine into groups for mutual assistance. It is both the greatness and glory of man that he is interdependent, that neither in his physical nor in his moral existence can he live alone without the support of his fellow beings. By himself man would have neither the time nor the strength to provide the means necessary for his bodily comfort, to say nothing of the arts and sciences which contribute to the blessedness and enrichment of life.[9] And as for the virtues of goodness, tenderness, justice, and morality, of what use or benefit would they be if man lived alone on a desert isle? Said Maimonides in the concluding chapter of *The Guide for the Perplexed*: "Imagine a person being alone, and having no connection whatever with any other person, all his good moral principles are at rest, they are not required, and give man no perfection whatever. These principles are only necessary and useful when man comes in contact with others." [10]

Zarik adam leshatef et azmo im ha-zibur, "It is the duty of man to associate himself with the community," may be said to be the guiding principle of Maimonides' social outlook. To be a Jew meant to him to harmonize and normalize one's life with the life and well-being of the Jewish group of which he is a part. He said: "One who separates himself from the community, even if he does not commit a transgression, but only holds himself aloof from the congregation of Israel, does not fulfill the religious precepts in common with his people, shows himself indifferent when they are in distress, does not observe their fasts, but goes his own way as if he were one of the Gentiles and did not belong to the Jewish people—such a person has no portion in the World-to-Come." [11]

Maimonides' Code is an encyclopedia of Jewish philosophy, theology, ethics, and ritual. It is also a treatise on commerce, industry, finance, property, inheritance, taxation, legal procedure, and penal law. It is a law book whose domain extends over almost every form of human activity. It legislates for the scholar, it provides for the trader, and prescribes for the shopkeeper. It seeks to guide and curb, to promote justice and restrain violence. It regards the simplest human activity and enterprise from the moral and ethical point of view. Its categorical imperative may be summed up in the words: "Act so as to find grace and favor in the eyes of God and man." Maimonides' Code secures the rights and privileges of the individual but holds the interests and welfare of society to be paramount in all things. Man may not be guided by his own likes and dislikes; he may not live, act, and behave as he will without squaring his conduct with the society or community in which he lives.

Moses Maimonides was not an economist, declares Professor Salo W. Baron in an exhaustive pioneer study of the jurist-philosopher's economic views in *Essays on Maimonides*. But Maimonides was certainly keenly aware of the life and affairs of the time in which he lived, and he devotes to them a considerable part of his Code. He was as deeply interested in the economic tasks and functions of life as he was in the religious and ritual observances. They are both part of the divine legislation. The road to perfection is not paved with men who negate the material life and would wish it to be destroyed. Time and again Maimonides demonstrated that the material world with its forms and functions is not unholy, and although it should be subordinated to the moral order, it should not be suppressed.

The social philosophy of Moses Maimonides is that while man has the right to work and acquire, and enjoy the fruit of his toil and labor, it is ethically required that such right should not run unreasonably counter to the rights of organized society. While Maimonides accepted the profit system of economic enterprises, he spoke out sharply against excessive profits, although he never quite defined what profits were reasonable and what were excessive. He was strenuously opposed to the monopolistic system of business, because of its damaging effect upon free enterprise. Though he abhorred competition, and would not have two shopkeepers do the same business in the same street, he allowed two elementary school teachers to establish themselves in the same locality if it was to the advantage of the religious training of the children. Residents of a city may prevent out-of-town traders from selling their merchandise. But spice merchants who travel from town to town cannot be hindered from plying their trade, because it is an enactment of Ezra to allow them to travel in order that perfume may be readily available to the daughters of Israel. They cannot, however, establish permanent residence without consent of the residents of the town.

Maimonides was particularly severe on those who lend money on interest, and he held the lender as well as the borrower equally culpable. The Torah calls such transaction *nesek*, because, Maimonides said, he who takes it bites his fellow, causes him pain, and eats his flesh. He condemned every form of deception, fraud, and misrepresentation, whether committed against a heathen or an Israelite. Weights and measures must be adjusted accurately, and if they are found to be faulty, restitution should be made to the defrauded party. Indeed, Maimonides wrote: "The punishment for incorrect measures is more severe than the punishment for immorality, for the latter is a sin against God only, the former against one's fellow-man." [12]

While the Maimonidean Code abounds in tenderest sentiments toward the poor and the needy, it has no words of praise for poverty. On the contrary, it urges upon every Jew the moral obligation of independence by earning a living and not becoming a public charge. Human life, Maimonides taught, is most worthily and ethically lived when one keeps the obligation he owes to society and the duty he owes to himself equally balanced. Thus, in accordance with a decision formed at Usha [13] Maimonides warned against the practice of ruinous charity, forbidding a person to dedicate all his property to the Temple or to distribute it to the poor without leaving anything for himself.

Notwithstanding the towering greatness of the *Mishneh Torah* and its immense service to Judaism, Maimonides was soon to discover that it was destined for no better fate at the hands of the professional scholars than was his *Mishnah Commentary*. For, while the friends and partisans of Maimonides hailed his work for what it was—a titanic achievement of rabbinic scholarship—and saluted the author for wielding his rod over the turbulent waters of the Talmud so that students of the Torah might pass safely through them, there were others whose judgment was less complimentary. Indeed, it was not merely criticism with which Maimonides' Code had met on its appearance, but reproach, attack, and ill-tempered abuse. Some critics opposed the work from motives of personal antagonism; others assailed the codification of the Talmud on the ground that it closed the door to free discussion; while still others of the more superficial variety of critics disapproved of the clear, lucid Hebrew style in which the book was written, preferring the difficult Aramaic dialect.

There were, however, more serious charges against the Code to which the author had left himself open and which were used effectively against him. Maimonides offended against the prevailing custom of his time by his failure to quote the sources of his legal decisions, an omission he regretted and which he intended to make good if time allowed; he often expressed himself in direct opposition to the Rabbis of the Talmud; his introduction of speculative material in the first section of the Code was disagreeable to men not trained in philosophical thinking; his insistence on the incorporeality of the Deity and his branding as heretics those who believed otherwise was not only contrary to the literalness of the Bible but was hard on people who from their youth had been brought up on the materiality of God; he conducted a vigorous campaign against the belief in witchcraft and demonology, ignoring the passage in the Talmud which makes the knowledge of witchcraft essential for membership in the Sanhedrin; he was vague to the point of disbelief in bodily Resurrection and he interpreted the delights and pleasures of *Olam ha-Ba* in spiritual rather than physical terms; he gave rise to the impression that the intellectual knowledge and contemplation of God were of greater importance than the carrying out of the precepts of His Torah. But by far the gravest charge that was leveled against Maimonides was that he intended by his Code to make the study of the Talmud less necessary, if not entirely to supersede it. To support the accusation, his detractors had but to quote Maimonides' own concluding words of his introduction to *Mishneh Torah:* "For this reason I called the name of this work *Mishneh Torah,* for all that a man has to do is to read first the Written Law and follow it up by this work, and he will know the entire Oral Law without the need of reading any other work between them." [14]

Rabbi Abraham ben David of Posquieres, France, abbreviated Rabad (1125–1198), a man of great wealth and learning, with a remarkable command of the whole Talmud, a contemporary of Moses Maimonides and one of his earliest critics, cannot be said to have been influenced by personal feelings in his intense opposition to the Code. While he was critical of Maimonides' method of smuggling into Judaism alien philosophical ideas under the cover of isolated talmudical passages, he was not himself a stranger to philosophy. What he feared in Maimonides, an objection he also registered against Alfasi, whom he greatly venerated, was, in the words of Dr. Louis Ginzberg ". . . that if Alfasi and Maimonides had not encountered such keen opposition, rabbinic Judaism would have degenerated into an exclusive study of the legal code, which would have been fatal to any original intellectual development in a considerable portion of the Jewish people." [15] He attacked Maimonides' dogmatic attitude toward Jewish beliefs and teachings, the airs of infallibility he allegedly gave himself, demanding, as it were, that his assertions be accepted without the need of citing superior authorities, his denouncing as apostates whosoever conceives God as a corporeal being, and the supposedly slighting manner with which he treated biblical personages.

The harshness, one may say, the extreme bitterness, with which the Provençe Rabbi prosecuted his case against Maimonides was the principal weakness of his criticism. Men fought hard in the Middle Ages; no quarter was given to an opponent. Thus, the French censor of Maimonides completely abandoning the caution of the Rabbis to take heed of one's words, speaks of his colleague in the Torah as "that man," and of his decisions as "mistaken," "not true," "I see here great confusion of thought," and when commenting on Maimonides' opposition to an anthropomorphic conception of the Deity, he caps the rudeness of his observations by the remark, "Why does he call such persons apostates? Men better and worthier than he have held this view (the materiality of God)."

But there was other opposition to Maimonides' work from less exalted quarters, antagonism based not on internal criticism of the Code but stemming from spite and malice. Thus, in Egypt, scholars forewent as much as opening the book lest they be suspected of turn- ing to it for information and knowledge. Dr. Alexander Marx reported in the name of a Spanish contemporary of Maimonides that "in many cases judges opposed the new work, for it enabled the laymen to check judicial decisions, since anybody could consult this well-organized book, written in a clear and easy language." [16]

While Maimonides was helpless against the petty saboteurs of the Code, he could not remain indifferent to the widespread charge that in writing it he aimed at the discouragement of the study of the Talmud and intended his work to take its place, a charge which, ridiculous though it was, persisted through the centuries. Maimonides indignantly refuted the accusation in a letter to Pinhas bar Meshulam of Alexandria. Where, he asked the *dayyan* of Alexandria,[17] had he given evidence of hostility to the Talmud, he whose whole life had been devoted to the Talmud and at the very time of writing was delivering lectures to students of the Talmud? Where, he wished to be told, had he said that all other books should be destroyed or burned except his own? On the contrary, he pleaded, his sole object in composing the Code was to further and spread the knowledge of the Talmud among those who were incapable of mastering it.

Maimonides' refutation did not disarm his opponents. When the skirmish showed signs of weakening on one front, the battle against him, well organized and directed, was carried to another front. So far the standard against the Sage of Fostat was raised by men of little official authority and political consequence; the man who took the field now was one who was famous alike for his talmudic learning and high official position and whose power over the Jewish communities extended all the way from Baghdad to Yemen, from Damascus to Egypt, even to distant Russia. He was Samuel bar Ali, a highly colorful personality, at once pious and arrogant, a literalist with a taste for the sciences who, as principal of the celebrated Baghdad academy "Geon Jacob" for about thirty years (1164–1193), delivered lectures on the Talmud from a gold-embroidered throne to hundreds of students who flocked to his school from nearly all parts of the world. He had no male children, but his daughter, a Jewish counterpart of Hypatia, famous alike for her beauty and learning, delivered lectures on the Talmud screened from the gaze of the students.

Samuel bar Ali Halevi, proud, ambitious and well-born—he traced his genealogy to the Prophet Samuel—was an energetic and resourceful man. He assumed the title Gaon and he regarded himself a successor to Saadia, Sherira (d. 900), and his son Rab Hai, who made the Babylonian gaonite famous in Jewish history. Under his administration, the Baghdad school rose to a position of unequaled authority and influence in Jewish life. He appointed rabbis, judges, and other synagogue and community functionaries and made his coffers swell with the revenues from the far-flung Jewish habitations under his rule. He conducted his personal life with an impressive show of dignity and importance. He had winter and summer homes, palatial residences maintained with an unsparing lavish hand. In imitation of an eastern potentate, he had slaves surround his throne, ready to scourge and punish at the nod of the master anyone who was disobedient of his command.

Petahya of Regensburg, a traveler at the end of the twelfth century who, like his colleague Benjamin of Tudela, had penetrated parts of the world not frequented by Jews in those days, was an eyewitness to the pomp and circumstance with which bar Ali had conducted himself. While the great man was the *pontifex maximus* of the court, he but rarely put in an appearance without being accompanied by nine subordinate judges, who delivered lectures and decided questions of law. When Samuel bar Ali lectured, he never spoke to his audience directly but through an interpreter who repeated word for word in a loud voice what he heard from the master.

Men ambitious and greedy for power are naturally fearful of rivals who might challenge their authority or question their greatness. There were rarely two men more unlike each other than the Gaon of Baghdad and the Sage of Fostat. They differed from each other in character, temperament, and outlook. One loved fame and glory, the other preferred the modest and humble life; one lived to order and command, the other to teach and guide; Samuel bar Ali ruled by reason of his official power and authority, Moses Maimonides by the simple moral and spiritual integrity of his life. Both—although by far not in the same measure—were profound students of the Law, but while to one every word and statement of the Talmud was of equal sinaitic revelation, Moses Maimonides sought to penetrate to its inner spirit.

A clash between the two men was inevitable. When vested interests meet with opposition, a conflict is unavoidable. Maimonides' rapidly spreading fame held a threat to Ali's spiritual empire. Egypt ostensibly belonged to the Gaon's diocese, but her Jews hung on the words of the Spanish scholar in their midst. While, as a matter of courtesy, the Jews of Yemen addressed their letters to the head of the Baghdad academy, in their hearts they acknowledged no higher authority than that of the son of Maimon who did so much to lighten their burden. Samuel bar Ali feared for his own prestige and the prestige of the Baghdad school, which alone, he maintained, was entitled to exercise religious and legal authority over all Jewry.

The clash between Baghdad and Fostat was spearheaded by a legal question which was far out of proportion to the controversy it aroused. The Gaon disputed a decision of Maimonides, that it was permissible to travel on a river on the Sabbath,[18] and he wrote him of his disagreement with him in a letter couched with much flattery and transparent insincerity, hypocritically adding that he need not fret over a mistake which scarcely a tyro in the Talmud could have made. On another occasion, likewise in a letter to Maimonides, Bar Ali assumed a patronizing attitude toward Maimonides, reminding him of the part he took against critics of his views on Resurrection and other controversial points in his "Book of Knowledge."

Maimonides, quick to recognize friend from foe behind the mask, answered his correspondent heatedly: "You seem to reckon me among those who are sensitive to every word of blame," he wrote. "You are making a mistake. God has protected me against this weakness, and I protest to you in His name, that if the most insignificant scholar, whether friend or foe, would point out to me an error, I would be grateful for the correction and instruction." [19] But it was not to correct an error or to "instruct" Maimonides that Samuel bar Ali sought, but to crush him, to question his learning, criticize his decisions, and even cast aspersion on his orthodoxy. This, indeed, he did through his disciples and camp-followers who spread a whispering campaign—more dangerous and effective in its consequences than open attack—in order to belittle Maimonides' importance in the eyes of the naïve and unsuspecting people. Every liberal view and tolerant attitude Maimonides expressed was ferreted out of his Code and paraded before the ignorant, or half-learned Jews, as heresies.

Samuel bar Ali was not alone in his attack; he infected others with his hostility to Maimonides. As a result of the campaign, critical voices were raised against Maimonides even in quarters usually friendly to him. His views on Immortality, Resurrection, the Messiah, the World-to-Come, his allegorizing of Bible stories, were made targets of sometimes malevolent, sometimes honest but disgruntled critics with limited range of vision. Thus, although a warm friend and admirer of Maimonides, as were all the Jews of his country, Nathaniel Ibn Al-Fayyumi of Yemen, father of Jacob to whom Maimonides wrote his famous "Letter," bitterly complained to the Gaon of Baghdad: "This [Maimonides' teaching of Resurrection and the Messiah] caused great confusion. Many people despair of Redemption, and many have taken to the reading of heretical writings. This is grievous to us. Our waters have failed, and there is none to show the nation the way of truth. And know, Sir, that revolt is rife among the Jews of the cities of Yemen."

Maimonides was alive to the storm raging about him. His friends kept him informed, and while relieving his hurt feeling by branding one of his critics as an ignoramus "imagining that he was learned," and passing some uncomplimentary remarks about bar Ali, whom he advised to confine himself to ritual matters, which were his province and not dabble in things which were beyond him, Maimonides was as a rule magnanimous toward his opponents and he called on his friends to desist from controversy. He thus wrote to Joseph Ibn Gabir: "I have been informed, although I do not know whether it is true, that there is in your city somebody who speaks evil against me and tries to gain honor by misrepresentation of my teachings. I have heard that you have protested against this and reprimanded the slanderer. Do not act this way! I forgive everybody who is opposed to me because of his lack of intelligence, even when he, by opposing, seeks his personal advantage. He does not harm me. . . . While he is pleased, I do not lose anything. . . . You trouble yourself with useless quarrels. I do not need the help of other men, and leave the people to follow their will." [19a]

He wrote in the same tenor to Joseph Ibn Aknin, begging him to abstain from entering into an argument with the Gaon, whose views were unsound and whose criticism inane, who was indeed nothing but a "chattering preacher," belonging to the class of men "who will sacrifice all modesty when their position is at stake." Maimonides sought no victory over his opponents. "Honor bids me," he wrote, "to avoid fools, not vanquish them. Better it is for me to spend my efforts in teaching those fitted and willing to learn than waste myself in winning victory over the unfit." [19b]

But however Maimonides may have laughed off his opponents or written sarcastically against them, as suggested by Dr. Joshua Finkel,[20] it was no mere harmless literary controversy on which Samuel bar Ali had entered with the Sage of Fostat but one which had more serious implications. By raising the question of Resurrection, the Gaon of Baghdad knew that he had a weapon in his hand with which to destroy his opponent. For resurrection from the dead was a cardinal principle of the Islamic faith, the denial of which no faithful Mohammedan would countenance with impunity. Saladin was a generous and chivalrous monarch, tolerant to a fault but unforgiving of anyone who taught a doctrine contrary to the teaching of the Prophet. "He detested philsophers, heretics, materialists, and all adversaries of orthodox religion." He believed in the literal interpretation of the Koran with its teaching of the resurrection of the bodies of the just in paradise and the punishment of the wicked in hell and frowned severely on the slightest deviation from it. Saladin had a prominent Mohammedan mystic-philosopher executed after long imprisonment, and although Maimonides was not a Moslem, he was a writer too well known to be overlooked if his heretical views were made known. It was, therefore, no laughing matter for Maimonides when the Resurrection issue was raised by his opponents, and, painful though it may have been to him, he wrote (probably in 1191) his treatise, *Ma'amar Tehiyat ha-Metim* (*Essay on Resurrection of the Dead*), in the Arabic language, which was twice translated into Hebrew.

Maimonides deplored that slander and misrepresentation had made it necessary for him to reaffirm his belief in Resurrection after he had already made his position on the subject clear in his *Mishnah Commentary* and *Mishneh Torah*. He refuted the assertion that references made in Scripture to the resurrection of the dead were to be taken allegorically. "We would premise," he writes, "that the dogma of the resurrection of the dead—universally acknowledged by our people, incorporated in our prayers, composed by wise and inspired men, and to which the Talmud frequently reverts—is capable of no other interpretation than the literal. . . . Whosoever, therefore, accuses us of having said that the biblical passages are figurative, has uttered a flagrant falsehood." If he dilated on the dogma of Immortality "offering appropriate proof and illustrations from Scripture and rabbinical authorities" and was brief in alluding to Resurrection, contenting himself with the mere assertion that it is an essential of our religion, it was because religious truths gain nothing by frequent repetition and lose nothing by rare and solitary mention.

Maimonides held that Resurrection was a matter of faith and not of reason, belonging to the realm of the miraculous where proof and demonstration must give way to hope and trust. But that need not necessarily lessen our confidence in the possibility of Resurrection, since the revival of the dead is not any more wonderful a miracle than that water should come out of a rock. "Still through a miracle water did issue of the rock, so will also the dead be revived by some marvellous miracle. . . . Whosoever believes that God has created the world out of nothing must concede the possibility of miracles, and, surely, none can consider himself a faithful follower of Abraham and Moses who doubts that verity." [21]

Maimonides' peculiar notion that those revived would live a long life in the Messianic Era, eat, drink, and procreate, and then die again to find eternal life in a bodyless spiritual form in the World-to-Come, instead of helping matters in the way of rehabilitating himself in the eyes of his critics, caused a fresh storm of criticism, this time spearheaded by his violent opponent, Meir ben Todros Abulafia (1180–1244), a scholar, poet and a man of unflinching piety, who voiced his dissent in the couplet: [22]

> If those that rise from death again must die,
> For lot like theirs I ne'er should long and sigh.
> If graves their bones once again shall confine,
> I hope to stay where first they bury mine.

While the opposition did not relax its campaign of malice and slander, the fame and reputation of Moses Maimonides in almost all parts of the Jewish world were so great that they overcame every voice that was raised against him. The name of many a captious critic survived oblivion and was recorded in history for no better reason than that it was linked to the name of the man he strove to defame. Letters of praise and adulation of Maimonides and his work arrived from many quarters of Jewry, so that, to quote Graetz, "It required all Maimonides' moral force not to be overpowered by the incense burned before him." Lavish titles were bestowed upon him, and men learned in the Law and recognized authorities in their respective communities willingly submitted themselves to his leadership.

The vindication of Maimonides and his Code was all the more striking since, in some instances, it came from men who were either neutral in the campaign against them or, in some special capacity, were related to the critics of Maimonides. Thus, Jonathan ben David Hakohen, an outstanding French talmudic authority and leading rabbi of Lunel, not only defended Maimonides against the criticism of Rabbi Abraham ben David (Rabad) of Posquieres but held the philosopher in the highest esteem and admiration. Addressing Maimonides in such extravagant terms as "holy man of the Lord," "luminary of the exile," and "enlightener of the eyes of Israel," Rabbi Jonathan wrote: "With thee, illustrious man . . . we feel connected in our souls. We bless thee on every Sabbath and on every month. But we are unable to repay truly all the good we have received from thee. . . . No weapon that is formed against thee shall prosper, and every tongue that shall rise against thee in judgment thou shalt split with the arrow of thy answer. . . . Our souls are linked with thy books in love. If they are here, everything is here. All is then certain, firm and true, we are not lacking in anything. There is no need for any other elucidation. The fountains of life rise from them." [23]

The Code, which was made the principal target of attack, was accepted everywhere as the supreme and final authority. Indeed, it became a "best seller," hundreds of copyists working hard to supply the demand for the book. In many places it was regarded as an act of piety and devotion to copy the whole work in one's own hand. It did not however become, as Moses Maimonides had hoped it would, the standard code of Jewish law and practice. That honor was reserved for the work of another Spanish-Jewish scholar, Rabbi Joseph Caro (1488–1575) who, about three hundred and fifty years after the death of Maimonides, composed the *Shulhan Aruk* (*Prepared Tables*) which became the Jews' popular lawbook to this day. But there is scarcely a scholar in the length and breadth of Jewry who will come to an important decision on a question of Jewish law without first wanting to know "what the *Rambam* says."

7. THE GUIDE FOR THE PERPLEXED

G REAT AS WAS Maimonides' reputation among the Jews, it was
not until the appearance of *The Guide for the Perplexed* that
he became universally famous. It was the climax of his literary
career, the first book, written by a Jew, after the Bible, to become
part of world literature. It is also the book with which, among Jews
and non-Jews—particularly the latter—the writer's name became
linked. Had Moses Maimonides rested on his laurels after his *Mishnah
Commentary* and the *Mishneh Torah* and written nothing else, the
Jews would remember him as the great *Rambam*, the master of
rabbinic lore, but Maimonides the philosopher, the man who with
prophetic vision gave the world a new view of God, Man, and the
World, might never have become known.

Through *The Guide for the Perplexed* not only Maimonides but
the Jews and Judaism may be said to have entered the orbit of the
world's thinking. Until the opening of the eighteenth century the
Guide was the main, indeed, the only channel through which post-
biblical Judaism spoke to the world. In the long and painful centuries of the Diaspora little cognizance was taken of the Jew as a
creative and contributing factor to civilization. His poets were not
known, his philosophers were not reckoned with; the world had but
a distorted knowledge of the Talmud, and even the Bible, the Jew's
greatest cultural contribution to mankind, was twisted and tortured
for partisan propaganda. The religion which mothered Christianity
and equipped Mohammedanism with many of its basic ideas was
written down as an empty, outlived superstition.

Moses Maimonides was the first Jew to have made himself heard in a society in which few Jewish voices had penetrated before, the first Jew to have posed problems and sought solutions to matters which troubled the minds of most men of faith. He held the stage of the world's thinking for a much longer time than was given to many other men of his position. In the long span of centuries thoughts and philosophies have changed, but after more than seven hundred and fifty years of his death, men still pay homage to the Sage of Fostat who, in an age of unreason and superstition, proclaimed the Sovereignty of Reason and taught that reason is the link which binds man to God and makes him God-like. "Maimonides was the teacher of the whole Middle Ages," Abraham Geiger (1810–1874) concludes his study of the Fostat philosopher, "and every enlightened mind that arose later drew eagerly from him and gladly acknowledged himself his pupil." [1]

There is something extraordinary about the way *The Guide for the Perplexed* caught the imagination of the world and spread rapidly among all classes of scholars. The book had no sooner left the hand of its writer than, almost overnight, it became a classic. It is one of the most widely translated and commented-upon philosophical works of all time. In less than a decade of its appearance, during the author's own lifetime, *Dalalat al-Harin*, the Arabic title of *The Guide for the Perplexed*, was translated twice into Hebrew, and shortly after Maimonides' death a Latin version of the book circulated all over Christian Europe. Mohammedan scholars had the Hebrew characters in which the *Guide* was composed transliterated into Arabic letters, wrote commentaries to parts of it, and a Moslem historian pronounced the work to be one of the most significant achievements of the age.

The spirit of the *Guide* had dug deep into medieval Christian thinking. Some of the most distinguished churchmen, anxious to found a Christian Aristotelian philosophy, discovered in the *Guide* a pattern for their thought. The work of the "Egyptian Moses" was studied assiduously and cited copiously by many of the towering Christian minds of the time. Albertus Magnus (1193–1280) was familiar with the Hebraeo-Arabic writers and quoted them frequently. He was acquainted with the writings of Avicebron (Solomon Ibn Gabirol), whose views he discussed extensively without knowing that he was a Jew. He was particularly partial to Maimonides, whose arguments on the nature of God, angels, and against the eternity of the world he had not only adopted but quoted verbatim. Although Thomas Aquinas (1225–1274), the greatest philosopher and Christian theologian of his time, was not known for partiality to Jews, he too availed himself of Maimonides' *magnum opus,* which he quoted copiously. Maimonides was in the background of William of Auvergne (d. 1249), learned teacher, philosopher, and Bishop of Paris, who, although he attacked the Jews violently, relied on the *Guide,* in which he displayed considerable proficiency; also, he recommended it warmly to his philosophical colleagues. Alexander of Hales (1170–1245), more favorably disposed to Jews than his Paris contemporary, was familiar with the *Guide* and adopted many of its biblical interpretations.[2]

Perhaps the most curious example of hostility to Jews but warm appreciations of their thinkers and their philosophical writings was the English "doctor mirabilis," Roger Bacon (1214–1294). He was a scholar, philosopher, scientist, and Orientalist who advocated, besides Greek, the study of Hebrew, Arabic, and "Chaldean" (probably meaning Aramaic) because of their significance to theology, science, commerce, and diplomacy. He was particularly keen on the study and knowledge of the language of the Bible, in which he believed God had revealed Himself to the world and which, incidentally, he felt would facilitate the conversion of Jews to Christianity. He entertained the medieval belief, reiterated by Judah Halevi and Maimonides, that the Jews were the first philosophers from whom philosophy percolated to the rest of the enlightened world. He enumerated about thirty famous Arabic—that is, Spanish—philosophers, among whom he lists Moses Maimonides first. Indeed, so pleased was he with the latter and his teaching that he did not hesitate to claim him for Christianity and had him write a "work" (meaning, no doubt, the *Guide*) against Judaism and in the defense of the Catholic faith.

Cecil Roth informs us of the great revival of Hebraic studies in England which in the seventeenth century, *inter alia,* included Maimonides. Edward Pocock (1604–1691), who occupied a chair in Hebrew at Oxford, made Latin translations from Maimonides' *Commentary* and *Mishneh Torah,*[3] and page after page of the writings of John Selden (1584–1654), English jurist, antiquarian and Orientalist, were filled with references to Moses Maimonides and elucidations of his teachings. "The study of Maimonides," writes Cecil Roth, "seems to have been especially favoured in England. It may, indeed, be said that after the Bible, his writings occupied the first place in the affections of English students of the Hebrew language and literature. . . . It is more than a mere coincidence that both Oxford and Cambridge made their débuts as centers of Hebrew scholarship with the publication of a Maimonides text. The younger University led the way, however, by upwards of half a century." [4]

Surprising as was the reception of *The Guide for the Perplexed* at the hands of the non-Jewish world, its impact on Maimonides' own co-religionists, for whom the book was primarily written, was extraordinary. It came almost with the force of a revelation. There were grumblings, and even bitter and passionate criticism because of its rationalist interpretation of Judaism; but when the smoke and thunder of battle had passed, even Maimonides' most violent opponents could not help remembering that he was the author of the *Commentary* and the *Mishneh Torah*, the two greatest works in rabbinic literature. As people formerly clamored for the *Mishneh Torah,* so they now implored the writer for copies of the *Guide*. Rumors of its completion had no sooner been circulated than requests for it came in from almost every group and section of enlightened Jewry. Jews to whom the language in which the book was written was incomprehensible besieged the author with demands that the book be translated into Hebrew. Rabbi Jonathan of Lunel wrote to Maimonides: "Thou holy man of the Lord, our teacher and master, thou luminary of the exile, grant the request of thy servants who are eager to draw from thy well, and let us find nourishment in *The Guide for the Perplexed*. The energy of thy righteous spirit has not relaxed, and now that thou hast surpassed all men . . . our souls are linked with thy books in love. If they are here, everything is here." [5]

The position of Moses Maimonides in the Jewish world was indeed unique. He was a multidimensional man—both rationalist and traditionalist, anchor-sheet of the Synagogue and follower of Aristotle, unshaken believer in the verbal inspiration of the Bible and an unconventional interpreter of its words and teachings. He was the first to dogmatize Judaism with his Thirteen Articles of Faith, and he was among the first to be accused of having adulterated Judaism by reducing it to a mere dogmatic faith in the manner of the Gentiles. Such is the man who flashed across the Jewish horizon. Men could not remain neutral with regard to him. He evoked both blame and admiration, wild censure and unmeasured enthusiasm. While on the one hand he was viciously attacked by Spinoza (1632–1677) for having falsified religion, Hermann Cohen, famous German-Jewish philosopher, thanked God two hundred and fifty years later for Moses Maimonides and *The Guide for the Perplexed* for his first training in philosophical reasoning. Whether approved or disapproved of, Maimonides was not the sort of man one could pass over in silence, nor his *Guide* be ignored.

Judaism was not the same after Maimonides, it was said—nor were the Jews, it may be added. The ferment the man and his book introduced was not limited to their time and place. It kept on working in the utmost reaches of Jewry and in the most obscure lands and places. The span of centuries had not dimmed the impact of *The Guide for the Perplexed* nor the authority and personality of its author. Indeed, as time went on, his spiritual image became clearer and more firmly and vividly fixed in the consciousness of the Jewish people. Throughout all phases of history, the position of Maimonides was that of a creative factor in Jewish life, as a teacher, guide, and enlightener to whom Jews turned in all the problems, difficulties, and perplexities of their existence. It was not so much the detailed teachings of the medieval philosopher that mattered as the pattern he set for a free philosophical interpretation of Judaism. Writes Ahad Ha'am (Asher Ginzberg, 1856–1927): "They [the Jews] did not feel it necessary to commemorate the death of one whom in spirit they regarded as still alive, and to whom they turned every day for advice and guidance in all their theoretical and practical difficulties. In those days it was almost impossible for an educated Jew (and most Jews then were educated) to pass a single day without remembering Maimonides; just as it was impossible for him to pass a single day without remembering Zion." [6]

Maimonides was the educator of generations of men. Some of the finest minds in Israel received their first training in rational thinking from *The Guide for the Perplexed*. Great movements of tremendous scope and influence arose in its wake—the *Haskalah* in Russia-Poland and the Jewish *Aufklärung* in Germany. There was scarce a Jewish home with any claim to enlightenment that did not harbor in its midst a copy of *Moreh Nebukim*, the Hebrew title of *The Guide for the Perplexed*. The book was on the study-tables of the religiously-trained scholars as well as on the reading-desks of the secularlyminded students. Students of the Torah secretly sat huddled over its pages, concealing the book from prying eyes lest they be suspected of "wasting" their time on speculations from which "no good could come."

Maimonides has fertilized more systems of philosophy than he is readily given credit for. Despite their religious and methodical differences, Spinoza was much more the disciple of Maimonides than he was of Descartes. What 'Isaac Husik said of Maimonides with regard to Abraham Ibn Daud "If not for Ibn Daud there would have been no Maimonides" [7] can certainly be applied to Spinoza with regard to Maimonides—if not for Maimonides there might have been no Spinoza. "Spinoza's own system has taken from Maimonides some essential features," [8] says Julius Guttmann. This is particularly apparent in his *Theological-Political Tractate*. Spinoza's insistence upon the love of God as the highest quality of human reason, his views on prophecy, miracles, immortality, interpretation, and general meaning of the Bible, as well as his strongly intellectual theory of ethics, "although written," says Leon Roth, "in ostensible opposition to Maimonides, are completely dependent on his arguments." [9]

"Even after the eighteenth century," remarks above-mentioned Julius Guttmann, "when the Jews entered the orbit of European culture and participated in its philosophical development, the connection of Jewish thought with Maimonides was not broken." [10] Solomon Maimon (1754–1800), the vagrant Polish-Jewish philosopher, a man of profound genius but disordered life, perhaps one of the keenest critics of Kant's critical philosophy, had assumed the name "Maimon" because of his great admiration for the author of *Moreh Nebukim;* when he came to Berlin his luggage consisted of an uncompleted commentary on *The Guide for the Perplexed*. Moses Mendelssohn (1729–1786), referred to as the German Socrates and founder of German-Jewish *Aufklärung,* playfully spoke of his hump as having been caused by his early brooding over the pages of *The Guide for the Perplexed*. "Ah," reflected Lessing's prototype of *Nathan the Wise* with a sigh of satisfaction, "Maimonides is the cause of my deformity. He spoiled my figure and ruined my constitution. But I bear him no grudge, for . . . if he has been unwittingly the cause of my physical disfigurement, has he not amply compensated me by invigorating my soul with sublime knowledge?" [11]

In neither of his two earlier works, the *Mishnah Commentary* and the *Mishneh Torah,* had Maimonides given any indication that he had in mind writing any such massive volume as *The Guide for the Perplexed.* In the Introduction to the *Commentary* he refers to a book on the Prophets and a treatise on the Midrashim, later abandoned for reasons stated in his Introduction to the *Guide.* What, then, might have moved him to embark on so stupendous a task after he had already demonstrated the fundamental philosophical principles of Judaism in his two preceding works, and when he might have known that any such book as the *Moreh Nebukim* would bring down upon him the odium of the orthodox? Writers on Maimonides attribute the genesis of the book to the philosopher's chance meeting with Joseph Ibn Aknin (1160–1226), a young man of twenty-five, from Morocco, who became his pupil, and to whom, indeed, the Sage of Fostat had dedicated his *magnum opus.* But plausible as this theory is, even deriving confirmation from Maimonides' letter to his famous pupil on the eve of completion of the *Guide* in 1189, it seems to the present writer highly improbable that the last and most famous work of the master, the fruit of his matured years, should owe its origin to no other impulse than to the author's accidental meeting with young Aknin, half the philosopher's age.

The more convincing theory of the origin of *The Guide for the Perplexed* seems to be the one suggested by Ahad Ha'am in his celebrated essay "The Sovereignty of Reason," [12] according to which Moses Maimonides, aiming at a rational philosophy of Judaism, was but mildly satisfied with the results he had obtained from his *Mishnah Commentary* and *Mishneh Torah.* In his early twenties, Maimonides started on his goal in the conventional manner of a commentary on the Mishnah in which he injected vigorous highly unconventional statements on Jewish beliefs. He even went so far as to catalogue the articles of the Jewish faith by which Judaism, in his opinion, stood or fell. It was a daring attempt, and "not every Jewish thinker," says Joseph H. Hertz, "has endorsed his articles of the Jewish creed, either because of the inclusion of this or that article among the dogmas of Judaism, or because of the omission of some principle of Jewish religion that seemed to the critic of fundamental importance." [13]

"But in his maturer years," to quote Asher Ginzberg directly, "with wider knowledge and greater self-confidence, Maimonides found the courage to attempt what he had not ventured in his youth. Still with the same object in view (to formulate a rational philosophy of Judaism), he decided to break new ground and to produce an original comprehensive work hitherto unknown in Jewish life." He wrote the *Mishneh Torah*, and by this clear-cut Code of Jewish life and practice he rescued Judaism from becoming lost in "the ocean of talmudic disputation." As before, but this time with clearer aim and more definite purpose, he introduced into the Code theological and philosophical views and opinions which were considerably at variance with the traditional orthodox norm. Maimonides' Code is a magnificent work, a tantalizing masterpiece of which only the genius of its creator was capable. But, still, it was a work for the *hamon,* ordinary men, by which to direct and guide their religious and secular life.

After having discharged his duty to the *hamon,* the multitude, with his *Commentary* and the Code with what basic conceptions of Judaism he thought it wise to introduce, Maimonides the intellectual aristocrat, the man who confessed that he cared more for the "few" than "for ten thousand fools," felt that the time had come to discharge his obligation to the *yehidim,* the select single ones, or that intellectual minority of Jews who were versed in the Torah and sincerely loved Judaism but were baffled by the anthropomorphic words and passages in the Bible which they could not reconcile with God's absolute spirituality. They felt dissatisfied and unhappy in their minds. They were puzzled and confused by the inconsistency they thought to exist between the demands of reason and the requirements of religion. Such men, Maimonides felt, must not be allowed to drift and be ultimately lost to Judaism. They must not be forced to choose between religion without reason and reason without religion. "The 'perplexed' had to be satisfied so that they could devote themselves peacefully to the acquisition of ideas without being disturbed by the thought that in so doing they were rejecting the fundamental principles of the Torah." These thoughts, which were long present in the mind of Moses Maimonides, did not, however, come to concrete expression until he wrote *The Guide for the Perplexed* after his acquantance with Joseph Ibn Aknin, who was typical of the bewildered intellectuals of the time.

The two men had no sooner met than they recognized in each other an intellectual kinship which developed into a "father and son" relationship. For all his popularity and greatness, Moses Maimonides was a lonely man. He missed the refined companionship which was so essential to his spirit. His environment was drab and ordinary; he had few friends and intimates, and what acquaintances he had were of the medical profession, with whom his relations were formal and perfunctory. Egypt was not Andalusia, and Cairo was a far cry from Cordova. He never forgot his youthful homeland, in spite of the pain and bitterness her name recalled to him. Maimonides had never ceased to regard himself as a Spaniard; to the day of his death he signed his letters and documents: "Moses, the son of Maimon, the Spaniard." One imagines his home life to have been rather drab and cheerless for want of the laughter of children. Not until Maimonides was fifty-one years old, did his second wife, a sister of Abn Almali, one of the royal secretaries, present him with a son.

Notwithstanding their discrepancy of age and intellectual stature, Maimonides and Joseph Ibn Aknin had much in common. They were both victims of the Almohade religious persecution, and both had chosen Egypt for their place of refuge. Although their literary and scholarly interests ran in different directions—one was a poet and devotee of the fine arts and the other regarded verse-making a waste of time—both had an overmastering love for Judaism and a desire to see it flourish in its alien environment. Both, too, for practical reasons and for the scientific interest it involved, took to the medical profession for a livelihood. And they contributed to each other enormously—one by stimulating the other's genius, and Maimonides by developing his junior friend's mental and spiritual faculties.

Like many of his "perplexed" young contemporaries, Joseph found it difficult to reconcile the teachings of the Bible with his philosophical studies. He was a persistent student of both Judaism and the secular sciences, but he found the gulf between them deep and impassable. He was a young man with scraps of knowledge of all sorts, but without a well-organized philosophy of Jewish life and thought. When the writings of Moses Maimonides fell into his hands he knew that he found the master from whom he wanted to seek instruction. Egypt was not very far from Morocco as the crow flies, but for a Jew who wore the mask of Mohammedanism it was a journey that was beset with many difficulties and perils.

Joseph arrived in Alexandria, where he established himself in a medical practice, but his heart was set on Fostat, where lived the man who was the aim and goal of his journey. Little knowing how odious poetry was to the great man, Joseph Ibn Aknin included in his letter, among other things, some of his Hebrew and Arabic verses. The mistake he made might have cost the young scholar the purpose of his mission had not Maimonides detected in the letter merits which made him forgive the writer's poetry. The sage of Fostat was touched by Joseph's ambition to learn and he wasted no time in inviting him to come.

Student and teacher were ideally suited to each other. Ibn Aknin found in Maimonides the teacher he had hoped for, and the latter discovered in his pupil a friend and associate worthy of his confidence. For two years master and pupil lived together, Maimonides instructing his disciple in mathematics and astronomy, in physics and metaphysics, in *ma'aseh bereshit* and *ma'aseh merkabah,* the very mysteries of the Torah forbidden to be taught even to one man except he be wise and able to understand by himself, and even then to explain to him only the "chapter headings." But Joseph Ibn Aknin, roving scholar (and probably moved by Bar Ali's persistent campaign against Maimonides), did not remain long under the master's tutelage, but set out for Baghdad after two years instruction so that he might all the better, in the enemy's own home town, defend his teacher in the face of his calumniators.

Their parting had not dissolved their friendship; if possible, it even brought them into closer intimacy with one another. For Joseph Ibn Aknin was in correspondence with his teacher, requesting further elucidation of the subjects they had studied together but which were interrupted by their separation; and Maimonides, after complimenting his disciple for the progress he had made under him, wrote: "When, by the will of God, we parted, and you went your way, our discussions aroused in me a resolution which had been long latent. Your absence has prompted me to compose this treatise [*The Guide for the Perplexed*] for you and those who are like you, however few they may be. I have divided it into chapters, each of which shall be sent to you as soon as it is completed." [14]

Because of the extreme delicacy of the subjects with which *The Guide for the Perplexed* dealt, Maimonides took every precaution that the book should not fall into the hands of the uninitiated and warned his pupil to conceal it from the masses, holding that metaphysics was a subject in which he who can swim will bring up pearls from its depths, but he who cannot swim may be drowned. He even went to the ridiculous extreme of trying to mystify the book, "though," observes Israel Friedlaender, "the logical mind of Maimonides was stronger than his intention, and the lucidity of his work is paralleled only by its depth."

"I have composed this work," Maimonides explained in the Introduction to the *Guide,* "neither for the common people, nor for beginners, nor for those who occupy themselves with the study of the Law as it was handed down without concerning themselves with its principles. The design of this work is rather to promote the understanding of the real spirit of the Law, to guide these religious persons who, adhering to the Torah, have studied philosophy and are embarrassed by the contradictions between the teachings of philosophy and the literal sense of the Torah. . . . In my larger work, the *Mishneh Torah,* I have contented myself with briefly stating the principles of our faith and its fundamental truths, together with such hints as approach a clear exposition. In this work, however, I address myself to those who have studied philosophy and acquired sound knowledge, and who, while firm in religious matters, are perplexed and bewildered on account of the ambiguous and figurative expressions found in the holy writings."

Aware of the obtuseness of the subjects with which his book dealt and the difficulty of mastering them, Maimonides prescribed for his pupils directions for the reading of his work: "If you desire," he said, "to grasp all that is contained in this book so that nothing shall escape your notice, consider the chapters in connected order. In studying each chapter, do not content yourself with comprehending its principal subject, but attend to every term mentioned therein, although it may seem to have no connection with the principal subject. For what I have written in this work was not the suggestion of the moment; it is the result of deep study and great application. Care has been taken that nothing that appeared doubtful should be left unexplained. Nothing of what is mentioned is out of place, every remark will be found to illustrate the subject-matter of the respective chapter. Do not read superficially, lest you do me an injury and derive no benefit for yourself. You must study thoroughly and read continually; for you will then find a solution of those important problems of religion, which are a source of anxiety to all intelligent men." [14a]

The Guide for the Perplexed penetrated into non-Arabic-speaking Europe chiefly through its Hebrew and Latin translations. The first

Hebrew translation of the *Guide* was done by the father-in-law of Jacob Anatoli (1194–1256) during its author's lifetime. Soon after a second Hebrew rendition of the book was made, likewise during Maimonides' lifetime, by Judah ben Solomon Alharizi (d. 1230), a celebrated Hebrew poet, traveler and wit. Although the latter rendering failed to meet with the requirements of an ideal translation and was criticized by Abraham Maimonides, the philosopher's son, it nevertheless served as text for the Latin version of the *Guide* in the early thirteenth century, probably by Jacob Anatoli, son-in-law of the Hebrew translator, who was a noted scholar and highly esteemed by Emperor Frederick II, by whom he was invited to Naples to found a university in 1224.

But it was Samuel Ibn Tibbon's Hebrew translation of the *Guide* (made at the request of Southern French scholars) which he called by the name agreed upon by the author, *Moreh Nebukim*, that gave the book the widest circulation in Jewish scholarly circles. Samuel Ibn Tibbon (1150–1230), who hailed from a family of translators, was not only careful to render the writer's every nuance but turned to him whenever he was in doubt about the meaning or wording of a difficult passage. It was to such correspondence between the philosopher and his translator that we are indebted for one of Maimonides's most interesting letters. After answering Samuel's questions and complimenting him on his "familiarity with the niceties of that [Arabic] language in the abstruse subjects," Maimonides laid down several rules on the art of translation.

Let me premise one rule [*wrote the author of the* Guide *to its translator*]. *Whoever wishes to translate, and aims at rendering each word literally, and at the same time adheres slavishly to the order of words and sentences in the original, will meet with much difficulty; his rendering will be faulty and untrustworthy. This is not the right method. The translator should first try to grasp the sense of the passage thoroughly and then state the author's intention with perfect clearness in the other language. This, however, cannot be done without changing the order of words, putting many words for one, or vice versa, and adding or taking away words, so that the subject may be perfectly intelligible in the language into which he translates. This method was followed by Honein Is'hak with the works of Galen and by his son Is'hak with the works of Aristotle. It is for this reason that all their versions are so peculiarly lucid, and therefore we should study them to the exclusion of all others. Your distinguished college ought to adopt this rule in all the translations undertaken for those honored men and the heads of the congregation. And may God grant that the spread of knowledge among the other communities of Israel be promoted by such works.*[15]

In Russian Poland another translation of the *Moreh Nebukim,* besides the classical ones of Alharizi and Ibn Tibbon, was made by one Mendel Levin (1741–1819), a forerunner of the *Haskalah* Movement, who conceived the idea of modernizing the medieval translations of the Jewish-Arabic classics by retranslating them into intelligible Hebrew. He furnished the example by recasting the first part of the *Guide* into lucid modern Hebrew, in striking contrast to the stiffness and obscurity of the Provencal Scholar's[16] (Samuel Ibn Tibbon) translation. It was however through Samuel Ibn Tibbon's Hebrew version that Maimonides' philosophical masterpiece penetrated into the Jewish scholarly circles and was studied and commented upon by them. Dr. Alexander Marx, the late head of the Jewish Theological Seminary Library, quotes Dr. Moritz Steinschneider (1816–1907) as having compiled a list of over sixty known commentaries on *The Guide for the Perplexed,* and there are still some others which escaped his notice.

When, in the course of time, Maimonides suffered neglect at the hands of the non-Jewish scholars, and his *magnum opus* was forgotten, Solomon Munk (1803–1867), a French Jewish savant, caused a sensation in the scholarly world by his discovery of the Arabic text of *The Guide for the Perplexed* in the Bibliothèque Nationale, which he annotated, translated, and published. The find was more than merely a literary curiosity, but brought about a revived interest in the work and personality of the man without whose liberal and intellectual insight the world would have been much poorer. A number of European editions and studies of the *Guide,* notably by German, English, and Italian scholars, followed Munk's translation. Michael Friedländer's translation of the *Guide* from the Arabic[17] has been frequently reprinted with and without his notes. Besides several helpful features with which the translator had provided the book, such as "The Life of Moses Maimonides," "The Moreh Nebukim Literature," and "Analysis of the Guide for the Perplexed," the author's mastery of style has been fully preserved in the translation, which makes the book delightful reading alike for scholars and laymen.

The Guide for the Perplexed is divided primarily into three principal parts, each part provided with an introduction, with as many subdivisions as the subjects with which the writer is dealing. The first fifty chapters of Part I are almost wholly exegetical, the author interpreting the figurative expressions in the Bible, the remaining twenty-six chapters consisting of Maimonides' theory of Attributes and Knowledge of God, as well as a lengthy exposition of the origin of *Kalam* (Arabic philosophy). In Part II the author discusses the Existence, Unity, and Incorporeality of God, the Spheres, Angels, Aristotle's theory of Creation, and the writer's argument against it. The subject of Prophecy and Prophets, the mental, moral, and physical faculties of the latter, together with the exceptional position of Moses among the prophets, is treated by Maimonides in forty-eight chapters. The concluding section of the book, or Part III, contains, besides the esoteric vision of Ezekiel, or *Ma'aseh Merkabah*, the all-important problems of Evil and God's relation to it. Trials and Temptations, God's Omniscience, Freedom of Will, Providence, and Job's and his friends' attitude toward it. Dr. Meyer Waxman is quite right in maintaining that the concluding chapters of the book—nearly one half of Part III—in which Maimonides rationalizes the precepts of the Torah and reflects in a magnificent poetic manner upon the true worship of God, can hardly be said to belong organically to the original plan of the work, but were added to it as a kind of striking appendix.

The Guide for the Perplexed, the third and last of Moses Maimonides' major works, is an outline of the writer's philosophy of Judaism, its beliefs and doctrines, its rites and ceremonies and, in a lesser degree, a summary of its social and ethical teachings, written in the form of letters to his favorite pupil, Joseph Ibn Aknin. The goal which already as a youth had been present in his mind, and which he pursued all his life, he realized in this stupendous work. The intellectual urge which prompted Maimonides to write the *Mishnah Commentary* and the speculative consciousness which achieved the *Sefer ha-Madda* (*Book of Knowledge*) resulted in the book in which not only the whole philosophical personality of the author comes to the fore but which marks an important event in the history of Jewish and world religious and philosophical thinking.

The Guide for the Perplexed is not easily and briefly summarized. It would indeed be presumptuous to attempt a capsule review of the book in view of the author's warning against a hasty and superficial reading. *The Guide for the Perplexed* is a book not to be read but to be studied, and the only way to get the best out of it, is to read it not all at once but in small portions, and in many sittings. "God knows," Maimonides wrote in his letter to Ibn Aknin, "that I hesitated very much in writing on subjects contained in this work, since they are profound mysteries; they are topics which, since the time of our captivity have not been treated by any of our scholars as far as we possess their writings." [18]

The Guide for the Perplexed is not so much a philosophical work as it is a philosophical interpretation of the Bible. The problem that faced Moses Maimonides was not to reconcile the truths of Judaism with the truths of the science and philosophy of his day for, in his opinion, their goals were the same and there was no conflict between them. In his depth of faith, Maimonides believed, as did many of his contemporaries, that "these [philosophical] theories are not opposed to anything taught by our Prophets or by our Sages." His problem was rather to explain the meaning and inner intention of the biblical words and narratives in relation to the Deity which baffled the intelligent reader. Maimonides himself leaves no doubt as to his intention and the purpose he had in mind for his book to serve. In his Introduction to the *Guide*, he wrote: "My primary object in this work is to explain certain words occurring in the prophetic books," and in a note to Part II, he stated his position with regard to the book more clearly:

It was not my intention when writing this treatise to expound natural science or discuss metaphysical systems; it was not my object to prove truths which have already been demonstrated, or describe the number or the properties of the spheres, for the books written on these subjects serve their purpose, and if in some points they are not satisfactory, I do not think that what I could say would be better than what has already been explained by others. But my intention was, as has been stated in the Introduction, to expound biblical passages which have been impugned, and to elucidate their hidden and true sense . . . I only desire to mention that which might, when well understood, serve as a means of removing some of the doubts concerning anything taught in Scripture; and, indeed, many difficulties will disappear when that which I am about to explain is taken into consideration.

Biblical Hebraism is anthropomorphic. God is interpreted in human qualities, experiences and emotions. The ancient Jew's all-too intimate familiarity with God attributed to Him a visible and tangible form. He created his God in his own image, so to say, and ascribed to Him corporeal tasks and functions. Thus, while in some passages of the Bible God is spoken of as Eternal, Omniscient, and Incorporeal, He is invested in other passages with bodily organs and characteristics. God is represented as seeing, hearing, acting, speaking; He is jealous, wrathful, vengeful, pleased, displeased, etc. To be sure, very early the ancient Rabbis became conscious of the incongruity and were emphatic in their assertion that the Torah merely meant to assist the simple-minded, and that such unseemly expressions concerning the Deity as are found in the Pentateuch and in the Prophets were not to be taken literally. Just the same, the mischief was done, so that not only the unphilosophical masses but their scholars and teachers as well mistook the metaphor as fact and the figure of speech as unquestioned designation of God.

Now, Moses Maimonides was, of course, a good traditional Jew. He believed in supernatural Revelation and made the divine origin of the Bible a fundamental creed of Judaism. The Bible was to him not so much a literary or historic document as it was the very word of God. He believed, to quote him, "that the whole of the Pentateuch now in our hands was revealed to us through Moses, that it is in its totality the word of God, that Moses only acted as a copyist to whom it was dictated." But, at the same time, Maimonides the rationalist, the philosopher, nurtured in the school of Greek philosophy, could not resign himself to the corporeal image of God fostered by the superficial reading of the Bible. Reason rebels against any such blasphemy, and the Book itself prohibits image-worship. Maimonides saw the Bible as a complex book with an outer and inner sense, the former for the plain and ordinary people, and the other for those who are capable to delve into its deeper meaning. To quote his own words: "This is also the reason why 'the Torah speaks the language of man,' for it is the object of the Torah to serve as a guide for the instruction of the young, of women, and of the common people; and as all of them are incapable to comprehend the true sense of the words, tradition was considered sufficient to convey all truths which were to be established, and as regards ideals, only such remarks were made as would lead toward a knowledge of their existence, though not to a comprehension of their true essence." [19] To speak of God as a transcended Being utterly removed from any physical representation would have been misunderstood by a generation accustomed to think of Him as a visible entity. "I compare such a person [of a low state of intelligence]," says Maimonides, "to an infant fed with wheaten bread, meat and wine; it will undoubtedly die, not because such food is naturally unfit for the human body, but because of the weakness of the child, who is unable to digest the food, and cannot derive benefit from it." [20]

Maimonides blazed new paths through the Bible. Awkward words and passages in the Holy Book in relation to the Deity he treated as metaphors and figures of speech. He invented, or rather, borrowed, from Aristotle, the term "homonyms," that is, words, phrases, and expressions having different meanings not related to each other. Thus, words like life, existence, kindness, mercy, knowledge, seeing, hearing, standing, etc., have a different meaning when applied to God than when used in relation to human beings. When we read in the Bible, "God stands," it means that He is constant, unchangeable; "He descends"—the intention is to convey His effect upon worldly matters; the Voice mentioned in the Sinaitic theophany is allegorized in a way so as to remove from it any semblance of materiality. "He also, thinks, in general," says Abraham Geiger, "that the ancients purposely express themselves in a manner which has an external sense suitable for those of an immature understanding, while the intelligent comprehend the deeper signification of it, that the men of the Bible and the Talmud had, like the ancient philosophers, sometimes purposely chosen expressions and forms of presentation which say also something for the ordinary human, without that he recognizes the complete truth, but which disclose the deeper wisdom for the thinker." [21] Maimonides extends the same interpretive method to the events, incidents, and narratives of the Bible on the general principle that there is nothing in the Torah which is not endowed with deeper spiritual significance than the stories seemingly convey.

With exquisite skill Maimonides proceeded to the task of analyzing, defining, and freeing from its metaphorical and sensory trapping every word in the Bible in relation to God. His painstaking study of the subject, the forty-seven chapters he devoted to it in the first part of the *Guide*, the originality and freshness of his exposition of the almost endless line of Hebrew verbs and nouns in any way suggesting an aspersion on God's spirituality, more properly belonging to a dictionary of the Bible than to a philosophical work, must indeed be put down as an extraordinary achievement of the man's genius. But Maimonides did not content himself with merely disposing of the anthropomorphisms of the Bible. In his hands, the exegesis became the keystone of a whole involved theological system. For if God cannot be conceived materially, no human attributes or qualities can be applied to Him. God is above and beyond human ken; He cannot be defined; He cannot be comprehended; time and space have no relation to Him. God is not matter, He is not mind; He is that deeper Unity in which mind and matter are one. He is the source of Reality. We can affirm nothing of Him, except that, in some way, He is our Creator and the source of all things that are. To know God, said Maimonides, *is to know what He is not*. To quote at the risk of repetition a classical passage from the *Guide*:

Those who believe in the essential attributes of God, viz., *Existence, Life, Power, Wisdom, and Will, should know that these attributes, when applied to God, have not the same meaning as when applied to us, but that the difference does not only consist in magnitude, or in the degree of perfection, stability, and duration. It cannot be said . . . that His existence is only more stable, His life more permanent, His power greater, His wisdom more perfect, and His Will more general than ours, and that the same definition applies to both. This is in no way admissible, for the expression "more than" is used in comparing two things as regards a certain attribute predicated of both of them in exactly the same sense, and consequently implies similarity [between God and His creatures].*[22]

In the very first verse of the Bible it is stated unequivocally that God created the world, while Aristotle, equally unequivocally, taught that, from the character of natural law, it was impossible for the world to have come into being by an act of creation but existed eternally. Here, for a man like Maimonides, with his implicit faith in the authority of the Bible and his no less implicit confidence in the authority and wisdom of Aristotle, whom he regarded as but a little lower than the Prophets, there was a contradiction that required no little ingenuity to straighten out. The creative power of God is nowhere challenged or questioned in the Bible; in almost innumerable passages He figures as the architect who brought the world into being out of His own free will without any external natural necessity, a doctrine which, according to Maimonides' own statement, is a rampart around the Law and is next in importance to the principle of God's Unity. Accepting the biblical dogma of *creatio ex nihilo,* every problem of God's relation to the world is solved and the basic identity of philosophy with the Torah is established. God is then the unfettered ruler of the Universe which He governs according to His will without any interference by any outside force. But rejecting it in favor of the Greek philosopher's theory of the Eternity of the Universe, a host of difficulties embarrassing to the religionist crop up, the most serious of which is God's uninhibited sovereignty in the world.

Maimonides found himself at odds with Aristotle on the problem of Creation, not so much for its own sake as because of the consequences which flowed from it. If there were no serious involvements in the philosopher's theory, and he—Maimonides—found convincing proof of the Eternity of the Universe, he would not have rejected it because Scripture taught the opposite, for "the gates of interpretation are not closed," and he would have found a way of getting around the Bible text. But, as Maimonides saw it, the theological consequences of Aristotle's teaching were, if possible, more serious than the theory itself. For if everything has not arisen from God, and Creation was the result not of a divine plan but of necessity, then God is not sovereign in the world, His "hands," so to say, are tied, and He cannot command nature to obey His will. The man anchored deep in Jewish tradition deemed the acceptance of the biblical affirmation of the world's origin so vital to Jewish belief that he protested both against the philosopher who taught the contrary doctrine as well as his fanatic followers "who consider it wrong to differ with Aristotle or think that he was wrong in anything. . . ." They reject the words of the Prophets, because they do not employ scientific language by which only a few persons could be instructed who are intellectually well prepared, but simply communicate the truth as received by Divine inspiration." [23] In Maimonides' opinion the uncontested acceptance of the Eternity of the World is tantamount to the belief that the Universe is the result of fixed laws, that nature does not change, and that there is no such thing as supernatural. We should then, he argues, necessarily be in opposition to the very foundation of our religion, disbelieve all miracles and signs, and certainly reject all hopes and fears derived from Scripture.

But it was not alone on religious ground that Maimonides took the field against the man he admired, and called "the chief of philosophers," and from whom he had imbibed many ideas. It was not merely with the unsure weapon of naïve faith in the biblical account of Creation that Maimonides proceeded to meet the greatest intellectual Goliath of all time. He tested his opponent's armor and detected its vulnerable spot. For, while insisting upon the Eternity of the Universe, Aristotle had failed to advance convincing proof, of which failure Maimonides was quick to take advantage. Indeed, so unsure was the Stagirite in his own mind that he freely confessed: "There are things concerning which we are unable to reason, or which we find too high for us; to say these things have a certain property is as difficult to decide as whether the universe is eternal or not." [24] Since, therefore, Maimonides argued, the opposition has not been satisfactorily established, he preferred to be on the side of the positive teaching of the Bible rather than on the negative unproved assertion of the philosopher.

Maimonides' repudiation of Aristotle on the question of Creation had the effect of validating the Bible on one of the most important principles of the Jewish faith. It rescued God's unrestricted rule over the world, and, what is equally important, it provided for the possibility of miracles. While admitting the systematic, orderly run of the cosmos, he at the same time did not rule out God's occasional interference with the events and happenings of the world. On the authority of curious rabbinic sources,[25] he made out miracles to have been in the original plan of Creation, so that their occurrence is as much part of the regular happening of things as is everything else in nature. Parenthetically, however, it may be remarked that Maimonides' conception of miracles is calculated to give but little comfort to the fundamentalist. For while to the orthodox a miracle can only take place in a miraculous manner, our philosopher so rationalized the Bible miracles as to deprive them of every semblance of the supernatural. For where he did not bring miracles within the realm of natural occurrences, he made them to be either the naïve imagining of the uninstructed or dream-visions beheld in a trance.

God created the Universe, but how does He control the world which he brought into existence? To put the question in other words, how does the purely spiritual God act upon the grossly material world? Maimonides made God relegate to the angels a share in the control of and contact with the things of the visible world. The angels, whose presence is conspicuous both in the Bible and in talmudic literature, make up, according to Maimonides, the heavenly hierarchy; they were created by God as intermediaries between Him and the existing things, to execute missions, to announce special events and, generally, to act as servants of the Lord. In other words, while the stream of causation flows directly from God, it filters through the material world through the agency of the angels. Although Maimonides' conception and function of the angels and their share in the governance of the world was more or less an adaptation of Aristotle's Intelligences, they differ from the latter in the fact that they are not beings co-existent with the First Cause, as the Greek philosopher would have them be, but completely subordinate to God who had created them.

Maimonides' conception of the angels is not unconnected with his doctrine of Divine Providence. For, while it is the function of the angelic messengers to foretell future happenings and warn against impending dangers, as they apprised Abraham of the birth of Isaac and the destruction of Sodom and announced to Manoah the birth of Samson, the larger working out of man's destiny is under the direct care and supervision of Divine Providence. After analyzing Aristotle's view of Providence, which holds that God's knowledge and care extend only to the species, and the theories of the Mohammedan religious sects, which maintain that God takes notice of all things, of the falling leaf and the destruction of the ant no less than of individual man, Maimonides declared that in the case of human beings, because they are the most perfect of all sublunary things and are endowed with the rational faculty, Providence is individual. But even in the case of man, Maimonides claims that Providence varies with a person's moral character and intellectual attainment. The more a man excels in these things, the greater is his share in Divine Providence. The Prophets, he says, enjoy a special Providence; the wise and holy men come next, while the ordinary men, the ignorant and disobedient, are reduced to the fate of the lower animals and are left to the rule of chance.

But Providence, in the philosophy of Moses Maimonides, does not imply predestination, and God's foreknowledge does not entail the abnegation of Freedom of the Will, which our philosopher rightly calls "the pillar of Israel's faith and morality." The difficulties inherent in the problem are grave and many, but there is no escaping Rabbi Akiba's famous saying, "Everything is foreseen and freedom of choice is given." [26] The prophetic and rabbinic tradition is at one on this point, and Maimonides marshals his most eloquent and convincing arguments in its favor. Man is free to live, act, and behave as he wills. He is not a creature of blind fate, a victim of an iron law of necessity. His very ethical and moral perfection depends upon this God-given gift. Well could our jurist philosopher write in his *Eight Chapters*, "If God were to decree concerning man whether he be righteous or wicked . . . what place would there have been for the Torah, and by what justice, or by what right, could he punish the wicked and reward the righteous?" Thus, while Spinoza, Maimonides' severest critic, decrees man's free will to be an intellectual resignation of submission to necessity, the philosopher of *The Guide for the Perplexed* insists that Free Will is the born prerogative of every man, that there is no predestination, but that every man may choose whether he will be good or evil, a wise man or a fool. [27]

Maimonides struggled with the problem of evil, as did most philosophers since the beginning of time—struggled without bringing up a final satisfactory word. He was obsessed with the ills of the world, with the aches, pains, hurts, and sufferings which afflict the heart of man. The Rabbis of the Talmud put it pithily, "The righteous suffer and the wicked prosper." How is it metaphysically possible for a limited and partially bad universe to have come from a perfect God? If God's Providence watches over the world, how explain its existent wrongs, injustice, and inadequacies? Since Maimonides had made God the ultimate cause of all things, why do life and the love of life encounter so many hindrances?

Maimonides did not meet the problem of evil head on. He did not and, indeed, he could not, absolve the All-Knowing of the knowledge of evil. What Maimonides did, and what, indeed, in this matter few others could have done any better, was to deny the existence of evil altogether, to rule it out of being, to refuse to recognize it as a positive quality. Evil, says Maimonides, is nonexistent, and what seems to be evil is nothing more than the absence of good, just as darkness is the absence of light, sickness the absence of health, and poverty the absence of wealth. Since God cannot have produced anything but what is good, evil cannot be said to be one of His creations. He castigates the Arabic philosopher who ventured to assert that there is more evil in the world than good. To paraphrase Maimonides: Whenever anything in the world seems absurd, ridiculous, or evil, it is because we have but a partial knowledge of things, and we want everything arranged according to our taste and reason. But when we look at life and the world from the aspect of the eternal scheme of things, we will find that what seems to us bad and shocking is because of our lack of knowledge and wisdom.

Moses Maimonides devoted ten chapters in the second part of his book to the subject of Prophets and Prophetism. Few men had delved deeper into the subject and with greater originality and penetration than he did. Next to his treatment of the anthropomorphisms of the Bible and the negative attributes of God, his views on the highly controversial subject of Prophets and Prophecy make perhaps the most unique and creative part of his work. "Maimonides has performed an important task," says R. V. Feldman. "He has elevated the status of the prophet beyond that which he enjoyed in the ancient world. The prophet had there degenerated into an oracle-monger or sooth-sayer, a state functionary or a civic official." [28] What was regarded as a supernatural inspiration, or an emanation from God regardless of the prophet's moral and intellectual qualities, Maimonides reduced to a discipline which calls for the highest cultivation of the would-be prophet's physical, rational, ethical, and imaginative faculties.

Between the ignorant who believed that God bestowed the spirit of prophecy upon whomsoever He willed, and the philosophers who stressed only the prophet's intellectual endowments, Maimonides made Prophetism a quality of soul and mind amounting to the highest stage of mental and spiritual development to which a man can attain. The illumination, or election, must, of course, come from God, who alone may grant or withhold it, but the human part is not to be neglected if the spark is to be ignited. Prophecy, in accordance with Maimonides' terms, is no simple or easy task, and no wonder that Jeremiah when he was called to prophesy would be excused the honor.[29] Maimonides enumerated a long list of qualifications for prophecy. The prophet must be in possession of perfect bodily health; he must not be subject to languid or depressive states of mind; his rational faculties must advance from the potential to the actual state; his desires and passions must be pure and equally balanced; his thoughts must be engaged in lofty matters, constantly directed toward the knowledge of God and His works.

The true prophet includes all the virtues of the genuine sage or philosopher. Indeed, the true prophet stands higher than the philosopher and sees more clearly than the scientist, for his truth proceeds directly from God. The true prophet not only teaches truth but he is the truth. His active intellect is developed to the highest possible perfection. Maimonides anticipated Ahad Ha'am when he said that the truth other men achieve slowly, stage by stage, by the gradual unfolding of their mental and spiritual faculties, the prophet receives instantly by his intuitive perception. The prophet is a courageous man—a narrow-minded zealot, one might call him. The ideal he holds masters his every feeling and passion, engrosses his whole being. He looks at life and looks at the world only through the mirror of his ideal, and he spends his whole life in fighting and agitating for it. He makes enemies, he lives in a hostile world, for only too often the world is not prepared for the message he brings.

Not all prophets, however, stand on the same level of equality. Maimonides enumerated eleven grades of prophets, with Moses occupying the highest rank. While other prophets received their communication from on high through an angel in a vision of the night, Moses received it directly from God whenever he wanted and in whichever state he was. His superiority over the other prophets was one not of degree but in the totality of the prophetic perception. His comprehension was clearer, his insight deeper, his manner of perceiving the truth was different from that of most other prophets. There was not a veil he did not pierce; no material hindrance stood in his way; he was the chosen of God from the whole of humankind.

Maimonides also pointed up the fact that, whereas all other prophets admonished Israel and did no more, Moses was both prophet and legislator. The patriarchs, particularly Abraham, did indeed communicate to others the truths they received, but they were not legislators in the manner Moses was. This grand and lofty peak of Prophet and Legislator, was scaled by Moses alone. He was both the Prophet of Righteousness and the Revealer of the Torah. Maimonides did not deny the gift of prophecy to the other nations of the earth. While Judah Halevi makes prophecy the peculiar hallmark of the Jewish national spirit, Maimonides granted that other nations at various times of their history had their men whose life was the life of an embodied idea.

Maimonides raised Judaism to the heights of a rational philosophical system. He was the first of Jewish philosophers to have probed the psychological manifestation of the prophetic activity. With the uniqueness and superiority of Moses over all prophets, not in degree but in principle, to which he devoted much space, Maimonides dealt a subtle but well-aimed blow at the Mohammedan claim that Mohammed was the greatest of prophets, and that his religion was therefore the greatest. Nevertheless the traditionalists were dissatisfied and made Maimonides' conception of prophecy one of the items in the storm of opposition that was raised against him. They resented the philosopher's making prophecy a natural phenomenon depending upon the prophet's intellectual and spiritual development, instead of an arbitrary selection by God. They likewise protested against his declaration that not all the Ten Commandments were communicated to the people at Mount Sinai, but only the first two, the rest having been imparted by Moses.

The Guide for the Perplexed is a philosophical expository work on the Bible. We have made this statement before, but it becomes all the more evident as we approach the conclusion of the book. It begins with the exposition of the anthropomorphisms of the Scriptures and concludes with an elaborate explanation of the precepts and ceremonial laws of the Torah. That between the beginning and end of the book the author treats of a large variety of other subjects, is because of his anxiety to equate the Holy Book with the rule and demands of reason.

As stated before, Maimonides never doubted the literal truth of the entire Law. The Torah was to him of divine origin, perfect and infallible in its every part. There was nothing in it without its higher meaning and purpose. Knowledge of the Torah confers the highest knowledge attainable to man. Those who questioned the rationality of its laws and commandments had not probed into their deeper meaning and significance. There are those, Maimonides said, who despair of finding a satisfactory rationale for some of the commandments of the Torah, and conclude that they have no basis in reason whatever. "They are led to adopt this theory by a certain disease in their soul. . . . For they imagine that these precepts if they were useful in any respect, and were commanded because of their usefulness, would seem to originate in the thought and reason of some intelligent being." [30] Maimonides rejected the assertion of the Rabbis that there were ordinances (*hukim*) in the Torah, for which no apparent reason had been assigned, but which are to be obeyed unquestioningly at the behest of God. He dismissed this assertion on the ground that

God cannot have imposed on man anything which defies reason and does not in some way serve a beneficial end.

The laws of the Torah, its commandments and prohibitions, Maimonides argued, are reasonable laws. Their binding-force is not arbitrary but moral and ethical. Their goal is the attainment of perfection—perfection of the soul and of the body. They aim at the attainment of the inner and outer harmony of man, the former by knowing and experiencing God, and the latter by the removal of injustice and violence in the world and the safeguarding the interests and well-being of society. If, therefore, we encounter in the Bible laws and precepts which on their surface have no influence upon the well-being of the soul nor do they affect in the training of man in the ways of truth and social and individual righteousness they must be explained so that their inner content might be revealed.

Maimonides then launched into a lengthy detailed discussion of the positive and negative commandments of the Torah about the usefulness of which people are in doubt. People, he said, are laboring under a wrong impression that the value and character of the divine laws would be endangered by attempting to establish their rationality. On the contrary, Maimonides argued, such exploration of the intent and purpose of the ceremonial laws of the Bible is not only not detrimental to their sanctity and their binding-force but removes any idea in the minds of the unthinking that the prescriptions of the Torah were in contradiction to the wisdom and justice of God.

Moses Maimonides was a scholar with a "comparative" outlook. He was the first philosopher of religion to detect a correspondence between the Mosaic ordinances whose moral or social purpose is not easily discernible and the customs of the neighboring religions. When, in 1685, John Spencer, the Cambridge orientalist and theologian, published his famous work, the *Laws of the Hebrews*, which was widely acclaimed as having laid the foundations for the whole science of comparative religion, "a work so much before its time that it was not followed up," he admittedly leaned heavily on the third part of Maimonides' *Guide for the Perplexed* which appeared in 1190.[31]

Maimonides was an avid reader; his literary range was extraordinarily wide. Besides medicine and philosophy, his intellectual curiosity was attracted by many other subjects. He had no taste for art, no liking for poetry, no ear for music, all of which he regarded as a waste of time, but primitive ideas, especially in their relation to religious customs and habits, engrossed him. He read what he could find on this subject in the Arabic language. He said himself that there was little on the subject of pagan religious rites, customs, practices, and superstitions with which he had not thoroughly acquainted himself. There are few parallels in his century to his interest in forms of religion other than his own. He not only studied the sources and collected the facts of the heathen forms of worship but proceeded on their basis to explain the origin of every law and precept of the Torah whose reason or meaning is not explicitly stated. In so doing, he collided with the strictly traditional view which held that every precept of the Law was divinely given and inspired, but the significance of his approach is incalculable.[31a]

Maimonides explained the motivation of some of the Mosaic ordinances on the ground of hygiene and self-discipline, and others on the score of the influence of the Sabeans, a widespread star-worshipping people in whose superstitious beliefs and manner of worship the Jews became so deeply habituated that it took the most solemn injunctions of the Torah to eradicate them. "If we knew all the particulars of the Sabean worship," said Maimonides, "and were informed of all the details of those doctrines, we should clearly see the reason and wisdom of every detail of the sacrificial service, and the laws concerning clean and unclean, and in other laws the object of which I am unable to state. I have no doubt that all these laws serve to blot out wrong principles from men's hearts, and to exterminate the practices which are useless." [32]

In his eagerness to rationalize the commandments, Maimonides often assigned reasons for them not specifically mentioned in the Bible. He thus explained the prohibition of prostitution not only as restraint on excessive sensuality but on the ground of maintaining domestic felicity. "Perfect love, brotherhood, and mutual assistance," said Maimonides, "is only found among those near to each other by relationship. The members of a family united by common descent from the same grandfather, or even from some more distant ancestor, have toward each other a certain feeling of love, help each other and sympathize with each other. . . . Professional harlotry was therefore not tolerated in Israel (Deut. 23:18), because their existence would disturb the above relationship between man and man. Their children are strangers to everybody; no one knows to what family they belong; nor does any person recognize them as relatives. And this is the greatest misfortune that can befall any child or father." [33]

While the primary purpose of circumcision is the curbing of excessive sensual lust and limiting sexual intercourse, Maimonides ascribes to this commandment a social and religious purpose. "It gives to all members of the same faith, i.e., to all believers in the Unity of God, a common bodily sign, so that it is impossible for any one that is a stranger to say that he belongs to them. . . . No one, however, should circumcize himself or his son for any other reason but pure faith. . . . It is also a fact that there is much mutual love and assistance among people that are united by the same sign when they consider it as [the symbol of] a covenant. Circumcision is likewise the [symbol of the] covenant which Abraham made in connection with the belief in God's Unity. So also every one that is circumcised enters the covenant of Abraham to believe in the Unity of God, in accordance with the words of the Law, 'To be a God unto thee, and to thy seed after thee' (Gen. 17:7)." [34]

The dietary laws of the Torah were explained by Maimonides on both hygienic and psychological grounds. Thus it is not because of their absence of scales and fins that certain species of fishes are disqualified for food, but because of their hygienic unfitness for consumption; carnivorous animals and birds beget a spirit of cruelty in persons that eat them; the fat of the intestines makes one full, interrupts digestion, and produces colds and thick blood; meat cooked in milk makes gross food, for which reason the Torah prohibited it, but also because it was used on heathen festivals; the Law put the prohibition of eating the blood of an animal on the same level with the prohibition of idolatry, because the Sabeans partook of it as the food of the spirits. They imagined that by eating the blood of slaughtered animals at their idolatrous ceremonies, they would establish a feeling of love, brotherhood, and friendship with the spirit-world. The aversion for pork is explained both because it contains more moisture than is necessary for human food and because of the loathsome habits of the animal. "If it were allowed to eat swine's flesh," said Maimonides, "the streets and houses would be more dirty than any cesspool. . . . A saying of our Sages declares, 'The mouth of a swine is as dirty as dung itself.' " [35]

Maimonides assumed Sabean origin of many of the beliefs, customs, and prohibitions current among the Israelites in pre-Mosaic times for which no reason is maintained. Such are the prohibitions of sorcery, wizardry, communion with the dead and with familiar spirits; passing through fire, observing of times; the laws concerning diverse seeds, grafting of trees, wearing of disguised garments, arraying oneself in wool and linen clothes; shaving the corners of the beard; the commandment concerning covering the blood of slaughtered beasts and birds; the law pertaining to the first-born of an ass, against eating the fruit of a tree during the first three years, and the like, all of which, according to Maimonides, have the distinct purpose of guarding us against the heathen customs, called by the Sages, "the ways of the Amorites," because they were connected with idolatry.

There had never been anyone before Maimonides who looked to pagan rites and customs for an explanation of the precepts and prohibitions of the Torah. But when he went a step further and boldly pulled down the glorified sacrificial service of the Temple from its lofty pedestal and branded it as an unholy notion of serving God which the ancient Israelites had absorbed from the idolatrous peoples among whom they lived, he shot a bolt at one of the most sanctified institutions of the Mosaic Legislation. Yet, daring for its time as the declaration was, Maimonides needed but point to the great prophets of Israel who manifested little enthusiasm about the sacrificial system of worship, who, indeed, in caustic language castigated the people for their overzealous addiction to animal sacrifices and burnt offerings. He needed but remind them that he was not any more daring in the matter of sacrifices than was Rabbi Levi, a Palestinian sage and scholar of the third century, who considered sacrifices a concession of God to the people who were disposed to idolatry in order to win them gradually for the true and pure faith.[36]

God, said Maimonides in his explanation of his theory of sacrifices, might have extirpated this pagan rite of worship as He did so many other things offensive to reason and the pure ideal of religion, but He suffered it to continue because of His concern for human weakness. God did not suddenly eradicate the then generally-accepted manner of worship because of the wrench it would have made in the hearts of the people to abruptly abandon that to which they had been long accustomed. "It would in those days have made the same impression as a prophet would make at present if he called us to the service of God and told us in His name that we should not pray to Him, not fast, not seek His help in time of trouble, that we should serve Him in thought, and not by any action." [37] For this reason, in His infinite wisdom, God refrained from proscribing what the people by their natural disposition would be incapable of obeying, but ordained instead to be transferred to Him that which formerly served as worship of created and unreal things. He commanded a temple to be built unto *Him*, to have an altar erected in *His* name, offer sacrifices and burn incense before *Him* and, contrary to the heathen system in which every man engaged in the temple service, God selected priests and Levites to minister before Him and ordered certain gifts to be assigned to them for their maintenance. By this Divine plan, said Maimonides, the traces of idolatry were blotted out "without deterring or confusing the minds of the people by the abolition of the service to which they were accustomed and which alone was familiar to them." [38]

Maimonides was not insensible to the deeper educational implications of the sacrificial system. It became imbedded in the consciousness of the people, and, besides the ideals of devotion and obedience it inculcated, it brought home to the mind many a high ethical and moral principle. From the sacrifices resulted the thought that whatever is done in the name of God must be of the finest and the best. God ordained that sacrifices brought to Him must be perfect in every respect. No blemished or maimed animal was permitted upon the altar. In the same way, everything that is done for the sake of Heaven should be done with the whole heart and ungrudging hand. If one builds a house of prayer, it should be executed beautifully and more resplendently than one's own home; when one clothes the naked, feeds the hungry, or assists the needy, it must be done unsparingly, with a full and generous hand.

Here Maimonides might have closed his book. He built a giant structure perfect in its every part. No man had undertaken a more heroic task and accomplished it more nobly. On the pillars of the intellect he reared his system, grand, solemn, and sublime. And it is not without color and warmth. There is the glow of faith in the pages of his book, and flashes of an intense love of God as clear and pure as sunlight. He makes philosophy infiltrate the Bible and the Bible soften and spiritualize philosophy. Stern and austere at times, the book pulsates with exalted moral and ethical maxims and teachings.

Maimonides was a man with an irresistible love and passion for

God. He loved knowledge not for its own sake but as a means of communion with and absorption in God. He is both the prophet and preacher of the intellectual love of God. Life with all its desires, activities, and possessions held for him no higher meaning than that it furnished the means of perfecting oneself in the knowledge and understanding of God. The knowledge and comprehension of God are for Maimonides no mere abstract thing but inspire piety, modesty, and good relations with one's fellow-men. In one of the characteristic passages of the closing chapters of the *Guide,* he wrote: "When the perfect bear this in mind, they will be filled with fear of God, humility, and piety, with true, not apparent, reverence and respect of God, in such a manner that their conduct, even when alone with their wives or in the bath, will be as modest as they are in public intercourse with other people." [39] The great men among our Sages, he says, felt themselves in the presence of God always, so that they "would not uncover their heads, because they believed that God's glory was round them and over them." [40]

The final chapter of the *Guide,* which may be regarded as the grand finale of the book, reflects the intellectual and spiritual personality of Maimonides perhaps more fully and clearly than anywhere else. The man who probed into the source and reason of the divine commandments is now, after his long odyssey, looking for the supreme life-ideal. What shall be the aim and purpose of human life; what is its essence; the goal it aspires for; the dreams, hopes, and ambitions which light up its path? In a large sense, Maimonides had already answered these questions. He advocated the primacy of reason; he preached the intellectual love of God; he spurned the pleasures of the senses, the imaginary delights of the terrestrial world; he made knowledge touched with the spirit of the Torah the necessary condition of the good life. But in the closing pages of the book all these things culminate in a grand summary which makes them all the more effective by its brevity and conciseness.

Maimonides looked around the world and found that there were really four "perfections," desires or ambitions, attainable by man. They are the acquisitive, the bodily, the moral, and the intellectual. There are men who hunger for power, property, belongings. This thing, this house, this land, they pride themselves, belong to me. But, in reality, they do not belong to them, they are purely imaginary possessions. They have no permanence; they are outside one's own self. Conditions change, and they are not any different than the lowest beggar.

The second mistaken perfection, one's physical strength and appearance although, in a sense, more closely related to us than the first, are likewise only relative and are far from being the ideal perfection. For they are at best not a human but an animal quality which we share with the lowest beasts. Moreover, however perfect our bodily strength and form, we cannot vie in these things with the denizens of the forest, who are stronger and physically more perfect than we are.

The third, or moral perfection, is more legitimately ours than any of the previous two, for virtue, morals, are purely human ethical qualities not shared by any one else. Religious teachings are designed for the attainment of this kind of perfection. Yet even moral perfection is not so completely ours that it can flourish independently of others around us. For moral perfection is a social quality in relation between man and man, a quality that would be vain and void were one to live on a desert island by oneself.

Only the fourth perfection—the knowledge of God and formation of correct metaphysical opinions—is truly ours, being peculiar to man alone; no one else has any share or portion in it. It is also the only legitimate aim and purpose of life. The prophets have stated unambiguously that neither the perfection of wealth, nor that of health, nor that of ethical qualities is the kind of perfection in which man may glory, "But let him that glorieth glory in this, that he understandeth and knoweth Me." [41]

8. AT THE COURT OF SALADIN

WHEN, WITH THE COMPLETION of *The Guide for the Perplexed*
Maimonides climaxed his literary and philosophical reputation,
his career as a physician had only just begun. Although the beginning
of his active medical practice dated back to the loss of his brother in
the Indian Ocean, it was not until he was discovered by Alfadhel,
Saladin's powerful Grand Vizier, who not only made him look after
his own health but appointed him as one of the doctors of the royal
court, that Maimonides may be said to have reached the summit of
his medical career.

His reputation spread rapidly. He became one of the most celebrated physicians of the Egyptian capital. His skill, tact, and warm
personality won for him many friends and admirers. Members of
Cairo fashionable society regarded it as a privilege to be treated by
the physician of Saladin's family. It was in 1190, when he was at the
height of his medical reputation, that he wrote to Joseph Ibn Aknin
in Aleppo that he had acquired great eminence in medicine and
counted among his patrons members of the nobility, although, observing obliquely, the income from that source was not great.

It was fortunate for Maimonides and fortunate for the world that
his success in the medical profession came to him comparatively late
in life, when he was about fifty-five years old or the works which
made him universally famous might never have been written. Hyperbolically he wrote to Rabbi Jonathan of Lunel complaining of the
heavy demands his new profession was making on his time, which
belonged to the study of Torah: "Although from my childhood the

Torah was betrothed to me and continues to hold my heart as the wife of my youth, in whose love I find constant delight, strange women whom I first took into my house as her handmaids, have become her rivals and take up much of my time." [1]

Maimonides referred to the medical science which became his absorbing task and unending study. To Maimonides medicine was not merely a profession for earning a livelihood, but a sacred calling, a religious occupation no less important and spiritually rewarding than the precepts of the Torah. He derived this attitude from the religion which made the preservation of life a divine commandment, from the religion of the people which refers to the physician as an instrument of the Almighty, and from the long line of scholars and thinkers through the centuries whose renown in the medical science matched their knowledge of the Torah.

What was the source of Moses Maimonides' medical education, and has he contributed to the healing art in any like measure he contributed to his philosophical and theological studies? Although more is known of the life of Maimonides than of most other Jewish scholars, there are gaps in his career which still remain to be explained. Writers on Maimonides refer to 1165, the time he arrived and settled in Egypt as the genesis of his interest in and study of medicine. But while that may have been the year when he first started on his medical practice, his study of the healing art and the proficiency he acquired in it must have been long before then.

One cannot read his *Mishnah Commentary* and the *Eight Chapters*, which were certainly the products of his wandering years and his brief residence in Fez, without being impressed with their numerous references, allusions to, and illustrations drawn from the medical science and practice. The fourth chapter of *Hilkot Deot* in the Code with its numerous health and sanitary prescriptions and regulations can be the work of none other than one who had long professional experience in scientific hygiene. Students of Maimonides speak of his interest in medicine, if he had not actually practiced it, sometime before his coming to Egypt, and they prove their assumption by the references in his works to medical teachers, students, and medical observations in Fez, and even in Spain, where he is said to have sought out the masters of medicine and learned their skill. What, then, in the mass of views and opinions, was the source of Maimonides' medical knowledge and training which made him one of the outstanding physicians of his time?

The medical science stood in high esteem in the Islamic lands. While the European leeches plied their trade against a background of ignorance and superstition, and were generally looked down upon and despised by the more enlightened people, in Moslem countries doctoring was a well remunerated and dignified profession. The Mohammedans loved life and they spent large sums of money for its preservation. Doctoring was a lucrative business, and we hear of at least one Baghdad physician who amassed a fortune from his profession amounting to 88,800,000 dirhams, the equivalent of $7,104,000.[2] Many renowned Mohammedan doctors were famous alike as philosophers and theologians. Will Durant tells of the portraits of Rhazes and Avicenna, the two greatest Moslem physician-philosophers, decorating the walls of the School of Medicine at the University of Paris.[3]

The Moslem Moors of Spain were not far behind their eastern brethren in the respect and honor they bestowed upon the medical profession and its practitioners. The medical art had more than kept pace with their highly developed progress in science, philosophy and literature. Andalusia was the focus and summit of Spanish intellectual life, and Cordova in the eleventh century was a favorite resort for patients who came to improve their delicate health. The Andalusian capital was celebrated for its medical schools, pharmacies, hospitals, and licensed physicians. Courses in medicine were on the curriculum of both the intermediary and higher schools of learning. No man's education was deemed complete without at least a rudimentary training in the medical art.

But great as were the medical advantages of the Cordova schools, Maimonides could not possibly have availed himself of them. He was but thirteen years old when the city was captured by the Almohades and he followed his family in exile. While even at that young age he amassed an almost unbelievable knowledge of the biblical and talmudic lore, he could not possibly have been expected to have added the study of medicine to his already overburdened program. During his wandering years, with his steadily shifting domicile—in his own words: "I was troubled by the suffering and exile which God had visited upon me, since I was driven from one end of the world to the other"—he was working consistently on his first great masterpiece, the *Mishnah Commentary* which, surely, left him no time for the intrusion of any other subject.

Had Maimonides taken up the study of medicine as a profession during his residence in Morocco, where he counted distinguished physicians and philosophers among his friends? The thought might—or should—have occurred to him as a practical solution of his insecure economic condition. With the Jews' unpredictable position in the world, often compelled in Christian and Mohammedan countries to change places on short notice and barred from most occupations, the medical profession was about the only calling they were permitted to follow, and in which, indeed, some had even attained distinction. In the very century Maimonides lived Jews exercised considerable influence both as teachers and practitioners of medicine and not a few of them served as doctors at the courts of Mohammedan princes.

The Almohade masters of Morocco were fanatic in their religion, but they were not hostile to the sciences. They abhorred philosophy, which they suspected of leading to heresy, but they did nothing to discourage the study of medicine, which they rightly considered as necessary for their physical well-being. Among Maimonides' Mohammedan friends in Morocco there were certainly scholars who combined the medical science with their more abstract studies in philosophy. If Maimonides did not have a formal education in medicine, had not attended a medical school nor had the advantage of a hospital, he acquired the art of healing, as did many others of his age—from the study of medical books and his own keen sense of observation.

Maimonides had the advantage of possessing an expert knowledge of the Jewish sources of medical science in the Bible and the Talmud. Moses and the Rabbis of the Talmud were the pioneer medical authorities from whom the Jews derived their first lesson in the preservation of life and health. The Jewish religious life is based on sanitary principles. The third book of Moses is a veritable text-book of sanitary laws and regulations. There is not a child who gambols his way into Judaism who is not made acquainted with its hygienic provisions. He learns of its preventive rules and principles, of communicable diseases and their isolation, of contagious illnesses and their cure. A person suspected of a dread malady was quarantined for a certain period of time until the diagnosis became more certain. Meats derived from loathsome or injured animals are forbidden, as are also contaminated food-stuffs.

Health and religion were closely allied in Bible times. Human life was held to be sacred and its preservation a religious duty. The principle was, "Take ye exceeding care of your life." [4] At a time when the science of medicine was in its infancy and trained physicians had not yet made their appearance, the priests were the supervisors of public sanitation. They were the guardians of the physical no less than the spiritual purity of the people. They treated infectious diseases not by incantations and amulets but by methods surprisingly in advance of their time.

From many allusions in the Bible, we infer that the science of medicine, which was carried on to comparatively great perfection in Egypt, where every disease had its own physician, was also cultivated in ancient Israel. That patients resorted to doctors and did not wholly depend on supernatural cure is evident from the sin of Asa who, when ailing in his feet, "he sought not to the Lord, but to the physicians." [5] Among the regular Temple officials, there was a medical man whose duty it was to attend to the priesthood who, from ministering barefoot, must have been specially liable to certain kinds of diseases.

The Talmud is not primarily a medical treatise. Its concern, besides jurisprudence, is principally with the religious, moral and ethical life of the Jews, containing at the same time extensive excursuses in history, philosophy, mathematics, astronomy and the natural sciences. But with the Jew's instinct for life and its physical well-being, medicine is frequently discussed by the Rabbis of the Talmud, and some even engaged in the practice of medicine. As on most other subjects, the Rabbis were accurate and keen observers of the laws of health, and their regulations are often far in advance of modern practice. They lacked the modern skills and methods, but they possessed a surprising knowledge of the symptoms and treatment of various types of diseases. "The creative ability and the wide scope of the talmudic scholars of that epoch attained a high standard," says Dr. Solomon Kagan in *Jewish Medicine*. "The scope of their knowledge of pathological anatomy and preventive medicine was considerably advanced over the accepted standards of medicine of that period."

Playfully the Rabbis of the Talmud sometimes poked fun at the doctors and passed caustic remarks at their expense, such as "The best of doctors deserves Gehenna," [6] and "Live not in a city whose chief is a medical man," [7] but in reality, the physician stood in high esteem among them. When in doubt on an important decision involving the life or health of a person they called in a skilled medical man in consultation. The Rabbis ordained that every town must have at least one physician who was also qualified to practice surgery, or else a physician and a surgeon.[8] There is at least one case on record of a talmudic medical practitioner who operated successfully for a cataract.[9] Ritual autopsies were made by the Rabbis of the Talmud upon animals for the purpose of meat inspection, and there is in the Babylonian Talmud a tractate of 242 folio pages which deals exclusively with the subject of animal anatomy and pathology.

It was but natural that Moses Maimonides who, through his biblical and talmudic studies was all but born and brought up in an atmosphere of medicine, should have wanted to perfect himself in the healing art in which so many Jewish and Islamic scholars had attained great fame and reputation. The age in which he lived was certainly of the physician-scientist. Medical works abounded in translation from the Greek, and original books were written. Every important mosque had its library, not only of theological but also of scientific and medical works. A great Moslem scholar tells of himself that to recover a lost manuscript by Galen, a Greek medical authority of the second century B.C., he searched all through Mesopotamia, Syria, Palestine, and Egypt, when at last he found about half of it in Damascus.[10]

During his comparatively brief stay in Alexandria, Maimonides had furthered and deepened his medical studies. His *Mishnah Commentary* was well on its way, and he felt safe in devoting some of his time to the secular studies which engrossed his attention. Indeed, Maimonides clearly stated in his Introduction to the Commentary, "I have devoted myself to the study of the sciences," which one surmises was the science of medicine. While Alexandria prided herself on a celebrated university with a medical faculty, it is not likely that Maimonides had availed himself of it. But with his customary thoroughness and ant-like diligence he mastered all he could find on the medical science in Arabic literature, not excluding the works of Isaac ben Solomon Israeli (832–932), which Maimonides honored more highly than his philosophical tomes. While Maimonides makes no mention of Asaf Judaeus, a Hebrew medical writer of the seventh century, as he rarely refers to any other Jewish medical or philosophical writer by name, one may assume that he had made himself

143

acquainted with his works which, as nearly as possible for their time, covered the entire field of the medical science. Thus, the man who was already famous as a great Rabbi and scholar, was preparing the ground for the new career which was to make him equally famous as a great physician.

But what is Moses Maimonides' place in the history of medicine as compared with his stature as a philosopher and theologian? While heeding Dr. Israel Wechsler's admonition not to permit one's devotional bias to credit men of the past with knowledge and scientific insights they did not possess,[11] it is generally acknowledged that working with what scientific tools the condition of his time provided Moses Maimonides had by his medieval writings a wider and more direct influence on medieval medical science than was given to many another man of his profession. The one regret that is registered by historians of medieval medical science is that medicine was not Maimonides' first and chief interest but that he entered upon it comparatively late in life after he had devoted his best matured powers to other studies.

Living in an age that was characterized by tradition, authority, and dependence, Maimonides, unlike many of his professional colleagues, was not a blind follower. He had implicit faith in personal observation and investigation. Man, he said, should believe in nothing but what can be attested by rational proof and the evidence of the senses. He proceeded against quackery in medicine as he was uncompromising against superstition in religion. He was a careful and conscientious diagnostician and was vigorous in his denunciation of doctors who attempted to treat patients without first thoroughly studying and analyzing the root and cause of their ailment. He served his patients with devotion and sympathy, never forgetting the responsibility of his calling.

It is not for this writer to pass judgment on Maimonides' medical activity, but men who speak with authority on the subject pay him the tribute of having been in advance of his time in medicine as he was in many other respects. He is credited with having been a pioneer in the science of preventive medicine, which made a distinguished medical writer observe, "This subject deserves careful attention to this day." He prescribed fresh air, plenty of sunshine, a proper diet and moderation in all things. He remarked that among one thousand men, only one dies a natural death, the rest succumb early in life due to an irregular and irrational mode of living. He prefers the curative power of nature to the use of drugs, and hygienic living to doctors' remedies. He was among the first physicians of his time who understood and wrote of the interdependence of the physical and the mental states, and to heal the latter he urged strongly to improve the physical condition. He emphasized the cleanliness of body and soul; he anticipated the modern trend of fruits before meals; he wrote on sexual hygiene, and condemned sexual overindulgence as one of the worst evils besetting the human race.

Maimonides has been credited with sixteen books on the theory and practice of medicine. But while some of the treatises attributed to him are spurious and were written by other hands than his, he is known to have authored at least ten volumes, some bulky tomes and some of the monograph size, besides his extensive treatment of medical and psychological subjects in the first section of the Code and in the *Eight Chapters*. Since the medical books were intended for general use and did not contain anything offensive to the religious sensibilities of Moslem readers, as was the case with his theological and philosophical writings, especially *The Guide for the Perplexed*, Maimonides composed them in the Arabic language and with Arabic characters.

Even conceding, as has been maintained, that as a medical writer Maimonides was more learned than original, more expository than creative, chiefly summarizing the results of Greek and Arabic scientific authorities, the volume and quality of his medical output are indeed amazing. For medicine was not Maimonides' only interest, and his ten books were the product of the last dozen years of his life, after he had battled for ten years with the *Mishneh Torah,* and another ten years with *The Guide for the Perplexed,* to say nothing of his extensive practice and several other occupations which kept him always active, always busy, giving to the quill and inkwell the time he owed his sleep and rest. If Maimonides was not as epoch-making in the medical science as he was in his theology and philosophy, his books were lucid and readable, marked for a style which was both fresh and novel, arresting the attention not only of their generation but of succeeding generations. As was the case with *The Guide for the Perplexed,* Maimonides' medical works did not wait long to be translated into other languages. Maimonides the physician was as popular and eminent a figure in the medieval medical circles as was Maimonides the theologian-philosopher in the medieval learned academies. Nearly all of Maimonides' medical writings appeared early in Latin and Hebrew versions, and due chiefly to the devoted service of Moritz Steinschneider, Hermann Kroner and Max Meyerhof, Harry Friedenwald, and George Sarton, modern attention has been called to them in the German, French and English languages.

Maimonides' medical writings cover almost the entire field of practical medicine which the time and the country he lived in were most in need of. He wrote on poisons and antidotes when Egypt was ravaged by bites of venomous animals and insects, such as snakes, scorpions, mad dogs, wasps and spiders. The book was greatly in vogue in the Middle Ages, and "one often feels in reading it that it is a modern work," says Dr. Harry Friedenwald. He wrote a discourse on asthma, in which he prescribed the dry, warm country climate and warned against the dangers of the vitiated city air. He composed a treatise on sexual hygiene at the request of a member of Saladin's royal family, in which he dwells on the dangers resulting from sexual intemperance, the temptations stimulating it, and how to overcome them.

Perhaps the most characteristic of Maimonides' medical writings, in which he figures in the combined capacities of doctor, preacher, moralizer, and philosopher, are the health regulations which he prepared for Sultan al-Malik al-Afdal, eldest son of Saladin during his short reign (1198–1200), whose frivolous, profligate life made him subject to all kinds of ailments, including distemper and fits of melancholia. After prescribing for his august patient the remedies of diet, exercises, avoidance of worry, and a hygienic course of life, he contrasts the philosopher's moral qualities which cause him happiness, prolong his life, and bring him nearer to God with the eternal misfortune which must befall those who make their existence depend upon the imaginary good and evils of the world. When the Sultan's condition did not improve and he fell into still deeper fits of melancholia bordering on madness, Maimonides ordered for the mentally dejected patient an hour-to-hour regimen, containing among other things, the use of wine and soft music to cheer his downcast spirit.

When Maimonides feared that by prescribing things offensive to the Moslem creed he might be hurting the religious sensibilities of his royal master, he tactfully appended to his discourse the significant paragraph, which we are quoting from Dr. Max Meyerhof (1874–

1945): "May our Master not blame his humble servant because he has prescribed in this discourse the preparation of wine and the use of music, which are abominable by the religious law. For the humble servant does not prescribe the use of these [forbidden] things, but he merely mentions all the things that are required by medical art. . . . Religion prescribes all that is useful and forbids all that is harmful in the next world, while the doctor indicates what is useful and harmful in this world."

The *Aphorisms, Pirke Moshe* in Hebrew, the bulkiest and most popular of Maimonides' medical writings on which his fame as physician in Christian Europe chiefly rested, is a systematic presentation of the practice of medicine in almost all its phases under various headings. While it is less an original work than a selection from Galen and other Greek medical authorities, Maimonides wants the reader to know that he had not merely compiled the aphorisms but edited them. This, indeed, he did, sometimes criticizing the authors, sometimes pointing out contradictions in their statements, and often amplifying them with observations of his own. As in the case of his *Mishneh Torah,* Maimonides states that he compiled the aphorisms for his own private use, but was led to publish them when he became convinced of their general usefulness. That the *Aphorisms,* which in its Latin translation (in 1489) covers some 260 pages and is divided into twenty-five chapters, was in great vogue in medical schools and among medical practitioners in the Middle Ages, is borne out by the fact that it saw five editions in the less than one hundred years between 1489 and 1579.[12] Writes Dr. Harry Friedenwald: "When we consider the maze of Galenic literature, we can easily understand how welcome such work was to the practicing physician. In it Maimonides shows the same amazing ability for which he is renowned. We realize that its composition was only possible because of his comprehensive knowledge, his philosophic mind, and not least, his marvelous memory."[13]

Maimonides' medical success was the well-merited reward of the years of study and labor he devoted to his new calling. The profession he adopted for purely economic reasons he came to love and follow for the larger humanitarian opportunities it offered. The *Doctor Perplexorum,* the healer of the intellectual and spiritual perplexities of his age, became a curer of the physical and psychic disorders of the people. The man who with almost mystic passion had all his life sought communion with God, had now found Him in the suffering of His afflicted creatures.

Maimonides knew no greater absorption in the last dozen years of his life after he penned the concluding pages of *The Guide for the Perplexed* than his devotion to the medical science which brought a new meaning and purpose to his declining years. The clinical experience of the practicing physician brought about a changed attitude in Maimonides' relations to the common people. The philosopher who speculated abstractly on the hurts and evils of the world became acquainted with human suffering in its stark horror and misery.

'Abd al-Latif (1161–1231) a celebrated Baghdad physician who visited Cairo and spent some time with Maimonides, commented on his great merits, but charged him at the same time with being excessively ambitious. But it was more than mere ambition that was responsible for Maimonides' medical success. His professional skill and learning, his uncommon wisdom, his winning personality, the sincerity and thoroughness with which he dedicated himself to his profession and, above all, his profound compassion and sympathy with the suffering, won for him the trust and confidence of his patients.

Evaluating Moses Maimonides as a scholar and physician in a commemorative address on the 750th anniversary of his death, Dr. George Sarton, late Professor Emeritus of the History of Science of Harvard University, remarked: "He (Maimonides) was not a great physician; he was not an inventor as al-Razi was, but he was a wise physician, and in those days objective medical knowledge and scientific methods of diagnosis or treatment were so few and shaky that wisdom and what one might call medical intuition counted for very much. Modern physicians still need those psychological qualities, but their judgment is solidly based on physical, chemical, and biological tests which did not exist, and could hardly be conceived until last century, almost seven centuries after his time of activity." [14]

Jewish physicians through the ages were wont to manifest in prayer the sense of the profound moral responsibility of their profession. Judah Halevi, the greatest Hebrew poet since Bible times who also attained considerable success as a practicing physician, prayed for divine assistance in the exercise of his calling:

My God, heal me and I shall be healed,
Let not Thy anger be kindled against me
so that I be consumed.
My medicines are of Thee, whether good or evil,
whether strong or weak.
It is Thou who shalt choose, not I,
Of Thy knowledge is the evil and the good.
Not upon my power of healing I rely;
Only for Thy healing do I watch.

The prayer composed and recited by the Fostat-Cairo physician which became famous in medical literature as the Prayer of Maimonides, was described by Sir William Osler as "one of the most precious documents of our profession, worthy to be placed beside the Hippocrates oath." Appearing in many versions, we have selected the briefer form of this lofty and beautiful petition:

O, God, Thou hast formed the body of man with infinite goodness. Thou hast united in him immeasurable forces incessantly at work like so many instruments so as to preserve in its entirety this beautiful house containing his immortal soul, and these forces act with all the order and harmony imaginable. But if weakness or violent passion should disturb this harmony, these forces would act against one another and the body return to the dust whence it came. Thou sendest to man Thy messenger the disease which announces the approach of danger and bids him prepare to overcome them. The eternal Providence has appointed me to watch o'er the life and health of Thy creatures. May the love of my art actuate me at all times; may neither avarice nor thirst for glory or ambition for reputation engage my mind, for enemies of truth and philanthropy they could easily deceive me and make me forgetful of my lofty aim of doing good to Thy children. Endow me with strength of mind and heart so that both be always ready to serve the rich and the poor, the good and the wicked, friend and foe, and that I may never see in the patient anything else but a fellow-creature in pain.

If physicians more learned than I wish to guide and counsel me, inspire me with confidence in, obedience toward recognition of them, for the study of the science is great. It is not given to one man alone to see what others see. May I be moderate in everything, except in the knowledge of this science; as far as it is concerned, may I be insatiable in the desire to learn. Grant me strength and opportunity to always correct what I have acquired, to always extend its [medicine's] domain, for knowledge is immense and the spirit of man can also extend infinitely to daily enrich itself with new acquirements. Today he can discover his errors of yesterday, and tomorrow he may obtain new light on what he thinks himself sure of today. O, God, Thou hast appointed me to watch o'er the health of Thy creatures; here am I ready for my vocation.

When a controversy developed over the authenticity of the Prayer, Sir William Osler (1849–1919), the noted Canadian physician, wrote to Dr. Joseph H. Hertz (1872–1946), the late Chief Rabbi of Great Britain, for an opinion. After due investigation, Dr. Hertz wrote: "The Prayer is the product of Dr. Markus Herz (1747–1803), a friend and pupil of Immanuel Kant and Moses Mendelssohn. He was a physician in the Jewish Hospital in Berlin. The Prayer was composed by him in the German language and was published in a Hebrew translation in the periodical *Ha-Meassef*. The current English version seems to be from the Hebrew translation and first appeared in the London paper *Voice of Jacob* on the 24th of December, 1841." [15]

Rabbi Hermann Kroner (1870–1930), a German Rabbi and authority on the medical works of Moses Maimonides, and Dr. Solomon R. Kagan, who made the Prayer the subject of special study, came to the conclusion on the basis of internal evidence of the Prayer, that Maimonides *was* its author, since in form and spirit it is in complete harmony with the Fostat philosopher-physician's other writings. In 1938, Dr. Kagan wrote a paper "evincing that the concept of medical ethics reflected in the Prayer appears repeatedly in the published books and letters of Maimonides," and postulated that one of his pupils compiled the Prayer from Maimonides' work, thus justifying the title, "Maimonides' Prayer." Even though the authorship of the Prayer may not be definitely established, it certainly emphasizes the traditional attitude of the Jewish physician toward the ethics of medical practice." [16]

While Maimonides' medical success was no doubt due to his professional conscientiousness, his accuracy of judgment and personal amiability, his reputation was no little advanced by his extraordinary skill as a writer. He was not only a profound thinker and proficient physician but also an uncommon literary master. He wrote with clearness and distinction, with ease and fluency. He was a gifted literary craftsman whose pen responded with equal grace and readiness no matter what subject he had it serve. Maimonides was a prolific writer, and being articulate in writing, Dr. Wechsler observes, was then, even more than now, the broad highway to fame. His vast knowledge of the medical literature of Greek and Arabic writers combined with his own acute observations contributed to his distinction and popularity as a medical writer.

Maimonides was one of the fortunate men who received the accolade of his colleagues. The doctors who worked with him at the royal court, or were associated with him in scientific medical studies, admitted their admiration for his skill and modesty. Scholars from foreign countries who visited Cairo availed themselves of the opportunity to meet the renowned Jewish physician and philosopher. Allusion was made to 'Abd al-Latif who, on visiting Maimonides, had unjustly characterized him as being ambitious with an inclination to pander to the rich and powerful, but it did not influence his judgment of the man as being the "Eagle of Physicians." Ibn Abi Usaibia (1172–1248), a learned physician and historian of Arabic medicine on whose work all modern histories of Moslem medical science are based, wrote of Maimonides that he was the most distinguished physician of his time both in the theory and practice of medicine, and he closes his sketch of the "Eagle Physician" with a poem by Al-Said Ibn Almulk in Reginald W. Feldman's version: [17]

> *Contrast Maimuni's with famed Galen's art:*
> *Health to the body Galen can impart,*
> *But the wise Hebrew, with a two-fold skill;*
> *Shows how base ignorance can hurt the soul,*
> *While wisdom, counteracting, makes it whole.*
> *Even the moon, obedient to his cure,*
> *From periodic taint would be secure;*
> *No spots the brightness of her disk would stain,*
> *Nor would rebirth entail her death again.*

Although Maimonides reached the pinnacle of his professional greatness when he was appointed to the medical staff of the royal palace, he was by no means the only Jew to be thus honored by an Egyptian monarch. Jews are known to have served as court physicians to the Caliphs of Egypt in all periods of the Egyptian monarchy. The most distinguished of them in the pre-Maimonidean time having been Isaac ben Solomon Israeli, to whom reference was made before, whose medical works were greatly in vogue in Latin translation all through the Middle Ages. He anticipated Maimonides in his admonition to doctors to use diet or curative foods in preference to drugs, "because most of them are enemies and opponents of nature." One cannot help quoting his observations on the high calling of the physician and his ethical conduct because of their sheer beauty and exalted idealism. "Let your deeds alone praise you," he counsels his medical colleagues in his *Guide for Physicians,* "and do not honor yourself by shaming colleagues. Be eager to visit and treat the poor and needy, for no virtuous act is greater than this. Quiet the patient and bring him tidings of his recovery even if you are not certain of it. The need of the physician is twofold: preserving health and curing disease, and the demand for the former is greater than for the latter."

Moses Maimonides must have met a number of his co-religionists and consulted with them, as he made the rounds of his patients in the royal palace, although he makes no mention of them in his medical writings. Although Maimonides was in active attendance on members of Saladin's court, his numerous wives, courtiers, and high officials, it is doubtful that he ever came in contact with the ruler himself. What influence Maimonides wielded was in all likelihood through Saladin's Grand Vizier, Alfadhel, who was both a friend and patient of the physician-philosopher. Saladin's life was a difficult one. A skillful general, a resolute fighter, a resourceful diplomat, and ruler of a vast empire extending all the way from Egypt to the Tigris, he had little time to spare for his capital and left its administration to his trusted Vizier and comrade, Alfadhel.

The last years of Moses Maimonides were compounded of good and evil. He was at the peak of his medical reputation; his fame was spreading rapidly far and wide. When Richard, the Lion-hearted king of England, sought his medical services and wanted him to accompany him to his country, Maimonides refused, preferring the peace and security of Cairo to the uncertain conditions of London. He stood high in the royal favor of el-Adid who, upon the death of 'Aziz, had made himself master of Egypt and the greater part of his brother Saladin's empire. He was cheered by the recognition and honor that were shown him by all Jewry, particularly the scholars of Lunel, whom he held in high esteem. But he was beginning to feel the burden of old age creeping upon him with its accompanying ills and weakness. He always referred to himself in his correspondence as an old and ailing man. Thus, even as early as 1190, when he had still fourteen more years to live, his letter to the Provençal Jews, in which he exhorted them to remain steadfast to their faith and the study of the Torah, concluded on the doleful note, "Do not rely upon my support, because I am an old man with grey hair. And know that for this not my age but my weakness is responsible." [18]

Maimonides was a much overworked man. He was mentally and bodily exhausted. His climb to fame was by a steep and narrow path strewn not with roses, but with hardships and obstacles. In view of his tantalizing activities in so many diverse directions, it is not surprising that he all but broke down under the strain. He worked incessantly from his early childhood and authored books each one of which in lesser hands than his might have been the undertaking of a lifetime. He knew little of the lighter side of life, and the air and sunshine he prescribed for his patients he rarely enjoyed himself. His physical weakness grew on him so that he could not attend to his duties at the court, and shortly after he suffered from the calamities that befell Egypt due to the failure of the Nile.

By the standard of his time, at sixty-seven Moses Maimonides was an old man who should have left off working to enjoy the leisure he had not known all his life. What more could he add to the record he had already written? His works in Jewish and secular scholarship were universally acclaimed, and tongues which were raised against them changed to praise and adulation. Indeed, in some quarters of the Jewish world the admiration for him was almost fulsome, and it must have embarrassed rather than pleased Maimonides. We have referred above to Rabbi Jonathan's letter in which the Sage of Fostat is addressed in terms almost more than human, "a man full of divine vision . . . unique, over whose head the sacred ointment is poured out" who "drew his people out of the waters of error" and had "sown the seed of holiness, and removed the sway of impurity from his people."

Maimonides had but three years to live, and he spent them not in idleness resting on his laurels but in incessant work. There was a surging burst of energy in his tired frame. He never stopped correcting his *Mishneh Torah,* revising and adding to his medical books, taking personal care of his heavy correspondence from many parts of Jewry, discharging at intervals his duties at the court, and when late in the day he returned home fatigued and exhausted, he attended to the patients who crowded to his door, listening to their complaints and advising and prescribing for them.

Toiling to the end, it was his literary work which kept Maimonides' blood aflow. Interest in *The Guide for the Perplexed* absorbed him to the last. Eleven years after the book's publication, it had conquered the Arabic-speaking Jewish world. But to non-Arabic Jewry which venerated Maimonides and hung on his every word, the *Guide* was a book sealed with seven seals, and many requests came in for its translation. We referred to the Jews of Lunel among whom Maimonides was venerated only second to Moses the Prophet, who pleaded to have the book made known to them in the language they understood, and even timorously suggested that the author undertake its translation himself, not knowing that it was already being done by Samuel Ibn Tibbon, to whom, strangely, the master stylist referred as a fine stylist and translator.

Supervising Samuel Ibn Tibbon's translation of *The Guide for the Perplexed*, which by mutual agreement they named *Moreh Nebukim*, was one of the last literary activities of Moses Maimonides. Ibn Tibbon was far from having been the fine Hebrew stylist Maimonides mistakenly thought him to be; his translation is rather turgid, heavy and hard to understand. But he aimed at accuracy, and when he came to a difficult passage, he did not hesitate to consult the writer. It was for such purpose, to clarify a number of difficulties in the book by personal consultation, that Samuel Ibn Tibbon communicated to Maimonides his desire to come to see him. Maimonides' reply, discouraging his friend and translator from his coming, is a striking revelation of the character and personality of the man and his manner of life.

Now God knows that in order to write this to you I have escaped to a secluded spot, where people would not think to find me, sometimes leaning for support against the wall, sometimes lying down on account of my excessive weakness, for I have grown old and feeble.

With regard to your wish to come here to me, I cannot but say how greatly your visit would delight me, for I truly long to commune with you, and would anticipate our meeting with even greater joy than you. Yet I must advise you not to expose yourself to the perils of the voyage, for beyond seeing me, and my doing all I could to honor you, you would not derive any advantage from your visit. Do not expect to be able to confer with me on any scientific subject, for even one hour either by day or by night, for the following is my daily occupation. I dwell at Misr [Fostat] and the Sultan resides at Kahira [Cairo]; these two places are two Sabbath days' journey [about one mile and a half] distant from each other. My duties to the Sultan are very heavy. I am obliged to visit him every day, early in the morning; and when he or any of his children, or any of the inmates of his harem, are indisposed, I dare not quit Kahira, but must stay during the greater part of the day in the palace. It also frequently happens that one or two of the royal officers fall sick, and I must attend to their healing. Hence, as a rule, I repair to Kahira very early in the day, and if nothing unusual happens, I do not return to Misr until the afternoon. Then I am almost dying with hunger. I find the antechamber filled with people, both Jews and Gentiles, nobles and common people, judges and bailiffs, friends and foes—a mixed multitude, who await the time of my return.

I dismount from my animal, wash my hands, go forth to my patients, and entreat them to bear with me while I partake of some slight refreshment, the only meal I take in the twenty-four hours. Then I attend to my patients, write prescriptions for their various ailments. Patients go in and out until nightfall, and sometimes even, I solemnly assure you, until two hours and more in the night. I converse and prescribe for them while lying down from sheer fatigue, and when night falls, I am so exhausted that I can scarcely speak.

In consequence of this, no Israelite can have any private interview with me except on the Sabbath. On this day the whole congregation, or at least the majority of the members, come to me after the morning service, when I instruct them as to their proceedings during the whole week; we study together a little until noon, when they depart. Some of them return, and read with me after the afternoon service until evening prayers. In this manner I spend that day. I have here related to you only a part of what you would see if you were to visit me. Now, when you have completed for our brethren the translation you have commenced, I beg that you will come to me but not with the hope of deriving any advantage from your visit as regards your studies; for my time is, as I have shown you, excessively occupied.[19]

Moses Maimonides was close to seventy. He had reached his goal. His life was slowly ebbing away amidst almost constant suffering. He was weary and worn out. A wanderer half his life, he was about to enter upon his last voyage. He did not live long enough to see the Hebrew translation of *The Guide for the Perplexed*, which would have given him the greatest satisfaction of his life. Maimonides was no longer in the land of the living when the last chapters of the book had reached his home. He died toiling to the end, on December 13, 1204, while dictating to his nephew, who acted as his scribe, the last chapter of the revised edition of his *Aphorisms,* known by its Hebrew title as *Pirke Mosheh.*

His death was mourned as an irreparable loss by all classes of Jewry, friends and antagonists alike. Even those who had differed with him during his life and had bitterly criticized him, felt that in his demise a great light had gone out in Israel, an incomparable guide and teacher. Public mourning was declared for him in Egypt for three days in which Moslems joined the Jews. In Jerusalem, solemn obsequies amid general fasting were observed. The whole Jewish population gathered in their synagogues and read from the Torah the maledictions predicted for Israel for disobedience of the Divine Law, and from the first Book of Samuel the story of the capture of the Ark of the Covenant by the Philistines was recited, concluding with the words: "The glory is departed from Israel, for the Ark of God is taken." [20]

It was Maimonides' wish that he be taken to Tiberias for burial, a city laden with so many historic memories for Jews. Maimonides' death, no less than his life, is overladen with myth and legend. Thus it is told that when the funeral procession was on its way, a company of Bedouins overtook it and wished to throw the coffin into the sea. But although there were many of them, they could not lift the casket because of its great weight. They then realized that it must be the body of a holy man that the Jews were taking for interment. They therefore not only gave up the attempt but begged to be permitted to join in the procession and assisted the mourners to bring the dead to his final resting place.

Maimonides' tomb became for Jews a holy place where to this day thousands come to pray and meditate upon the life and teachings of the man who marks a lofty peak in the nation's intellectual and spiritual life. On Maimonides' grave an inscription penned by an unknown hand, likens the theologian-philosopher-physician to a celestial being:

> *Here lies a man, yet not a man,*
> *And if a man, conceived by angels;*
> *By human mother only born in light;*
> *Perhaps himself a spirit pure—*
> *Not a child by man and woman fostered—*
> *From God above an emanation bright.*

THE TEACHINGS OF MAIMONIDES

When the chief of philosophers [Aristotle] was about to inquire into some very profound subjects, and to establish his theory by proof, he commenced his treatise with an apology and requested the reader to attribute the author's inquiries not to presumption, vanity, egotism, or arrogance, as though he were interfering with things of which he had no knowledge, but rather to his zeal and his desire to discover and establish true doctrines, as far as it lay in human power.

We take the same position, and think that a man when he commences to speculate, ought not to embark at once on a subject so vast and important, but he should previously adapt himself to the study of the several branches of science and knowledge, should most thoroughly refine his moral character and subdue his passions and desires, the offspring of his imagination; when in addition he obtained a knowledge of the true fundamental propositions, a comprehension of the several methods of inference and proof, and the capacity of guarding against fallacies, then he may approach the investigation of this subject. He must, however, not decide any question by the first idea that suggests itself to his mind, or at once direct his thoughts and force them to obtain a knowledge of the Creator, but he must wait modestly and patiently, and advance step by step.

Guide, I, 5

9. GOD AS HE IS

The beginning and the end, the goal and the substance of all religious teaching is that there is a Supreme Power, Ruler, Ordainer, and Sovereign Master of the Universe from whom all existing things proceed and without whom the life-process of the world would be unthinkable. This God-consciousness, common to almost all mankind, is particularly strong among the Jews. It is the pillar of their faith, the bastion of their religious convictions, the essence of their lifelong contest with the various forms of heathenism from the patriarch Abraham down through the ages.

There is no exact word in the Hebrew language equivalent to "atheism" in its modern connotation. From the Jewish point of view, a godless Judaism is the strangest of all paradoxes. It was only the villain (nabal) who "says in his heart, There is no God" (Ps. 14:1). The conflict between the Prophets and their opponents was not around the controversy whether there was or was not a God, but whether the God the Prophets preached of was the only legitimate God of Israel. There are a number of designations applied in rabbinic literature to heretics, deniers, and perverters of the faith, but none that would seem to describe exactly the atheist in the usual acceptation of the term. When the Rabbis speak of the man who asserts, "There is neither judgment nor a judge above and beyond" (B.B. 16b), they have in mind not so much the atheist as the one who is skeptical of the moral order of the world.

It was, therefore, but natural that Moses Maimonides should introduce his great Code, the Mishneh Torah, *containing as it does the theoretical as well as the practical teachings of Judaism, with an elaborate exposition of the Jewish conception of the Deity.*

GOD IS

The basic principle of all principles and the pillar of all sciences is to realize that there is a First Being who brought every existing thing into being. All existing things, whether celestial, terrestrial, or belonging to an intermediate class, exist only through His true Existence. If it could be supposed that He did not exist, it would follow that nothing else could possibly exist. If, however, it were supposed that all other things were non-existent, He alone would still exist. Their non-existence would not involve His non-existence. For all beings are in need of Him; but He, blessed be He, is not in need of them nor of any of them. This is what the prophet means when he says, "But the Eternal is the true God" (Jer. 10:10); that is, He alone is real, and nothing else has reality like His reality. The same thought the Torah expresses in the text: "There is none else beside Him" (Deut. 4:35); that is: There is no being beside Him that is really like Him.

This being is the God of the Universe, the Lord of all Earth. And He it is who controls the Sphere (of the Universe) with a power that is without end or limit, with a power that is without cessation. For the sphere is always revolving, and it is impossible for it to revolve without something making it revolve. God, blessed be He, it is, who, without hand or body, causes it to revolve. To acknowledge this is an affirmative precept, as it is said, "I am the Lord, thy God" (Ex. 20:2). And whoever permits the thought to enter his mind that there is another deity besides this God, violates a prohibition; as it is said, "Thou shalt have no other gods before me" (Ex. 20:3; Deut. 5:7), and denies the essence of religion—this doctrine being the great principle on which everything depends.

Fundamental Principles of the Torah, 2

Everything existing and endowed with a form, is whatever it is, through its form, and when that form is destroyed its whole existence terminates and is obliterated. The same is the case as regards between God and all distant causes of existing beings; it is through the existence of God that all things exist, and it is He who maintains their existence by that process which is called emanation [in Hebrew, *shepha*]. . . . In this sense it may be said that God is the ultimate form, that He is the form of all forms; that is to say, the existence

and continuance of all forms in the last instance depend on Him. . . .
On that account God is called in the sacred language, *he ha-'olamim,*
"the life of the Universe," . . .

Some of the scholars belonging to the Mutakallemim [Mohamme-
dan theologians], went so far in their folly and in their vainglory as
to say that the non-existence of the Creator, if that were possible,
would not necessarily imply the non-existence of the things created
by Him, i.e., the Universe; for a production need not necessarily
cease to exist when the producer, after having produced it, has ceased
to exist. They would be right if God were only the maker of the
Universe, and if its permanent existence were not dependent on Him.
The storehouse does not cease to exist at the death of the builder, for
he does not give permanent.existence to the building. God, however,
is Himself the form of the Universe . . . and it is He who causes continuance and permanency. It is therefore wrong to say that a thing
can remain durable and permanent after the thing that made it durable and permanent has ceased to exist, since that thing can possess no
more durability and permanence than it has received from that being.

Guide, I, 69

GOD IS ONE

The Unity of God, in Hebrew, yihud ha-Shem, *is the first and foremost article of the Jewish faith. It was proclaimed on Sinai, was crystallized into
a dogma in Israel's eternal battle-cry* Shema Yisrael, *and was through the
centuries heroically defended by the Jews with their lives. God's Unity is
the principal doctrine which marks off the Jews from the followers of other
religious sects with their own notions of the Deity. Maimonides succinctly
reiterates this principle of Jewish religious belief:*

This God is One. He is not two nor more than two, but One; so
that none of the things existing in the Universe to which the term
one is applied is like unto His Unity; neither such a unit as a species
which comprises many units (i.e., sub-species), nor such a unit as a
physical body which consists of parts. His Unity is such that there
is no other Unity like it in the world.

If there were plural deities, these would be physical bodies; because
entities that can be enumerated and are equal in their essence are only
distinguishable from each other by the accidents that happen to physical bodies. If the Creator were a physical body, He would have

161

bounds and limits, for it is impossible for a physical body to be without limits; and where a body is limited and finite, its energy is also limited and finite. And our God, blessed be His name, since His power is infinite and unceasing . . . His power is not the energy of a physical body. And since He is not a physical body, the accidents that happen to physical bodies do not apply to Him, so as to distinguish Him from another being. Hence it is impossible that He can be anything but One. To realize this truth is an affirmative precept, as it is said, "The Eternal our God, is One God" (Deut. 6:4).

Fundamental Principles of the Torah, 1

Following more closely the subject of God's Unity in the Guide (II, 1), *Maimonides writes:*

It has been demonstrated by proof that the whole existing world is one organic body, all parts of which are connected together. . . . Hence it is impossible to assume that one deity be engaged in forming one, and another deity in forming another part of the organic body of which all parts are closely connected together. A duality could only be imagined in this way, either that at one time the one deity is active, the other at another time, or that both act simultaneously, nothing being done except by both together. The first alternative is certainly absurd for many reasons; if at the time the one deity be active, the other could also be active, there is no reason why the one deity should then act and the other not; if, on the other hand, it be impossible for one deity to act when the other is at work, there must be some other cause [besides these deities] which [at a certain time] enables the one to act and disables the other. . . . Besides, if two deities existed in this way both would be subject to the relations of time, since their actions would depend on time; they would also in the moment of acting pass from potentiality to actuality and require an agent for such transition; their essence would besides include possibility of existence.

It is furthermore absurd to assume that both together produce everything in existence, and that neither of them does anything alone; for when a number of forces unite for a certain result, none of these forces acts of its own accord, and none by itself is the immediate cause of that result, but their union is the immediate cause. It has, furthermore, been proved that the action of the absolute cannot be due to an [external cause]. The union is also an act which presupposes a cause effecting that union, and if that cause be one, it is undoubtedly God; but if it also consists of a number of separate forces, a cause is required for the combination of these forces, as in the first case. Finally, one simple being must be arrived at that is the cause of the existence of the Universe which is one whole. It would make no difference whether we assumed that the First Cause had produced the Universe by *creatio ex nihilo,* or whether the Universe co-existed with the First Cause. It is thus clear that we can prove the Unity of God from the fact that this Universe is one whole.

Guide, II, 1

Maimonides pursues the subject of God's Oneness with his inexorable logic, illustrating his thesis by an instance from practical, everyday life:

The circumstance which caused men to believe in the existence of divine attributes is similar to that which caused others to believe in the corporeality of God. The latter have not arrived at that belief by speculation, but by following the literal sense of certain passages in the Bible. The same is the case with attributes, when in the Prophets and in the Law, God is described by attributes, such passages are taken in their literal sense, and it is then believed that God possesses attributes, as if He were to be exalted above corporeality, and not above things connected with corporeality, i.e., the accidents, I mean psychical dispositions, all of which are qualities [and connected with corporeality]. Every attribute which the followers of this doctrine assume to be essential to the Creator, you will find to express, although they do not distinctly say so, a quality similar to those which they are accustomed to notice in the bodies of all living beings. We apply to all such passages the principle "The Torah speaks in the language of man," (Ber. 31b) and say that the object of all these terms is to describe God as the most perfect being, not as possessing those qualities which are only perfections in relation to created living beings. Many of the attributes express different acts of God, but that difference does not necessitate any difference as regards Him from whom the acts proceed.

This fact, *viz.,* that from one agency different effects may result, although that agency has not free will, and much more so if it has free will, I will illustrate by an instance taken from our own sphere.

Fire melts certain things and makes others hard, it boils and burns, it bleaches and blackens. If we described the fire as bleaching, blackening, burning, boiling, hardening, and melting, we should be correct, and yet he who does not know the nature of fire, would think that it included six different elements, one by which it blackens, another by which it bleaches, a third by which it boils, a fourth by which it consumes, a fifth by which it melts, a sixth by which it hardens things—actions which are opposed to one another, and of which each has its peculiar property. He, however, who knows the nature of fire, will know that by virtue of one quality in action, namely, by heat, it produces all these effects. If this is the case with that which is done by nature, how much more is it the case with regard to beings that act by free will, and still more with regard to God, who is above all description. If we, therefore, perceive in God certain relations of various kinds—for wisdom in us is different from power, and power from will—it does by no means follow that different elements are really contained in him, that He contains one element by which He knows, another by which He wills, and another by which he exercises power, as is, in fact, the signification of the attributes of God, according to the Attributists. Some of them express it plainly, and enumerate the attributes as elements added to the essence. Others, however, are more reserved with regard to this matter, but indicate their opinion, though they do not express it in distinct and intelligible words. Thus, e.g., some of them say: "God is omnipotent by His essence, wise by His essence, living by His essence, and endowed with a will by His essence."

I will mention to you, as an instance, man's reason which being one faculty and implying no plurality, enables him to know many arts and sciences; by the same faculty man is able to sow, to do carpenter's work, to weave, to build, to study, to acquire a knowledge of geometry, and to govern a state. These various acts resulting from one simple faculty, which involves no plurality, are very numerous; their number, that is, the number of the actions originating in man's reason, is almost infinite. It is therefore intelligible how in reference to God, those different actions can be caused by one simple substance, that does not include any plurality or any additional element. The attributes found in Holy Scripture are either qualifications of His actions, without any reference to His essence, or indicate absolute perfection, but do not imply that the essence of God is a compound of various elements. . . .

Therefore we, who truly believe in the Unity of God, declare, that as we do not believe that some element is included in His essence by which He created the heavens, another by which He created the (four) elements, a third by which He created the ideals, in the same way we reject the idea that His essence contains an element by which He has power, another element by which He has will, and a third by which He has a knowledge of His creatures. On the contrary, He is a simple essence, without any additional element whatever; He created the Universe, and knows it, but not by an extraneous force. There is no difference whether these various attributes refer to His actions or to His relations between Him and His works; in fact, these relations, as we have also shown, exist only in the thoughts of men. This is what we must believe concerning the attributes occurring in the books of the Prophets; some may also be taken as expressive of the perfection of God by way of comparison with what we consider as perfection in us. . . .

Guide, I, 53

GOD IS INCORPOREAL

Maimonides was concerned more with establishing the absolute spirituality of God by removing every trace of materiality with which the Bible and post-biblical literature had encrusted His Being than to demonstrate His existence. For while the people whom he addressed believed in God and did not doubt His existence, they entertained strange notions about Him which seriously compromised His unqualified intangible existence. In order to make God comprehensible to the people, the Prophets deliberately describe Him in vivid human images, attribute to Him human qualities and attributes, such as jealousy, wrath, vengeance, kindness, mercy, and compassion, not even sparing such ordinary functions as seeing, hearing, speaking, smelling, walking, and the like. "It would seem," remarks Solomon Schechter, "that the Rabbis felt actual delight in heaping human qualities upon God whenever opportunity was offered." Attempts were made to explain away the unseemly, and even offensive expressions concerning the Deity, but the habit persisted down to Maimonides' time, when outstanding scholars defended the literal anthropomorphic phrases in the Bible.

It was one of Moses Maimonides' greatest contributions to the cause of rational religion that he established the immateriality of God by devoting much of the first part of the Guide *to an interpretation of the anthropor-*

phisms of the Scriptures which impugn His incorporeality, explaining some of them as naive, figurative expressions intended for the immature understanding, and others as containing deep esoteric wisdom for the more advanced minds. He illustrates this by the well-known verse in Prov. 25:11: "A word fitly spoken is like apples of gold in a setting of silver." "To him who stands afar like a near-sighted person," Maimonides says, "only the silver shell is visible, the more valuable contents within is hidden from him. But he who approaches nearer, like one gifted with sharp eyes, recognizes the golden apples through the silver shell. Therefore, the intelligent must look deeper into such corporeally-sounding expression of the Bible in order to comprehend their truth."

In a note at the beginning of the second part of the Guide, *after he demolished in twenty-six propositions the position of the Mutakallimim with regard to the Unity, Eternity, and Incorporeality of God, Maimonides made clear the real purpose which impelled him to write his book.*

"It was not my intention," he said, "when writing this treatise to expound natural science or discuss metaphysical systems; it was not my object to prove truths which have already been demonstrated, or describe the number and the properties of the spheres; for the books written on these subjects serve their purpose, and if in some points they are not satisfactory, I do not think that what I could say would be better than what has already been explained by others. But my intention was, as has already been stated in the Introduction, to expound biblical passages which have been impugned, and elucidate their hidden and true sense, which is above the comprehension of the multitude . . . I only desire to mention that which might, when well understood, serve as means of removing some of the doubts concerning anything taught in Scripture; and indeed many difficulties will disappear when that which I am about to explain is taken into consideration." Guide (II, 2).

Thus it was for a rational religion through a rational interpretation of the Bible that Maimonides was seeking. But where was he to begin? How shall he proceed? He found his clue in the very first chapter of the Book of Genesis, verse 26: "Let us make man in our zelem (image)." What? Is it possible? Can this expression be taken literally when reason teaches us that God is an invisible, immaterial, intangible Intelligence? The inference is that there are words and phrases in the sacred Book which are homonyms (a term borrowed from Aristotle), having a double meaning, the one usual and obvious, the other figurative or allegorical, and zelem is one of such words. But let Maimonides speak for himself:

Some have been of opinion that by the Hebrew *zelem* the shape and figure of a thing is to be understood, and this explanation led men to believe in the corporeality [of the Divine Being]; for they

166

thought that the words "Let us make man in our *zelem*" implied that God had the form of a human being, i.e., that He had figure and shape, and that, consequently, He was corporeal. They adhered faithfully to this view, and thought that if they were to relinquish it they would *eo ipso* reject the truth of the Bible; and further, if they did not conceive God as having a body possessed of face and limbs, similar to their own in appearance, they would have to deny even the existence of God. The sole difference they admitted, was that He exalted in greatness and splendor, and that His substance was not flesh and blood. Thus far went their conception of the greatness and glory of God. . . . I hold that the Hebrew equivalent of "form" in the ordinary acceptance of the word, viz., the figure and shape of a thing is *toar*. Thus we find "(And Joseph was) beautiful in *toar* [form], and beautiful in appearance" (Gen. 39:6). It is also applied to form produced by human labor, as "He maketh its form [*toar*] with a line," "and he maketh its form [*toar*] with a compass" (Is. 44:13). This term is not at all applicable to God. The term *zelem*, on the other hand, signifies the specific form, viz., that which constitutes the essence of a thing, whereby the thing is what it is; the reality of a thing in so far as it is that particular being. In man the "form" is that constituent which gives him human perception; and on account of this intellectual perception the term *zelem* is employed in the sentences "In the *zelem* of God He created him" (Gen. I, 27). It is therefore rightly said, "Thou despisest their *zelem*" (Ps. 73:20): the "contempt" can only concern the soul—the specific form of man, not the properties and shape of his body. I am also of the opinion that the reason why this term is used for "idols" may be found in the circumstance that they are worshipped on account of some idea represented by them, not on account of their figure and shape. . . ."

Guide, I, 1

As man's distinction consists in a property which no other creature on earth possesses, viz., intellectual perception, in the exercise of which he does not employ his senses, nor move his hand or his foot, this perception has been compared—though only apparently, not in truth—to the Divine perception, which requires no corporeal organ. On this account, i.e., on account of the Divine intellect with which man has been endowed, he is said to have been made in the form and likeness of the Almighty, but far from it be the notion that the Supreme Being is corporeal, having a material form.

Ibid.

THE TORAH SPEAKS IN THE LANGUAGE OF MAN

You, no doubt, know the talmudical saying, which includes in itself all the various kinds of interpretation connected with our subject. It runs thus: "The Torah speaks according to the language of man" (Ber. 31b), that is to say, expressions, which can easily be comprehended and understood by all, are applied to the Creator. Hence the description of God by attributes implying corporeality, in order to express His existence; because the multitude of people do not easily conceive existence unless in connection with a body, and that which is not a body nor connected with a body has for them no existence. Whatever we regard as a state of perfection, is likewise attributed to God, as expressing that He is perfect in every respect, and that no imperfection or deficiency whatever is found in Him. But there is not attributed to God anything which the multitude consider a defect or want; thus, He is never represented as eating, drinking, sleeping, being ill, using violence, and the like.

Ibid., 26

Onkelos the Proselyte who was thoroughly acquainted with the Hebrew and Chaldaic languages, made it his task to oppose the belief in God's corporeality. Accordingly, any expression employed in the Pentateuch in reference to God, and in any way implying corporeality he paraphrases in consonance with the context. All expressions denoting any mode of motion, are explained by him to mean the appearance or manifestation of a certain light that had been created [for the occasion], i.e., the Shekinah [Divine Presence] or Providence. Thus he paraphrases "the Lord will come down" (Ex. 19:11), "The Lord will manifest Himself"; and does not say "And God came down"; "I will go down now and see" (Gen. 18:21), he paraphrases, "I will manifest myself now and see." This is his rendering [of the word *yarad*], "he went down [when used in reference to God] throughout his version. . . .

In the passage (Ex. 24:10), "And there was under his feet like the action of the whiteness of a sapphire stone," Onkelos, as you know, in his version, considers the word *raglav* "his feet" as a figurative expression and a substitute for "throne"; the words "under his feet" he therefore paraphrases, "And under the throne of his glory." Consider this well, and you will observe with wonder how Onkelos keeps free from the corporeality of God, and from everything that leads thereto, even in the remotest degree.

Ibid., 27-28

When we are told that God addressed the Prophets and spoke to them, our minds are merely to receive a notion that there is a Divine knowledge to which the Prophets attain; we are to be impressed with the idea that the things which the Prophets communicate to us came from the Lord, and are not altogether the products of their own conceptions and ideas. . . . We must not suppose that in speaking God employed a voice or a sound, or that He has a soul in which the thoughts reside, and that these thoughts are things superadded to His essence.

Ibid., 64

The corporeal element in man is a large screen and partition that prevents him from perfectly perceiving abstract ideals; this would be the case even if the corporeal element were as pure and superior as the substance of the spheres; how much more must this be the case with our dark and opaque body. However great the exertion of our minds may be to comprehend the Divine Being or any of the ideals, we find a screen and partition between Him and ourselves. Thus the prophets frequently hint at the existence of a partition between God and us. They say, He is concealed from us in vapors, in darkness, in mist, or in a thick cloud; or use similar figures to express that on account of our bodies we are unable to comprehend His essence. This is the meaning of the words, "Clouds and darkness are round about Him" (Ps. 97:2).

The Prophets tell us that the difficulty consists in the grossness of our substance; they do not imply, as might be gathered from the literal meaning of their words, that God is corporeal and is invisible because He is surrounded by thick clouds, vapors, darkness, or mists. This figure is also expressed in the passage, "He made darkness his secret place" (Ps. 18:12). The object of God revealing Himself in thick clouds . . . was to teach this lesson; for every prophetic vision contains some lesson by means of allegory; that mighty vision, therefore, though the greatest of all visions, and above all comparisons, viz., His revelation in a thick cloud, did not take place without any purpose, it was intended to indicate that we cannot comprehend Him on account of the dark body that surrounds us. It does not surround God, because He is incorporeal. A tradition is current among our people that the day of the Revelation on Mount Sinai was misty, cloudy, and a little rainy. "Lord, when Thou wentest forth from Seir, when Thou marchest out of the fields of Edom, the earth trembled, and the heavens dropped water" (Jud. 5:4). The same idea is expressed by the words "darkness, clouds, and thick darkness" (Deut. 4:11). The phrase does not denote that darkness surrounds God, for with Him there is no darkness, but the great, strong, and permanent light, which, emanating from Him, illuminates all darkness, as is expressed by the prophetic simile, "And the earth shined with His glory" (Ez. 43:2).

Guide, III, 9

GOD'S ATTRIBUTES

Closely connected, indeed, identical, with Maimonides' doctrine of the anthropomorphisms of the Bible, is his theory of Attributes, or certain qualities assigned to God, both together practically conveying the quintessence of his whole philosophy. Jewish scholars in all ages considered it unlawful to assign to God positive attributes for fear that they might lead to dualism, to believe in God and His attributes as two distinct beings, because attributes can so easily be personalized and addressed as separate deities. The gist of Maimonides' argument is that no attribute coming under the head of corporeality in its widest sense can be predicated to God, but man can come nearer to the knowledge and comprehension of God by the negative attributes. In other words, we can know that God is, but not what He is:

If you have a desire to rise to a higher state, *viz.*, that of reflection, and truly to hold the conviction that God is One and possesses true unity, without admitting plurality or divisibility in any sense whatever, you must understand that God has no essential attributes in any form or in any sense whatever, and that the rejection of corporeality implies the rejection of essential attributes. Those who believe that God is One, and that He has many attributes, declare the Unity with their lips and assume plurality in their thoughts. This is like the doctrine of the Christians, who say that He is one and He is three, and that the three are one. Of the same character is the doctrine of those who say that God is One, but that He has many attributes; and

that He and His attributes are One, although they deny corporeality
and affirm His most absolute freedom from matter, as if our object
were to seek forms of expression, not subjects of belief.

Guide, I, 50

God exists without possessing the attributes of existence. Similarly,
He lives without possessing the attributes of life; knows without possessing the attributes of knowledge; is omnipotent without possessing
the attributes of omnipotence; is wise without possessing the attributes of wisdom . . . He is one without possessing the attributes
of unity. . . . The same is the case when we say God is the first
[Kadmon], to express that He has not been created; the term "First"
is decidedly inaccurate, for it can in its true sense only be applied to
a being that is subject to the relation of time. . . . Besides, the attribute "first" is a relative term, being in regard to time the same as the
term "long" and "short" are in regard to a line.

Ibid., 57

. . . those who believe in the essential attributes of God, viz.,
Existence, Life, Power, Wisdom, and Will, should know that these
attributes, when applied to God, have not the same meaning as when
applied to us, and that the difference does not only consist in magnitude, or in the degree of perfection, ability and durability. It cannot
be said as they practically believe, that His existence is only more
stable, His life more permanent, His power greater, His wisdom more
perfect, and His will more general than ours, and that the same definition applies to both. This is in no way admissible, for the expression
"more than" is used in comparing two things as regards a certain
attribute predicated of both of them in exactly the same sense, and
consequently implies similarity [between God and His creatures].

Ibid., 56

Consider all these and similar attributes and you will find that they
cannot be employed in reference to God. He is not a magnitude that
any quality resulting from quantity as such could be possessed by
Him; He is not affected by external influences and therefore does not
possess any quality resulting from emotion. He is not subject to physical conditions, and therefore does not possess strength or similar
qualities; He is not an animate being, that he should have a certain

171

disposition of the soul, or acquire certain properties, as meekness, modesty, etc., or be in a state to which animate beings as such are subject, as, e.g., in that of health or of illness.

Ibid., 52

WHAT MAN CAN KNOW OF GOD

What was it that Moses sought to comprehend, when he said "Show me, I beseech Thee, Thy glory"? (Ex. 33:18). He sought to have so clear an apprehension of the truth of God's existence that the knowledge might be like that which one possesses of a human being, whose face one has seen and whose image is imprinted on the mind and whom, therefore, the mind distinguishes from other men. In the same way, Moses, our teacher, asked that the truth of God's existence might be distinguished in this mind from other beings, and that he might thus know the truth of God's existence, as it really is. God replied that it is beyond the mental capacity of a human creature, composed of body and soul, to obtain in this regard clear knowledge of the truth. The Almighty, however, imparted to Moses what has been vouchsafed to no man before or since. Moses attained so much knowledge of the truth of the Divine Existence that God was, in his mind, distinct from other beings, in the same way as an individual, whose back is seen, whose physical form and apparel are perceived, is distinguished in the observer's mind from the physical form of other individuals. And Scripture hints this in the text "Thou shalt see My rearward but my face shall not be seen" (Ex. 33:23).

Fundamental Principles of the Torah

Human knowledge is limited. As long as the soul dwells in the body it cannot know what is beyond matter. Knowledge is restricted to matter, and the intellect cannot visualize and see what is beyond it. The mind that attempts to penetrate further will realize the impossibility thereof and the subtlety of the subject. Only what is part of nature can be perceived and understood.

Responsum to Hasdai ha-Levi of Alexandria; *Kobez*, II, 23

Another accepted axiom of metaphysics is that human reason cannot fully conceive God in His true essence, because of the perfection of God's essence and the imperfection of our own reason, and because

His essence is not due to cause through which it may be known. Furthermore, the inability of our reason to comprehend Him may be compared to the inability of our eyes to gaze at the sun, not because of the weakness of the sun's light, but because that light is more powerful than that which seeks to gaze into it.

Eight Chapters, 8

From what we have said, it has been demonstrated also that we cannot comprehend God's knowledge, that our minds cannot grasp it all, for He is His knowledge, and His knowledge is He. This is an especially striking idea, but those [who raise the question of God's knowledge of the future] fail to grasp it to their dying day. They are, it is true, aware that the divine essence, as it is, is comprehensible, yet they strive to comprehend God's knowledge, so that they may know it, but this is, of course, impossible. If the human reason could grasp His knowledge, it would be able also to define His essence, since both are one and the same, as the perfect knowledge of God is the comprehension of Him as He is in His essence, which consists of His knowledge, His will, His life, and all His other majestic attributes. Thus, we have shown how utterly futile is the pretension to define His knowledge. All that we can comprehend is that just as we know that God exists so are we cognizant of the fact that He knows. If we are asked "What is the nature of God's knowledge?" we answer that we do not know any more than we know the nature of His true existence. Fault is found, moreover, with him who tries to grasp the truth of the divine existence as expressed by the words, "Canst thou by searching find out God? Canst thou find out the Almighty unto perfection?

Ibid.

GOD KNOWS HIMSELF

The Holy One, blessed be He, realizes His true being, and knows it as it is, not with a knowledge external to himself, as is our knowledge. For our knowledge and ourselves are separate. But as for the Creator, blessed be He, his knowledge and His life are One, in all aspects, from every point of view, and however we conceive Unity. If the Creator lived as other living creatures live, and his knowledge were external to Himself, there would be a plurality of deities, namely: He himself, His life, and His knowledge. This however, is not so. He is One in every aspect, from every angle, and in all ways in which Unity is conceived. Hence the conclusion that God is One who knows, is known, and is the knowledge [of Himself]—all these being One. This is beyond the power of speech to express, beyond the capacity of the ear to hear, and of the human mind to apprehend clearly. Scripture accordingly says "By the life of Pharaoh" and "by the life of thy soul" but not "By the life of the Eternal." The phrase employed is "As God liveth"; because the Creator and His life are not dual, as is the case with the life of living bodies or of angels. Hence too, God does not apprehend creatures and know them because of them, as we know them, but He knows them because of Himself. Knowing Himself, He knows everything, for everything is attached to Him, in His being.

Fundamental Principles of the Torah, 11

GOD IS INCOMPARABLE TO MAN

Do not think that what we have said on the importance, obscurity, and difficulty of the subject, and its unsuitableness for communication to ordinary persons, includes the doctrines of God's incorporeality and His exemption from all affections. This is not the case. For in the same way as all people must be informed, and even children must be trained in the belief that God is One, and none besides Him is to be worshipped, so must all be taught by simple authority that God is incorporeal; that there is no similarity in any way whatsoever between Him and His creatures; that His existence is not like the existence of His creatures, His life not like that of any living being, His wisdom not like the wisdom of the wisest of men; and that the difference between Him and His creatures is not merely quantitative, but absolute [as between two individuals of two different classes]; I mean to say that all must understand that our wisdom and His, or our power and His, do not differ quantitatively or qualitatively, or in a similar manner; for two things, of which the one is strong and the other weak, are necessarily similar, belong to the same class, and can be included in one definition. The same is the case with all other comparisons; they can only be made between two things belonging to the same class, as has been shown in works on natural science. Anything predicated of God is totally different from our attributes; no definition can comprehend both; therefore His existence and that

of any other being totally differ from each other, and the term existence applied to both is homonymous. . . .

That God is incorporeal, that He cannot be compared with His
creatures, that He is not subject to external influence; these are things
which must be explained to everyone according to his capacity, and
they must be taught by way of tradition to children and women, to
the stupid and ignorant, as they are taught that God is One, that He
is eternal, and that none but He is to be worshipped. . . . When persons have received this doctrine, and have been trained in this belief
and are in consequence at a loss to reconcile it with the writings of
the Prophets, the meaning of the latter must be made clear and explained to them by pointing out the homonymity and the figurative
application of certain terms. . . . Their belief in the unity of God and in
the words of the Prophets will then be a true and perfect belief. . . .

Guide, I, 35

The idea [that God cannot be the object of human comprehen-
sion] is best expressed in the Book of Psalms, "Silence is praise to
Thee" (65:2). It is a very expressive remark on this subject; for
whatever we utter with the intention of extolling and praising Him,
contains something that cannot be applied to God, and includes de-
rogatory expressions; it is therefore more becoming to be silent, and
be content with intellectual reflection, as has been recommended by
men of the highest culture, in the words "Commune with your own
heart upon your beds, and be still" (Ps. 4:5). You must surely know
the celebrated passage in the Talmud (Ber. 33b)—would that all
passages in the Talmud were like that!—although it is known to you,
I quote it literally, as I wish to point out to you the idea contained
in it: "A certain person, reading prayers in the presence of Rabbi
Haninah, said, 'God the great, the valiant, and the tremendous, the
powerful, the strong, and the mighty.'—The Rabbi said to him,
'Have you finished all the praises of the Master? The three epithets,
"God the great, the valiant, and the tremendous," we should not have
applied to God, had Moses not mentioned them in the Law, and had
not men of the Great Synagogue come forward subsequently and
established their use in the prayer; and you say all this! Let this be
illustrated by a parable. There was once an earthly king possessing
millions of gold coin; he was praised for owning millions of silver
coin; was not this really mispraise to him.'" Thus far the opinion

of the pious rabbi. . . . If slander and libel is a great sin, how much greater is the sin of those who speak with looseness of tongue in reference to God, and describe Him by attributes which are far below Him; and I declare that they commit not only an ordinary sin but unconsciously at least incur the guilt of profanity and blasphemy. This applies both to the multitude that listens to such prayers, and to the foolish man that recites them. Men, however, who understand the fault of such compositions, and, nevertheless recite them, may be classed, according to my opinion, among those to whom the following words may be applied: "And the children of Israel used words that were not right against the Lord their God" (II Kings 17:9), and "utter errors against the Lord" (Is. 32:6). If you are of those who regard the honor of their Creator, do not listen in any way to them, much less utter what they say, and still less compose such prayers, knowing how great is the offense of one who hurls aspersions against the Supreme Being. There is no necessity at all for you to use positive attributes of God with the view of magnifying Him in your thoughts, or go beyond the limits which the men of the Great Synagogue have introduced in the prayers and in the blessings, for this is sufficient for all purposes, and even more than sufficient, as Rabbi Haninah said.

Ibid., 59

Obsessed with the idea of ascribing the non-qualities to God, Maimonides evolved the theory of negative attributes, according to which God may be known better by what He is not than by what He is.

Know [writes Maimonides] that the negative attributes of God are the true attributes: they do not include any incorrect notions of any deficiency whatever in reference to God, while positive attributes imply polytheism, and are inadequate. . . . It is now necessary to explain how negative expressions can in a certain sense be employed as attributes and how they are distinguished from positive attributes. Then I shall show that we cannot describe the Creator by any means except by negative attributes.

An attribute does not exclusively belong to the one object to which it is related; while qualifying one thing, it can also be employed to qualify other things, e.g., if you see an object from a distance, and on inquiring what it is, are told that it is a living being, you have certainly learned an attribute of the object seen, and although that attribute does not exclusively belong to the object perceived, it expresses that the object is not a plant or a mineral. Again, if a man is in a certain house, and you know that something is in the house but not exactly what, you ask what is in that house, and you are told not a plant nor a mineral. You have thereby obtained some special knowledge of the thing; you have learnt that it is a living being, although you do not yet know what kind of a living being it is. The negative attributes have this in common with the positive, that they necessarily circumscribe the object to some extent, although such circumscription consists only in the exclusion of what otherwise would be excluded. The positive attributes although not peculiar to one thing, describe a portion of what we desire to know, either some part of its essence or some of its accidents; the negative attributes, on the other hand, do not, as regards the essence of the thing which we desire to know, in any way tell us what it is, except it be indirectly, as has been shown in the instance given by us.

After this introduction, I would observe that—as has already been shown—God's existence is absolute, that it includes no composition . . . and that we comprehend only the fact that He exists, not His essence. Consequently it is a false assumption to hold that He has any positive attribute; for He does not possess existence in addition to His essence; it therefore cannot be said that the one may be described as an attribute [of the other]; much less has He [in addition to His existence] a compound essence consisting of two constituent elements to which the attribute could refer; still less has He accidents which could be described by an attribute. Hence it is clear that He has no positive attribute whatever.

Ibid.

THE NAMES OF GOD

God figures in the Bible and in rabbinic literature under a number of names which, with the exception of one, which is His true identity, are descriptions of His actions and His relation to the world and men.

It is well known that all the names of God occurring in Scripture are derived from His action, except one, namely, the Tetragrammaton, which consists of the letters *yod, he, vau* and *he*. This name is applied exclusively to God, and is on that account called *Shem ha-meforash*, "the nomen proprium." It is the distinct and exclusive

177

designation of the Divine Being; whilst His other names are common nouns, and are derived from actions, to which some of our own are similar. Even the name *Adonay*, "Lord," which has been substituted for the Tetragrammaton, is derived from the appellative "lord"; compare "The man who is the lord [*adonay*] of the land spake roughly to us" (Gen. 43:30). An angel is also addressed *Adonay*, e.g., "*Adonay* [My lord], pass not away, I pray thee" (*ibid.*, 18:3). I have restricted my explanation to the term *Adonay*, the substitute for the Tetragrammaton, because it is more commonly applied to God than any of the other names which are in frequent use, like *dayyan*, "judge," *shaddai*, "almighty," *zaddik*, "righteous," *hannun*, "gracious," *rahum*, "merciful," *elohim*, "chief"; all these terms are unquestionably appellations and derivatives.

The derivation of the name, consisting of *yod*, *he*, *vau* and *he*, is not positively known, the word having no additional signification. This sacred name, which, as you know, was not pronounced except in the sanctuary by the appointed priests, when they gave the sacerdotal blessing, and by the high priest on the Day of Atonement, undoubtedly denotes something which is peculiar to God, and is not found in any other being. It is possible that in the Hebrew language, of which we have now but a slight knowledge, the Tetragrammaton, in the way it was pronounced, conveyed the meaning of "absolute Existence." In short, the majesty of the name and the great dread of uttering it, are connected with the fact that it denotes God Himself, without including in its meaning any names of the things created by Him. Thus our Sages say: " 'My name' (Nu. 6:27) means the name which is peculiar to Me." All other names of God have reference to quality, and do not signify a simple substance, but a substance with attributes, they being derivatives. . . . Such is the meaning of all derivative names; they imply the presence of some attribute and its substratum, though this be not distinctly named. As, however, it has been proved that God is not a substratum capable of attributes, we are convinced that those appellatives, when employed as names of God, only indicate the relation of certain actions to Him, or they convey to us some notion of His perfection.

Guide, I, 61

Our Sages knew in addition a name of God which consisted of twelve letters inferior in sanctity to the Tetragrammaton. I believe that this was not a single noun, but consisted of two or three words, the sum of their letters being twelve, and that these words were used by our Sages as a substitute for the Tetragrammaton, whenever they met with it in the course of their reading the Scriptures in the same manner as we at present substitute for it *aleph, dalet,* etc. [i.e., *Adonay,* the Lord]. There is no doubt that this name also, consisting of twelve letters, was in this sense more distinctive than the name *Adonay:* it was never withheld from any of the students; whoever wished to learn it, has the opportunity given to him without any reserve: Not so the Tetragrammaton; those who knew it did not communicate it except to a son or to a disciple, once in seven years. When, however, unprincipled men had become acquainted with that name which consists of twelve letters and in consequence had become corrupt in faith—as is sometimes the case when persons with imperfect knowledge become aware that a thing is not such as they had imagined—the Sages concealed also that name and only communicated it to the worthiest among the priests, that they should pronounce it when they bless the people in the Temple, for the Tetragrammaton was then no longer uttered in the sanctuary on account of the corruption of the people.

Ibid., 62

There was also a name of forty-two letters known among them. Every intelligent person knows that one word of forty-two letters is impossible. But it was a phrase of several words which had together forty-two letters. There is no doubt that the words had such a meaning as to convey a correct notion of the essence of God, in the way we have stated. This phrase of so many letters is called a name because, like other proper nouns, they represent one single object, and several words have been employed in order to explain more clearly the idea which the name represents; for an idea can more easily be comprehended if expressed in many words . . . *Shem ha-meforash* applied neither to the name of forty-two letters nor to that of twelve, but only to the Tetragrammaton, the proper name of God, as we have explained. Those two names must have included some metaphysical ideas. It can be proved that one of them conveyed profound knowledge, from the following rule laid down by our Sages: "The name of forty-two letters is exceedingly holy; it can only be entrusted to him who is modest, in the midway of life, not easily provoked to anger, temperate, gentle, and who speaks kindly to his fellow men. He who understands it, is cautious with it, and keeps it in purity, is loved above and is liked here below; he is respected by his fellow men; his learning remaineth with him, and he enjoys both this world and the world to come." (Kid. 71a).

Ibid.

SUPERSTITIOUS USE OF GOD'S NAME

The "holy and awesome" multi-lettered names of God were often used by practitioners of medieval Jewish magic to produce certain occult results, and Maimonides, an avowed enemy of every form of superstition, warned sternly against it.

When bad and foolish men were reading such passages, they considered them to be a support of their false pretensions and of their assertion that they could by means of an arbitrary combination of letters, form a *shem* [Name] which would act and operate miraculously when written or spoken in a certain particular way. Such fictions, originally invented by foolish men, were in the course of time committed to writing, and came into the hands of good but weak-minded and ignorant persons who were unable to discriminate between truth and falsehood, and who made a secret of these *shemot*. When after the death of such persons those writings were discovered among their papers, it was believed that they contained truths; for, "The simple believeth every word" (Prov. 14:15).

Ibid.

You must beware of sharing the error of those who write amulets [*kameot*]. Whatever you hear from them, or read in their works, especially in reference to the names which they form by combination, is utterly senseless; they call these combinations *shemot* [names] and believe that their pronunciation demands sanctification and purification, and that by using them they are enabled to work miracles. Rational persons ought not to listen to such men, nor in any way believe their assertions.

Ibid., 61

GOD TEACHES MOSES HIS EXISTENCE

When God appeared to our Teacher Moses and commanded him to address the people and bring them the message, Moses replied that he might first be asked to prove the existence of God in the Universe, and that only after doing so he would be able to announce to them that God had sent him. For all men, with few exceptions, were ignorant of the existence of God; their highest thought did not extend beyond the heavenly sphere, its forms or its influence. They could not yet emancipate themselves from sensation and had not yet attained to any intellectual perfection.

Then God taught Moses how to teach them, and how to establish amongst them the belief in the existence of Himself, namely, by saying *Ehye asher Ehye*, a name derived from the verb *hayah* in the sense of "existing," for the verb *hayah* denotes "to be," and in Hebrew no difference is made between the verbs "to be" and "to exist." The principal point in this phrase is that the same word which denotes "existence" is repeated as an attribute. The word *asher*, that corresponds to the Arabic *illadi* and *illati*, and is an incomplete noun that must be completed by another noun; it may be completed by the subject of the predicate that follows. The first noun which is to be described as *ehyeh*; the second by which is described, is likewise *ehyeh*, the identical word, as if to show that the object which is to be described and the attribute by which it is described are in this case necessarily identical. This is, therefore, the expression of the idea that God exists, but not in the ordinary sense of the term; or, in other words, He is "the existing Being which is the Existing Being," that is to say, the Being whose existence is absolute. The proof which he was to give consisted in demonstrating that there is a Being of absolute existence that has never been and never will be without existence.

God thus showed Moses the proofs by which His existence would be firmly established among the wise men of His people. Therefore the explanation of the name is followed by the words, "Go, gather the elders of Israel," and by the assurance that the elders would understand what God had shown to him, and would accept it, as is stated in the words, "And they will hearken to thy voice." Then Moses replied as follows: They will accept the doctrine that God exists convinced by these intelligible proofs. But, said Moses, by what means shall I be able to show that this existing God has sent me? Thereupon God gave him the sign. We have thus shown that the question, "What is His name?" means "Who is that Being which according to thy belief has sent thee?" The sentence, "What is His name" [instead of Who is He], has here been used as a tribute of praise and homage, as though it had been said, Nobody can be ignorant of Thy essence and of Thy real existence; if, nevertheless I ask what is Thy name, I mean, What idea is to be expressed by the name? (Moses considered it inappropriate to say to God that any person was ignorant of God's existence, and therefore described the Israelites as ignorant of God's name, not as ignorant of Him who was called by that name.)

Ibid., 63

HOW TO FIND GOD: A PARABLE

One of the characteristic features of Maimonides' literary craftsmanship is his liberal use of the allegory, or parable, to drive home an abstract thought. The following illustration of the diverse ways of seeking and finding God is particularly striking:

A king is in his palace, and all his subjects are partly in the country and partly abroad. Of the former, some have their backs turned toward the king's palace, and their faces in another direction; and some are desirous and zealous to go to the palace, seeking "to inquire in his temple," and to minister before him, but have not yet seen even the face of the wall of the house. Of those that desire to go to the palace, some reach it, and go round about in search of the entrance gate; others have passed through the gate, and walk about in the antechamber; and others have succeeded in entering into the inner part of the palace, and being in the same room with the king in the royal palace. But even the latter do not immediately on entering the palace see the king, or speak to him; for, after having entered the inner part of the palace, another effort is required before they can stand before the king—at a distance, or close by—hear his words, or speak to him.

I will now explain the simile which I have made. The people who are abroad are all those that have no religion, neither one based on speculation nor one received by tradition. I consider these as irrational beings, and not as human beings, they are below mankind but above monkeys, since they have the form and shape of men, and a mental faculty above that of the monkey.

Those who are in the country, but have their backs turned toward the king's palace, are those who possess religion, belief and thought, but happen to hold false doctrines, which they either adopted in consequence of great mistakes made in their own speculations, or received from others who misled them. Because of these doctrines they recede more and more from the royal palace the more they seem to proceed. These are worse than the first class. . . . Those who desire to arrive at the palace, and to enter it, but have never yet seen it, are the mass of religious people; the multitude that observe the divine commandments, but are ignorant. Those who arrive at the palace, but go round about it, are those who devote themselves exclusively to the study of the practical law; they believe traditionally in true principles of faith, and learn the practical worship of God, but are not trained in philosophical treatment of the principles of the Law, and do not endeavor to establish truth of their faith by proof. Those who undertake to investigate principles of religion, have come into the ante-chamber; and there is no doubt that these can also be divided into different grades. But those who have succeeded in finding a proof for everything that can be proved, who have a true knowledge of God, so far as a true knowledge can be obtained and are near the truth, wherever an approach to the truth is possible, they have reached the goal, and are in the palace in which the king lives.

My son [he wrote to Joseph Ibn Aknin], so long as you are engaged in studying the Mathematical Sciences and Logic, you belong to those who go round about the palace in search of the gate. Thus, our Sages figuratively used the phrase: "Ben-Zoma is still outside." When you understand Physics, you have entered the hall; and when, after completing the study of Natural Philosophy, you master Metaphysics, you have entered the innermost court, and are with the king in the same palace. You have attained the degree of the wise men, who include men of different grades of perfection. There are some who direct all their mind toward the attainment of perfection in Metaphysics, devote themselves entirely to God, exclude from their thought every other thing, and employ all their intellectual faculties in the study of the Universe, in order to derive therefrom a proof for the existence of God, and to learn in every possible way how God rules all things; they form the class of those who have entered the palace, namely, the class of prophets. One of these has attained so much knowledge and has concentrated his thoughts to such an extent in the idea of God, that it could be said of him, "And he was with the Lord forty days," (Ex. 34:28); during that holy communion he could ask Him, answer Him, speak to Him, and be addressed by Him, enjoying beatitudes in that which he had obtained to such a degree that "he did neither eat bread nor drink water" (*ibid.*) ; his intellectual energy was so predominant that all coarser functions of the body, especially those connected with the sense of touch, were in abeyance. . . . This is the worship peculiar to those who have acquired a knowledge of the highest truths; and the more they reflect on Him, and think of Him, the more are they engaged in His worship. Those, however, who think of God, and frequently mention His name, without any correct notion of Him, but merely following some imagination, or some creed received from another person, are, in my opinion, like those who remain outside the palace and distant from it. They do not mention the name of God in truth, nor do they reflect on it. That which they imagine and mention does not correspond to any being in existence; it is a thing invented by their imagination. . . . The true worship of God is only possible when correct notions of Him have previously been conceived. When you have arrived by way of intellectual research at a knowledge of God and His works, then commence to devote yourselves to Him, try to approach Him and strengthen the intellect which is the link that joins you to Him. Thus the Lord distinctly states that the highest kind of worship . . . is only possible after the acquisition of the knowledge of God. For it is said, "To love the Lord your God, and to serve Him with all your heart and with all your soul," (Deut. 11:13). . . . The Divine Service enjoined in these words, must, accordingly, be preceded by the love of God. Our Sages have pointed out to us that it is a service of the heart, which explanation I understand to mean this: man concentrates all his thoughts on the First Intellect, and is absorbed in these thoughts as much as possible. . . . He accomplishes this generally by seclusion and retirement. Every pious man should therefore seek retirement and seclusion, and should only in case of necessity associate with others.

Guide, III, 51

WORSHIP IS MAN'S LINK TO GOD

I have shown you that the intellect is the link that joins us to God. You have it in your power to strengthen that bond, if you choose to do so, or to weaken it gradually till it breaks, if you prefer this. It will only become strong if you employ it in the love of God, and seek that love; it will be weakened when you direct your thoughts to other things. You must know that even if you were the wisest man with respect to the true knowledge of God, you break the bond between you and God whenever you turn entirely your thoughts to the necessary food or any necessary business; you are then not with God, and He is not with you, for that relation between you and Him is actually interrupted in those moments. The pious were therefore particular to restrict the time on which they could not meditate upon the name of God, and cautioned others about it, saying, "Let not your minds be vacant from reflection upon God." In the same sense did David say, "I have set the Lord always before me; because He is at my right hand I shall not be moved" (Ps. 16:8); i.e., I do not turn my thoughts away from God. . . .

We must bear in mind that all such religious acts as reading the Law, praying and the performance of other precepts, serve exclusively as the means of causing us to occupy and fill our mind with the precepts of God, and free it from worldly business; for we are thus, as it were, in communion with God, and undisturbed by any other thing. If we, however, pray with the motion of our lips, and our face toward the wall, but, at the same time think of our business; if we read the Law with our tongue whilst our heart is occupied with the building of our house, and we do not think of what we are reading; if we perform the commandments only with our limbs, we are like those who are engaged in digging in the ground, or hewing wood in the forest, without reflecting on the nature of those acts, or by whom they are commanded, or what is their object. . . .

The first thing you must do is this: Turn your thoughts away from everything while you read *Shema* or during the *Tefillah*. . . . When you have successfully practised this for many years, try, in reading the Law or listening to it, to have all your heart and all your thought occupied with understanding what you read or hear. After some time when you have mastered this, accustom yourself to have your mind free from all other thoughts when you read any portion of the other books of the Prophets, or when you say any blessing; and to have your attention directed exclusively to the perception and the understanding of what you utter. When you have succeeded in properly performing these acts of divine service, and you have your thought, during their performance, entirely abstracted from worldly affairs, take care then that your thought be not disturbed by cares for your wants or for superfluous food. In short, think of worldly matters when you eat, drink, bathe, talk with your wife and little children, or when you converse with other people. These times, which are frequent and long, I think, must suffice to you for reflecting on everything that is necessary as regards business, household, and health. But when you are engaged in the performance of religious duties, have your mind exclusively directed to what you are doing.

When you are alone by yourself, when you are awake on your couch, be careful to meditate in such precious moments on nothing but the intellectual worship of God, *viz.*, to approach Him and to minister before Him in the true manner which I have described to you—not in hollow emotion. This I consider as the highest perfection wise men can attain by the above training.

When we have acquired a true knowledge of God, and rejoice in that knowledge in such a manner that while speaking with others, or attending to our bodily wants, our mind is all that time with God; when we are with our heart constantly near God, even whilst our body is in the society of men; when we are in that state which the Song on the relation between God and man poetically describes in the following words: "I sleep but my heart waketh; it is the voice of my beloved that knocketh" (Song 5:2):—then we have attained not only the height of ordinary prophets but of Moses our Teacher of whom Scripture relates: "And Moses alone shall come near before the Lord" (*ibid.*, 34:28). . . . The Patriarchs likewise attained this degree of perfection; they approached God in such a manner that with them the name of God became known in the world. Thus we read in Scripture: "The God of Abraham, the God of Isaac, and the God of Jacob. . . . This is my name forever" (Ex. 3:15). Their mind was so identified with the knowledge of God that He made a lasting covenant with each of them: "Then will I remember my covenant with Jacob," etc. (Lev. 26:42). . . . It was the chief aim of their whole life to create a people that should know and worship God. . . . The object of all their labors was to publish the Unity of God in the world, and to induce people to love Him; and it was on this account that they succeeded in reaching that high degree; for even those [worldly] affairs were for them a perfect worship of God.

Ibid.

LOVE AND FEAR OF GOD

The love of God describes a feeling of constant joyful longing for Him, a yearning for His nearness and craving for union with Him, and the fear

*of God indicates a desire to express our love and gratitude to Him in speech
and action. Both are the result of our irresistible impulse to make known
to Him our reverence, faith, and obedience to His will.*

This God, honored and revered, it is our duty to love and fear;
as it is said "Thou shalt love the Lord, thy God" (Deut. 6:5), and it
is further said "Thou shalt fear the Lord, thy God" (Deut. 6:13).

And what is the way that will lead to the love of Him and the
fear of Him? When a person contemplates His great wondrous works
and creatures and from them obtains a glimpse of His wisdom which
is incomparable and infinite, he will straightway love Him, praise
Him, glorify Him, and long with an exceeding longing to know His
great Name; even as David said "My soul thirsteth for God, for the
living God" (Ps. 42:3). And when he ponders these matters, he will
recoil affrighted, and realize that he is a small creature, lowly and
obscure, endowed with slight and slender intelligence, standing in the
presence of Him who is perfect in knowledge. And so David said
"When I consider Thy heavens, the work of Thy fingers—what
is man that Thou art mindful of Him?" (Ps. 8:4-5). In harmony
with these sentiments, I shall explain some large, general aspects of
the Works of the Sovereign of the Universe, that they may serve
the intelligent individual as a door to the love of God, even as our
sages have remarked in connection with the theme of the love of
God, "Observe the Universe and hence, you will realize Him who
spake and the world was."

Fundamental Principles of the Torah, 2

How We Are to Love God

We are to dwell upon and contemplate His commandments, His
words and His (wondrous) deeds, so that we may obtain [in a measure a true] conception of Him, and in conceiving Him attain absolute joy, this procedure constituting the love of Him. . . . In the
words of the Siphre: "Since it is said, 'And thou shalt love the Lord
thy God' (Deut. 6:5), the question arises, how is one to manifest
his love for the Lord? Scripture therefore states, 'And these words
which I command thee this day, shall be upon thy heart (*ibid.* 6),'
for through this [i.e., the contemplation of His words] you will learn
to discern Him who has called the Universe into existence."

. . . this commandment also embodies (the obligation) that we should call upon all mankind to serve Him, praised be He, and to have faith in Him. Just as in the case of someone you love you recount his praises, enlarging upon them, and calling upon other people to love him, even so it is on attaining true love of Him, blessed be He, and on gaining in a measure a conception of His true essence, you will undoubtedly call upon the foolish and ignorant to [seek] a knowledge of the truth which you have already acquired.

Sefer ha-Mitzvot, Com. 3

Whoever serves God out of love, occupies himself with the study of the Law and the fulfillment of commandments and walks in the paths of wisdom, impelled by no external motive whatsoever, moved neither by fear of calamity nor by the desire to obtain material benefits; such a man does what is truly right because it is truly right, and ultimately, happiness comes to him as a result of his conduct. This standard is indeed a very high one; not every sage attained to it. It was the standard of the patriarch Abraham whom God called His lover, because he served only out of love. It is the standard which God, through Moses, bids us achieve, as it is said, "And thou shalt love the Lord, thy God" (Deut. 6:5). When one loves God with the right love, he will straightway observe all the commandments out of love.

What is the love of God that is befitting? It is to love the Eternal with a great and exceeding love, so strong that one's soul shall be knit up with the love of God, and one should be continually enraptured by it, like a love-sick individual, whose mind is at no time free from his passion for a particular woman, the thought of her filling his heart at all times, when sitting down or rising up, when he is eating or drinking. Even intenser should be the love of God in the hearts of those who love him. And this love should continually possess them, even as He commanded us in the phrase, "with all thy heart, and with all thy soul" (Deut. 6:5). This Solomon expressed allegorically in the sentence, "for I am sick with love" (Song of Songs 2:5). The entire Song of Songs is indeed an allegory descriptive of this Love.

Fundamental Principles of the Torah, Repentance, 10

10. THIS CREATED WORLD

Although hidush ha-olam, *the belief in God as the author and Creator of the Universe had been proclaimed as a fundamental principle of the Jewish faith, the doctrine has not been universally accepted without considerable discussion and controversy. There were philosophers who maintained that the first chapter of Genesis was incompatible with the dictates of reason, and held with Aristotle and his followers that corporeal objects cannot be produced without corporeal substance. Rabbi Judah Halevi and Saadia Gaon had grappled with the problem and decided in favor of the Bible, and Abraham Ibn Ezra inferred from the Scripture account of Creation the existence of primeval chaotic matter. Although Maimonides in the first of his Thirteen Articles of Faith states that God "is the Author and Guide of everything that had been created, and that He alone has made, does make and will make all things," there is a conspicuous absence of the belief in* creatio ex nihilo. *He is equally timid in expressing himself on the subject in* Sefer ha-Madda, *the "Book of Knowledge" of his great Code.*

In The Guide for the Perplexed, *however, he subjects the Creation and Eternity of the World to a profound and careful investigation, and comes to the conclusion that* creatio ex nihilo *"is undoubtedly a fundamental principle of the Law of our teacher Moses; it is next in importance to the principle of God's unity. . . . Abraham, our father, was the first who taught it, after he had established it by philosophical research"* (Guide, II, 13). *He came to this conclusion after he became convinced that the question of the Eternity or the Creation of the world cannot be mathematically demonstrated, and that there was nothing in the biblical statement that is not admissible to reason. "Everything produced comes into existence from non-existence," says Maimonides, "even when the substance of a thing has been in existence, and has only changed form, the thing itself, which has gone*

189

*through the process of genesis and development, has arrived at its final
state, has now different properties from those which it possessed at the commencement of the transition from potentiality to reality."*

LIMITATION OF HUMAN REASON

*Maimonides admits the difficulty of dealing with the problem of Creation,
a difficulty, among other things, arising from the limitation of human reason:*

A boundary is undoubtedly set to the human mind which it cannot pass. There are things beyond that boundary which are acknowledged to be inaccessible to human understanding, and man does not
show any desire to comprehend them, being aware that such knowledge is impossible, and that there are no means of overcoming the
difficulty. . . . Do not imagine that what we have said of the insufficiency of our understanding and of its limited extent is an assertion
founded only on the Bible; for philosophers likewise assert the same
and perfectly understand it, without having regard to any religion or
opinion. It is a fact which is only doubted by those who ignore things
fully proved.

Guide, I, 31

. . . Aristotle was well aware that he had not proved the Eternity
of the Universe. He was not mistaken in this respect. He knew that
he could not prove his theory, and that his arguments and proofs
were only apparent and plausible. . . . Later philosophers, disciples of
Aristotle, assume that he has proved the Eternity of the Universe,
and most of those who believe that they are philosophers blindly follow him in this point, and accept all his arguments as conclusive
and absolute proofs. They consider it wrong to differ from Aristotle,
or to think that he was ignorant or mistaken in anything. . . . Is
Aristotle ignorant of the difference between argument and proof?
between opinion which may be received more or less favorably, and
truths capable of demonstration? . . . Certainly not. . . . My conviction is, that what Aristotle says on the Eternity of the Universe, the
cause of the variety in the motion of the spheres and the order of
the Intelligences, cannot be proved, and that Aristotle never intended to prove these things. I agree with him that the ways of proving this have their gates closed before us, there being no foundation
on which to build up the proof. His words on this subject are well
known. He says, "There are things concerning which we are unable

to reason, or which we find too high for us; to say why these things have a certain property is as difficult as to decide whether the Universe is eternal or not." . . . We have mentioned these things only because we know that the majority of those who consider themselves wise, although they know nothing of science, accept the theory of the Eternity of the Universe on the authority of famous scholars. They reject the words of the Prophets because the latter do not employ any scientific method by which only a few persons would be instructed who are intellectually well prepared, but simply communicate the truth as received by Divine inspiration.

Guide, II, 15

ETERNITY IS NOT PROVEN

Maimonides declares that he would have accepted the Eternity theory if it were proved and would have interpreted the Bible accordingly, since many passages in Scripture lend themselves to such interpretation.

We do not reject the Eternity of the Universe because certain passages in Scripture confirm the creation; for such passages are not more numerous than those in which God is represented as a corporeal being; nor is it impossible or difficult to find for them a suitable interpretation. We might have explained them in the same manner as we did in respect to the Incorporeality of God. We should perhaps have had an easier task in showing that the Scriptural passages referred to are in harmony with the theory of the Eternity of the Universe, if we accepted the latter, than we had in explaining the anthropomorphism in the Bible when we rejected the idea that God is corporeal. For two reasons, however, we have not done so, and have not accepted the Eternity of the Universe. First the Incorporeality of God has been demonstrated by proof; those passages in the Bible which, in their literal sense contain statements which can be refuted by proof, must and can be interpreted otherwise. But the Eternity of the Universe has not been proved; a mere argument of a certain theory is not sufficient reason for rejecting the literal meaning of a biblical text, and explaining it figuratively when the opposite theory can be supported by an equally good argument.

Ibid., 25

Secondly . . . , if we were to accept the Eternity of the Universe as taught by Aristotle, that everything in the Universe is the result of fixed laws, that nature does not change, and that there is nothing supernatural, we should necessarily be in opposition to the foundation of our religion, we should disbelieve all miracles and signs, and certainly reject all hopes and fears derived from Scripture, unless the miracles are also explained figuratively. The Allegorists amongst the Mohammedans have done this, and have thereby arrived at absurd conclusions. . . . Accepting the Creation, we find that miracles are possible, that Revelation is possible, and that every difficulty in this question is removed. . . . Owing to the absence of all proof, we reject the theory of the Eternity of the Universe.

Ibid.

Although in one place Maimonides regards the principle of Creation as a "high rampart erected round the Law able to resist all the missiles directed against it," (Guide, II, 17), he declares in another place:

The account given in Scripture of the Creation is not, as is generally believed, intended to be in all its parts literal. For if this were the case wise men would not have kept its explanation secret, and our Sages would not have employed figurative speech [in treating of Creation] in order to hide its true meaning nor would they have objected to discuss it in the presence of the common people. The literal meaning of the words might lead us to conceive corrupt ideas and to form false opinions about God, or even entirely abandon and reject the principles of our faith. It is therefore right to abstain and refrain from examining this subject superficially and unscientifically. We must blame the practice of some ignorant preachers and expounders of the Bible, who think that wisdom consists in knowing the explanation of words, and that greater perfection is attained by employing more words and longer speech. It is, however, right that we should examine the Scriptural texts by the intellect, after having acquired knowledge of demonstrative science, and of the true hidden meaning of the prophecies. But if one has obtained knowledge of this matter he must not preach on it, as I stated in my Commentary on the Mishnah (Hagigah II, 7), and our Sages said distinctly: From the beginning of the book to this place—after the account of the sixth day of the Creation—it is "the glory of God to conceal a thing" (Prov. 25:2).

Ibid., 11

CREATION IS NOT A MYTH

Maimonides walked on slippery ground and was not little criticized for his more or less wabbly stand on the question of Creation. "In truth, however," says M. Friedlander (The Jewish Religion, London, 1922), "the method of Maimonides is neither strange nor arbitrary. There is no doubt that figurative language is extensively used in the Scriptures, especially in the poetical and prophetical books. . . . Maimonides is therefore justified in saying that so long as reason does decide against the teaching of the Bible in its literal sense he would adhere to the latter, and only if reason were to decide against the creatio ex nihilo, he would follow reason and interpret Scripture accordingly." The impression however gained is that Maimonides was less interested in establishing the truth of the biblical doctrine of Creation as the consequences that would follow its rejection. He, therefore, in a decisive statement on the subject, comes out vigorously in favor of the traditional doctrine of Creation:

Those who follow the Law of Moses, our Teacher, hold that the whole Universe, i.e., everything except God, has been brought by Him into existence out of non-existence. In the beginning God alone existed, and nothing else; neither angels, nor spheres, nor the things that are contained within the spheres existed. He then produced from nothing all existing things, such as they are by His will and desire. Even time itself is among the things created; for time depends on motion, i.e., on an accident in things which move, and the things upon whose motion time depends are themselves created beings which have passed from non-existence into existence. . . . We consider time a thing created; it comes into existence in the same manner as other accidents. . . . If you admit the existence of time before Creation, you will be compelled to accept the theory of the Eternity of the Universe. . . . You will have to assume that something [beside God] existed before the Universe was created, an assumption which it is our duty to oppose.

Ibid., 13

THE MECHANICS OF CREATION

An inquiry into the mechanics of Creation will reveal that the four bodies "fire, air, earth and water" are the basic elements of all created things that are beneath the firmament. All things—man and beast, birds, reptile, fish, plant, minerals, precious stones and pearls, stones for building, mountains and clods of earth are, as far as their matter is concerned, composed of these four elements. And accordingly, apart from the four elements, all bodies beneath the firmament are composed of substance and form—this substance consisting of a combination of the four elements. Each of these four elements, however, consist of form and matter only.

These four bodies are without souls. They have neither knowledge nor perception, and are thus like dead bodies. Each of them has a governing principle of which it has no knowledge nor apprehension, and which it cannot alter. . . . Everything made up of these four elements ultimately disintegrates. This process takes place in the case of some things after a few days; in the case of others, after several years. But everything compounded of them must ultimately revert to them. Even gold and the carnelian cannot but disintegrate and return to their original elements; part becoming fire, part water, part air, and part earth.

Fundamental Principles of the Torah, 3

These four bodies, namely: fire, air, earth and water, are the basic elements of all created things that are beneath the firmament. All things—man and beast, bird, reptile, fish, plant, minerals, precious stones and pearls, stones for building, mountains and clods of earth are, as far as their matter is concerned, composed of these four elements. And accordingly, apart from the four elements, all bodies beneath the firmament are composed of a substance and form—this substance consisting of a combination of the four elements. Each of these four elements, however, consists of form and matter only.

Ibid., 4

These four elements are ceaselessly, daily and hourly, changing into each other. How so? That part of earth which is nearest in its nature to water, alters, crumbles and becomes water; that part of water which is nearest in its nature to air, becomes attenuated and turns into air; that portion of air most akin to fire is transformed into fire. And so a reverse process takes place slowly, gradually, and in the course of a long period. Nor does the whole of the element change to the extent that all the water in a body turns into air; or all of the air into fire; for it is impossible that an element should altogether disappear, but part only turns from fire into air or vice versa, and such mutual change takes place in all the four elements in a perpetual cycle.

The changes arise from the movement of the Sphere. This causes the four elements to combine and produce other substances—those of human beings and other animals, vegetables, stones and minerals. To each of these substances God gives its suitable form through the angels of the tenth degree, called *ishim*, "individuals."

Ibid.

MATTER AND FORM

You can never see matter without form, or form without matter. But the human mind divides in thought an existing body into its constituents and recognizes that it is made up of matter and form. It also knows that in some objects, the matter is composed of the four elements; while in others, it is simple, consisting of one substance. The forms that are devoid of matter cannot be perceived with the physical eye but only with the mind's eye; in the same way as we are conscious of the Lord of the Universe, without physical vision.

The vital principle of all flesh is the form which God has given it. The superior intelligence in the human soul is the specific form of the mentally normal human being. To this form, the Torah refers in the text "Let us make man in our image, after our likeness" (Gen. 1:26). This means that man should have a form that knows and apprehends idealistic beings that are devoid of matter, such as the angels which are forms without substance, so that [intellectually] man is like the angels. The text, above quoted, does not refer to the visible features—the mouth, nose, cheeks, and other distinguishing bodily marks. These are comprehended in the nomenclature "features." Nor does it refer to the vital principle in every animal by which it eats, drinks, reproduces, feels, and broods. It is the intellect which is the human soul's specific form. And to this specific form of the soul, the Scriptural phrase "in our image, after our likeness" alludes. This form is frequently called *nephesh, rauch* (soul, spirit). One must therefore, in order to avoid mistakes, pay special attention to the meaning of these terms which, in each case, has to be ascertained from the context.

This form of the Soul is not compounded of elements into which it would again dissolve. Nor does it exist by the energy of the vital principle [common to all animals] so that the latter would be necessary to its existence in the way that the vital principle requires a physical body for its existence. But it comes directly from God in Heaven. Hence when the material portion of our being dissolves its component elements and physical life perishes—since that only exists in association with the body and the needs of the body for its functions, this form of the Soul is not destroyed, as it does not require physical life for its activities. It knows and apprehends the Intelligences that exist without material substance; it knows the Creator of all things, and it endures forever. Solomon in his wisdom said, "And the dust returneth to the earth as it was, and the spirit returneth to God who gave it" (Ecc. 12:7).

Ibid.

DESIGN IN CREATION

Maimonides repudiates Aristotle's theory of natural necessity, and shows by proof and illustration that the whole scheme of Creation from the spheres down to the least considered creature demonstrate the existence of a voluntary determination which designed them all.

It has been shown that, according to Aristotle and according to all that defend his theory, the Universe is inseparable from God. He is the cause; and the Universe the effect; and this effect is a necessary one; and as it cannot be explained why or how God exists in this particular manner, namely, being One and incorporeal, so it cannot be asked concerning the whole Universe why or how it exists in this particular way. For it is necessary that the whole, the cause as well as the effect, exist in this particular manner, it is impossible for them not to exist or to be different from what they actually are. This leads to the conclusion that the nature of everything remains constant, that nothing changes its nature in any way, and that such a change is impossible in any existing thing. It would also follow that the Universe is not the result of design, choice, and desire; for if this were the case, they would have been non-existing before the design had been conceived.

We, however, hold that all things in the Universe are the result of design, and not merely of necessity; He who designed them may change them when He changes His design. But not every design is subject to change; for there are things which are impossible and their nature cannot be altered. . . .

Everything according to him [Aristotle] is the result of a law of Nature and not the result of the design of a being that designs as it likes, or the termination of a being that determines as it pleases. He has not carried out the idea consistently, and it will never be done. He tries indeed to find the cause why the sphere moves from east and not from west; why some spheres move with greater velocity, others with less velocity, and he finds the cause of these differences in their different positions in reference to the uppermost sphere. He further attempts to show why there are several spheres for each of the seven planets, while there is only one sphere for the large number of the fixed stars. For all these he endeavors to state the reason, so that to show that the whole order is the necessary result of the laws of Nature. He has not attained his object. . . . There is no doubt that Aristotle knew the weakness of his argument in tracing and describing the cause of these things, and therefore he prefaces his researches on these things as follows:—"We will now thoroughly investigate two problems which it is our proper duty to investigate and to discuss according to our capacity, wisdom, and opinion. Thus our attempt must not be attributed to presumption and pride, but to our extraordinary zeal in the study of philosophy, when we attempt the highest and grandest problems, and endeavor to offer some proper solution, every one that hears it should rejoice and be pleased."

Guide, II, 19

EVIDENCE OF DESIGN

According to our theory of the Creation, all this can easily be explained; for we say that there is a being that determines the direction and the velocity of the motion of each sphere; but we do not know the reason why the wisdom of that being gave to each sphere its peculiar property. There is a phenomenon in the spheres which more clearly shows the existence of voluntary determination; it cannot be explained otherwise than by assuming that some being designed it: this phenomenon is the existence of the stars. . . .

It is well known that the veins and nerves of an individual dog or ass are not the result of chance; their magnitude is not determined by chance; nor is it by chance, but for a certain purpose, that one vein is thick, another thin; that one nerve has many branches, another has none; that one goes down straight, whilst another is bent; it is well known that all this must be just as it is. How, then, can any reasonable person imagine that the position, magnitude, and number of the stars, or the various courses of their spheres, are purposeless, or the result of chance. There is no doubt that every one of these things is necessary and in accordance with a certain design; and it is extremely improbable that these things should be the necessary result of natural laws, and not that of design.

Ibid.

THE PURPOSE OF CREATION

Intelligent persons are much perplexed when they inquire into the purpose of Creation. . . . The question "what is the purpose thereof?" cannot be asked about anything which is not the product of an agent; therefore we cannot ask what is the purpose of the existence of God. He has not been created. . . . It is a recognized fact in Natural Philosophy that everything in nature has its object, or its final cause. . . . Aristotle repeatedly says that Nature produces nothing in vain, for every natural action has a certain object. Thus, Aristotle says that plants exist for animals; and similarly he shows of other parts of the Universe for what purpose they exist. . . . The existence of a final cause in the various parts of Nature has compelled philosophers to assume a primal cause apart from Nature; it is called by Aristotle the intellectual or divine cause, and this cause creates one thing for the purpose of another. Those who acknowledge the truth will accept as the best proof for the Creation the fact that everything in Nature serves a certain purpose, so that one thing exists for the benefit of another . . . and shows that there is design in Nature. But the existence of design in nature cannot be imagined unless it be assumed that Nature has been produced.

Guide, III, 13

It seems clear that, according to Aristotle, who assumes the Eternity of the Universe, there is no occasion for the question what is the object of the existence of the Universe. But of those who accept our theory that the whole Universe has been created from nothing, some hold that the inquiry after the purpose of Creation is necessary, and assume that the Universe was only created for the sake of man's existence, that he might serve God. Everything that is done, they believe, is done for man's sake; even the spheres move only for his benefit, in order that his wants might be supplied. . . . If the sphere existed for the sake of man, how much more must this be the case with all other living beings and plants. On examining this opinion an intelligent person ought to examine all different opinions, he shall discover the errors it includes. Those who hold this view, namely, that the existence of man is the object of the whole Creation . . . and man existed for the purpose of serving God, as has been mentioned, the question remains, What is the end of serving God? He does not become more perfect if all His creatures serve Him and comprehend Him as far as possible; nor would He lose anything if nothing existed beside Him. It might perhaps be replied that the service of God is not intended for God's perfection; it is intended for our own perfection—it is good for us, it makes us perfect. But then the question might be repeated, What is the object of our being perfect? We must in continuing the inquiry as to the purpose of the Creation at last arrive at the answer, It was the will of God, or His Wisdom decreed it, and this is the correct answer. . . . I consider, therefore, the following opinion as most correct according to the teaching of the Bible, and best in accordance with the results of philosophy, namely, that the Universe does not exist for man's sake, but that each being exists for its own sake, and not because of some other thing.

Ibid.

The question of the purpose of the Universe has been the subject of discussion among philosophers down through the ages. While Maimonides accepts purpose in relation to God, he maintains Creation to have been the result of His Will and Wisdom.

[Man's] actions are divided as regard their object into four classes: they are either *purposeless, unimportant, in vain,* or *good.* An action is *in vain* if the object which is sought by it is not obtained on account of some obstacle. Thus people frequently use the phrase "thou hast worked in vain" in reference to a person who looks out for some one and cannot find him, or who undertakes the troubles of a journey for his business without profit. Our endeavors and exertions are *in vain* as regards a patient that is not cured. This applies to all actions which are intended for certain purposes that are not realized. *Purposeless* are such actions which serve no purpose at all. Some persons, e.g., do something with their hands while thinking of something else. The actions of the insane and confused are of this kind.

Unimportant are such actions by which a trivial object is sought, an object that is not necessary and is not of great use. This is the case when a person dances without seeking to benefit his digestion by that exercise, or performs certain actions for the purpose of causing laughter. Such actions are certainly mere pastimes. Whether an action belongs to this class or not depends on the intention of those who perform it, and on the degree of their perfection. For many things are necessary or very useful in the opinion of one person and superfluous in the opinion of another. E.g., bodily exercise, in its different kinds, is necessary for the proper preservation of health in the opinion of him who understands the science of medicine; writing is considered as very useful by scholars. When people take exercise by playing with the ball, wrestling, stretching out the hands or keeping back the breathing, or do certain things as preparation for writing, shape the pen and get the paper ready, such actions are mere pastime in the eyes of the ignorant, but the wise do not consider them as unimportant. *Useful* are such actions as serve a proper purpose; being either necessary or useful for the purpose which is to be attained. This division [of man's actions] is, as I believe, not open to any objection. For every action is either intended for a certain purpose or is not intended; and if intended for a certain purpose that purpose may be important or unimportant, is sometimes attained and sometimes missed.

Ibid., 25

God's Actions Are Not in Vain

After having explained this division, I contend that no intelligent person can assume that any of the actions of God can be vain, purposeless, or unimportant. According to our view and the view of all that follow the Law of Moses, all actions of God are "exceedingly good." Thus Scripture says, "And God saw everything that He had made, and behold, it was very good" (Gen. I:31). And that which God made for a certain thing is necessary for the existence of that thing or is [at least] very useful. Thus food is necessary for the existence of living beings; the possession of eyes helps to make life more agreeable, although food only serves to sustain living beings a certain time, and the senses are only intended to procure to animals the advantages of sensation.

Ibid.

The philosophers likewise assume that in Nature there is nothing in vain, so that everything that is not the product of human industry serves a certain purpose, which may be known or unknown to us. There are thinkers that assume that God does not create one thing for the sake of another, that existing things are not to each other in relation of cause and effect; that they are all the direct result of the Will of God, and do not serve any purpose. According to this opinion, we cannot ask why has He made this and not that; for He does what pleases Him, without following a fixed system. Those who defend this theory must consider the actions of God as purposeless, and even as inferior to purposeless actions; for when we perform purposeless actions, our attention is engaged by other things and we do not know what we are doing; but God, according to these theorists, knows what He is doing, and knowingly does it for no purpose or use whatever.

The absurdity of assuming that some of God's actions are trivial is apparent even at first sight, and no notice need be taken of the nonsensical idea that monkeys were created for our pastime. Such opinions originate only in man's ignorance of the nature of transient beings, and in his overlooking the principle that it was intended by the Creator to produce in its present form everything whose existence is possible; a different form was not decreed by the Divine Wisdom, and the existence [of objects of a different form] is therefore impossible, because the existence of all things depends on the decree of God's wisdom.

Ibid.

THE PURPOSE OF THE UNIVERSE

Those who hold that God's works serve no purpose whatever, believe that an examination of the totality of existing things compels them to adopt this theory. They ask what is the purpose of the whole Universe? they necessarily answer like all those who believe in the Creation, that it was created because God willed it so, and for no other purpose. The same answer they apply to all parts of the Universe, and do not admit that the hole in the uvea and the transparency of the cornea are intended for the purpose of allowing the *spiritus visus* to pass and to perceive certain objects; they do not assume that these circumstances are causes for the sight; the hole in the uvea and the transparent matter over it are not there because of the sight, but because of the Will of God, although the sense of sight could have been created in a different form. There are passages in the Bible which at first sight we might understand to imply this theory, e.g., "The Lord hath done whatever He pleased" (Ps. 135:6); "His soul desired it and He made it" (Job 23:13); Who will say unto Thee, what doest Thou? (Ecc. 8:4). The meaning of these and similar verses is this: whatever God desires to do is necessarily done; there is nothing that could prevent the realization of His will. The object of His will is only that which is possible, and of the things possible only such as His wisdom decrees upon.

When God desires to produce the best work, no obstacle or hindrance intervenes between Him and that work. This is the opinion held by all religious people, also by the philosophers; it is also our opinion. For although we believe that God created the Universe from nothing, most of our wise and learned men believe that the Creation was not the exclusive result of His will; but His wisdom, which we are unable to comprehend, made the actual existence of the Universe necessary. The same unchangeable wisdom found it as necessary that non-existence should precede the existence of the Universe. Our Sages frequently express this idea in the explanation of the words "He hath made everything beautiful in His time" (Eccl. 3:11), only in order to avoid that which is objectionable, viz., the opinion that God does things without any purpose whatever. This is the belief of most of our Theologians; and in a similar manner have the Prophets expressed the idea that all parts of natural products are well arranged in good order, connected with each other and stand to each other in the relation of cause and effect; nothing of them is purposeless, trivial, or vain; they are all the result of great wisdom. Comp. "O Lord, how manifold are Thy works! in wisdom hast Thou made them all; the earth is full of thy riches" (Ps. 104:24); "and all His works are done in truth" (Ibid., 33:4); "The Lord by wisdom hath founded the earth" (Prov. 3:19). . . .

Guide, III, 25

MAN IS NOT THE SOLE GOAL OF CREATION

Know that the difficulties which lead to confusion in the question what is the purpose of the Universe or of any of its parts, arise from two causes: first, man has an erroneous idea of himself, and believes that the whole world exists only for his sake; secondly, he is ignorant both about the nature of the sublunary world, and about the Creator's intention to give existence to all beings whose existence is possible, because existence is undoubtedly good. The consequences of that error and of the ignorance about the two things named, are doubts and confusion, which lead many to imagine that some of God's works are trivial, others purposeless, and others vain. . . . I have already told you the view, which is set forth in Scripture on this question, and which is proper to accept. It is this: it is not unreasonable to assume that the works of God, their existence and preceding non-existence, are the result of His wisdom, but we are unable to understand many of the ways of His wisdom in His works. On this principle the whole Law of Moses is based; it begins with this principle; (and) "And God saw all that He had made, and, behold, it was very good" (Gen. 1:31); and it ends with this principle: "The Rock, perfect in His work" (Deut. 32:4).

Ibid.

Things Exist for Themselves

The wise men in Israel have therefore introduced in our prayers the following passage:—"Thou hast distinguished man from the beginning and chose him to stand before Thee; who can say unto Thee, What dost Thou? And if he be righteous, what does he give Thee?" (Day of Atonement Neilah service. See Silverman, *High Holiday Prayer Book*) They have thus clearly stated that it was not a final cause that determined the existence of all things, but only His Will. This being the case, we who believe in the Creation must admit that God could have created the Universe in a different manner as regards the cause and effect contained in it, and this would lead to the absurd conclusion that everything except man existed without any purpose, as the principal object, man, could have been brought into existence without the rest of the creation. I consider therefore the following opinion to be the most correct according to the teaching of the Bible, and best in accordance with the results of philosophy; namely that the Universe does not exist for man's sake, but that each being exists for its own sake, and because of some other thing. Thus we believe in the Creation, and yet need not inquire what purpose is served by each species of the existing things, because we assume that God created all parts of the Universe by His will; some for their own sake, and some for the sake of other beings, that in-

203

clude their own purpose in themselves. In the same manner as it was the will of God that man should exist, so it was His will that the heavens with their stars should exist, that there should be angels, and each of these beings is itself the purpose of its own existence.

Ibid.

CREATION AND MIRACLES

The Bible abounds in "signs" and "wonders"; every extraordinary occurrence is regarded as a supernatural miraculous event. Talmudic Judaism has not only accepted the biblical miracles but has added greatly to them. The medieval Jewish philosopher endeavored as much as possible to limit the miracles by bringing them within the sphere of natural occurrences without, however, totally rejecting them. Maimonides was led to renounce the Eternity of the Universe because it would fetter God's ruling power over the world. But while he recognized the Bible miracles as "a fundamental principle of our religion" and would not allegorize them as he did so many Scriptural narratives, the miracles had for him quite another meaning than what they had for the naive, simple believers. He recognized that some miracles were miracles only in appearance due to the people's imperfect knowledge of nature, while others implied temporary and not permanent changes of properties.

For although the rod was changed into a serpent, the water into blood, the pure and noble hand into a leprous one, without the existence of any natural cause that could effect these or similar phenomena, these changes were *not permanent*, they have not become a physical property. On the contrary, the Universe since continues its regular course. This is my opinion; this should be our belief.

Our Sages, however, said very strange things as regards miracles; they are found in *Bereshit Rabba,* and in *Midrash Kohelet,* namely, that the miracles are to some extent also natural; for they say, when God created the Universe with its present physical properties, He made it part of these properties, that they should produce certain miracles at certain times, and the sign of a prophet consisted in the fact that God told him to declare when a certain thing will take place, but the thing itself was effected according to the fixed laws of Nature. If this is really the meaning of the passage referred to, it testifies to the greatness of the author, and shows that he held it to be impossible that there should be a change in the laws of Nature, or a change in the will of God [as regards the physical properties of things] after they have once been established. He therefore assumes, e.g., that God gave the waters the property of joining together, and of flowing in a downward direction, and of separating only at the time when the Egyptians were drowned, and only in a particular place. I have already pointed out the source of this passage, and it only tends to oppose the hypothesis of a new creation. It is said there: R. Jonathan said, God made an agreement with the sea that it should divide before the Israelites; thus it is said: "And the sea returned to its strength when the morning appeared" (Ex. 14:27). R. Jeremiah, son of Elazar, said: Not only with the sea but with all that has been created in the six days of the beginning [was the agreement made]; this is referred to in the words, "I, even my hands have stretched out the heavens and all their host have I commanded" (Is. 45:12); i.e., I have commanded the sea to divide, the fire not to hurt Hananiah, Mishael, and Azariah, the lions not to harm Daniel, and the fish to spit out Jonah. The same is the case with the rest of the miracles.

We have thus clearly stated and explained our opinion that we agree with Aristotle in one half of his theory. For we believe that this Universe remains perpetually with the same properties with which the Creator has endowed it, and that none of these will ever be changed except by way of miracle in some individual instances, although the Creator has the power to change the whole Universe, to annihilate it, or to remove any of its properties.

Guide, II, 29

THE WORLD IS INDESTRUCTIBLE

While Maimonides parts company with Aristotle on the problem of Creation, he holds with him that the world is not subject to destruction and cites proof from Holy Writ to substantiate his contention.

We have stated already that the belief in the Creation is a fundamental principle of our religion; but we do not consider it a principle of our faith that the Universe will again be reduced to nothing. It is not contrary to the tenets of our religion to assume that the Universe will continue to exist forever. It might be objected that everything produced is subject to destruction; consequently the Universe, having had a beginning, must come to an end. The axiom cannot be applied according to our views. We do not hold that the Universe came into existence like all things in Nature as a result of the laws of Nature. For whatever owes its existence to the action of physical laws is, according to the same laws, subject to destruction: the same law which caused the existence of a thing after a period of non-existence, is also the cause that the thing is not permanent since the previous non-existence proves that the nature of that thing does not necessitate its permanent existence.

Guide, II, 27

According to our theory, taught in Scripture, the existence and non-existence of things depends solely on the will of God and not on fixed laws, and, therefore, it does not follow that God must destroy the Universe after having created it from nothing. It depends on His will. He may, according to His desire, or according to the decree of His wisdom either destroy it, or allow it to exist, and it is therefore possible that He will preserve the Universe forever, and let it exist permanently as He Himself exists. It is well known that our Sages never said that the throne of glory will perish, although they assumed that it has been created. No prophet or Sage ever maintained that the throne of glory will be destroyed or annihilated; but, on the contrary, the Scriptural passages speak of its permanent existence. We are of the opinion that the souls of the pious have been created, and at the same time we believe that they are immortal. . . . In short, reasoning leads to the conclusion that the destruction of the Universe is not a certain fact. There remains only the question as to what the prophets and our Sages say on this point; whether they affirm that the world will certainly come to an end, or not. Most people amongst us believe that such statements have been made, and that the world will at one time be destroyed. I will show you that this is not the case; and that, on the contrary, many passages in the Bible speak of the permanent existence of the Universe. Those passages which, in the literal sense, would indicate the destruction of the Universe, are undoubtedly to be understood in a figurative sense.

Ibid.

KING SOLOMON AND THE WORLD

Many of our co-religionists thought that King Solomon believed in the Eternity of the Universe. This is very strange. How can we suppose that any one that adheres to the Law of Moses, our Teacher, should accept that theory? If we were to assume that Solomon has on this point, God forbid, deviated from the Law of Moses, the question would be asked, Why did most of the Prophets and of the Sages accept it of Him? Why have they not opposed him, or blamed him for holding that opinion, as he has been blamed for having married strange women, and for other things? The reason why this has been imputed to him is to be found in the following passage: "They desired to suppress the book Kohelet, because its words inclined toward scepticism." It is undoubtedly true that certain passages in this book include, when taken literally, opinions different from those taught in the Law, and they must therefore be explained figuratively. But the theory of the Eternity of the Universe is not among those opinions, the book does not even contain any passage that implies this theory; much less a passage in which it is clearly set forth.

There are, however, in the book, some passages which imply the indestructibility of the Universe, a doctrine that is true; and from the fact that the indestructibility of the Universe is taught in this book, some persons wrongly inferred that the author believed in the Eternity of the Universe. The following are the words that refer to the indestructibility of the Universe: "And the earth remaineth forever." . . . David has also in other passages clearly spoken of the incorruptibility of the heavens, the perpetuity and immutability of their laws, and of all the heavenly beings. He says, "Praise ye the Lord from the heavens, etc. For He commanded, and they were created. He hath also established them forever and ever; He hath made a decree which shall not pass" (Ps. 148:1-6); that is to say, there will never be a change in the decrees which God made, or in the sources of the properties of the heavens and the earth, which the Psalmist has mentioned before. But he distinctly states that they have been created. . . . The works of God being most perfect, admitting no addition or deduction, must remain the same forever. It is impossible that anything should exist that could cause a change in them.

Ibid., 28

THE UNIVERSE IS PERPETUAL

We believe this Universe remains perpetually with the same properties the Creator has endowed it, and that none of these will ever be changed except by way of miracle in some individual instances, although the Creator has the power to change the whole Universe, to annihilate it, or to remove any of its properties. The Universe had, however, a beginning and commencement, for when nothing was yet in existence except God, His wisdom declared that the Universe be brought into existence at a certain time, that it should not be annihilated or changed as regards any of its properties, except in some instances; some of these are known to us, whilst others belong to the future, and are therefore unknown to us. This is our opinion and the basis of our religion.

Ibid., 29

THE SPHERES AND THE ANGELS

Maimonides believed with Aristotle that the spheres are animated intellectual beings, capable of fully comprehending the principia of their existence, were created by God to serve as the intermediate element between Him and the material world.

Scripture supports the theory that the spheres are animate and intellectual, i.e., capable of comprehending things; that they are not, as ignorant persons believe, inanimate masses like fire and earth, but are, as the philosophers assert, endowed with life, and serve their Lord, whom they mightily praise and glorify; comp. "The heavens declare the glory of God," etc. (Ps. 19, 2). It is a great error to think that this is a mere figure of speech; for the verbs "to declare" and "to relate," when joined together, are, in Hebrew, only used of intellectual being. . . .

As to the opinion of our Sages, I do not see any necessity for expounding or demonstrating it. Consider only the form they gave to the blessing recited in seeing the new moon, the ideas repeatedly occurring in the prayers and the remarks in the Midrash on the following and similar passages:—"And the host of heaven worshippeth thee" (Neh. 9:6): "When the morning stars sang together, and all the sons of God shouteth for joy" (Job 38:7). In *Bereshit Rabba*, on the passage—"And the earth was empty and formless" (Gen. 1, 2), our Sages remark as follows: "The words *tohu* and *bohu* mean mourning and crying; the earth mourned and cried on account of her evil lot, saying, 'I and the heavens were created together, and yet the beings above live forever, and we are mortal.'" Our Sages, by this remark, indicate their belief that the spheres are animated beings, and not inanimate matter like the elements.

Guide, II, 5

There are angels in the Bible and in rabbinic literature and none of the medieval Jewish philosophers doubted their existence. They figure as the celestial host surrounding God's throne to execute His will, announce events, and serve as intermediaries between God and the world. Maimonides not only believed in the reality of angels but connected the belief in them with the belief in God.

As for the existence of angels, there is no necessity to cite any proof from Scripture where the fact is frequently mentioned. The term *elohim* signifies "judges"; comp. "The cause of both parties shall come before the 'judges'" (*ha-elohim*, Ex. 22:8). It has been figuratively applied to angels, and to the Creator as being Judge over the angels. When God says, "I am the Lord your God," the pronoun "your" refers to all mankind; but in the phrase *elohe ha-elohim*, He is described as the God of the angels, and *adone ha-adonim*, as the Lord of the spheres and the stars, which are the masters of the rest of the corporeal creation. . . . The phrases there admit of no other meaning than this: God is the Judge over the judges; i.e., over the angels and the Lord over the spheres.

Ibid., 6

We have already stated above (I, 49) that the angels are incorporeal. This agrees with the opinion of Aristotle: there is only this difference in the names employed—he uses the term "Intelligences," and we say instead "angels." His theory is that the Intelligences are intermediate beings between the Prime Cause and existing things, and that they effect the motion of the spheres, on which motion the existence of all things depends. This is also the view we meet with in all parts of Scripture; every act of God is described as being performed by angels. But "angel" means "messenger"; hence everyone that is entrusted with a certain mission is an angel. . . . The elements are also called angels. Comp. "Who maketh winds His angels, flaming fire His minister" (Ps. 104:4). There is no doubt that the word "angels" is used of a messenger sent by man; e.g., "And Jacob sent angels (Gen. 32:4). . . . It is also used of ideals, perceived by prophets in prophetic vision, and of man's animal powers. . . .

When we assert that Scripture teaches that God rules this world through angels, we mean such angels as are identical with the Intelligences. In some passages the plural is used of God, e.g., "Let us make

209

man in our image" (Gen. 1:26); "Go to, let us go down, and there confound their language (*ibid.*, 11:7). Our Sages explain this in the following manner: God, as it were, does nothing without contemplating the host above. I wonder at the expression "contemplating," which is the very expression used by Plato: God, as it were "contemplates the world of ideals, and thus produces the existing beings." In other passages our Sages expressed it more decidedly; "God does nothing without consulting the host above" [the word *familia,* used in the original, is a Greek noun, and signifies "host"].

Ibid.

Angels Are Intelligences Without Matter

The angels are incorporeal; they are Intelligences without matter, but they are nevertheless created beings, and God created them. In Bereshit Rabba (Gen. 3:24) we read the following remark of our Sages: "The angel is called 'the flame of the sword which turned every way' (Gen. 3:24), in accordance with the words 'His ministers a flaming fire' (Ps. 104:4); the attribute, 'which turned every way' is added, because angels are changeable in form; they appear at one time as males, and another as females; now as spirits; now as angels." By this remark they clearly stated that angels are incorporeal, and have no permanent bodily form independent of the mind (of him who perceives them), they exist entirely in prophetic vision, and depend on the action of the imaginative power. As to the words "At another time as females," which imply that the Prophets in prophetical vision perceived angels also in the form of women, they refer to the vision of Zechariah (5:9), "And behold, there came out two women, and the wind was in their wings."

Guide, I, 49

You know very well how difficult it is for men to form a notion of anything immaterial and entirely devoid of corporeality, except after considerable training; it is especially difficult for those who do not distinguish between objects of the intellect and objects of the imagination, and depend mostly on the mere imaginative power. They believe that imagined things exist or at least have the possibility of existing; but that which cannot be imagined does not exist, and cannot exist. For persons of this class—and the majority of thinkers belong to it—cannot arrive at the true solution of any question, or at the explanation of anything doubtful. On account of this difficulty the prophetic books contain expressions which, taken literally, imply that angels are corporeal, moving about, endowed with human form, receiving commands of God, obeying His word and performing whatever He wishes, according to His command. All this only serves to lead to the belief that angels exist and are alive and perfect, in the same way as we have explained in reference to God.

If the figurative representation of angels were limited to this, their true essence would be believed to be the same as the essence of God, since, in reference to the Creator expressions are likewise employed, which literally imply that He is corporeal, living, moving and endowed with human form. In order, therefore, to give to the mind of man the idea that the existence of angels is lower than the existence of God, certain forms of lower animals were introduced in the description of angels. It is thereby shown, that the existence of God is more perfect than that of angels, as much as man is more perfect than the lower animals. Nevertheless no organ of the brute creation was attributed to the angels, except wings. Without wings the act of flying appears as impossible as that of walking without legs; for these two modes of motion can only be imagined in connection with these organs. The motion of flying has been chosen as a symbol to represent that angels possess life, because it is the most perfect and most sublime movement of the brute creation. Men consider this motion a perfection to such an extent that they themselves wish to be able to fly, in order to escape easily what is injurious, and to obtain quickly what is useful, though it be at a distance. For this reason this motion has been attributed to the angels.

There is besides another reason. The bird in its flight is sometimes visible, sometimes withdrawn from our sight; one moment near to us, and in the next far off; and these are exactly the circumstances which we must associate with the idea of angels. This imaginary perfection, the motion of flight, being the exclusive property of the brute creation, has never been attributed to God. You must not be misled by the passage, "And he rode upon a cherub, and he did fly" (Ps. 18:11), for it is the cherub that did fly, and the simile only serves to denote the rapid arrival of that which is referred to in that passage. Comp.: "Behold the Lord rideth upon a swift cloud, and shall come into Egypt" (Is. 19:1); that is, the punishment alluded to will come down quickly upon Egypt. Nor should expressions like "the face of an ox," "the face of a lion" "the face of an eagle" "the sole of the foot of a calf," found in the prophecies of Ezekiel (1, 10 and 7) mislead you. . . . The prophet only describes the animals [*hayot*].

Ibid.

THE NAMES AND STATIONS OF THE ANGELS

The variety of names that the angels bear has reference to the difference in their rank. They are called *Hayoth Hakodesh*—these are the highest; *Ophanim, Erelim, Hashmalim, Seraphim, Malachim, Elohim, Bene Elohim, Cherubim* and *Ishim*. These ten names, by which the angels are called, correspond to their ten degrees. The highest rank, above which there is no degree higher but that of God, blessed be He, is that of the form called *Hayoth*. In the prophetic literature it is therefore said that the *Hayoth* are beneath the Throne of Glory. To the tenth degree, belongs the form of those termed *Ishim*. They are the angels that commune with the prophets and appear to them in the prophetic vision. They are called *Ishim* [individuals, men], because their rank approximates to that of the intelligence of human beings.

Fundamental Principles of the Torah, 2

When we say that one angel is below another, this does not refer to position in space as when we think of an individual who occupies a higher seat than another, but to superiority in rank, as when one says in reference to two scholars, one of whom has more wisdom than the other, that he is the higher in degree, or when one says of the cause that it is higher than the effect.

Ibid.

What then is meant when the Prophets say that they saw an angel of fire, possessing wings? Such descriptions are to be understood as prophetic visions and are to be taken in an allegorical sense. They are meant to indicate that the angel is not corporeal and has no gravity like bodies which have weight. Thus too, it is said "For the Lord, thy God, is a devouring fire" (Deut. 4:24). Yet God is not fire. The expression is a metaphor. Similarly it is said "He makes his angels winds" (Ps. 104:4).

Ibid.

THE PITFALLS OF METAPHYSICS

Of the opinion that metaphysics was not a popular subject which could be taught safely to the uninitiated, Maimonides devotes a whole chapter enumerating five reasons why instruction in it should be withheld from the masses. When Maimonides sent the Guide *to Joseph Ibn Aknin, for whom, indeed, the book was written, he instructed him not to teach or expound the work publicly, holding that the metaphysical problems with which it deals cannot be made a subject of popular treatment.*

You must know that it is very injurious to begin with this branch of philosophy, viz., Metaphysics; or to explain [at first] the sense of the similes occurring in prophecies, and interpret the metaphors which are employed in historical accounts and which abound in the writings of the Prophets. On the contrary, it is necessary to initiate the young and to instruct the less intelligent according to their comprehension; those who appear to be talented and to have capacity for the higher method of study, i.e., that based on proof and on true logical argument, should be gradually advanced towards perfection either by tuition or by self-instruction. He, however, who begins with Metaphysics will not only become confused in matters of religion but will fall into complete infidelity. I compare such a person to an infant fed with wheaten bread, meat and wine; it will undoubtedly die, not because such food is naturally unfit for the human body, but because of the weakness of the child who is unable to digest the food, and cannot derive benefit from it. The same is the case with the true principles of science. They were presented in enigmas, clad in riddles, and taught by all wise men in the most mysterious way that could be devised, not because they contain some secret evil, or are contrary to the fundamental principles of the Law [as fools think who are only philosophers in their own eyes], but because of the incapacity of man to comprehend them at the beginning of his studies: only slight allusions have been made to them to serve for the guidance of those who are capable of understanding them. These sciences were, therefore, called Mysteries [*sodoth*], and Secrets of the Law [*sitre torah*], as we shall explain.

There are five reasons why instruction should not begin with metaphysics but should at first be restricted to pointing out what is fitted for notice and what may be made manifest to the multitude.

First Reason. The subject itself is difficult, subtle and profound,

"Far off and exceeding deep, who can find it out?" (Ecc. 7:24). The following words of Job may be applied to it: "Whence, then, cometh wisdom? and where is the place of understanding?" (Job 28:20). Instruction should not begin with abstruse and difficult subjects. In one of the similies contained in the Bible wisdom is compared to water, and amongst other interpretations given by our Sages of this simile, occurs the following: He who can swim may bring up pearls from the depth of the sea, he who is unable to swim will be drowned, therefore only such persons as have had proper instruction should expose themselves to the risk.

Second Reason. The intelligence of man is at first insufficient; for he is not endowed with perfection at the beginning, but first possesses perfection only *in potentia*, not in fact. Thus it is said, "And man is born a wild ass" (Job 11:12). If a man possess a certain faculty *in potentia* it does not follow that it must become in him a reality. He may possibly remain deficient either on account of some obstacle, or from want of training in practices which would turn the possibility into a reality. Thus it is distinctly stated in the Bible, "Not many are wise" (*ibid.*, 32:9); also our Sages say, "I noticed how few were those who attained to a higher degree of perfection" (Suk. 45b). . . .

Third Reason. The preparatory studies are of long duration, and man, in his natural desire to reach the goal, finds them frequently too wearisome, and does not wish to be troubled by them. Be convinced that, if man were able to reach the end without preparatory studies, such studies would not be preparatory but tiresome and utterly superfluous. Suppose you awaken any person even the most simple, as if from sleep, and you say to him, Do you not desire to know what the heavens are, what is their number and their form; what beings are contained in them; what the angels are; how the creation of the whole world took place; what is its purpose, and what is the relation of its various parts to each other; what is the nature of the soul; how it enters the body; whether it has an independent existence, and if so, how it can exist independently of the body; by what means and to what purpose, and similar problems. He would undoubtedly say, "Yes," and show a natural desire for the true knowledge of these things; but he will wish to satisfy that desire and to attain to that knowledge by listening to a few words from you. Ask him to interrupt his usual pursuits for a week, till he learn all this, he would not do it, and would be satisfied and contented with imaginary and misleading notions; he would refuse to believe that there is anything which requires preparatory studies and persevering research. . . .

The fourth Reason is taken from the physical constitution of man. It has been proved that moral conduct is a preparation for intellectual progress, and that only a man whose character is pure, calm and steadfast can attain to intellectual perfection; that is, acquire correct conceptions. Many men are naturally so constituted that all perfection is impossible; e.g., he whose heart is very warm and is himself very powerful, is sure to be passionate, though he tries to counteract that disposition by training; . . . You also find persons of great levity and rashness, whose excited manners and wild gestures prove that their constitution is in disorder, and their temperament is so bad that it cannot be cured. Such persons can never attain to perfection; it is utterly useless to occupy oneself with them in such a subject [as Metaphysics]. For this science is, as you know, different from the science of Medicine and Geometry, and, from the reason already mentioned, it is not every person who is capable of approaching it. It is impossible for a man to study it successfully without moral preparation. . . . Therefore it was considered inadvisable to teach it to young men, nay, it is impossible for them to comprehend it on account of the heat of their blood and the flame of youth, which confuses their minds. That heat which causes all the disorder must first disappear; they must have become moderate and settled, humble in their hearts, and subdued in their temperament; only then will they be able to arrive at the highest degree of the perception of God, i.e., the study of Metaphysics, which is called Ma'aseh Mercaba.

Fifth Reason. Man is disturbed in his intellectual occupation by the necessity of looking after the material wants of the body, especially if the necessity of providing for wife and children is superadded; much more so if he seeks superfluities in addition to his ordinary wants, for by custom and bad habits these become a powerful motive. Even the perfect man to whom we have referred, is too busy with these necessary things, much more so if busy with unnecessary things, and filled with a great desire for them—must weaken or altogether lose his desire for study, to which he will apply himself with interruption, lassitude, and want of attention. He will not attain to that for which he is fitted by his abilities, or he will acquire imperfect knowledge, a confused mass of true and false ideas. For these reasons it was proper that the study of Metaphysics should have been exclusively cultivated by privileged persons, and not entrusted to the common people. It is not for the beginner, and he should abstain from it, as the little child has to abstain from taking solid food and from carrying heavy weights.

Guide, I, 34

11. GOD AND THE EXISTENCE OF EVIL

Philosophers have speculated on God's Omniscience. They generally agreed that God realizes His own true being. But does He know what exists beside Himself, and if so, by what manner of knowledge does He perceive things different from human knowledge? Does God know only what is constant and unchangeable or is the whole process of life and nature in all their variations and accidents unrolled before Him so that nothing escapes Him? Maimonides deals with this problem in great detail in both Mishneh Torah *and* The Guide for the Perplexed.

IT IS UNDOUBTEDLY an innate idea that God must be perfect in every respect and cannot be deficient in anything. It is almost an innate idea that ignorance of anything is a deficiency, and God can therefore not be ignorant in anything. But some thinkers assume . . . that God knows certain things and is ignorant of certain other things. They did so because they imagined that they discovered a certain absence of order in man's affairs, most of which are not only the result of physical properties but also of those faculties which he possesses as a being endowed with free will and reason. The Prophets have already stated the proof which the ignorant persons offer for their belief that God does not know our actions; viz., the fact that wicked people are seen in happiness, ease and peace. This fact leads the righteous and pious persons to think that it is of no use for them to aim at that which is good and to suffer for it through the opposition of other people. . . . David likewise shows how general this view was in his time, and how it led and caused people to sin and to oppress one another. At first he argues against this theory, and then he declares that God is omniscient. He says as follows; "They slay the widow and the stranger, and murder the fatherless. Yet they say, The Lord shall not see, neither shall the God of Jacob regard it. Understand, ye brutish among the people, and ye fools, when will you be wise? He that planteth the ear shall he not hear? He that formed the eye shall he not see? He that chastiseth nations, shall not he correct? Or he that teacheth man knowledge" (Ps. 94:4-10).

Guide, III, 19

THE WORLD IS GOOD

The world is good, since it was in love and goodness that God created it. Every act of creation is stamped with the words, "And behold, it was good." But the religious consciousness of man found it difficult to reconcile the professed goodness of God with the existing flagrant physical and moral evils with which one meets everywhere. How can the Omnipotent Being suffer His creation, conceived in goodness, to be so disfigured and distorted? Should not the All-Good God have averted the pain and bitterness, the sins and passions which darken His universe?

The philosophers of all ages had dealt with the problem and came up with unsatisfactory solutions. It was one of Maimonides' memorable accomplishments that he cut the Gordian knot by simply repudiating the reality of evil and thereby absolved God from all responsibility for the misdeeds in His world. For evil, he maintains, has no positive existence of its own; it is the negation of good, just as darkness is the negation of light, sickness the negation of health, and poverty the negation of riches. But let Maimonides speak for himself:

The [so-called evils] are evils only in their relation to a certain thing, and that which is evil in reference to a certain existing thing, either includes the non-existence of that thing or the non-existence of some of its good conditions. The proposition has therefore been laid down in the most general terms "All evils are negations." Thus for man death is evil; death is his non-existence. Ignorance, poverty, and illness are evils for man; all these are privations of properties. If you will examine all single cases to which this general proposition applies, you will find that there is not one case in which the proposition is wrong, except in the opinion of those who do not make any distinction between negative and positive properties.

Guide, III, 12

EVIL DOES NOT EXCEED THE GOOD

Men frequently think that the evils in the world are more numerous than the good things. . . . They say that a good thing is only exceptional, whilst evil things are numerous and lasting. Not only common people make this mistake but even many who believe that they are wise. Al-Razi wrote a well-known book. . . . Among other mad and foolish things, it contains also the idea, discovered by him, that there exists more evil than good. . . . The origin of the error is to be found in the circumstance that this ignorant man, and his party among the common people, judge the whole universe by examining one single person. For an ignorant man believes that the whole universe only exists for him, as if nothing else required any consideration. If therefore, anything happens to him contrary to his expectation, he at once concludes that the whole universe is evil. If, however, he would take into consideration the whole universe, form an idea of it, and comprehend what a small portion he is of the universe, he will find the truth.

Ibid.

What we have, in truth, to consider is this: The whole mankind at present in existence, and *a fortiori,* every other species of animals, form an infinitesimal portion of the permanent universe. . . . It is of great advantage that man should know his station, and not erroneously imagine that the whole universe exists only for him. We hold that the universe exists because the Creator wills it so; that mankind is low in rank as compared with the uppermost portion of the universe, viz., with the spheres and the stars; but as regards the angels, there cannot be any real comparison between man and angels, although man is the highest of all beings on earth; i.e., of all beings formed of the four elements. Man's existence is nevertheless a great boon to him, and his distinction and perfection is a divine gift. The numerous evils to which individual persons are exposed are due to the defects existing in the persons themselves. We complain and seek relief from our own faults; we suffer from the evils which we, by our own free will, inflict on ourselves and ascribe them to God, who is far from being connected with them.

Ibid.

GOD ONLY PRODUCES EXISTENCE

After these propositions (that evils "are not things in positive existence") it must be admitted as a fact that it cannot be said of God that He directly creates evil, or He has the direct intention to produce evil; this is impossible. His works are all perfectly good. He only produces existence, and all existence is good, whilst evils are of a negative character, and cannot be acted upon. He creates evil only in so far as He produces the corporeal element . . . and is on that account the source of all destruction and evil. Those beings that do not possess the corporeal element are not subject to destruction or evil; consequently the true work of God is all good, since it is existence. The book which enlightened the darkness of the world, says therefore, "And God saw everything that He had made, and, behold, it was very good" (Gen. I:31). Even the existence of this corporeal element, low as it in reality is, because it is the source of death and all evils, is likewise good for the permanence of the universe and the continuation of the order of things, so that one thing departs and the other succeeds. Rabbi Meir therefore explains the words "and behold it was very good" [*tob me'od*], that even death was good in accordance with what we have observed.

Ibid., 10

All great evils which men cause to each other because of certain intentions, desires, opinions, or religious principles, are likewise due to non-existence, because they originate in ignorance, which is absence of wisdom. A blind man, for example, who has no guide, stumbles constantly, because he cannot see, and causes injury and harm to himself and to others. In the same manner, various classes of men, each man in proportion to his ignorance, bring great evils upon themselves and upon other individual members of the species. If man possessed wisdom, which stands in the same relation to the form of man as sight to the eyes, they would not cause any injury to themselves or to others, for the knowledge of truth removes hatred and quarrels, and prevents mutual injuries. This state of society is promised to us by the prophet in the words, "And the wolf shall dwell with the lamb," etc.; "and the cow and the bear shall feed together," etc.; and "the suckling child shall play on the hole of the asp" (Is. 11, 6 *seq.*). The prophet also points out what will be the cause of this change; for he says that hatred, quarrel, and fighting will come to an end, because men will have then a true knowledge of God. "They will not hurt nor destroy in all my holy mountain; for the earth shall be full of the knowledge of the Lord, as the waters cover the sea" (*ibid.*, ver. 9).

Ibid., 11

THE THREE EVILS OF MAN

The first kind of evil is that which is caused to man by the circumstance that he is subject to genesis and destruction, or that he possesses a body. It is on account of that body that some persons happen to have great deformities or paralysis of the organs. . . . You will, nevertheless, find that the evils of the above kind which befall man are very few and rare; . . . there are thousands of men who are in perfect health, deformed individuals are a strange and exceptional occurrence . . . they are not one-hundredth, not even one-thousandth part of those that are perfectly normal.

The second class of evils comprises such evils as people cause to each other, when, e.g., some of them use their strength against others. These evils are more numerous than those of the first kind, their causes are numerous and known; they likewise originate in ourselves, though the sufferer himself cannot avert them. This kind of evil is nevertheless not widespread in any country in the whole world. It is of rare occurrence that man plans to kill his neighbor or to rob him of his property by night.

The third class of evils comprises those which man causes to himself by his own action. This is the largest class, and is by far more numerous than the second class. It is especially of these evils that all men complain—only few men are found that do not sin against themselves by this kind of evil. Those who are afflicted by it are therefore justly blamed in the words of the prophet, "This hath been by your means" (Mal. I, 9). In reference to this kind of evil, Solomon says, "The foolishness of man perverteth his way" (Prov. 6:32). . . . This class of evil originates in man's vices, such as excessive desire for eating, drinking, and love; indulgence in these things in undue measure, or in improper manner, or partaking of bad food. This cause brings diseases and afflictions upon body and soul alike. . . . The soul when accustomed to superfluous things, acquires a strong habit of desiring things which are neither necessary for the preservation of the individual nor for that of the species. This

221

desire is without a limit, whilst things which are necessary are few in number and restricted within certain limits, but that which is superfluous is without end—e.g., you desire to have your vessels of silver, but golden vessels are still better, others have even vessels of sapphire, or perhaps they can be made of emerald or rubies, or any other substance that could be suggested. Those who are ignorant and perverse in their thought are constantly in trouble and pain because they cannot get as much of the superfluous things as a certain other person possesses. They as a rule expose themselves to great danger, e.g., by sea voyage or service of kings, and all this for the purpose of obtaining that which is superfluous and not necessary. When they thus meet with the consequences of the course which they adopt, they complain of the decrees and judgments of God; they begin to blame the times, and wonder at the want of justice in its changes, that it has not enabled them to acquire great riches, . . . for the purpose of driving themselves to voluptuousness beyond their capacities, as if the whole universe existed exclusively for the purpose of giving pleasure to these low people.

The error of the ignorant goes so far as to say that God's power is insufficient, because He has given to this universe the properties which they imagine cause these great evils, and which do not help all evil disposed persons to obtain the evil which they seek, and to bring their evil souls to the aim of their desires, though these, as we have shown, are really without limit. The virtuous and wise, however, see and comprehend the wisdom God displayed in the universe. Thus David says, "All the paths of the Lord are mercy and truth unto such as keep His covenant and His testimonies" (Ps. 25:10). For those who observe the nature of the universe and the commandments of the Law, and know their purpose, see clearly God's mercy and truth in everything: They seek, therefore, that which the Creator intended to be the aim of man, viz., comprehension. Forced by the claims of the body, they seek also that which is necessary for the preservation of the body, "bread to eat and garment to clothe," and this is very little; but they seek nothing superfluous; with very slight exertion man can obtain it, so long as he is contented with that which is indispensable. All the difficulties and troubles we meet in this respect are due to the desire for superfluous things; when we seek unnecessary things, we have difficulty even in finding that which is indispensable. For the more we desire to have that which is superfluous, the more we meet with difficulties; our strength and possessions are spent in unnecessary things, and are wanting when required for that which is necessary.

Guide, III, 12

NATURE'S GIFTS

Observe how Nature proves the correctness of this assertion. The more necessary a thing is for living beings, the more easily it is found and the cheaper it is; the less necessary it is, the rarer and dearer it is, e.g., air, water, and food are indispensable to man; air is most necessary, for if man is without air a short time he dies; whilst he can be without water a day or two. Air is also undoubtedly found more easily and cheaper [than water]. Water is more necessary than food; for some people can be four or five days without food, provided they have water; water also exists in every country in larger quantities than food, and is also cheaper. The same proportion can be noticed in the different kinds of food; that which is more necessary in a certain place exists there in larger quantities and is cheaper than that which is less necessary. No intelligent person, I think, considers musk, amber, rubies, and emeralds as very necessary for man except as medicines; and they, as well as other like substances, can be replaced for this purpose by herbs and minerals. This shows the kindness of God to His creatures, even to us weak beings.

Guide, III, 12

ACTS OF GOD

With regard to evils befalling man by causes outside himself, Maimonides says:

His [God's] actions towards mankind also include great calamities, which overtake individuals and bring death to them, or affect whole families and even entire regions, spread death, destroy generation after generation, and spare nothing whatsoever. Hence there occur inundations, earthquakes, destructive storms, expeditions of one nation against the other for the sake of destroying with the sword and blotting out its memory, and many other evils of the same kind. Whenever such evils are caused by us to any person, they originate in great anger, violent jealousy, or a desire for revenge. God is therefore called because of these acts "jealous," and "revengeful," "wrathful" and "keeping anger" (Nahum 1:2); that is to say, He performs acts similar to those which, when performed by us, originate in certain psychical dispositions, in jealousy, desire for retaliation, revenge or anger; they are in accordance with the guilt of those who are to be punished, and not the result of any emotion, for He is above all defects! The same is the case with all divine acts; though resembling those acts which animate from our passions and psychical dispositions, they are not due to anything superadded to His essence.

Guide, I, 54

TRIALS ARE TESTS OF FAITH

After Maimonides established that evil does not proceed from God, he vindicates the disciplinary effect of the trials and hardships of life. He also considers the unquestioning faith, the test of the true lover of God.

The doctrine of trials is open to great objections; it is in fact more exposed to objections than any other thing taught in Scripture. It is mentioned in Scripture six times. People have generally the notion that trials consist in afflictions and mishaps sent by God to man, not as punishments for past sins, but as giving opportunity for great reward. This principle is not mentioned in Scripture in plain language, and it is only in one of the six places referred to that the literal meaning conveys this notion. . . . The principle taught in Scripture is exactly the reverse; for it is said "He is a God of faithfulness, and there is no inquity in Him" (Deut. 32:4).

The teaching of our Sages, although some of them approve this general belief [concerning trials], is on the whole against it. For they say "There is no death without sin, and no affliction without transgression" (Sab. 55a). Every intelligent religious person should have this faith, and should not ascribe any wrong to God, who is far from it; he must not assume that a person is innocent and perfect and does not deserve what has befallen him. The trials mentioned in Scripture in the [six] passages, seem to have been tests and experiments by which God desires to learn the intensity of the faith and the devotion of a man or a nation. [If this were the case] it would be very difficult to comprehend the objects of the trials, and yet the sacrifice of Isaac seems to be a case of this kind, as none witnessed it, but God and the two concerned [Abraham and Isaac]. Thus God says to Abraham, "For now I know that thou fearest God," etc. (Gen. 22:12). In another passage it is said: "For the Lord your God proveth you to know whether ye love" (Deut. 13:4). Again, "And to prove thee to know what was in thine heart," etc. (*ibid.*, 8:2).

Guide, III, 24

TRIALS TEACH US WHAT TO DO AND HOW TO ACT

The sole object of all the trials mentioned in Scripture is to teach man what he ought to do or believe; so that the event which forms the actual trial is not the end desired; it is but an example for our instruction and guidance. . . . Having shown that the term "to know" means "that all the people may know" we apply this interpretation to the following words [said in reference to the manna]: "To humble thee and to prove thee, to know what is in thine heart, whether thou wouldst keep His commandments, or not" (Deut. 8:2). All nations shall know, it shall be published throughout the world, that those who devote themselves to the service of God are supported beyond their expectation. . . . This might induce us to think that God sometimes afflicts man for the purpose of increasing his reward. But in truth this is not the case. . . . The Hebrew term *le-nassoteka* means "to accustom thee"; the word is used in this sense in the following passage: "She has not *accustomed (nisseta)* the sole of her foot to set it upon the ground" (*ibid.*, 28:56). The meaning of the above passage would then be: "God has first trained you in the hardships of the wilderness, in order to increase your welfare when you enter the land of Canaan."

Ibid.

It is indeed a fact that the transition from trouble to ease gives more pleasure than continual ease. It is also known that the Israelites would not have been able to conquer the land and fight with its inhabitants if they had not previously undergone the trouble and hardship of the wilderness. Scripture says in reference to this: "For God said, Lest peradventure the people repent when they see war and they return to Egypt. But God led the people about, through the way of the wilderness of the Red Sea; and the Children of Israel went up harnessed out of the land of Egypt" (Ex. 13:17, 18). Ease destroys bravery, whilst trouble and care for food create strength; and this was [also for the Israelites] the good that ultimately came out of their wanderings in the wilderness.

Ibid.

THE TEST OF ABRAHAM

The account of Abraham our father binding his son, includes two great ideas or principles of our faith. It shows us the extent and limit of the fear of God. Abraham is commanded to perform a certain act, which is not equalled by any surrender of property or by any sacrifice of life, for it surpasses everything that can be done, and belongs to the class of actions which are believed to be contrary to human feelings. He had been without child, and had been longing for a child; he had great riches, and was expecting that a nation should spring from his seed. After all hope of a son had already been given up, a son was born unto him. How great must have been his delight in the child! how intensely must he have loved him! And yet because he feared God, and loved to do what God commanded, he thought little of that beloved child, and set aside all his hopes concerning him, and consented to kill him after a journey of three days. If the act by which he showed his readiness to kill his son had taken place immediately when he received the commandment, it might have been the result of confusion and not of consideration. But the fact that he performed it three days after he had received the commandment, proves the presence of thought, proper consideration, and careful examination of what is due to the Divine command and what is in accordance with the love and fear of God. . . . For Abraham did not hasten to kill Isaac out of fear that God might slay him or make him poor, but solely because it is man's duty to love and to fear God even without hope of reward or fear of punishment. . . . This is the way how we have to understand the accounts of trials; we must not think that God desires to examine us and to try us in order to know what He did not know before. Far is this from Him; He is far above that which ignorant and foolish people imagine concerning Him, in the evil of their thoughts.

Ibid.

JOB AND HIS FRIENDS

In two of the most remarkable chapters of the Guide *conceived, as the author claims, by inspiration, Maimonides finds support in the Book of Job for his theory that the trials and sufferings of the just and upright do not constitute an indictment against divine justice. For the truly good and perfect man will not only not be discouraged by his personal adverse experience and rebel against God but will rise above them by his true love and knowledge of Him. Maimonides seems to differentiate between the two Jobs: the one who knew God only by hearsay and found his imaginary happiness in such things as health, possessions, and children, and therefore fell into confusion and perplexities and spoke ill of Him, and the other Job who, realizing God, also realized his true happiness and rose above his afflictions.*

Maimonides dwells with peculiar affection upon "the strange and wonderful Book of Job," a subject of speculation and controversy among the ancients, the very existence and historical identity of the man having been put to question, and says:

But whether he has existed or not, that which is related of him is an experience of frequent occurrence, is a source of perplexity to all thinkers and has suggested opinions on God's Omnipotence and Providence. This perplexity is caused by the account of a simple and perfect person, who is upright in his actions, and very anxious to abstain from sin, is afflicted by successive misfortunes, namely, by loss of property, by the death of his children, and by bodily disease, though he has not committed any sin. According to both theories, *viz.*, the theory that Job did exist, and the theory that he did not exist, the introduction to the book is certainly a fiction; I mean the portion which relates to the words of the adversary, the word of God to the former, and the handing over of Job to him. This fiction, however, is so far different from other fictions that it includes profound ideas and great mysteries, removes great doubts, and reveals the most important truths.

The Catastrophe

Job, the simple and righteous man, is given and handed over to the adversary; whatever evils and misfortunes befell Job as regards his property, children, and health, were all caused by the adversary. When this idea is sufficiently indicated, the writer begins to reflect on it; one opinion Job is represented to hold, whilst other opinions are defended by his friends. . . . Job, as well as his friends were of opinion that God Himself was the direct agent of what happened, and that the adversary was not the intermediate cause. It is remarkable in this account that wisdom is not ascribed to Job. The text does not say he was an intelligent, wise, or clever man; but virtue and uprightness, especially in actions, are ascribed to him. If he were wise he would not have any doubt about the cause of his suffering. . . . Besides, his misfortunes are enumerated in the same order as they rank in man's estimation. There are some who are not perplexed or discouraged by the loss of property, thinking little of it, but are terrified when they are threatened with the loss of their children and are killed by their anxiety. There are others who bear without shock or fainting even the loss of their children, but no one endowed with sensation is able to bear bodily pain. We generally extol God in words, and praise Him as righteous and benevolent when we prosper and are happy, or when the grief we have to bear is moderate. But [it is otherwise] when such troubles as are described in Job come over us. Some of us deny God, and believe that there is no rule in the Universe, even if only their property is lost. Others retain their faith in the existence of justice and order, even when suffering from loss of property, whereas loss of children is too much affliction for them. Others remain firm in their faith, even with the loss of their children; but there is no one who can patiently bear the pain that reaches his own person; he then murmurs and complains of injustice either in his heart or with his tongue.

THE ARGUMENT

Assuming the first part of the history of Job as having actually taken place, the five, viz., Job and his friends, agreed that the misfortune of Job was known to God, and that it was God that caused Job's suffering. They further agree that God does no wrong, and that no injustice can be ascribed to Him. You will find these ideas frequently repeated in the words of Job. When you consider the words of the five who take part in the discussion, you will easily notice that things said by one of them are also uttered by the rest. The arguments are repeated, mixed up, and interrupted by Job's description of his acute pain and troubles, which had come upon him in spite of his strict righteousness, and by an account of his charity, humane disposition, and good acts. The replies of the friends to Job are likewise interrupted by exhortations to patience, by words of comfort, and other speeches tending to make him forget his grief. He is told by them to be silent; that he ought not to let loose the bridle of his tongue, as if he were in dispute with another man; that he ought silently to submit to the judgments of God. Job replies that the intensity of his pains did not permit him to bear patiently, to collect his thoughts and to say what he ought to say. The friends, on the other hand, contend that those who act well receive reward, and those who act wickedly are punished. When a wicked and rebellious person is seen in prosperity, it may be assumed for certain that a change will take place; he will die, or troubles will afflict him and his house. When we find a worshipper of God in misfortune, we may be certain that God will heal the stroke of his wound. This idea is frequently repeated in the words of the three friends, Eliphaz, Bildad, and Zofar, who agree in this opinion.

JOB QUESTIONS MORAL GOVERNANCE OF THE WORLD

It is, however, not the object of this chapter to describe in what they agree, but to define the distinguishing characteristic of each of them, and to elucidate the opinion of each as regards the question why the most simple and upright man is afflicted with the greatest and acutest pain. Job found in this fact a proof that the righteous and the wicked are equal before God, who holds all mankind in contempt. Job therefore says (9:22, 23): "This is one thing, therefore I said it, He destroyeth the perfect and the wicked. If the scourge slay suddenly, he will laugh at the trial of the innocent." He thus declares that when a scourge comes suddenly, killing and destroying all it meets, God laughs at the trial of the innocent. He further confirms this view in the following passage: "One dieth in his full strength, being wholly at ease and quiet. His vessels are full of milk, etc. And another dieth in the bitterness of his soul, and never eateth with pleasure. They shall lie down alike in the dust, and the worms shall cover them" (*ibid.*, 11:23, 26). In a similar manner he shows the good condition and prosperity of wicked people; and is even very explicit on this point. He speaks thus: "Even when I remember I am afraid, and trembling taketh hold on my flesh. Wherefore do the wicked live, become old, yea, are mighty in power? Their seed is established in their sight with them,' etc. (*ibid.*, 6-8). Having thus described their prosperity, he addresses his opponents, and says to them: "Granted that as you think, the children of this prosperous atheist will perish after his death, and their memory will be blotted out, what harm will the fate of his family cause him after his death? For what pleasure hath he in his house after him, when the number of his months is cut off in the midst?" (*ibid.*, 21). Job then explains that there is no hope after death, so that the cause [of the misfortune of the righteous man] is nothing else but entire neglect on the part of God. He is therefore surprised that God has not abandoned the creation of man altogether; and that after having created him, He does not take any notice of him. He says in his surprise: "Hast thou not poured me out as milk, and curdled me like cheese?" etc. (*ibid.*, 10:10, *seq.*). This is one of the different views held by some thinkers on Providence. Our Sages (B.B. 16*a*) condemned this view of Job as mischievous, and expressed their feeling in words like the following: "dust should have filled the mouth of Job"; "Job wished to upset the dish"; "Job denied the resurrection of the dead"; "He commenced to blaspheme." When, however, God said to Eliphaz and his colleagues, "You have not spoken of me the thing that is right, as my servant Job hath" our Sages assume as the cause of this rebuke, the maxim "Man is not punished for that which he utters in his pain"; and that God ignored the sin of Job [in his utterances], because of the acuteness of his suffering. But this explanation does not agree with the object of the whole allegory. The words of God are justified, as I will show, by the fact that Job abandoned his first very erroneous opinion, and himself proved that it was an error. It is the opinion which suggests itself as plausible at first thought, especially in the minds of those who meet with mishaps, well knowing that they have not merited them through sins. This is admitted by all, and therefore this opinion was assigned to Job. But he is represented to hold this view only so long as he was without wisdom, and knew God only by tradition, in the same manner as religious people generally know Him. As soon as he had acquired a true knowledge of God, he confessed that there is undoubtedly true felicity in the knowledge of God; it is attained by all who acquire that knowledge, and no earthly trouble can disturb it. So long as Job's knowledge of God was based on tradition and communication, and not on research, he believed that such imaginary good as it possessed in health, riches, and children, was the utmost that men can attain; this was the reason why he was in perplexity, and why he uttered the above-mentioned opinions, and this is also the meaning of his words: "I have heard of thee by the hearing of the ear; but now mine eye seeth thee. Wherefore I abhor myself, and repent because of dust and ashes" (42:5, 6); that is to say, he abhorred all that he had desired before, and that he was sorry that he had been in dust and ashes; comp. "and he sat down among the ashes" (2:8). On account of this last utterance, which implies true perception, it is said afterwards in reference to him, "for you have not spoken of me the thing that is right, as my servant Job hath."

The opinion set forth by Eliphaz in reference to Job's suffering is likewise one of the current views on Providence. He holds that the fate of Job was in accordance with strict justice. Job was guilty of sins for which he deserved his fate. Eliphaz therefore says to Job: "Is not thy wickedness great, and thine iniquities infinite?" (12:5). He then points out to him that his upright actions and his good ways, on which he relies, need not be so perfect in the eyes of God that no punishment should be inflicted on him. "Behold, he putteth no trust in his servants; and his angels he chargeth with folly: how much less in them that dwell in houses of clay," etc. (4:17-18). Eliphaz never abandoned his belief that the fate of man is the result of justice, that we do not know all our shortcomings for which we are punished, nor the way how we incur the punishment through them.

Bildad the Shuhite defends in this question the theory of reward and compensation. He therefore tells Job that if he is innocent and without sin, his terrible misfortunes will be the source of great reward, will be followed by the best compensation, and will prove a boon to him as the cause of great bliss in the future world. This idea is expressed in the words: "If thou be pure and upright, surely now he will awake for thee, and make the habitation of thy righteousness prosperous. Though thy beginning was small, yet thy latter end will greatly increase" (8:6-8). This opinion concerning Providence is widespread.

Zofar the Naamathite holds that the Divine Will is the source of everything that happens; no further cause can be sought for His actions, and it cannot be asked why He has done this and why He has not done that. That which God does can therefore not be explained by the way of justice or the result of wisdom. His true Essence demands that He does what He wills; we are unable to fathom the depth of His wisdom, and it is the law and rule of this wisdom that whatever He does is done because it is His will and for no other cause. Zofar therefore says to Job: "But oh that God would speak, and open his lips against thee; and that he would show thee the secrets of wisdom, for wisdom hath two portions! Know, therefore, that God exacteth of thee less than thine iniquity deserveth. Canst thou by searching find out God? canst thou find out the Almighty unto perfection?" (11:6-7).

BOOK OF JOB REFLECTS DIVERSE VIEWS OF DIVINE PROVIDENCE

In this manner consider well how the Book of Job discusses the problem, which has perplexed many people, and led them to adopt in reference to Divine Providence some one of the theories I have explained. The problem is described either by way of fiction or in accordance with real fact, as having manifested itself in a man famous for his excellency and wisdom. The view ascribed to Job is the theory of Aristotle. Eliphaz holds the opinion taught in Scripture, Bildad's opinion is identical with that of the Mu'tazilah, whilst Zofar defends the theory of the Asha'riyah. These were the ancient views on Providence; later on a new theory was set forth, namely, that ascribed to Elihu. For this reason he is placed above the others, and described as younger in years but greater in wisdom. He censures Job for his foolishly exalting himself, expressing surprise at such great troubles befalling a good man, and dwelling on the praises of his own deeds. He also tells the three friends that their minds have been weakened by great age. A profound and wonderful discourse then follows. Reflecting on his words we may at first thought be surprised to find that he does not add anything to the words of Eliphaz, Bildad, and Zofar; and that he only repeats their ideas in other terms and more explicitly. For he likewise censures and rebukes Job, attributes justice to God, relates His wonders in nature, and holds that God is not affected by the service of the worshipper, nor by the disobedience of the rebellious. All this has already been said by his colleagues. But after due consideration we see clearly the new idea introduced by Elihu, which is the principal object of his speech, an idea which has not been uttered by those who spoke before him. . . .

The new idea, which is peculiar to Elihu and has not been mentioned by the others, is contained in his metaphor of the angel's intercession. It is a frequent occurrence, he says, that a man becomes ill, approaches the gates of death, and is already given up by his neighbours. If then an angel, of any kind whatever, intercedes on his behalf and prays for him, the intercession and prayers are accepted; the patient rises from his illness, is saved, and returns to good health. This result is not always obtained; intercession and deliverance do not always follow each other; it happens only twice, or three times. Elihu therefore says: "If there be an angel with him, an interpreter, one among a thousand, to show unto man his uprightness," etc. (33:23).

He then describes man's condition when convalescent and the rejoicing at his recovery, and continues thus: "Lo, all these things worketh God twice, three times with man" (*ibid.*, 29). The idea occurs only in the words of Elihu. His description of the method of prophecy in preceding verses is likewise new. He says: "Surely God speaketh in one way, yea in two ways, yet man perceiveth it not. In a dream, in a vision of the night when deep sleep falleth upon man, in slumberings upon the bed" (*ibid.*, 14, 15). He afterwards supports and illustrates his theory by a description of many natural phenomena, such as thunder, lightning, rain, and winds; with these are mixed up accounts of various incidents of life, e.g., an account of pestilence contained in the following passage: "In a moment they die, and at midnight; the people become tumultuous and pass away" (34:20). Great wars are described in the following verse: "He breaketh in pieces mighty men without number, and setteth others in their stead" (*ibid.*, 24). There are many more passages of this kind. In a similar manner the Revelation that reached Job (chap. 38, chap. 41), and explained to him the error of his whole belief, constantly describes natural objects, and nothing else; it describes the elements, meteorological phenomena, and peculiarities of various kinds of living beings. The sky, the heavens, Orion and Pleiades are only mentioned in reference to their influence upon our atmosphere, so that Job's attention is in this prophecy only called to things below the lunar sphere. Elihu likewise derives instruction from the nature of various kinds of animals. Thus he says: "He teacheth us through the beasts of the earth, and maketh us wise through the fowls of heaven" (35:11). He dwells longest on the nature of the Leviathan, which possesses a combination of bodily peculiarities found separate in different animals, in those that walk, those that swim, and those that fly.

Job's Faith Rebuilt through Vision of God's Action in Nature

The description of all these things serves to impress on our minds that we are unable to comprehend how these transient creatures come into existence, or to imagine how their natural properties commenced to exist, and that these are not like the things which we are able to produce. Much less can we compare the manner in which God rules and manages His creatures with the manner in which we rule and manage certain beings. We must content ourselves with this, and believe that nothing is hidden from God, as Elihu says: "For his eyes are upon the ways of man, and he seeth all his goings. There is no darkness nor shadow of death, where the workers of iniquity may hide themselves" (34:21, 22). But the term management, when applied to God, has not the same meaning which it has when applied to us; and when we say that He rules His creatures we do not mean that He does the same as we do when we rule over other beings. The term "rule" has not the same definition in both cases; it signifies two different notions, which have nothing in common but the name. In the same manner, as there is a difference between works of nature and productions of human handicraft, so there is a difference between God's rule, providence, and intention in reference to all natural forces, and our rule, providence, and intention in reference to things which are the objects of our rule, providence, and intention.

This lesson is the principal object of the whole Book of Job; it lays down this principle of faith, and recommends us to derive a proof from nature, that we should not fall into the error of imagining His knowledge to be similar to ours, or His intention, providence, and rule similar to ours. When we know this we shall find everything that may befall us easy to bear; mishap will create no doubts in our hearts concerning God, whether He knows our affairs or not, whether He provides for us or abandons us. On the contrary, our fate will increase our love of God; as is said in the end of this prophecy: "Therefore I abhor myself and repent concerning the dust and ashes" (42:6); and as our Sages say: "The pious do everything out of love, and rejoice in their own afflictions." (B. T. Shabb. 88*b*.).

Guide, III, 22-23

12. DIVINE PROVIDENCE AND FREE WILL

The belief in Divine Providence is deeply ingrained in the hope and faith of man. It is one of those religious principles which came in response to man's desperate need of God's encompassing love and care. But is Providence concerned with the welfare of each individual or is it extended only to the preservation of the human species? On this the philosophers are divided, Maimonides holding that while there is special or individual Providence in the case of human beings, all other created things, such as plants and animals, are ruled by chance. But even with regard to man, his share in Divine Providence varies with his character and intellectual achievement.

FOUR THEORIES OF PROVIDENCE

There are four different theories concerning Divine Providence; they are all ancient, known since the time of the Prophets, when the true Law was revealed to enlighten these dark regions.

EPICUREAN VIEW

There is no Providence at all for anything in the Universe. All parts of the Universe, the heavens and what they contain owe their origin to accident and chance. This is the theory of Epicurus, who assumes also that the Universe consists of atoms, that they have combined by chance, and have received their various forms by accident. There have been atheists among the Israelites who have expressed the same view. It is reported of them: "They have denied the Lord, and said He is not" (Jer. 5:12). Aristotle has proved the ambiguity of the theory, that the whole Universe could have originated by chance;

he has shown that, on the contrary, there is a being who rules and governs the Universe.

ARISTOTLE'S THEORY

Whilst one part of the Universe owes its existence to Providence, and is under the control of a ruler and governor, another part is abandoned and left to chance. This is the view of Aristotle about Providence. . . . He holds that God controls the spheres and what they contain; therefore the individual beings in the spheres remain permanently in the same form. In the same manner it is said that Providence sends forth [from the spheres to the earth] sufficient influence to secure immortality and constancy of the species without securing at the same time permanence for the individual beings of the species. But the individual beings in each specie have not been entirely abandoned. . . . The portion of the *materia prima* which is still more refined and is endowed with the intellectual faculty, possesses a special property by which each individual, according to the degree of his perfection, is enabled to manage, to calculate, and to discover what is conducive both to the temporary existence of the individual and to the preservation of the species. All other movements, however, which are made by the individual members of the species are due to accident; they are not, according to Aristotle, the result of rule and management.

Aristotle sees no difference between the falling of a leaf or a stone and the death of good and noble people in a ship; nor does he distinguish between the destruction of a multitude of ants caused by an ox depositing on them his excrement and the death of worshippers killed by the fall of the house when the foundations give way; nor does he discriminate between the case of a cat killing a mouse that happens to come in her way, or that of a spider catching a fly, and that of a hungry lion meeting a prophet and tearing him. In short, the opinion of Aristotle is this: Everything is the result of management [Providence] which is constant, which does not come to an end and does not change any of its properties, as, e.g., the heavenly beings, and everything which continues according to a certain rule, and deviates from it only rarely and exceptionally, as is the case of objects in Nature. All these are the result of management i.e., in a close relation to Divine Providence. But that which is not constant, and does not follow a certain rule, as incidents in the individual beings in each species of plants or animals, whether rational or irrational, is due to chance and not to management; it is in no relation to Divine Providence.

PROVIDENCE ACCORDING TO THE ASHARIYAH

This theory is the reverse of the second. According to this theory, there is nothing in the whole Universe, neither a class nor an individual being, that is due to chance; everything is the result of will, intention, and rule. It is a matter of course that he who rules must know [that which is under his control]. The Mohammedan Ashariyah adhere to this theory. . . . The Ashariyah were compelled to assume that motion and rest of living beings are predestined, and that it is not in the power of man to do a certain thing or leave it undone. . . . It follows also from this theory that precepts are perfectly useless, since the people to whom the law is given are unable to do anything; they can neither do that what they are commanded or abstain from what they are forbidden. The supporters of this theory hold that it was the will of God to send prophets, to command, to forbid, to promise, and to threaten, although we have no power [over our actions]. . . . When we see a person born blind or leprous, who could not have merited the punishment for previous sins, they say, It is the will of God, when a pious worshipper is tortured and slain, it is likewise the will of God, and no injustice can be asserted to Him for that, for according to their opinion it is proper that God should afflict the innocent and do good to the sinner.

THE MUTAZILITE VIEW

Man has free will; it is therefore intelligible that the Law contains commands and prohibitions, with announcements of reward and punishment. All acts of God are due to wisdom; no injustice is found in Him, and He does not afflict the good. The Mu'tazila profess this theory, although they do not believe in man's absolute free will. They hold also that God takes notice of the falling of the leaf and the destruction of the ant, and that His Providence extends over all things. . . . The fact that some people are born with defects, although they have not sinned previously, is ascribed to the wisdom of God, it being better for such persons to be in such a condition than to be in a normal state, though we do not see why it is better; and they do not suffer thereby any punishment at all, but, on the contrary, enjoy

God's goodness. In similar manner the slaughter of the pious is explained as being for them the source of an increased reward in future life. They go even further in their absurdities. We ask them why is God just to man and not to other beings, and how has the irrational animal sinned that it is condemned to slaughter? and they reply it is good for the animal, for it will receive reward for it in the world to come; also the flea and the mouse will there receive compensation for their untimely death. . . .

WHERE JUDAISM STANDS

This is our theory, or that of our Law. . . . The theory of man's perfectly free will is one of the fundamental principles of the Law of our Teacher Moses, and of those who follow the Law. According to this principle, man does what is in his power to do, by his nature, his choice, and his will; and his action is not due to any faculty created for the purpose. All species of irrational animals likewise move by their own free will. This is the will of God; that is to say, it is due to the eternal divine will that all living beings should move freely, and that man should have power to act according to his will or choice within the limits of his capacity. . . .

Another fundamental principle taught by the Law of Moses is this: Wrong cannot be ascribed to God in any way whatever; all evils and afflictions, as well as all kinds of happiness of man, whether they concern one individual person or a community, are distributed according to justice; they are the result of strict judgment that admits no wrong whatever . . . and the words of our Sages generally express the same idea. They clearly say: "There is no death without sin, no suffering without transgression. (Sab. 55a). Again: "The deserts of man are meted out to him in the same measure which he himself employs (Mish. Sotah I, 7)." But they contain an additional doctrine not contained in the Law; viz., the doctrine of "affliction of love," as taught by some of our Sages (Ber. 5a). According to this doctrine it is possible that a person be afflicted without having previously committed any sin, in order that his reward may be increased. . . .

MAIMONIDES' THEORY OF PROVIDENCE

My opinion on this principle of Divine Providence . . . is this: In the lower or sublunary portion of the Universe Divine Providence does not extend to the individual members of species, except in the case of mankind. It is only in this species that the incidents in the existence of the individual being, their good and evil fortunes, are the result of justice, in accordance with the words, "For all His ways are judgment" (Deut. 32:4). But I agree with Aristotle as regards all other living beings, and *a fortiori* as regards plants and all the rest of earthly creatures. For I do not believe that it is through the interference of Divine Providence that a certain leaf drops [from a tree], nor do I hold that when a certain spider catches a certain fly, that this is the direct result of a special decree and will of God in that moment; it is not by a particular decree that the spittle of a certain person moved, fell on a certain gnat in a certain place and killed it; nor is it by the direct will of God that a certain fish catches and swallows a certain worm on the surface of the water. In all these cases the action is, according to my opinion, entirely due to chance, as taught by Aristotle. . . .

It may be by mere chance that a ship goes down with all her contents, as in the above mentioned instance, or the roof of a house falls upon those within; but it is not due to chance, according to our view, that in the one instance the men went into the ship, or remained in the house in the other instance; it is due to the will of God, and is in accordance with the justice of His judgments, the method of which our mind is incapable of understanding. I have been induced to accept this theory by the circumstances that I have not met in any of the prophetical books with a description of God's Providence otherwise than in relation to human beings. The Prophets even express their surprise that God should take notice of man, who is too little and too unimportant to be worthy of the attention of the Creator; how, then, should other living creatures be considered as proper objects for Divine Providence! Comp. "What is man that Thou takest knowledge of him?" (Ps. 144:3). "What is man that Thou art mindful of him?" (*ibid.*, 8:8). It is clearly expressed in many Scriptural passages that God provides for all men, and controls all their deeds—e.g., "He fashioneth their hearts alike, He considereth all their works" (*ibid.*, 33:15); "For Thine eyes are open all the ways of the sons of men, to give every one according to his way" (Jer. 32:19). . . .

The view that other living beings are only governed by Divine Providence in the way described by Aristotle, is supported by the words of the Prophet Habakuk when he perceived the victories of

Nebuchadnezzar, and saw the multitude of those slain by him, he said, "O God, it is as if men were abandoned, neglected, and unprotected like fish and like worms of the earth" (1:14). He thus shows that these classes are abandoned. This is expressed in the following passage: "And makest men as the fishes of the sea, as the creeping things, that have no ruler over them. They take up all of them with the angle" (*ibid.*, I:15, 15). The Prophet then declares that such is not the case; for the events referred to are not the result of abandonment, forsaking, and absence of Providence, but are intended as a punishment for the people, who well deserved all that befell them. He therefore says: "O Lord, Thou hast ordained them for judgment, and O mighty God, Thou hast established them for correction" (*ibid.*, v. 12). . . .

Aristotle likewise holds that this kind of Providence is necessary, and is in actual existence. Alexander also notices this fact in the name of Aristotle, viz., that every species has its nourishment prepared for its individual members; otherwise the species would undoubtedly have perished. It does not require much consideration to understand this. There is a rule laid down by the Sages that it is directly prohibited by the Law to cause pain to an animal, and it is based on the words: "Wherefore hast thou smitten thine ass?" (Nu. 22:32). But the object of this rule is to make us perfect; that we should not assume cruel habits, and that we should not cause useless pain to others; that, on the contrary, we should be prepared to show pity and mercy to all living creatures, except when necessity demands the contrary: "When thy soul longeth to eat flesh, etc." (Deut. 12:20). We should not kill animals for the purpose of practicing cruelty, or for the purpose of play.

PROVIDENCE IS RELATED TO THE INTELLECT

There can be no objection to this theory, Why should God select mankind as the object of His special Providence and not other living things? For he who asks this question must also inquire, Why has man alone, of all species of animals, been endowed with intellect? The answer to this second question must be, according to the three aforementioned theories: It was the Will of God, it is the decree of His Wisdom, or it is in accordance with the laws of Nature. The same answer applies to the first question . . . I hold that the Divine Providence is related and closely connected with the intellect, because

Providence can only proceed from an intelligent being, from a being that is itself the most perfect intellect. Those creatures, therefore, which receive part of that intellectual influence will become subject to the action of Providence in the same proportion as they are acted upon by the intellect. This theory is in accordance with reason and with the teaching of Scripture, while the other theories previously mentioned either exaggerate Divine Providence or detract from it.

Guide, III, 17

Having shown that of all living things mankind alone is directly under the control of Divine Providence, I will now add the following remarks: It is an established fact that species have no existence except in our mind. Species and other classes are merely ideas formed in our minds, whilst everything in real existence is an individual object, or an aggregate of individual objects. This being granted, it must further be admitted that the result of the existing Divine influence, that reaches mankind through the human intellect, is identical with individual intellects really in existence with which, e.g., Zeid, Amr, Kaled, and Bekr, are endowed.

Hence it follows . . . that the greater the share in which a person has obtained of this Divine influence, on account of both his physical predisposition and his training, the greater must also be the effect of Divine Providence upon him, for the action of Divine Providence is proportional to the endowment of intellect, as has been mentioned above. The relation of Divine Providence is therefore not the same to all men; the greater the human perfection a person has obtained, the greater the benefit he derives from Divine Providence.

Ibid., 18

THE PROPHETS' SHARE IN PROVIDENCE

This benefit is very great in the case of prophets, and varies according to the degree of their prophetic faculty; as it varies in the case of pious and good men according to their piety and uprightness. For it is the intensity of the Divine intellectual influence that has inspired the prophets, guided the good in their actions, and perfected the wisdom of the pious. In the same proportion as ignorant and disobedient persons are deficient in that Divine influence, their condition is inferior, and their rank equal to that of irrational beings; and they are "like unto the beasts" (Ps. 49:21). . . . This belief that God

241

provides for every individual human being in accordance with his merits is one of the fundamental principles on which the Law is founded.

Ibid.

We have already stated in the chapters which treat of Divine Providence, that Providence watches over every rational being according to the amount of intellect which that being possesses. Those who are perfect in their perception of God, whose mind is never separated from Him, enjoy always the influence of Providence. But those who, perfect in their knowledge of God, turn their mind sometimes away from God, enjoy the presence of Divine Providence only when they meditate on God; when their thoughts are engaged in other matters Divine Providence departs from them. The absence of Providence in this case is not like its absence in the case of those who do not reflect on God at all; it is in this case less intense, because when a person perfect in his knowledge [of God] is busy with worldly matters, he has not knowledge in actuality, but only knowledge in potentiality [though ready to become actual]. This person is then like a trained scribe when he is not writing.

Divine Providence is constantly watching over those who have obtained the blessing which is prepared for those who endeavor to obtain it. If man frees his thoughts from worldly matters, obtains a knowledge of God in the right way, and rejoices in that knowledge, it is impossible that any kind of evil should befall him while he is with God, and God with him. When he does not meditate on God, when he is separated from God, when God is also separated from him, then he is exposed to any evil that might befall him; for it is only that intellectual link with God that secures the presence of Providence and protection from evil accidents. Hence it may occur that the perfect man is at times not happy, whilst no evil befalls those who are imperfect; in these cases what happens to them is due to chance.

Ibid., 51

When we see that some escape plagues and mishaps whilst others perish by them, we must not attribute this to difference in the properties of their bodies, or in thier physical constitution, for "not by strength shall man prevail" (I Sam. 2:9); but it must be attributed to their different degrees of perfection, some approaching God, whilst others move away from Him. Those who approach Him are best protected, and "He will keep the feet of His holy ones (*Ibid.*); but those who keep far away from Him are left exposed to what may befall them; there is nothing that could protect them from what might happen; they are like those who walk in darkness and are certain to stumble. . . . The philosophers have likewise discussed this subject. Abu-nasr, in the Introduction to his *Commentary on Aristotle's Nicomachean Ethics*, says, as follows: Those who possess the facility of raising their souls from virtue to virtue obtain, according to Plato, Divine Protection to a higher degree. . . .

Now consider how by this method of reasoning we have arrived at the view taught by the Prophets, that every person has his individual share of Divine Providence in proportion to his perfection. For philosophical research leads to this conclusion, if we assume, as has been mentioned above, that Divine Providence is in each case proportional to the person's intellectual development. It is wrong to say that Divine Providence extends only to the species, and not to individual beings, as some of the philosophers teach. For only individual beings have real existence, and individual beings are endowed with Divine Intellect; Divine Providence acts, therefore, upon these individual beings.

Ibid., 18

FREEDOM OF WILL

There is no direct statement in the Bible which emphasizes freedom of will, although a number of verses in the Book point to it. But the moral order of the world and the dignity and greatness of man demand that his life and actions be free and not determined by the iron law of necessity. Indeed, it is his freedom of choice, the ability to will and act without any exterior moral or physical compulsion, which distinguishes man from the lower animals. While most other Jewish philosophers had dealt with the problem of Free Will, it finds in Maimonides its clearest expression. The importance he attaches to the question may be seen by the fact that he calls it "a pillar of the Law and the commandments." While he, of course, affirms the freedom of man's will and action, he at the same time endeavors to square it with God's Omniscience and Omnipotence.

Free Will is bestowed on every human being. If one desires to turn towards the good way and be righteous, he has the power to do so. If one wishes to turn towards the evil way and be wicked, he is at liberty to do so. And thus it is written in the Torah, "Behold, the man is become as one of us, to know good and evil" (Gen. 3:22)—which means that the human species has become unique in the world—there being no other species like it in the following respect, namely, that man, of himself and by the exercise of his own intelligence and reason, knows what is good and what is evil, and there is none who can prevent him from doing that which is good or that which is evil. And since this is so (there is reason to fear) "lest he put forth his hand, etc."

Repentance, 5

Let not the notion, expressed by foolish gentiles and most of the senseless folk among Israelites, pass through your mind that at the beginning of a person's existence the Almighty decrees that he is to be either righteous or wicked. This is not so. Every human being may become righteous like Moses, our teacher, or wicked like Jeroboam; wise or foolish, merciful or cruel; niggardly or generous; and so with all other qualities. There is no one that coerces or decrees what he is to do, or draws him to either of the two ways; but every person turns to the way which he desires, spontaneously and of his own volition. Thus Jeremiah said, "out of the mouth of the Most High, proceedeth not evil and good" (Lam. 3:38); that is to say, the Creator does not decree either that a man shall be good or that he shall be wicked. Accordingly it follows that it is the sinner who has inflicted injury on himself; and he should therefore weep for, and bewail what he has done to his soul—how he has mistreated it.

This doctrine is an important principle, the pillar of the Law and the commandment, as it is said, "See, I set before thee this day life and good, and death and evil" (Deut. 30:15); and again it is written, "Behold, I set before you this day a blessing and a curse" (*ibid.*, 11:26) This means that the power is in your hands, and whatever a man desires to do among the things that human beings do, he can do whether they are good or evil; and, because of this faculty, it is said, "O that they had such a heart as this always" (*ibid.*, 5:26), which implies that the Creator neither puts compulsion on the children of man nor decrees that they should do either good or evil, but it is all left to their discretion.

If God had decreed that a person be either righteous or wicked, or if there were some force inherent in his nature which irresistibly drew

244

him to a particular course, or to a special branch of knowledge, to special views or activities, as the foolish astrologers, out of their own fancy pretend, how would the Almighty have charged us through His prophets: "Do this and do not do that, improve your ways, do not follow your wicked impulses," when from beginning of his existence his destiny had already been decreed, or his innate constitution irresistibly drew him to that from which he could not set himself free? What room would there be for the whole of the Torah? By what right or justice could God punish the wicked or reward the righteous? "Shall not the Judge of all the earth act justly?" (Gen. 18:25).

Ibid.

I have entered into this subject so that thou mayest not believe the absurd ideas of astrologers, who falsely assert that the constellation at the time of one's birth determines whether one is to be virtuous or vicious, the individual being thus necessarily compelled to follow out a certain line of conduct. We, on the contrary, are convinced that our Law agrees with Greek philosophy, which substantiates with convincing proofs the contention that man's conduct is entirely in his own hands, that no compulsion is exerted, that no external influence is brought to bear upon him that constrains him to be either virtuous or vicious. . . . Were a man compelled to act according to the dictates of predestination, then the commands and prohibitions of the Law would become null and void, and the Law would be completely false, since man would have no freedom of choice in what he does. Moreover, it would be useless, in fact, absolutely in vain, for man to study, to instruct, or attempt to learn an art, as it would be entirely impossible for him, on account of the external force compelling him, according to the opinion of those who hold this view, to keep from doing a certain act, from gaining certain knowledge, or from acquiring a certain characteristic. Reward and punishment would be pure injustice, both as regards man toward man, and as between God and man. . . . This theory is, therefore positively unsound, contrary to reason and common sense, subversive of the fundamental principles of religion, and attributes injustice to God (far be it from Him). In reality, the undoubted truth of the matter is that man has full sway over all his actions. If he wishes to do a thing, he does it; if he does not wish to do it, he need not, without any external compulsion controlling him. Therefore God very properly commanded man, saying, "See, I have set before thee this day life and good, death and evil . . . therefore choose thou life," (Deut. 30:15, 19), giving us, as regards these, freedom of choice.

Eight Chapters, 8

Keep in mind that one of the principles of Moses' faith, accepted also by all the philosophers, is that man's actions are determined by his own will; there is no force that determines his action. If a man decides to worship God, to acquire wisdom, he may do so; if he decides to associate with the wicked, with thieves, or with adulterers, he is free to do so; nobody is by nature or astrological elements compelled to choose either one way or the other. This fact alone makes it possible to demand of him: "Do this" and "Don't do that."

I know that you could find in the Talmud, the Mishnah, or the Midrash statements of our teachers to the effect that, at the hour of birth, the stars caused this or that. Let this not disturb you. One should not abandon a matter of reason that is proved true and adhere to the opinion of one of the Sages who might have forgotten the right answer, or might have alluded to something else, or offered his view for a special time, or for a certain occasion. One should never abandon reason; the eyes look forward and not backward.

Hebrew Union College Annual, 1926

There are many verses in the Pentateuch and in the Prophets which seem to contradict this fundamental doctrine. And they lead most people astray and make them think that God decrees that a person shall do good or evil, and that a man's heart is not under his control, to incline him in whichever direction he pleases. I will therefore expound an important principle by which you will learn the meaning of those verses. When an individual sins or the inhabitants of a country sin, and the sinner commits an offense, consciously and voluntarily, it is proper that he be punished. God knows the way in which punishment should be enacted. In the case of some sins, justice requires that the sinner should be punished for his sin in this world, corporeally or pecuniarily or through his little children; for a man's little children, who have as yet no understanding and have not arrived at the age of religious obligations, are their father's quasi-property, and the text "Every man shall be put to death for his own sin" (Deut. 24:16) implies that one is not personally liable till he is an adult. Again, there are sins where justice requires that the punishment be inflicted in the life hereafter and the transgressor suffers no hurt here on earth. Other sins again there are, for which the penalty is exacted here and hereafter.

Repentance, 6

13. REPENTANCE

Since every human being has free will, a man should strive to repent, make verbal confession of his sins, and renounce them so that he may die penitent and thus be worthy of life in the world to come.

AT THE PRESENT time when the Temple no longer exists, and we have no altar for atonement, nothing is left but repentance. Repentance atones for all transgressions. Even if a man was wicked all the days of his life and repented at the end, nothing of his wickedness is recalled to him.

Repentance, 1

Repentance is one of those principles which are an indispensable element in the creed of the followers of the Law. For it is impossible for a man to be entirely free from error and sin; he either does not know the opinion which he has to choose, or he adopts a principle, not for its own merits, but in order to gratify his desire or passion. If we were convinced that we could never make our crooked ways straight, we should forever continue in our errors and perhaps add other sins to them since we did not see that any remedy was left to us. But the belief in the effect of repentance causes us to improve, to turn to the best of the ways, and to become more perfect than we were before we sinned.

Guide, III, 36

THE ESSENCE OF CONFESSION

With regard to all the precepts of the Torah, affirmative or negative, if a person transgresses any one of them, either wilfully or in error, and repents and turns away from his sin, he is under a duty to confess before God, blessed be He, as it is said, "When a man or woman shall commit any sin that men commit, to do a trespass against the Lord, and that person be guilty, then they shall confess the sin which they have done" (Nu. 5:6-7); this means confess *in words;* and this confession is an affirmative precept. How does he confess? The penitent says "I beseech Thee, O Lord, I have sinned, I have acted perversely; I have transgressed before Thee, and have done thus and thus, and lo, I repent and am ashamed of my deeds, and I will never do this again." This constitutes the essence of Confession. The fuller and more detailed the confession one makes, the more praiseworthy is he. . . . So too, those who incurred the judicial penalty of death or punishment of stripes, do not obtain forgiveness by suffering death or receiving stripes unless they repent and confess. Similarly, one who inflicted a wound upon another person, or caused him monetary damage, even though he pays what is due the injured party, does not obtain pardon until he confesses and penitently resolves never to commit the same offense again; as it is said "[when a man or woman] shall commit any sin that men commit . . . then they shall confess" (Nu. 5:6-7).

Repentance, 1

THE PERFECT REPENTANCE

What is perfect repentance? It is so when an opportunity presents itself for repenting an offense once committed, and the offender, while able to commit the offense, nevertheless refrains from doing so, because he is penitent and not out of fear or failure of vigor. For instance, if a man had sinful intercourse with a woman, and after a time was alone with her, his passion for her persisting, his physical powers unabated while he continued to live in the same district where he had sinned, and yet he refrains and does not transgress, he is a sincere penitent. . . . If, however, a person only repented in old age, at a time when he is no longer capable of doing what he had done— although this is not an excellent mode of repentance, it nevertheless avails him and he is accepted as a penitent. Even if one transgressed all his life and only repented on the day of his death and dies penitent, all his iniquities are pardoned to him, as it is said "Before the sun and the light and the moon and the stars are darkened and the clouds return after the rain" (Eccles. 12:2)—which is an allusion to the day of death. Hence the inference that if one remembers his Creator and repents before death, he is forgiven.

Repentance, 2

Although repentance and supplication are always good, they are particularly so and are immediately accepted during the ten days intervening between the New Year and the Day of Atonement, as it is said, "Seek the Lord while He may be found" (Is. 55:6).

Ibid.

THE CALL OF THE SHOFAR

Although the sounding of the Shofar on the New Year is a decree of Holy Writ, still it has a deep meaning, as if saying, "Awake, awake, O sleepers, from your sleep; O slumberers, arouse ye from your slumbers; and examine your deeds, return in repentance, and remember your Creator. Those of you who forget the truth in the follies of the times and go astray, the whole year, in vanity and empti-ness, which neither profit nor save, look to your souls; improve your ways and works. Abandon, everyone of you, his evil course and the thought that is not good."

Ibid.

The Day of Atonement is the time of repentance for all, for the individual as well as for the multitude. It is the goal of the penitential season, appointed unto Israel for pardon and forgiveness. Hence, all are under the obligation of repenting and making confession on the Day of Atonement. . . . And notwithstanding that he had already made confession, he confesses again on the night of the Day of Atone-ment, during the evening service, and again in the morning service, additional, afternoon and concluding services. At which part of the service is the confession made? It is recited by the individual after the *Amidah;* by the reader of the congregation, during the *Amidah,* in its fourth blessing.

Ibid.

REPENTANCE AND RESTITUTION

Repentance and the Day of Atonement only secure forgiveness for transgressions against God; as, for example, when one has partaken of forbidden food or indulged in illicit intercourse, and so forth. But transgressions against one's fellowmen, as for instance, if one wounds, curses or robs his neighbour or commits similar wrongs, are never pardoned till the injured party has received the compensation due to him and has also been appeased. Even though he has made the compensation, the wrong-doer must also appease the one he has injured and ask his forgiveness. Even if a person only annoyed another in words, he has to pacify the latter and entreat him till he has obtained his forgiveness.

Repentance, 2

REPENTANCE AND FORGIVENESS

It is forbidden to be obdurate and not allow oneself to be appeased. On the contrary, one should be easily pacified and find it difficult to become angry. And, when asked by an offender for forgiveness, one should forgive with a sincere mind and willing spirit. Even if one had been much vexed and grievously wronged, he is not to avenge nor bear a grudge. Not so are the hard-hearted heathens. "His resentment keeps for ever" (Amos 1:11). Thus, of the Gibeonites who did not forgive and refused to be appeased, it is said, "Now the Gibeonites were not of the children of Israel" (11 Sam. 21:2).

Repentance, 2

When a man sins against another, the injured party should not hate the offender and keep silent, as it is said concerning the wicked "And Absalom spake to Amnon neither good nor evil, for Absalom hated Amnon" (2. Sam. 13:22). But it is his duty to inform the offender and say to him "Why did you do this to me? Why did you sin against me in this matter?" And thus it is said "Thou shalt surely rebuke thy neighbour" (Lev. 19:17). If the offender repents and pleads for forgiveness, he should be forgiven. The forgiver should not be obdurate, as it is said "And Abraham prayed unto God (for Abimelech)" (Gen. 20:17).

Ethical Conduct (Deot), 6

If a person sinned against another and the latter died before pardon was sought, the sinner should bring ten men, station them at the grave of the deceased, and, in their presence, make the declaration: "I sinned against the Lord God of Israel and against this individual, having committed such and such a wrong against him." If he owed the deceased money, he should pay it to the heirs. If he did not know of any heirs, he should deposit the amount in Court, and make confession.

Repentance, 2

What is Repentance? It consists in this, that the sinner abandon his sin, remove it from his thoughts, and resolve in his heart never to repeat it, as it is said, "let the wicked forsake his way, and the man of iniquity his thoughts" (Is. 55:7); that he regret the past, as it is said "Surely, after that I turned I repented, after that I was instructed, I smote upon my side" (Jer. 31:19); that he calls Him who knows all secrets to witness that he will never return to this sin again, as it is said, "neither will we call any more the works of our hands our God, for in Thee the fatherless findeth mercy" (Hos. 14:4). It is also necessary that he make oral confession and utter the resolutions which he made in his heart.

He who confesses in words and has not in his heart resolved to forsake his sin is like one who immerses himself and keeps in his hands a creeping thing. Unless he casts it away, his immersion is useless. And thus it is said "but who so confesseth and forsaketh [them] shall obtain mercy." (Prov. 28:13). Moreover, it is necessary to specify the sin, as it is said, "O, This people have sinned a great sin, and have made them a god of gold" (Ex. 32:31).

Some of the modes of manifesting repentance are that the penitent cries continuously before the Lord with tears and supplications; gives charity according to his means; keeps far away from that wherein he sinned; changes his name, as much as to say: "I am another individual and not the one who committed those deeds"; changes all his activities for a better course, for the righteous way; and exiles himself from his former place of residence, since exile atones for iniquity, inducing, as it does, humility, meekness, and lowliness of spirit.

Ibid.

It is highly praiseworthy in a penitent to make public confession, openly avow his transgressions and disclose to others his sins against his fellow-men; he should say to them: "Truly, I have sinned against so and so, and did thus and thus to him; and lo, this day I repent and feel remorse." He, however, who is proud and does not publish his trespasses but conceals them, has not achieved complete repentance, as it is said, "He who covereth his transgressions shall not prosper" (Prov. 28:13). This only applies to transgressions in matters between man and man. But sins committed against God, the penitent need not publish. Indeed, it is a mark of effrontery on his part if he does so, but he should repent of them before the Almighty, blessed be He, declaring in detail his sins before Him, and make public confession in general terms; and it is well for him that his iniquity has not become known, as it is said, "Happy is he whose transgression is forgiven, whose sin is covered" (Ps. 32:1).

Ibid.

A person whose iniquities exceed his merits, perishes forthwith in his wickedness, as it is said, "For the multitude of thy iniquity" (Hos. 9:7). So, too, a country, the iniquities of whose inhabitants preponderate, perishes forthwith, as it is said, "The cry of Sodom and Gomorrah, because it is great" (Gen. 18:20). So, with the entire world, if the iniquities of its human population exceed their merits, they are destroyed forthwith, as it is said, "And the Lord saw that the wickedness of man was great in the earth" (Gen. 6:5). This valuation takes into account not the number but the magnitude of merits and iniquities. There may be a single merit that outweighs many iniquities, as it is said, "Because in him there is found some good thing" (I Kings, 14:13). And there may be iniquity that counterbalances many merits, as it is said "But one sinner destroyeth much good" (Ecc. 9:19). The valuation is according to the knowledge of the Omniscient God. He alone knows how to set off merit against iniquities.

Ibid., 3

Whoever regrets the precepts that he had fulfilled and wonders at his meritorious deeds, saying to himself, "What profit have I of them? Would that I had not done them," forfeits the credit for all of them, and none of his meritorious deeds is ever remembered in his favor, as it is said "The righteousness of the righteous shall not deliver him on the day of his transgression" (Ez. 33:12); that is, if he regrets his former good deeds. And even as a man's meritorious deeds and iniquities are balanced at the hour of death, so are the iniquities of every single inhabitant of the earth weighed against his merits annually on the New Year Feast. He who is found righteous is sealed unto life; he who is found wicked is sealed unto death. If one belongs to the intermediate class, sentence on him is suspended till the Day of Atonement. If he repents, he is sealed unto life; if he does not do so, he is sealed unto death.

Ibid.

Do not say that one need only to repent of sinful deeds such as fornication, robbery and theft. Just as a man needs to repent of these sins involving acts, so he needs to investigate and repent of any evil dispositions that he may have, such as hot temper, hatred, jealousy, quarreling, scoffing, eager pursuit of wealth or honors, greediness in eating, and so on. Of all these faults one should repent.

Ibid., 7

Let not the penitent suppose that he is kept far away from the degree attained by the righteous, because of the iniquities and sins that he had committed. This is not so. He is beloved by the Creator, desired by Him, as if he had never sinned. Moreover, his regard is great; since though having tasted sin, he renounced it and overcame his evil passions. The Sages say, "Where penitents stand, the completely righteous cannot stand." This means that the degree attained by penitents is higher than that of those who had never sinned, the reason being that the former had had to put forth a greater effort to subdue their passions than the latter.

The right way for penitents is to be exceedingly humble and meek. If fools taunt them with their former deeds and say to them, "But last night thou didst thus and thus; last night thou wast saying this and that," thou should not be unpleasantly affected by them, but should listen and rejoice, realizing that this will be accounted a merit unto them. For when they are ashamed of their past deeds and humiliated because of them, their merit is increased and their worth enhanced.

All the prophets charged the people concerning repentance. Only through repentance will Israel be redeemed, and the Torah already offered the assurance that Israel will, in the closing period of his exile, finally repent, and thereupon be immediately redeemed, as it is said, "And it shall come to pass, when all these things are come upon thee, the blessing and the curse, which I have set before thee, and thou shalt take it to heart among all the nations, whither the Lord thy God hath driven thee, and shalt return unto the Lord thy God, and hearken to His voice according to all that I command thee this day, thou and thy children with all thine heart, and with all thy soul that the Lord thy God will turn thy captivity, and have mercy upon thee, and will return and gather thee from all the nations, whither the Lord thy God hath scattered thee" (Deut. 30, 1-3).

Great is repentance, for it brings man near to the Divine Presence, as it is said, "Return, O Israel, unto the Lord, thy God" (Hosea 14:2) . . . Further, "If thou return, O Israel, to Me shalt thou return" (Jer. 4:1), which means, 'If thou returnest in repentance, thou wilt cleave to Me,' Repentance brings near those who are far away. But yesterday this person was odious before God, abhorred, estranged, an abomination. Today he is beloved, desirable, near [to God], a friend. So you find that the same expression with which God thrusts sinners away from Him, He employs to bring the penitent near to Him, whether they are individuals or communities, as it is said, "And instead of that which was said unto them: 'Ye are not my people' it shall be said unto them: 'Ye are children of the living God' " (Hosea 2:1).

Ibid.

14. GOD AND TORAH

Maimonides uses "Torah" in its widest sense, including both the Written and the Oral Law. He held to the traditional belief that not only is the Pentateuch of divine origin but also its accepted interpretation, and he branded as unbeliever with no share in the World-to-Come whoever denied the Sinaitic origin of either. Maimonides made the study of Torah transcend all things and incumbent upon all Jews, no matter their station and condition of life. He raised the study of Torah to the highest ideal of young and old, of great and small, more important than the practice of all the laws. Indeed, according to the Talmud, "God Himself sits and studies the Torah" (Ab.Zorah 3b.).

THE THREE CROWNS

With three crowns was Israel crowned—with the crown of the Torah, with the crown of the priesthood and with the crown of sovereignty. The crown of the priesthood was bestowed upon Aaron, as it is said "And it shall be unto him and unto his seed after him, the covenant of an everlasting priesthood" (Num. 25:13). The crown of sovereignty was conferred upon David, as it is said, "His seed shall endure forever, and his throne as the sun before Me" (Ps. 89:37). The crown of the Torah, however, is for all Israel, as it is said, "Moses commanded us a law, an inheritance of the congregation of Jacob" (Deut. 33:4). Whoever desires it can win it. Do not suppose that the other two crowns are greater than the crown of the Torah, for it is said, "By me, kings reign and princes decree justice. By me, princes rule"

(Prov. 8:15, 16). Hence the inference, that the crown of the Torah is greater than the other two crowns.

Study of Torah, 3

Every Israelite is under an obligation to study Torah, whether he is poor or rich, in sound health or ailing, in the vigor of youth or very old and feeble. Even a man so poor that he is maintained by charity or goes begging from door to door, as also a man with a wife and children to support, are under the obligation to set aside a definite period during the day and at night for the study of the Torah, as it is said, "But thou shalt meditate therein day and night" (Joshua 1:8).

Ibid., 1

Until what period in life ought one to study Torah? Until the day of one's death, as it is said, "And lest they (the precepts) depart from thy heart all the days of thy life" (Deut. 4:9). Whenever one ceases to study, one forgets.

Ibid.

Of all precepts, none is equal in importance to the study of the Torah. Nay, study of the Torah is equal to them all, for the study leads to practice. Hence, study always takes precedence of practice.

Ibid., 3

He whose heart prompts him to fulfil the duty properly, and to be crowned with the crown of the Torah, must not allow his mind to be diverted to other subjects. He must not aim at acquiring Torah as well as riches and honor at the same time. "This is the way for the study of Torah: A morsel of bread with salt must thou eat, and water by measure thou must drink; thou must sleep upon the ground and live a life of hardship, the while thou toilest in the Torah" (Ethics of the Fathers 6:4) . . . "The recompense will be proportional to the pains" (*ibid.*, 5:26).

At the Judgment hereafter, a man will first be called to account in regard to his fulfilment of the duty of study, and afterwards concerning his other activities. Hence, the sages said, "A person should always occupy himself with the Torah, whether for its own sake or for other reasons. For the study of the Torah, even when pursued from interested motives, will lead to study for its own sake."

Ibid.

THE STUDY OF TORAH IS NOT IMPOSED ON WOMEN

A woman who studies Torah will be recompensed, but not in the same measure as a man, for study was not imposed on her as a duty, and one who performs a meritorious act which is not obligatory will not receive the same reward as one upon whom it is incumbent and who fulfills it as a duty, but only a lesser reward. And notwithstanding that she is recompensed, yet the Sages have warned us that a man shall not teach his daughter Torah, as the majority of women have not a mind adequate for its study.

Ibid., 1

The Sages said, "A bastard who is a scholar takes precedence to an ignorant High Priest; for it is said, 'More precious is it than rubies' (Prov. 3:15), that is, more to be honored is the scholar than the High Priest who enters the Innermost sanctuary."

Ibid.

TORAH IS NOT IN HEAVEN

In the Torah it is written, "It is not in heaven . . . neither is it beyond the sea" (Deut. 30:12-13). "It is not in heaven," this means that the Torah is not to be found with the arrogant; "nor beyond the seas," that is, it is not found among those who cross the ocean. Hence, our Sages said, "Nor can one who is engaged overmuch in business grow wise" (Ethics of the Fathers 2:6). They have also exhorted us, "Engage little in business and occupy thyself with the Torah" (*Ibid.* 4:12).

Ibid.

TORAH BROOKS NO POSTPONEMENT

Possibly you will say: When I shall have accumulated money, I shall resume my studies; when I shall have provided for my needs and have leisure from my affairs, I shall resume my studies. Should such thought enter your mind, you will never win the crown of Torah. "Rather make the study of the Torah your fixed occupation" (Ethics of the Fathers 1:15) and let your secular affairs engage you casually, and do not say: "When I shall have leisure, I shall study; perhaps you never may have leisure" (*ibid.*, 2:15).

Ibid., 1

How and When Torah Is To Be Studied

The words of the Torah do not abide with one who studies listlessly, nor with those who learn amidst luxury, and high living, but only with one who mortifies himself for the sake of the Torah, constantly enduring physical discomfort, and not permitting sleep to his eyes nor slumber to his eyelids. "This is the Law, when a man dieth in a tent" (Nu. 19:14). The Sages explain the text metaphorically thus: "The Torah only abides with him who mortifies himself in the tents of the wise." . . . The Sages said, "There is a solemn covenant that any one who toils at his studies in the Synagogue will not quickly forget." He who toils privately in learning, will become wise, as it is said, "With the lowly [literally, "the reserved"] is wisdom" (Prov. 11:2). If one recites aloud while studying, what he learns will remain with him. But he who reads silently soon forgets.

Ibid.

Maimonides follows an Arabic custom which uses the night hours for study. He bases his assertions, however, on a verse from the Bible which he quotes.

While it is a duty to study by day and by night, most of one's knowledge is acquired at night. Accordingly, when one aspires to win the crown of the Torah, he should be especially heedful of all his nights and not waste a single one of them in sleep, eating, drinking, idle talk, and so forth, but devote all of them to study of the Torah and words of wisdom. The Sages said, "That sound of the Torah has worth, which is heard by night, as it is said, 'Arise cry out in the night' " (Lam. 2:19): and whoever occupies himself with the study of the Torah at night—a mark of spiritual grace distinguishes him by day, as it is said, "By day the Lord will command His loving kindness, and in the night His song shall be with me, even a prayer unto the God of my life" (Ps. 42:9) . . . One who is able to occupy himself with the Torah and does not do so, or who has read Scripture and learned Mishnah and gave them up for worldly inanities, and abandoned and completely renounced this study, is in-

259

cluded in the condemnation, "Because he hath despised the Word of the Lord." The Sages say, whoever neglects the Torah because of wealth, will at last be forced to neglect it owing to poverty. And whoever fulfils the Torah in poverty, will ultimately fulfil it amidst wealth (Ethics of the Fathers, 4:9, with order of sentences reversed).

Study of Torah, 3

A man should always first study Torah and then marry; for if he takes a wife first, his mind will not be free for study. But if his physical desires are so overpowering as to preoccupy his mind, he should marry and then study Torah.

Ibid., 1

TORAH IS NOT FOR THE ARROGANT

The words of the Torah have been compared to water, as it is said, "O every one that thirsteth, come ye for water" (Is. 55:1); this teaches us that just as water does not accumulate on a slope but flows away, while in a depression it stays, so the Words of the Torah are not to be found in the arrogant or haughty but only in him who is contrite and lowly in spirit, who sits in the dust at the feet of the wise and banishes from his heart lusts and temporal delights; works a little daily, just enough to provide for his needs, if he would otherwise have nothing to eat, and devotes the rest of the day and night to the study of the Torah.

Ibid., 3

A SCROLL OF THE LAW

The "Scroll of the Law" applies only to the Five Books of Moses. The writing calls for considerable expertness, and is usually done by a professional scribe (Sofer). It is written on parchment of "clean" animals and then sewn together.

He [God] has commanded us that every man among us is to write a Scroll of the Law for himself. If he write it with his own hand Scripture considers it as if he received it from Mount Sinai. If he himself cannot write it, he is obliged to purchase one, or he is to hire a scribe who will write it for him. This injunction finds expression in His words, "Now, therefore, write ye this song for you (Deut. 31:19)." Now since it is permissible to write [a Scroll of the Law containing only] certain sections of it, it follows of necessity that by His words, "this song," He has intended to say [that we are to write] in its entirety the Torah which includes "this song."

In the words of the Gemara, Rabba said: "Although one's parents have left him a Scroll of the Law he is nevertheless commanded to write one from his own means, for it is said, 'Now therefore write ye [this song] for you' [—the implication here being that all Israelites are so commanded]. Thereupon Abaye objected: '[We have been taught] The king is to write a Scroll of the Law for himself so that he may not take undue pride in that of his ancestors.' [From this it would appear] that it is only the king who must write a Scroll even where his parents left him one, but that a commoner [is under no such obligation]. To this the reply was: This [teaching] merely points to (the obligation the king is under to write) two Scrolls of the Law, as we have been taught, 'He shall write him [a copy of the Law].' " That is to say there is this difference between the king and a commoner; every man must write only one Scroll of the Law, but the king must write two, as it has been explained in the second chapter of [Tractate] Sanhedrin.

Sefer ha-Mitzvot, Com. 18

THE AIM OF TORAH

The general object of the Law is twofold: the well-being of the soul and the well-being of the body. The well-being of the soul is promoted by correct opinions communicated to the people according to their capacity. Some of these opinions are therefore imparted in plain form, others allegorically. . . . The well-being of the body is established by a proper management of the relations in which we live one to another. This can be attained in two ways; first by removing all violence from our midst; that is to say that we do not do every one as he pleases, desires and is able to do, but every one of us does what contributes towards the common welfare. Secondly by teaching every one of us such good morals as must produce a good social state.

Of these two objects, the well-being of the soul, or the communication of correct opinions, comes undoubtedly first in rank, but the other, the well-being of the body, the government of state and the establishment of the best possible relations among men, is anterior in nature and time. The latter object is required first; it is also treated [in the Law] most carefully and minutely, because the well-being of the soul can only be obtained after that of the body has been secured.

It is clear that the second and superior kind of perfection (well-being) can only be attained when the first perfection has been acquired; for a person that is suffering from great hunger, thirst, heat, or cold, cannot grasp an idea even if communicated by others, much less can he arrive at it by his own reasoning.

The true Law which, as we said, is one, and beside which there is no other Law, *viz.*, the Law of our teacher Moses, has for its purpose to give us the twofold perfection. It aims first at the establishment of good mutual relations among men by removing injustice and creating the noblest feelings. In this way the people in every land are enabled to stay and continue in one condition, and every one can acquire his first perfection. Secondly, it seeks to train us in faith, and to impart correct and true opinions when the intellect is sufficiently developed.

Guide, III, 27

It indicates a high degree of excellence in a man to maintain himself by the labor of his hands. And this was the normal practice of the early saints. Thus, one secures all honor and happiness here and hereafter, as it is said, "When thou eatest of the labor of thine hands, happy shalt thou be, and it shall be well with thee" (Ps. 128:2). Happy shalt thou be in this world, and it shall be well with thee in the world to come, which is altogether good.

Study of Torah, 3

Among the great sages of Israel, some were hewers of wood, drawers of water, while others were kings. Nevertheless, they devoted themselves by day and by night to the study of the Torah. They are included among the transmitters of the tradition in the direct line from Moses.

The ancient sages said: "Peradventure," you will say, "I will study Torah, in order that I may become rich, that I may be a Rabbi, that I may receive a reward in the world to come." It is therefore said, "To love the Lord." Whatever you do, do it out of love only.

Repentance, 10

The sensible course is for a man first to choose an occupation that will give him a livelihood, then buy himself a home; and after that, take a wife. . . . But the foolish first marry; then if one of this sort can afford it, he purchases a house; and, last of all, towards the end of his life, he sets about seeking a trade or lives on charity. Thus it is said in *The Imprecations*, "A wife shalt thou betroth . . . a house shalt thou build . . . a vineyard shalt thou plant" (Deut. 28:30); that is, all your activities shall be in the reverse order of what they should be, so that you will not prosper in your ways. And a blessing is conveyed in the Scriptural text "And David had success in all his ways; and the Lord was with him" (1 Sam. 18:14).

Ethical Conduct, 5

MISUSE OF TORAH

One however who makes up his mind to study Torah and not work but live on charity, profanes the name of God, brings the Torah into contempt, extinguishes the light of religion, brings evil upon himself and deprives himself of life hereafter, for it is forbidden to derive any temporal advantage from the words of the Torah. The sages said, "Whoever derives a profit for himself from the words of the Torah is helping on his own destruction" (Ethics of the Fathers 4:17). They have further charged us, "Make not of them a crown wherewith to aggrandise thyself, nor a spade wherewith to dig" (*Ibid*. 4:7). They likewise exhorted us, "Love thy work, hate lordship" (*Ibid*. 1:10). "All study of the Torah, not conjoined with work, must, in the end, be futile, and become a cause of sin" (*Ibid*. 2:2). The end of such a person will be that he will rob his fellow-creatures.

Study of Torah, 3

REWARDS OF TORAH

Learning was held high among Jews and scholars enjoyed special privileges and immunities, but are warned against taking undue advantage of their position.

It is a duty to honor every scholar, even if he is not one's teacher, as it is said, "Thou shalt rise up before the hoary head, and honor the face of the old man" (Lev. 19:32). The word *Zaken* [rendered "old man"] refers to one who has acquired wisdom. When ought people rise up before him? At the moment that he has approached within four cubits [and they should keep standing] till he has passed out of sight.

Study of Torah, 6

It is improper for a sage to put the people to inconvenience by deliberately passing before them, so that they should have to stand up before him. He should use a short route and endeavor to avoid notice so that they should not be troubled to stand up. The sages were wont to use circuitous and exterior paths, where they were not likely to meet those who might recognize them, so as not to trouble them.

Ibid.

One rises up before an old man, advanced in years, even if he is not a sage. Even a learned man who is young rises up before a man of advanced age. He is not obliged, however, to rise to his full height but need only raise himself sufficiently to indicate courtesy. Even a gentile who is aged should be shown courtesy in speech; and one should extend a hand to support him, as it is said, "Thou shalt rise up before the hoary head," without qualification.

Ibid.

TORAH AND THE SCHOLAR

Scholars do not go out with the rest of the community in building, digging or similar work for the state, so as not to lose the respect of the common people. Nor are they assessed for the cost of building the walls, repairing the gates, paying the watchman's wages, etc., or making a gift to the king. Nor are they obliged to pay a tax, jointly or severally levied upon the inhabitants of a city, as it is said, "Yea, though they hire among the nations, now will I gather them up, and they begin to be diminished by reason of the burden of kings and princes" (Hos. 8:10). So too, if a scholar has goods for sale, he is to be given the opportunity of disposing of them first; and no one else in the market is to be permitted to sell, till the scholar has first sold his stock. Similarly, if he has a cause pending and he is standing among a large number of suitors his cause is taken first, and [during the hearing] he is seated.

Study of Torah, 6

It is exceedingly iniquitous to contemn sages or hate them. Jerusalem was only destroyed when its scholars were treated with contumely, as it is said "But they mocked the messengers of God and despised His words, and scoffed at His prophets" (11 Chron. 36:16).

This means that they "despised those who taught His words." So too, the text "And if ye shall abhor My statutes" (Lev. 26:15) means "if ye abhor the teachers of My statutes." Whoever contemns the sages will have no portion in the world to come, and is included in the censure "For the word of the Lord hath he despised" (Num. 15:31).

Ibid.

ETERNITY OF THE LAW

It is clearly and explicitly set forth in the Torah that its ordinances will endure forever without variation, diminution or addition; as it is said, "All this word which I command you, that shall ye observe to do; thou shalt not add to it, nor take away from it" (Deut. 13:1); and further it is said "but the things that are revealed belong unto us and to our children forever, that we may do all the words of this Law" (Deut. 29:28). Hence the inference that to fulfil all the behests of the Torah is an obligation incumbent upon us forever, as it is said, "It is an everlasting statute throughout your generations." . . . Accordingly, if any one should arise, whether among the Gentiles or among the Israelites, and, showing a sign and token, declare that God had sent him to add a precept to the Torah or take away a precept from the Torah, or give an interpretation to any of the commandments, such as we had not heard from Moses; or should assert that the commandments ordained to Israel are not of perpetual obligation for all generations but only temporary, such a man is a false prophet, because he sets out to deny the prophecy of Moses.

Fundamental Principles of the Torah, 9

While the Law is eternal and may not be changed, much less abrogated, exceptional circumstances make temporary modification of the law permissible.

God knew that the judgments of the Law will always require an extension in some cases and curtailments in others, according to the variety of places, events, and circumstances. He therefore cautioned against such increase and diminution, and commanded, "Thou shalt not add thereto nor diminish from it" (Deut. 13:1): for constant changes would tend to disturb the whole system of the Law, and would lead people to believe that the Law is not of Divine origin. But permission is at the same time given to the wise men, i.e., the great court (Sanhedrin) of every generation to make fences round the judgments of the Law for their protection and to introduce by-laws (fences) in order to insure the keeping of the Law. Such fences once erected remain in force forever. The Mishnah therefore teachs "And make a fence around the Law" (Ab. 1:1). In the same manner they have the power temporarily to dispense with some religious act prescribed in the Law, or to allow that which is forbidden if exceptional circumstances and events require it; but none of the laws can be abrogated permanently. . . . By this method the Law will remain perpetually the same, and will yet admit at all times and under all circumstances such temporary modifications as are indispensable. If every scholar had the power to make such modifications, the multitude of disputes and differences of opinion would have produced an injurious effect. Therefore it was commanded that of the Sages only the great Sanhedrin, and none else, should have this power.

Guide, III, 41

ON CLEAVING UNTO SAGES

The Talmud abounds in illustrations of disciples going to extreme lengths in their earnest desire to learn the ways and customs, conduct and conversation of the Sages (Ber.62a).

He has commanded us that we are to attach ourselves to the Sages, uniting ourselves with them, and being perpetually in their company, associating ourselves with them in every possible manner of fellowship . . . to the end that we may [succeed] in imitating them [in respect of] their deeds [and manner of conduct], and [to the end that] from their words we may acquire faith in the Truth. . . .

Likewise in proof of the obligation [that one] is to take in marriage the daughter of a Sage [and in proof of the obligation we are under] to support the Sages, and to favor them in business [the Sages have cited] His words, "And to Him shalt thou cleave," their explanation [being offered] in the following terms: "How is it ever possible for a man to cleave unto the Divine Presence," it being written, "For the Lord thy God is a devouring fire (Deut. 10:4)"? [Hence we must conclude] that everyone who gives his daughter in marriage to a Sage, or who marries the daughter of a Sage, and he who by means of any possessions, confers a benefit upon a Sage, must be considered in the light [of] this verse as if he were cleaving unto the Divine Presence.

Sefer ha-Mitzvot, Com. 6

THE WAYS OF THE SAGE

If a sage grown old in wisdom, a *nasi,* or *Ab-Bet-Din,* committed a grave offense, he is under no circumstances, to be publicly excommunicated, unless he acted like Jeroboam, the son of Nebat and his confederates. But if he committed other sins less heinous, he is punished with stripes privately, as it is said "Therefore shalt thou stumble in the day and the prophet also shall stumble with thee in the night" (Hosea 4:5): this means that even if he stumbled, conceal it as in the darkness of the night. And we also say to him "Save your self-respect and stay at home" (II Kings 14:16). So too, if any scholar rendered himself liable to excommunication, the Court is forbidden to act precipitately and hastily put him under the ban. The members of the Court should flee from such a procedure, and take no part in it. The saints among the sages gloried in the fact that they never sat in a quorum of Judges to excommunicate a scholar, though they might sit as judges in a court that sentenced a scholar to be punished with stripes, if he had incurred that penalty, and even if the sentence was for contumacy.

Study of Torah, 7

THE SAGE IS MODEST AND FORGIVING

Although a scholar has the right to pronounce the ban to safeguard his honor, it is not creditable for a scholar to accustom himself to this procedure. He should rather close his ears to remarks of the illiterate and take no notice of them, as Solomon, in his wisdom, said "Also pay not heed to all the words that are spoken" (Eccles. 7:21). Such, too, was the way of the ancient saints. They heard themselves reviled and made no reply. Yet more, they forgave the reviler and pardoned him. Great sages, glorying in their commendable practices, said that they never, for the sake of personal honor, imposed on any one the lighter or severer ban. This is the way of scholars, which it is right to follow. It however only applied to cases where one has been reviled in private. But a scholar, who has been treated with contumely or been reviled in public, may not forgive the wrong done to his honor. If he does so, he is punished, for this is contempt of

267

the Torah. We should relentlessly pursue the matter, till the offender begs his pardon, after which he should be forgiven.

Ibid.

THE SAGE IS RECOGNIZED BY HIS CONDUCT

Not only his wisdom and learning win for the scholar the regard of his fellow-men but his inner worth and dealings in the ordinary affairs of life. He must always be on his guard not to lower the dignity of the Torah which he represents.

Even as a sage is recognized by his wisdom and moral principles which distinguish him from the rest of the people, so ought he to be recognized in all his activities, in his food and drink, in the fulfillment of his marital obligations, . . . in his talk, walk, dress, management of his affairs and business transactions.

Ethical Conduct (Deot), 5

A scholar, when speaking, will not shout or scream, like domestic cattle or wild beasts. He will not raise his voice unduly. His speech with all men will be gentle. But while speaking gently, he will be careful to avoid exaggeration which would make his speech sound affected, like the speech of the haughty. He will be the first to greet every one he meets, so that they will be well disposed towards him. He will judge every one favorably. He will dwell on the merits of others and never speak disparagingly of anybody. He loves peace and ensues it. If he feels that his words will be effective and heeded, he will speak; otherwise, he will remain silent. For instance, he will not attempt to appease his neighbour when the latter is exasperated, nor question him concerning his vows immediately after he has made them, but will wait until the man's mind has become cool and composed. He will not attempt to console the mourner while the dead still lies unburied; for till the body is interred, the mourner's mind is preoccupied. And thus he will behave in circumstances of a similar kind. He will not show himself in his neighbor's presence when that person is in disgrace, but will avoid meeting him. He will not deviate from the truth; neither add to it nor detract from it, except in the interest of peace or similar worthy aims. In short, he will limit his speech to topics of wisdom, benevolence, and the like. He will not

268

enter into conversation with a woman on the street, not even with his wife, sister or daughter.

Ibid.

The sage must not be neglectful of his outward appearance. He should be moderate in all his actions so as not to incur the reproach of his fellow-men.

A scholar's dress will be becoming and clean. It is an offense for such a man if a stain or grease or the like is found on his garment. He should not put on robes befitting royalty, such as those embroidered with gold or purple, which attract universal attention; nor, on the other hand, shabby garments such as are worn by the poor, which bring contempt upon the wearer, but he will wear apparel suitable to the middle classes and that is neat.

Ibid.

The sage manages his affairs with judgment and prudence; spends on food, drink, and maintenance of his household, in accordance with his income and the state of his finances. He will not put himself to excessive trouble [to be considered wealthy].

Ibid.

The scholar conducts his business affairs honestly and in good faith. His nay is nay; his yea, yea. In his accounts, he is strict [in meeting his obligations]. At the same time, when buying, he is liberal and does not drive a hard bargain. He pays promptly for his purchases. He declines to act as a surety or trustee; nor will he accept a power of attorney. In commercial matters, he acknowledges liability even where the law would not hold him liable; his principle being to keep his word and not change it. If others have been adjudged liable to him, he is considerate, and even forgives them the amount due. He grants benevolent loans and does favors. He will not encroach on another man's business, and throughout his life will not vex a human being. In short, he belongs to the class of those who are persecuted but do not persecute, who are reviled but do not revile. A man who acts thus is commended in the Scriptural text "And He said unto me, thou art my servant, Israel, in whom I glory" (Is. 49:3).

Ibid.

15. THE PRECEPTS OF THE TORAH

Few other parts of The Guide for the Perplexed *provoked the censure of Maimonides' opponents as the one in which the author attempted to submit to the test of reason the laws and precepts of the Pentateuch, especially the dietary prescriptions, for which thentofore no rational explanation had been offered.*

As THEOLOGIANS are divided on the question whether the actions of God are the result of His wisdom, or only of His will without being intended for any purpose whatever, so they are also divided as regards the object of the commandments which God gave us. Some of them hold that the commandments have no object at all, and are only dictated by the will of God. Others are of opinion that all commandments and prohibitions are dictated by His wisdom and serve a certain aim; consequently there is a reason for each one of the precepts; they are enjoined because they are useful. All of us, the common people as well as the scholars, believe that there is a reason for every precept, although there are commandments the reason of which is unknown to us, and in which the ways of God's wisdom are incomprehensible to us.

There are commandments which are called *hukim,* "ordinances," like the prohibition of wearing garments of wool and linen [*sh'atnez*], boiling meat and milk together, and the sending of the goat [into the wilderness on the Day of Atonement]. Our Sages use in reference to them [such words as] the following: "These are things which I have fully ordained for thee, and you dare not criticize them" (Yoma 67b). But our Sages generally do not think that such precepts have no cause whatever and serve no purpose, for this would lead us to assume that God's actions are purposeless. On the contrary, they hold that even these ordinances have a cause and certainly are intended for some use, although it is not known to us, owing either to the deficiency of our knowledge or the weakness of our intellect. Consequently there is a cause for every commandment; every positive or negative precept serves a useful object. In some cases the usefulness is evident, e.g., the prohibition of murder and theft; in others the usefulness is not so evident, e.g., the prohibition of enjoying the fruit of a tree in the first three years (Lev. 19:23), or the vineyard in which other seeds have been growing (Deut. 22:9).

Guide, III, 26

It is necessary to bear in mind that Scripture only teaches the chief points of those true principles which lead to the true perfection of man, and . . . demands faith in them. Thus Scripture teaches the Existence, the Unity, the Omniscience, the Omnipotence, the Will, and the Eternity of God. All this is given in the form of final results, but they cannot be understood fully and accurately except after the acquisition of many kinds of knowledge. Scripture further demands belief in certain truths, the belief which is indispensable in regulating our social relations; such is the belief that God is angry with those who disobey Him, for it leads us to the fear and dread of disobedience [to the will of God]. There are other truths in reference to the whole of the Universe, which form the substance of the various and many kinds of speculative sciences. . . . But Scripture does not so distinctly prescribe the belief in them as it does in the first case; it is implied in the commandment, "to love the lord" (Deut. 11:13).

But there are other precepts concerning which people are in doubt, and of divided opinion, some believing that they are mere commands, and serve no purpose whatever, whilst others believe that they serve a certain purpose which, however, is unknown to man. Such are those precepts which in their literal meaning do not seem to further any of the above-named results; to impart some truth, to teach some moral, or to remove injustice. They do not seem to have any influence upon the well-being of our soul . . . or upon the well-being of the

271

body by suggesting such ways and rules as are useful in the government of a state, or in the management of a household. . . .

Ibid., 28

I am prepared to tell you my explanation of all these comm-ndments, and to assign for them a true reason supported by proof, with the exception of some minor rules and a few commandments. . . . I will show that all these and similar laws must have some bearing upon one of the following three things, *viz.*, the regulation of our opinions, or the improvement of our social relations, which implies two things, the removal of injustice, and the teaching of good morals.

Ibid.

DIETARY LAWS

Here follows Maimonides' explanation of the reason and purpose of the commandments of the Bible, particularly the ceremonial precepts which apparently have no rational meaning:

I maintain that the food which is forbidden by the Law is unwholesome. There is nothing among the forbidden kinds of food whose injurious character is doubted, except pork (Lev. 11:7), and fat (ibid. 7:23). But also in these cases the doubt is not justified. For pork contains more moisture than necessary [for human body], and too much of the superfluous matter. The principal reason why the Law forbids swine's flesh is to be found in the circumstance that its habits and its food are very dirty and loathsome. It has already been pointed out how emphatically the Law enjoins the removal of the sight of loathsome objects, even in the field and in the camp; how much more objectionable is such a sight in towns. But if it were allowed to eat swine's flesh, the streets and houses would be more dirty than any cesspool, as may be seen at present in the country of the Franks. A saying of our Sages declares: "The mouth of a swine is as dirty as dung itself" (Ber. 25a).

The fat of the intestine makes us full, interrupts the digestion, and produces cold and thick blood; it is more fit for fuel [than for human food].

Blood (Lev. 17:12) and *nebelah*, i.e., the flesh of an animal that died of itself (Deut. 14:21), are indigestible and injurious as food; *trefah*, an animal in a diseased state (Ex. 22:30), is on the way of becoming a *nebelah*.

The characteristics given in the Law (Lev. 11, and Deut. 14) of the permitted animals, *viz.*, chewing the cud and divided hoofs for cattle, and fins and scales for fish, are in themselves neither the cause of the permission when they are present, nor the prohibition when they are absent; but merely signs by which the recommended species of animals can be discerned from those that are forbidden.

The reason why the sinew that shrank is prohibited is stated in the Law (Gen. 32:33).

It is prohibited to cut off the limb of a living animal and eat it, because such acts produce cruelty, and develop it; besides, the heathen kings used to do it; it was also a kind of idolatrous worship to cut off a certain limb of a living animal and eat it.

Meat boiled in milk is undoubtedly gross food, and makes overfull; but I think most probably it is also prohibited because it is somehow connected with idolatry, forming perhaps part of the service, or being used on some festival of the heathen. . . . This I consider as the best reason for the prohibition; but as far as I have seen the books on Sabean rites, nothing is mentioned of this custom.

The commandment concerning the killing of animals is necessary, because the natural food of man consists of vegetables and of the flesh of animals; the best meat is that of the animals permitted to be used for food. No doctor has any doubt about this. Since, therefore, the desire for procuring good food necessitates the slaying of animals, the Law enjoins that the death of the animal should be the easiest. It is not allowed to torment the animal by cutting the throat in a clumsy manner, by poleaxing, or by cutting off a limb whilst the animal is alive.

It is forbidden to kill an animal with its young on the same day (Lev. 22:28), in order that people should be restrained and prevented from killing the two together in such a manner that the young is slain in the sight of the mother; for the pain of the animals under such circumstances is very great. There is no difference in this case between the pain of man and the pain of other living beings, since the love and tenderness of the mother for her young ones is not produced by reasoning but by imagination, and this faculty exists not only in man but in most living beings. This law applies only to ox and lamb, because of the domestic animals used as food these alone are permitted to us, and in these cases the mother recognizes her young.

The same reason applies to the law which enjoins that we should let the mother fly away when we take the young. The egg over which the bird sits and the young that are in need of their mother, are generally unfit for food, and when the mother is sent away she does not see the taking of her young ones, and does not feel any pain. In most cases, however, this commandment will cause man to leave the whole nest untouched because [the young or the eggs], which he is allowed to take, are, as a rule, unfit for food. If the law provides that such grief should not be caused to cattle or birds, how much more careful must we be that we should not cause grief to our fellow-men. . . .

The reason why we cover the blood when we kill animals, and why we do it only when we kill clean beasts and clean birds [in order] that the people should not assemble round the blood for the purpose of eating there as did the Abeans because they thought it was the food of the spirits).

Guide, III, 48

CIRCUMCISION

As regards circumcision, I think that one of its objects is to limit sexual intercourse, and to weaken the organ of generation as far as possible, and this causes men to be moderate. . . . Circumcision simply counteracts excessive lust; for there is no doubt that circumcision weakens the power of sexual excitement, and sometimes lessens the natural enjoyment; the organ necessarily becomes weak when it loses blood and is deprived of its covering from the beginning.

There is, however, another important object in this commandment. It gives to all members of the same faith, i.e., to all believers of the Unity of God, a common bodily sign, so that it is impossible for any one that is a stranger to say that he belongs to them. For sometimes people say so for the purpose of obtaining some advantage, or in order to make some attack upon the Jews. No one, however, should circumcise himself or his son for any other reason but pure faith; for circumcision is not like an incision on the leg, or a burning in the arm, but a very difficult operation. It is also a fact that there is much mutual love and assistance among people that are united by the same sign when they consider it as [the symbol] a covenant. Circumcision is likewise the [symbol of the] covenant which Abraham made in connection with the belief in God's Unity. So also every one that is circumcised enters the covenant of Abraham to believe in the Unity of God, in accordance with the words of the Law, "To be a God unto thee, and to thy seed after thee" (Gen. 17:7). This purpose of circumcision is as important as the first, and perhaps more important.

This law can only be kept and perpetuated in its perfection, if circumcision is performed when the child is very young, and this for three good reasons. First, if the operation were postponed till the boy had grown up, he would perhaps not submit to it. Secondly, the young child has not much pain, because the skin is tender, and the imagination weak; for grown-up persons are in dread and fear of things which they imagine as coming, sometime before these actually occur. Thirdly, when a child is very young, the parents do not think much of him; because the image of the child that leads the parents to love him, has not yet taken a firm root in their minds. That image becomes stronger by the continual sight; it grows with the development of the child, and later on the image begins again to decrease and to vanish. The parents' love for a new born child is not so great as when the child is one year old; and when one year old, it is less loved by them than when six years old. The feeling and love of the father for the child would have led him to neglect the law if he were allowed to wait two or three years, whilst shortly after birth the image is very weak in the mind of the parent, especially of the father who is responsible for the execution of this commandment. The circumcision must take place on the eighth day (Lev. 12:3), because all living beings are after birth, within the first seven days, very weak and exceedingly tender, as if they were still in the womb of their mother; not until the eighth day can they be counted among those that enjoy the life of the world. That this is also the case with beasts may be inferred from the words of Scripture: "Seven days shall it be under the dam" (Lev. 22:27), as if it had no vitality before the end of that period. In the same manner man is circumcised after the completion of seven days, the period has been fixed and has not been left to everybody's judgment.

Guide, III, 49

FORBIDDEN INTERCOURSE

Perfect love, brotherhood and mutual assistance is only found among those near to each other by relationship. The members of a family united by common descent from the same grandfather, or even from some more distant ancestor, have toward each other a certain feeling of love, help each other, and sympathize with each other. To effect this is one of the chief purposes of the Law. Professional harlots were therefore not tolerated in Israel (Deut. 23:18), because their existence would disturb the above relationship between man and man. Their children are strangers to everybody; no one knows to what family they belong; nor does any person recognize them as relatives. And this is the greatest misfortune that can befall any child or father. . . .

Another effect of this prohibition, is the removal of a cause for strife; for if the prohibition did not exist, several persons might by chance come to one woman and would naturally quarrel with each other; they would in many cases kill one another, or they would kill the woman. This is known to have occurred in days of old, "And they assembled themselves by troops in a harlot's house" (Jer. 5:7). In order to prevent these great evils, and to effect the great boon that all men should know their relationship to each other, prostitutes (Deut. 23:17) were not tolerated, and sexual intercourse was only permitted when man has chosen a certain female, and married her openly; for if it sufficed merely to choose her, many a person would bring a prostitute into his house at a certain time agreed upon between them, and say that she was his wife. Therefore it is commanded to perform the act of engagement by which he declares that he has chosen her to take her for his wife, and then to go through the public ceremony of marriage. Comp. "And Boaz took ten men" etc. (Ruth 4:2).

Guide, III, 49

DIVORCE

It may happen that husband and wife do not agree, live without love and peace, and do not enjoy the benefit of a home; in that case he is permitted to send her away. If he had been allowed to divorce her by a mere word, or by turning her out of his house, the wife would wait for some negligence [on the part of the husband], and then come out and say that she was divorced; or having committed adultery, she and the adulterer would contend that she had then been divorced. Therefore the law is that divorce can only take place by means of a document which can serve as evidence, "He shall write her a bill of divorcement" (Deut. 24:1).

Guide, III, 49

FESTIVALS

The object of Sabbath is obvious and requires no explanation. The rest it affords to man is known. One seventh of the life of man, whether small or great, passes thus in comfort, and in rest from trouble and exertion. This the Sabbath effects in addition to the perpetuation and confirmation of the grand doctrine of the Creation.

The object of the Fast of Atonement is evident. The Fast creates a sense of repentance; it is the same day on which the chief of all prophets came down [from Mount Sinai] with the second tables, and announced to the people the divine pardon of their great sin; the day was therefore appointed forever as a day devoted to repentence and true worship of God. For this reason all material enjoyment, all trouble and care for the body, are interdicted, no work may be done; the day must be spent in confession; every one shall confess his sins and abandon them.

Other holy days are appointed for rejoicing and for such pleasant gathering as people generally need. They also promote the good feeling that men should have toward each other in their social and political relations. The appointment of the special days for such purposes has its cause.

The reason for the Passover is well known. It is kept seven days, because the period of seven days is the unit of time intermediate between a day and a month. It is also known how great is the importance of this period in Nature, and in many religious duties. For the Law always follows Nature, and in some respects brings it to perfection; for Nature is not capable of designing and thinking, whilst the Law is the result of the wisdom and guidance of God, who is the author of the intellect of all rational beings.

FEAST OF WEEKS

The Feast of Weeks is the anniversary of the Revelation on Mount Sinai. In order to raise the importance of this day, we count the days that pass since the preceding festival, just as one who expects his most intimate friend on a certain day counts the days and even the hours. This is the reason we count the days that pass since the offering of the Omer, between the anniversary of our departure from Egypt and the anniversary of the Lawgiving. The latter was the aim and object of the exodus from Egypt, and thus God said, "I brought you unto myself" (Ex. 19:4). As that great Revelation took place only on one day, so we keep its anniversary only one day; but if the eating of unleavened bread on Passover were only commanded for one day, we should not have noticed it, and its object would not have been manifest.

NEW YEAR

New Year is likewise kept for one day; for it is a day of repentance, on which we are stirred up from our forgetfulness. For this reason the Shofar is blown on this day. The day is, as it were, a preparation for and introduction to the day of the Fast, as is obvious from the national tradition about the days between New Year and the Day of Atonement.

FEAST OF TABERNACLES

The Feast of Tabernacles, which is a feast of rejoicing and gladness, is kept seven days, in order that the idea of the festival may be more noticeable. The reason why it is kept in the autumn is stated in the Law, "When thou hast gathered in thy labors out of the field" (Ex. 23:16); that is to say, when you rest and are free from pressing labors. . . . Another reason is that in this season it is possible to dwell in tabernacles, as there is neither great heat nor troublesome rain.

The two festivals, Passover and the Feast of Tabernacles, imply also the teaching of certain truths and certain moral lessons. Passover teaches us to remember the miracles which God wrought in Egypt, and to perpetuate their memory; the Feast of Tabernacles reminds of the miracles wrought in the wilderness. The moral lessons derived from these feasts is this: Man ought to remember his evil days in his days of prosperity. He will thereby be induced to thank God repeatedly, to lead a modest and humble life. We eat, therefore, unleavened bread and bitter herbs on Passover in memory of what has happened unto us, and leave [on Succoth]our houses in order to dwell in tabernacles, as inhabitants of desert do that are in want of comfort. We shall thereby remember that this has once been our condition. . . . We join to the Feast of Tabernacles the Feast of the Eighth Day, in order to complete our rejoicing, which cannot be perfect in booths but in comfortable and well-built houses.

As regards the four species of the branches [the branches of the palm tree, the citron, the myrtle, and the willows of the brook] our Sages gave a reason for their use by way of an Agadaic interpretation, the method of which is well known to those who are acquainted with the style of our Sages. . . . I believe that the four species are a symbolical expression of our rejoicing that the Israelites changed the wilderness, "no place of seeds, or figs, or of vines, or of pomegranates, or of water to drink" (Nu. 20:5), to a country full of fruit-trees and rivers. In order to remember this we take the fruit which is the most pleasant of the fruit of the land, branches which smell best, most beautiful leaves, and also the best of herbs, i.e., the willows of the brook. These four kinds have also those three purposes. First, they were plentiful in those days in Palestine, so that every one could easily get them. Secondly, they have a good appearance, they are green; some of them viz., the citron and the myrtle, are also excellent as regards their smell, the branches of the palm-tree and the willow having neither good nor bad smell. Thirdly, they keep fresh and green for seven days, which is not the case with peaches, pomegranates, asparagus, nuts, and the like.

Guide III, 46

RELIGIOUS PRECEPTS OF PAGAN ORIGIN

[We] should not follow the customs of the gentiles, nor imitate them in dress or in their way of trimming the hair, as it is said "And ye shall not walk in the customs of the nation [which I cast out before you]" (Lev. 20:23); "neither shall ye walk in their statutes" (Lev. 18:3); "Take heed to thyself that thou be not ensnared to follow them" (Deut. 12:30). These texts all refer to one theme and warn against imitating them. The Israelite shall, on the contrary, be distinguished from them and recognizable by the way he dresses and in his other activities, just as he is distinguished from them by his knowledge and his principles. And thus is it said, "And I have set you apart from the peoples" (Lev. 20:26). He shall not put on a garment like that specially worn by them nor let the lock of his hair grow in the way they do. Thus, he shall not cut the hair of the head at the sides, leaving the hair in the center untouched as they do—this is called "growing the forelock." Nor shall he cut the hair in front from ear to ear, leaving the hair at the back to grow, as they do. He shall not rear edifices resembling idolatrous temples for the gathering of multitudes, as they do. Whoever does these or similar things is punished with stripes.

Idolatry, 2; *Guide* III, 37

The corners of the head are not to be shaved as the idolators and their priests used to do, as it is said, "ye shall not round the corners of your heads" (Lev. 19:27). Accordingly, if one shaves both temples, even at one time and after one warning, he is punished with stripes twice. Whether he shaves the corners only, leaving the rest of the head untouched, or shaves the entire head at one time, he is punished with stripes, because he shaved the corners. The liability attaches to the man who shaves. But the man who is shaved is not punished with stripes, unless he assisted the barber. One who shaves the corners of a male child's head is punished with stripes.

Ibid.

A woman may not adorn herself with men's special ornaments; as for instance, by placing a mitre or helmet on her head, or putting on a coat of mail or anything similar, or cutting her hair short, after the fashion of a man. And a man must not adorn himself in the modes peculiar to women, as for example, by wearing garments of bright hues, or golden jewelry, in localities where such garments or jewels are only worn by women. In this respect the custom of the country governs. A man who has put on a woman's garment, or a woman who adorns herself in the modes peculiar to men, is punished with stripes. Whoever plucks out white hairs in his beard or in his head from among the dark, is punished with stripes—even if he has removed only one hair—the offense being the use of adornment peculiar to women. So too, one who dyes his hair a dark color, even if he has only dyed a single white hair, is punished with stripes. One whose sex is indetermined and an hermaphrodite may not put on woman's apparel nor cut the hair of their heads in man's fashion; if they do so, they are not punished with stripes.

Ibid., 12

An Israelite, having access to royalty, who has to appear before gentile sovereigns, and to whom it would be a disgrace not to look like gentiles, is permitted to put on apparel like theirs, and cut his hair in front, after their fashion.

Ibid., 11

Tattooing mentioned in the Torah (Lev. 19:28) consists in cutting the flesh and filling up the cut with pigments, ink, or other printing matter which leaves an indelible mark. This is the custom of the heathens who used to mark themselves for idolatry, as much as to say that the tattooed was a slave sold to the idol and marked for its service. As soon as one prints with any material that leaves an indelible mark, having previously made an incision in any part of the body, whether it be a man or woman, that person incurs the punishment of stripes. . . .

Ibid., 12

SACRIFICES

Maimonides shot his boldest bolt when he pulled off the sacrificial system from its lofty pedestal with its elaborate prescriptions and regulations and priestly functionaries, and declared it to be nothing more than a superstitious cult of pagan idolatrous worship tolerated in Judaism only because of its strong hold on primitive Israel.

It is impossible to go suddenly from one extreme to the other; it is therefore according to the nature of man impossible for him suddenly to discontinue everything to which he has been accustomed. Now God sent Moses to make [the Israelites] a kingdom of priests and holy nation (Ex. 19:6) by means of the knowledge of God. . . . The Israelites were commanded to devote themselves to His service. . . . But the custom which was in those days general among all men, and the general mode of worship in which the Israelites were brought up, consisted in sacrificing animals in the temples which contained certain images, to bow down to those, and to burn incense before them. It was in accordance with the wisdom and plan of God, as displayed in the whole Creation, that He did not command us to give up and to discontinue all these manners of service; for to obey such a commandment would have been contrary to the nature of man, who generally cleaves to that to which he is used. It would in those days

281

have made the same impression as a prophet would make at present if he called us to the service of God and told us in His name that we should not pray to Him, not fast, not seek His help in time of trouble, that we should serve Him in thought and not by any action.

For this reason God allowed this kind of service to continue; He transferred to His service that which had formerly served as a worship of created beings, and of things imaginary and unreal, and commanded us to serve Him in the same manner; *viz.*, to build Him a temple; to have the altar erected in His name; to offer sacrifices to Him; to bow down to Him, and to burn incense before Him. He has forbidden to do any of these things to any other being. He selected priests for the service in the temple. He made it obligatory that certain gifts of the Levites and the priests should be assigned to them for their maintenance while they are engaged in the service of the Temple and its sacrifices. By this Divine plan it was effected that the traces of idolatry were blotted out, and the truly great principles of our faith, the Existence and Eternity of God, were established.

As the sacrificial system is not the primary object [of the commandments about sacrifice], whilst supplications, prayers, and similar kinds of worship are nearer to the primary object, and indispensable for obtaining it, a great difference in the Law was made between these two kinds of service. The one kind which consists of offering sacrifices, although the sacrifices are offered in the name of God, has not been made obligatory for us to the same extent as it had been before. We were not commanded to sacrifice in every place, and in every time, or to build a temple in every place, or to permit any one who desires to become priest and to sacrifice. On the contrary, all this is prohibited unto us. Only one temple has been appointed, "in the place which the Lord shall choose" (Deut. 12:26); in no other place is it allowed to sacrifice, and only the members of a particular family were allowed to officiate as priests. All these restrictions served to limit this kind of worship and keep it within those bounds which God did not think necessary to abolish sacrificial service altogether. But prayer and supplication can be offered everywhere and by every person. . . .

Because of this principle, the Prophets in their books are frequently found to rebuke their fellow-men for being over-zealous and exerting themselves too much in bringing sacrifices; the prophets thus distinctly declared that the object of the sacrifices is not very essential, and that God does not require them. Samuel therefore said, "Hath the Lord as great delight in burnt-offerings and sacrifices as in obeying the voice of the Lord?" (I Sam. 15:22) Isaiah exclaimed, "To what purpose is the multitude of your sacrifices unto me? saith the Lord" (Isa. I, 11). Jeremiah declared: "For I spake not unto your fathers, nor commanded them in the day that I brought them out of the land of Egypt, concerning burnt-offerings, sacrifices. But this thing commanded I them, saying, Obey my voice, and I will be your God, and ye shall be my people" (Jer. 7:22,23).

Guide, III, 32

16. EDUCATION

The religious and moral training of children is one of the basic principles of the Jewish pattern of living. In the Shema *the Unity and love of God is coupled with the admonition, "And thou shalt teach them diligently unto thy children." In Bible times, the instruction of the Hebrew child was made mandatory upon the father, but with the changed economic condition and because not every parent could carry out the behest of the Torah, education became a highly specialized institution with trained teachers and state support. Joshua ben Gamla was credited with having pioneered in the education of the young. As far back as the second century he revolutionized the system of education by instituting public schools for boys of six and seven in all the cities of Palestine for which he received the praise of his colleagues that he prevented the Torah from being forgotten in Israel.*

Moses Maimonides was not himself a teacher nor was he the head of an academy, but he devised rules and methods of education which justly assign him a place among the foremost pedagogues. While he reflects in the main the thoughts and ideas of the Rabbis of the Talmud, he reveals at times attitudes which make him stand out as an independent philosopher of Jewish education. He gives priority to education; he makes it equal, if not superior to all the precepts of the Torah; he makes the greatest demands on the teacher, and he would not have him engage in any other occupation; he is solicitous about the pupil's physical health and well-being; he demands that the teacher be proficient in the Bible and in Hebrew grammar, a qualification not demanded by any other man before him. That Maimonides did not include women in his scheme of education was due to the influence of the Rabbis who felt that their wifely and motherly duties were superior to their every other occupation.

284

A FATHER'S DUTY TO HIS SON

It is a duty of the father to teach his young son Torah; as it is said, "And ye shall teach them, to your children, talking of them" (Deut. 11:19). A woman is under no obligation to teach her son, since only one whose duty it is to learn has a duty to teach.

Study of Torah, 1

Just as it is a man's duty to teach his son, so it is his duty to teach his grandson, as it is said, "Make them known unto thy children and thy children's children" (Deut. 4:9). This obligation is to be fulfilled not only toward a son and grandson. A duty rests on every scholar in Israel to teach all disciples [who seek instruction from him], even if they are not his children, as it is said "And thou shalt teach them diligently unto thy children" (Deut. 6:7). On traditional authority, the term "thy children" includes disciples, for disciples too are called children, as it is said "And the sons of the prophets came forth" (II Kings 2:3). This being so, why does the precept [concerning instruction] specifically mention (Deut. 4:9) a man's son and a son's son? To impress upon us that the son should receive instruction in preference to a grandson, and a grandson in preference to another man's son.

If a father has not had his son taught, it is the duty of the latter, as soon as he realizes his deficiencies, to acquire knowledge for himself, as it is said "That ye may learn them and observe to do them" (Deut. 5:1). And so, too, you will find that study in all cases takes precedence to practice, since study leads to practice, but practice does not lead to study.

When should a father commence his son's instruction in Torah? As soon as the child begins to talk, the father should teach him the text "Moses commanded us a law" (Deut. 33:4), and the first verse of the *Shema* ["Hear O Israel, the Lord our God, the Lord is One"] (Deut. 6:4). Later on, according to the child's capacity, the father should teach him a few verses at a time, till he attains the age of six or seven years, when he should take him to a teacher of young children.

Ibid.

If a man needs to learn Torah and has a son who needs instruction, his own requirements are to be satisfied first. But if his son has better capacity and greater ability to grasp what he learns, then the son's education takes precedence. Still, even in this case, the father must not wholly neglect the study of the Torah. For, just as it is incumbent on him to have his son taught, so is he under an obligation to obtain instruction for himself.

Ibid.

TEACHER AND PUPIL

Maimonides follows the rabbinic tradition on the appointment of teachers and the age and number of children but, as physician, he adds "the strength of the individual child and its physical development" must be considered.

Teachers of young children are to be appointed in each province, district and town. If a city has made no provision for the education of the young, its inhabitants are placed under a ban, till such teachers have been engaged. And if they persistently neglect this duty, the city is excommunicated, for the world is only maintained by the breath of school children.

Study of Torah, 2

Children are to be sent to school at the age of six or seven years, according to the strength of the individual child and its physical development. But no child is to be sent to school under six years of age. The teacher may chastise his pupils to inspire them with awe. But he must not do so in a cruel manner or in a vindictive spirit. Accordingly, he must not strike them with whips or sticks, but only use a small strap. He is to teach them the whole day and part of the night, so as to train them to study by day and by night. And there is to be no holiday except on the eve of the Sabbath or festival, towards the close of the day, and on festivals. On Sabbaths, pupils are not taught a new lesson, but they repeat what they have already learnt previously, even if only once. Pupils must not be interrupted at their studies, even for the rebuilding of the Temple.

Twenty-five children may be put in charge of one teacher. If the number in the class exceeds twenty-five but is not more than forty, he should have an assistant to help with the instruction. If there are more than forty, two teachers must be appointed.

Ibid.

With Maimonides' known hostility to remunerative instruction in the Law he is making a large concession in the case of training of children.

If it is the custom of the country for a teacher of children to receive remuneration, the father is to pay the fee, and it is his duty to have his son taught, even if he has to pay for the instruction, till the child has gone through the whole of the Written Law. Where it is the custom to charge a fee for teaching the Written Law, it is permissible to take payment for such instruction. It is forbidden however to teach the Oral Law for payment, for it is said "Behold, I have taught you statutes and ordinances, even as the Lord, my God, commanded me" (Deut. 4:5). This means: "Even as I [Moses] learnt [from God] without payment, so have ye learnt from me, gratuitously. And throughout the Generations, whenever you teach, do so gratuitously, even as you learnt from me." If a person cannot find any one willing to teach him without remuneration, he should engage a paid teacher, as it is said "Buy the truth" (Prov. 23:23).

Ibid., 1

The time allotted to study should be divided into three parts. A third should be devoted to the Written Law; a third to the Oral Law; and the last third should be spent in reflection, deducing conclusions from premises, developing implications of statements, comparing dicta, studying the hermeneutical principles by which the Torah is interpreted, till one knows the essence of these principles, how to deduce what is permitted and what is forbidden from what one has learned traditionally. This is termed Talmud.

Ibid.

A teacher who leaves the children and goes out (when he should be teaching them), or does other work while he is with them, or teaches lazily, falls under the ban "Cursed be he that doeth the work of the Lord with a slack hand" (Jer. 48:10). Hence, it is not proper to appoint any one as teacher unless he is God-fearing and well versed in reading and in grammar.

Ibid., 2

A child may be transferred from one teacher to another who is more competent in reading or grammar, only, however, if both the teacher and the pupil live in the same town and are not separated by a river. But we must not take the child to a school in another town or even across a river in the same town, unless it is spanned by a firm bridge, nor likely soon to collapse.

If one of the residents in an alley or even in a court wishes to open a school, his neighbors cannot resent it. Nor can a teacher, already established, object to another teacher opening a school next door to him, either for new pupils or even with the intention of drawing away pupils from the existing school, for it is said, "The Lord was pleased for His righteousness' sake, to make the Torah great and glorious" (Is. 42:21).

Ibid.

If the teacher taught and his pupils did not understand, he should not be angry with them or fall into a rage, but should repeat the lesson again and again till they have grasped the full meaning of the *halakah* [rule] he is expounding. So also, the pupil should not say "I understand" when he has not understood, but should ask again and again. And if the master is angry with him and storms at him, he should say "Master, it is Torah. I need to learn, and my intellectual capacities are deficient."

Ibid., 4

A disciple should not feel ashamed before his fellow-students who grasp the lesson after hearing it once or twice, while he needs to hear it several times before he knows it. For if this makes him feel ashamed, he will go through school without having learnt anything. The ancient sages accordingly said, "A bashful man cannot learn, nor a passionate man teach" (Ethics of Fathers 2:6). These observations only apply when the students' lack of understanding is due to the difficulty of the subject or to their mental deficiency. But if the teacher clearly sees that they are negligent and indolent in their study of the Torah and that this is the cause of their failure to understand, it is his duty to scold them and shame them with words of reproach, and so stimulate them to be keen. And in this regard, the sages said "Arouse awe in the pupils."

Ibid.

Reverence must be shown by pupil to his teacher. But, on the other hand, it is the teacher's duty to win his pupil's respect and affection. "Much have I learned from my teachers, more from my fellow-students, most from my pupils."

Just as a person is commanded to honor and revere his father, so he is under an obligation to honor and revere his teacher, even to a greater extent than his father; for his father gave him life in this world, while his teacher who instructs him in wisdom, secures for him life in the world to come. If he sees an article that his father had lost and another article that his teacher had lost, the teacher's property should be recovered first, and then the father's. If his father and his teacher are loaded with burden, he should first relieve his teacher and then his father. If his father and teacher are in captivity, he should first ransom his teacher. But if his father is a scholar, though not of the same rank as his teacher, he should first recover his father's lost property and then his teacher's.

There is no honor higher than that which is due to the teacher; no reverence profounder than that which should be paid him. The Sages said "Reverence for thy teacher shall be like the fear of Heaven" (Ethics of the Fathers 4:15). They further said "Whoever distrusts the authority of his teacher—it is as if he disputes with the *Shekinah!*; as it is said "When they strove against the Lord" (Nu. 26:9). Whoever starts a quarrel with his teacher, it is as if he started a quarrel with the *Shekinah;* as it is said, "Where the children of Israel strove with the Lord, and He was sanctified in them" (Nu. 20:13). And whoever cherishes resentment against his teacher—it is as if he cherishes resentment against the Lord, as it is said "Your murmurings are not against us, but against the Lord" (Ex. 16:8). Whoever harbors doubts about his teacher—it is as if he harbors doubts about the *Shekinah;* as it is said, "And the people spoke against God and against Moses" (Nu. 21:3).

Ibid., 5

If a pupil saw his teacher violating the ordinances of the Torah, he should say to him, "Thus and thus hast thou taught us." Whenever a pupil recites a dictum in his teacher's presence, he should say, "Thus, our master, hast thou taught us." He should never quote a dictum that he has not heard from his teacher without the authority for it. When his teacher dies, he rends all the garments he wears till he bares his breast. These rents he never sews up. These rules apply only to the chief teacher from whom he has learnt most of what he knows. But his relation to one from whom he did not acquire most of his knowledge is that of a junior to a senior fellow-student. . . .

Ibid.

As pupils are bound to honor their teacher, so a teacher ought to show courtesy and friendliness to his pupils. The Sages said "Let the honor of thy disciples be as dear to thee as thine own" (Ethics of the Fathers 4:15). A man should take an interest in his pupils and love them, for they are his spiritual children who will bring him happiness in this world and in the world hereafter.

Ibid., 4

Disciples increase the teacher's wisdom and broaden his mind. The sages said, "Much wisdom I learnt from my teachers, more from my colleagues; from my pupils, most of all." Even as a small piece of wood kindles a large log, so a pupil of small attainments sharpens the mind of his teacher, so that by his questions, he elicits glorious wisdom.

Ibid.

THE HEBREW LANGUAGE

You know how we condemn lowness of speech, and justly so, for speech is likewise peculiar to man and a boon which God granted to him that he may be distinguished from the rest of living creatures. Thus God says, "Who gave a mouth to man?" (Ex. 4:11); and the prophet declares, "The Lord God hath given me a learned tongue" (Is. 50:4). This gift, therefore, which God gave us in order to enable us to perfect ourselves, to learn and to teach, must not be employed in doing that which is for us most degrading and perfectly disgraceful; we must not imitate the songs and tales of ignorant and lascivious people. It may be suitable to them, but is not fit for those who are told, "And ye shall be unto me a kingdom of priests and a holy nation" (Ex. 19:6). Those who employ the faculty of thinking and speaking in the service of that sense which is no honor to us, who think more than necessary of drink and love, or even sing of these things; they employ and use the divine gift in acts of rebellion against the Giver, and in the transgression of His commandments. To them the following verse may be applied: "And I multiplied her silver and gold, which they prepared for Baal" (Hos. 2:10).

Guide, III, 8

I have also a reason and cause for calling our language the holy language—do not think it is exaggeration or error on my part, it is perfectly correct—the Hebrew language has no special name for the organ of generation in females or in males, not for the act of generation itself, nor for semen, nor for secretion. The Hebrew has no original expression for these things, and only describes them in figurative language and by way of hints, as if to indicate thereby that these things should not be mentioned and should therefore have no names; we ought to be silent about them, and when we are compelled to mention them, we must manage to employ for that purpose some suitable expressions, although these are generally used in a different sense.

Ibid.

JEWS AND THE SCIENCES

Like many others of his time, Maimonides held that the Jews were formerly ardent followers of the sciences in which they obtained brilliant results but which were subsequently forgotten both because of their misfortunes and owing to the fact that they were taught orally and did not have it written down. He also gives the reason why the "Oral Law" remained "oral" and was not more widely disseminated among the people.

We have already mentioned that these theories [the constitution of the Universe] are not opposed to anything taught by our Prophets or by our Sages. Our nation is wise and perfect, as has been declared by the Most High through Moses, who made us perfect; "Surely this great nation is a wise and understanding people" (Deut. 4:6). But when wicked barbarians have deprived us of our possessions, put an end to our science and literature, and killed our wise men, we have become ignorant; this has been foretold by the Prophets, when they pronounced the punishment for our sins: "The wisdom of their wise men shall perish, and the understanding of their prudent men shall be hid" (Isa. 29:14). We are mixed up with other nations; we have learned their opinions, and followed their ways and acts. The Psalmist deploring this imitation of the actions of other nations, says, "They were mingled among the nations, and learned their works" (Ps. 106:35). Isaiah likewise complained that Israelites adopted the opinions of their neighbors and says, "And they please themselves in the children of strangers" (Isa. 2:6); or, according to the Aramaic version of Jonathan, son of Uziel, "And they walk in the ways of the nations." Having been brought up among persons untrained in philosophy, we are inclined to consider these philosophical opinions as foreign to our religion, just as uneducated persons find them foreign to their own notions. But, in fact, it is not so.

Guide, II, 11

Know that many branches of science relating to the correct solution of these problems, were once cultivated by our forefathers, but were in the course of time neglected, especially in consequence of the tyranny which barbarous nations exercised over us. Besides, speculative studies were not open to all men . . . only the subjects taught in the Scriptures were accessible to all. Even the traditional Law was not originally committed to writing, in conformity with the rule to which our nation generally adhered, "Things which I have communicated to you orally, you must not communicate to others in writing." With reference to the Law, this Law was very opportune; for while it remained in force, it averted the evils which happened subsequently, viz., great diversity of opinion, doubts as to the meaning of written words, slips of the pen, dissensions among the people, formation of new sects, and confused notions about practical subjects. The traditional teaching was in fact, according to the words of the Law, entrusted to the Great Tribunal, as we have already stated in our works on the Talmud.

Introduction to *Mishneh Torah* and
Mishnah Commentary

Care having been taken for the sake of obviating injurious influences, that the Oral Law should not be recorded in a form accessible to all, it was but natural that no portion of "the secrets of the Law" [i.e., metaphysical problems] would be permitted to be written down or divulged for the use of all men. These secrets . . . were orally communicated by a few able men to others who were equally distinguished. Hence the principle applied by our teachers, "The secrets of the Law can only be entrusted to him who is a counsellor, a cunning artificer, etc." The natural effect of this practice was that our nation lost the knowledge of those important disciplines. Nothing but a few remarks and allusions are to be found in the Talmud and the Midrashim, like a few kernels involved in such a quantity of husk that the reader is generally occupied with the husk, and forgets that it encloses a kernel.

Ibid.

17. PROPHECY, PROPHETS, AND MOSES

Prophecy is the product of a peculiar gift of the spirit endowed by God corresponding to the man's character, intellectual and moral perfection and the development of one's imaginative faculty. The Divine Influence does not rest upon every prophet in the same degree. Maimonides enumerates eleven degrees of prophets with Moses occupying the highest rank.

IT IS ONE of the basic principles of religion that God inspires men with the prophetic gift. But the spirit of prophecy only rests upon the wise man who is distinguished by great wisdom and strong moral character, whose passions never overcome him in anything whatsoever, but who by his rational faculty always has his passions under control, and possesses a broad and sedate mind. When one, abundantly endowed with these qualities and physically sound, enters the "Paradise" . . . and continuously dwells upon those great and abstruse themes, having the right mind capable of comprehending and grasping them; sanctifying himself, withdrawing from the ways of the ordinary run of men who walk in the obscurities of the times, zealously training himself not to have a single thought of the vanities of the age and its intrigues, but keeping his mind disengaged, concentrated on higher things . . . on such a man the Holy Spirit will promptly descend. And when the spirit rests upon him, his soul will mingle with the angels called *Ishim*. . . . He will be changed into another man and will realize that he is not the same as he had been, and has been exalted above other wise men, even as it is said of Saul

"And thou shalt prophesy with them, and shalt be turned into another man" (1 Sam. 10:6).

Fundamental Principles of the Torah, 7

OPINIONS CONCERNING PROPHECY

There are as many different opinions concerning Prophecy as concerning the Eternity or Non-Eternity of the Universe. For we have shown that those who assume the existence of God as proved may be divided into three classes, according to the view they take of the question, whether the Universe is eternal or not. Similarly there are three different opinions on Prophecy. I will not notice the view of the Atheist; he does not believe in the Existence of God, much less in Prophecy; but I will content myself with discussing the various opinions [on Prophecy] held by those who believe in God.

Among those who believe in Prophecy, and even among our coreligionists, there are some ignorant people who think as follows: God selects any person He pleases, inspires him with the spirit of Prophecy, and entrusts him with a mission. It makes no difference whether that person be wise or stupid, old or young; provided he be, to some extent, morally good. For these people have not yet gone so far as to maintain that God might also inspire a wicked person with His spirit. They admit that this is impossible, unless God has previously caused him to improve his ways.

The philosophers hold that prophecy is a certain faculty of man in a state of perfection, which can only be obtained by study. Although the faculty is common to the whole race, yet it is not fully developed in each individual, either on account of the individual's defective constitution, or on account of some other external cause. This is the case with every faculty common to a class. It is only brought to a state of perfection in some individuals, and not in all; but it is impossible that it should not be perfect in some individual of the class; and if the perfection is of such a nature that it can only be produced by an agent, such an agent must exist. Accordingly, it is impossible that an ignorant person should be a prophet; or that a person being no prophet in the evening, should, unexpectedly on the following morning, find himself a prophet, as if prophecy were a thing that could be found unintentionally. But if a person, perfect in his intellectual and moral faculties, and also perfect, as far as possible, in his imaginative faculty, prepares himself in the manner

294

which will be described, he must become a prophet; for prophecy is a natural faculty of man. It is impossible that a man who has the capacity for prophecy should prepare himself for it without attaining it, just as it is impossible that a person with a healthy constitution should be fed well, and yet not properly assimilate his food; and the like.

The third view is that which is taught in Scripture, and which forms one of the principles of our religion. It coincides with the opinion of the philosophers in all points except one. For we believe that, even if one has the capacity for prophecy, and has duly prepared himself, it may yet happen that he does not actually prophesy. It is in that case the will of God [that withholds from him the use of the faculty]. According to my opinion, this fact is as exceptional as any other miracle, and acts in the same way. For the laws of Nature demand that every one should be a prophet, who has a proper physical constitution, and has been duly prepared as regards education and training. If such a person is not a prophet, he is in the same position as a person who, like Jeroboam (I Kings 13:4), is deprived of the use of his hand, or of his eyes, as was the case with the army of Syria, in the history of Elisha (II Kings 6:18). As for the principle which I laid down, that preparation and perfection of moral and rational faculties are the *sine quâ non*, our Sages say exactly the same: "The spirit of prophecy only rests upon persons who are wise, strong, and rich." We have explained these words in our Commentary on the Mishnah, and in our large work. We stated there that the Sons of the Prophets were constantly engaged in preparation. That those who have prepared themselves may still be prevented from being prophets, may be inferred from the history of Baruch, the son of Nerijah; for he followed Jeremiah, who prepared and instructed him; and yet he hoped in vain for prophecy; comp., "I am weary with my sighing, and rest have I not found." He was then told through Jeremiah, "Thus saith the Lord, Thus shalt thou say to him, Thou seekest for thee great things, do not seek" (Jer. 45:5). It may perhaps be assumed that prophecy is here described as a thing "too great" for Baruch. So also the fact that "her prophets did not find visions from the Lord" (Lam. 2:9), may be considered as the result of the exile of her prophets.

There are, however, numerous passages in Scripture as well as in the writings of our Sages, which support the principle that it depends chiefly on the will of God who is to prophesy, and at what time; and that He only selects the best and the wisest. We hold that fools and ignorant people are unfit for this distinction. It is as impossible for any one of these to prophesy as it is for an ass or a frog; for prophecy is impossible without study and training; when these have created the possibility, then it depends on the will of God whether the possibility is to be turned into reality. We must not be misled by the words of Jeremiah (4:5), "Before I formed thee in the womb I knew thee, and before thou camest forth from the womb I have sanctified thee"; for this is the case with all prophets; there must be a physical preparation from the beginning of their existence, as will be explained. As to the words, "For I am young" (*ibid.*, ver. 6), it is well known that the pious Joseph, when he was thirty years old, is called by the Hebrew "young" (*na'ar*); also Joshua, when he was nearly sixty years old. For the statement, "and his minister Joshua, the son of Nun, was young," occurs in the account of the Golden Calf (Exod. 33:11). Moses was then eighty-one years old, he lived one hundred and twenty years; Joshua, who survived him fourteen years, lived one hundred and ten years and must consequently have been at least fifty-seven years old at the time when the Golden Calf was made, and yet he is called *na'ar*, "young." Nor must we be misled by prophecies like the following: "I will pour out my spirit over-all flesh, and your sons and your daughters shall prophesy"; since it is distinctly stated what is meant by "prophesy" in this place, viz., "Your old men will dream dreams, your young men shall see visions." For we call also prophets all those who reveal something unknown by surmises, or conjectures, or correct inferences. Thus "prophets of Baal" and "of Asherah" are mentioned in Scripture. And God says, "If there arise among you a prophet or a dreamer of dreams," etc. (Deut. 13:2). As for the revelation on Mount Sinai, all saw the great fire, and heard the fearful thunderings, that caused such an extraordinary terror; but only those of them who were duly qualified were prophetically inspired, each one according to his capacities. Therefore it is said, "Come up unto the Lord, thou and Aaron, Nadab and Abihu." Moses rose to the highest degree of prophecy, according to the words, "And Moses alone shall come near the Lord." Aaron was below him, Nadab and Abihu below Aaron, and the seventy elders below Nadab and Abihu, and the rest below the latter, each one according to his degree of perfection. Similarly our Sages wrote:

Moses had his own place and Aaron his own. Since we have touched upon the revelation on Mount Sinai, we will point out in a separate chapter what may be inferred as regards the nature of that event, both from the Scriptural text, in accordance with reasonable interpretation, and from the words of our Sages.

Guide, II, 32

MOSES ON MOUNT SINAI

It is clear to me that what Moses experienced at the revelation on Mount Sinai was different from that which was experienced by all the other Israelites, for Moses alone was addressed by God, and for this reason the second person singular is used in the Ten Commandments; Moses then went down to the foot of the mount and told his fellow-men what he had heard. Comp., "I stood between the Lord and you at that time to tell you the word of the Lord" (Deut. 5:5). Again, "Moses spake, and God answered him with a loud voice" (Exod. 19:19). In the Mechilta our Sages say distinctly that he brought to them every word as he had heard it. Furthermore, the words, "In order that the people hear when I speak with thee" (Exod. 19:14), show that God spoke to Moses, and the people only heard the mighty sound, not distinct words. It is to the perception of this mighty sound that Scripture refers in the passage, "When ye hear the sound" (Deut. 5:20); again it is stated, "You heard a sound of words" (*ibid.*, 4:12), and it is not said "You heard words"; and even where the hearing of the words is mentioned, only the perception of the sound is meant. It was only Moses that heard the words, and he reported them to the people. This is apparent from Scripture, and from the utterances of our Sages in general. There is, however, an opinion of our Sages frequently expressed in the Midrashim, and found also in the Talmud, to this effect: The Israelites heard the first and the second commandments from God, i.e., they learnt the truth of the principles contained in these two commandments in the same manner as Moses, and not through Moses. For these two principles, the existence of God and His Unity, can be arrived at by means of reasoning, and whatever can be established by proof is known by the prophet in the same way as by any other person; he has no advantage in this respect. These two principles were not known through prophecy alone. Comp., "Thou hast been shown to know that," etc. (Deut. 4:35). But the rest of the commandments are of an ethical and authoritative character, and do not contain [truths] perceived by the intellect.

Notwithstanding all that has been said by our Sages on this subject, we infer from Scripture as well as from the words of our Sages, that the Israelites heard on that occasion a certain sound which Moses understood to proclaim the first two commandments, and through Moses all other Israelites learnt them when he in intelligible sounds repeated them to the people. Our Sages mention this view, and support it by the verse, "God hath spoken once; twice have I heard this" (Ps. 62:12). They state distinctly, in the beginning of *Midrash Hazita*, that the Israelites did not hear any other command directly from God; comp. "A loud voice, and it was not heard again" (Deut. 5:19). It was after this first sound was heard that the people were seized with the fear and terror described in Scripture, and that they said, "Behold the Lord our God has shown us, etc., and now why shall we die, etc. Come thou near," etc. Then Moses, the most distinguished of all mankind, came the second time, received successively the other commandments, and came down to the foot of the mountain to proclaim them to the people, whilst the mighty phenomena continued; they saw the fire, they heard the sounds, which were those of thunder and lightning during a storm, and the loud sound of the shofar; and all that is said of the many sounds heard at that time, e.g., in the verse, "and all the people perceived the sounds," etc., refers to the sound of the shofar, thunder, and similar sounds. But the voice of the Lord, that is, the voice created for that purpose, which was understood to include the diverse commandments, was only heard once, as is declared in the Law, and has been clearly stated by our Sages in the places which I have indicated to you. When the people heard this voice their soul left them; and in this voice they perceived the first two commandments. It must, however, be noticed that the people did not understand the voice in the same degree as Moses did.

Guide, II, 33

THE ESSENCE OF PROPHECY: IMAGINATION
AND DIVINE INFLUENCE

Prophecy is, in truth and reality, an emanation sent forth by the Divine Being through the medium of the Active Intellect, in the first instance to man's rational faculty, and then to his imaginative faculty; it is the highest degree and greatest perfection man can attain; it consists in the most perfect development of the imaginative faculty. Prophecy is a faculty that cannot in any way be found in a person, or acquired by man, through a culture of his mental and moral faculties; for even if these latter were as good and perfect as possible, they would be of no avail, unless they were combined with the highest natural excellence of the imaginative faculty. You know that the full development of any faculty of the body, such as the imagination, depends on the condition of the organ, by means of which the faculty acts. This must be the best possible as regards its temperament and its size, and also as regards the purity of its subtance. Any defect in this respect cannot in any way be supplied or remedied by training. For when any organ is defective in its temperament, proper training can in the best case restore a healthy condition to some extent, but cannot make such an organ perfect. But if the organ is defective as regards size, position, or as regards the substance and the matter of which the organ is formed, there is no remedy. You know all this, and I need not explain it to you at length.

Part of the functions of the imaginative faculty is, as you well know, to retain impressions by the senses, to combine them, and chiefly to form images. The principal and highest function is performed when the senses are at rest and pause in their action, for then it receives, to some extent, divine inspiration in the measure as it is predisposed for this influence. This is the nature of those dreams which prove true, and also of prophecy, the difference being one of quantity, not of quality. Thus our Sages say, that dream is the sixtieth part of prophecy (Ber. 57b); and no such comparison could be made between two things of different kinds, for we cannot say the perfection of man is so many times the perfection of a horse. In *Bereshit Rabba* (sect. xvii.) the following saying of our Sages occurs, "Dream is the *nobelet* (the unripe fruit) of prophecy." This is an excellent comparison, for the unripe fruit (*nobelet*) is really the fruit to some extent, only it has fallen from the tree before it was fully developed and ripe. In a similar manner the action of the imaginative faculty during sleep is the same as at the time when it receives a prophecy, only in the first case it is not fully developed, and has not yet reached its highest degree. But why need I quote the words of our Sages, when I can refer to the following passage of Scripture: "If there be among you a prophet, I, the Lord, will make myself known

unto him in a vision, in a dream will I speak to him" (Num. 12:6).
Here the Lord tells us what the real essence of prophecy is, that it is
a perfection acquired in a dream or in a vision (the original *mareh*
is a noun derived from the verb *raah*); the imaginative faculty acquires such an efficiency in its action that it sees the thing as if it came
from without, and perceives it as if through the medium of bodily
senses. These two modes of prophecy, vision and dream, include all
its different degrees. It is a well-known fact that the thing which
engages greatly and earnestly man's attention whilst he is awake and
in the full possession of his senses forms during his sleep the object
of the action of his imaginative faculty. Imagination is then only influenced by the intellect in so far as it is predisposed for such influence. It would be quite useless to illustrate this by a simile, or to explain it fully, as it is clear, and every one knows it. It is like the
action of the senses, the existence of which no person with common
sense would ever deny.

After these introductory remarks you will understand that a
person must satisfy the following conditions before he can become
a prophet: The substance of the brain must from the very beginning
be in the most perfect condition as regards purity of matter, composition of its different parts, size and position; no part of his body
must suffer from ill-health; he must in addition have studied and
acquired wisdom, so that his rational faculty passes from a state of
potentiality to that of actuality; his intellect must be as developed
and perfect as human intellect can be; his passions pure and equally
balanced; all his desires must aim at obtaining a knowledge of the
hidden laws and causes that are in force in the Universe; his thoughts
must be engaged in lofty matters; his attention directed to the knowledge of God, the consideration of His works, and of that which he
must believe in this respect. There must be an absence of the lower
desires and appetites, of the seeking after pleasure in eating, drinking,
and cohabitation; and, in short, every pleasure connected with the
sense of touch. (Aristotle correctly says that this sense is a disgrace
to us, since we possess it only in virtue of our being animals; and
it does not include any specifically human element, whilst enjoyments connected with other senses, as smell, hearing, and sight,
though likewise of a material nature, may sometimes include [intel-
lectual] pleasure, appealing to man as man, according to Aristotle.
This remark, although forming no part of our subject, is not superflu-

ous, for the thoughts of the most renowned wise men are to a great extent affected by the pleasures of this sense, and filled with a desire for them. And yet people are surprised that these scholars do not prophesy, if prophesying be nothing but a certain degree in the natural development of man.)

It is further necessary to suppress every thought or desire for unreal power and dominion; that is to say, for victory, increase of followers, acquisition of honour, and service from the people without any ulterior object. On the contrary, the multitude must be considered according to their true worth; some of them are undoubtedly like domesticated cattle, and others like wild beasts, and these only engage the mind of the perfect and distinguished man in so far as he desires to guard himself from injury, in case of contact with them, and to derive some benefit from them when necessary. A man who satisfies these conditions, whilst his fully developed imagination is in action, influenced by the Active Intellect according to his mental training,—such a person will undoubtedly perceive nothing but things very extraordinary and divine, and see nothing but God and His angels. His knowledge will only include that which is real knowledge, and his thought will only be directed to such general principles as would tend to improve the social relations between man and man.

PROPHECY CALLS FOR A CHEERFUL DISPOSITION

We have thus described three kinds of perfection: mental perfection acquired by training, perfection of the natural constitution of the imaginative faculty, and moral perfection produced by the suppression of every thought of bodily pleasures, and of every kind of foolish or evil ambition. These qualities are, as is well known, possessed by the wise men in different degrees, and the degrees of prophetic faculty vary in accordance with this difference. Faculties of the body are, as you know, at one time weak, wearied, and corrupted, at others in a healthy state. Imagination is certainly one of the faculties of the body. You find, therefore, that prophets are deprived of the faculty of prophesying when they mourn, are angry, or are similarly affected. Our Sages say, Inspiration does not come upon a prophet when he is sad or languid. This is the reason why Jacob did not receive any revelation during the period of his mourning, when his imagination was engaged with the loss of Joseph. The same was the case with Moses, when he was in a state of depression through the

301

multitude of his troubles, which lasted from the murmurings of the Israelites in consequence of the evil report of the spies, till the death of the warriors of that generation. He received no message of God, as he used to do, even though he did not receive prophetic inspiration through the medium of the imaginative faculty, but directly through the intellect. We have mentioned it several times that Moses did not, like other prophets, speak in similes.

Guide, II, 36

DIVINE INFLUENCE IN PROPORTION TO THE ACTIVE INTELLECT

It is necessary to consider the nature of the divine influence, which enables us to think, and gives us the various degrees of intelligence. For this influence may reach a person only in a small measure, and in exactly the same proportion would then be his intellectual condition, whilst it may reach another person in such a measure that, in addition to his own perfection, he can be the means of perfection for others. The same relation may be observed throughout the whole Universe. There are some beings so perfect that they can govern other beings, but there are also beings that are only perfect in so far as they can govern themselves and cannot influence other beings. In some cases the influence of the [Active] Intellect reaches only the logical and not the imaginative faculty; either on account of the insufficiency of that influence, or on account of a defect in the constitution of the imaginative faculty, and the consequent inability of the latter to receive that influence: this is the condition of wise men or philosophers. If, however, the imaginative faculty is naturally in the most perfect condition, this influence may, as has been explained by us and by other philosophers, reach both his logical and his imaginative faculties: this is the case with prophets. But it happens sometimes that the influence only reaches the imaginative faculty on account of the insufficiency of the logical faculty, arising either from a natural defect, or from a neglect in training. This is the case with statesmen, lawgivers, diviners, charmers, and men that have true dreams, or do wonderful things by strange means and secret arts, though they are not wise men; all these belong to the third class. It is further necessary to understand that some persons belonging to the third class perceive scenes, dreams, and confused images, when awake, in the form of a prophetic vision. They then believe that they are prophets; they wonder that they perceive visions, and think that they

302

have acquired wisdom without training. They fall into grave errors as regards important philosophical principles, and see a strange mixture of true and imaginary things. All this is the consequence of the strength of their imaginative faculty, and the weakness of their logical faculty, which has not developed, and has not passed from potentiality to actuality.

It is well known that the members of each class differ greatly from each other. Each of the first two classes is again subdivided, and contains two sections, namely, those who receive the influence only as far as is necessary for their own perfection, and those who receive it in so great a measure that it suffices for their own perfection and that of others. A member of the first class, the wise men, may have his mind influenced either only so far, that he is enabled to search, to understand, to know, and to discern, without attempting to be a teacher or an author, having neither the desire nor the capacity; but he may also be influenced to such a degree that he becomes a teacher and an author. The same is the case with the second class. A person may receive a prophecy enabling him to perfect himself but not others; but he may also receive such a prophecy as would compel him to address his fellow-men, teach them, and benefit them through his perfection. It is clear that, without this second degree of perfection, no books would have been written, nor would any prophets have persuaded others to know the truth. For a scholar does not write a book with the object to teach himself what he already knows. But the characteristic of the intellect is this: what the intellect of one receives is transmitted to another, and so on, till a person is reached that can only himself be perfected by such an influence, but is unable to communicate it to others, as has been explained in some chapters of this treatise (chap. xi.). It is further the nature of this element in man that he who possesses an additional degree of that influence is compelled to address his fellow-men, under all circumstances, whether he is listened to or not, even if he injures himself thereby. Thus we find prophets that did not leave off speaking to the people until they were slain; it is this divine influence that moves them, that does not allow them to rest in any way, though they might bring upon themselves great evils by their action, e.g., when Jeremiah was despised like other teachers and scholars of his age, he could not, though he desired it, withhold his prophecy, or cease from reminding the people of the truth which they rejected. Comp. "For the word of the Lord was unto me a reproach and a mocking all day, and I said, I will not mention it, nor will I again speak in His name; but it was in mine heart as a burning fire, enclosed in my bones, and I was wearied to keep it, and did not prevail" (Jer. 20:8, 9). This is also the meaning of the words of another prophet, "The Lord God hath spoken, who shall not prophesy?" (Amos 3:8).

Ibid., 35-37

MOSES AND THE OTHER PROPHETS

In what respects was the prophecy of Moses distinguished from that of the other prophets? All the prophets received their inspired messages in a dream or in a vision; Moses while awake and standing, as it is said, "And when Moses went into the tent of meeting, that he might speak with Him, then he heard the Voice speaking unto him" (Num. 7:89). All the prophets received their messages through the medium of an angel. Hence, what they saw, they saw as an allegory or riddle—Moses received his message not through an angel, as it is said, "Mouth to mouth will I speak with him" (Num. 12:8), "The Lord spake unto Moses face to face" (Exod. 33:11); furthermore "And the similitude of the Lord doth he behold" (Num. 12:8); that is to say, that it was no allegory that was revealed to Moses but he realized the prophetic message clearly, without riddle and without parable. To this, the Torah testifies in the text, "Even manifestly, not in dark speeches" (Num. 12:8), which means that he received his prophecy not as a riddle, but had a clear and lucid vision. All the prophets (when receiving their messages) were filled with fear and consternation and became physically weak. Not so, our teacher Moses, of whom Scripture says, "As a man speaketh unto his neighbor" (Ex. 33:11). Just as a man is not startled when he hears the words of his fellow-man, so the mind of Moses was vigorous enough to comprehend the words of prophecy while retaining his normal state. None of the prophets could prophesy at their pleasure. It was otherwise with Moses. He was invested with the prophetic spirit and was clothed with the power of prophecy whenever he pleased. There was no need for him specially to concentrate his mind and prepare for the prophetic manifestations; since he was ever intent and in readiness like the ministering angels.

Guide, II, 35-37

NOT BECAUSE OF SIGNS AND WONDERS . . .

Israel did not believe in Moses, our Teacher, on account of the tokens he showed. For when one's faith is founded on tokens, a lurking doubt always remains in the mind that these tokens may have been performed with the aid of occult arts and witchcraft. After all signs Moses showed in the wilderness, he performed because they were needed, and not to support his prophetic claims. . . . What then were the grounds of the faith in him? The Revelation on Sinai which we saw with our own eyes, and heard with our own ears, not having to depend on the testimony of others, we ourselves witnessing the fire, the thunder, the lightning, Moses entering the thick darkness after which the Divine Voice spoke to him, while we heard the call, Moses, Moses, go, tell them thus and thus." And so it is said, "The Lord spoke with you, face to face" (Deut. 5:4), and furthermore, "The Lord made not this covenant with our fathers only, [but with us, *even us*, who are all of us here alive this day"] (Deut. 5:3). Whence do we know that the Sinaitic Revelation is the sole proof that Moses' prophetic mission is true? From the text, "Lo, I come unto thee in a thick cloud, that the people may hear when I speak unto thee, and may also believe in thee forever." (Ex. 19:9). Hence the inference that before that event they did not believe with a faith that would endure forever, but only with a faith followed by hesitating and doubting speculation.

Fundamental Principles of the Torah, 8

BY HIS CONDUCT YE SHALL KNOW HIM . . .

The gift of prophecy may be vouchsafed to a prophet intended for him alone, to develop his mind, to increase his knowledge, so that he may know what hitherto he had not known concerning exalted themes. Sometimes the prophet is sent on a special mission to a particular people or to the inhabitants of a certain city or kingdom, to direct them aright, teach them what they are to do or restrain them from the evil course they were pursuing. And when so sent a sign or token may be given him, so that the people might know that God had in truth sent him. Not every one showing a sign or token is on that account accepted as a prophet. Only if a man by reason of his wisdom and conduct wherein he stands preeminent among his contemporaries, is already recognized as worthy of the prophetic gift, and his life, in its sanctity and renunciation, is favorable to the prophetic calling—then when he shows a sign or token and asserts that God had sent him, is it one's duty to listen to his message, as it is said, "Unto him ye shall hearken" (Deut. 18:15).

It is, however, possible that such a man may show a sign and token and yet not be a prophet. The sign may be a mystery. Nevertheless, it is a duty to listen to him for, being a great and wise man, worthy of the prophetic gift, we give him the benefit of the presumption. . . . On these and suchlike matters, it is said, "The secret things belong unto the Lord, our God; but the things that are revealed belong to us and to our children" (Deut. 29:28). And further it is said, "For man looketh on the outward appearance, but the Lord looketh on the heart" (I Sam. 16:7).

Ibid., 7

QUALIFICATIONS OF PROPHETS

Know . . . that no prophet received the gift of prophecy unless he possessed all the mental virtues and a great majority of the most important moral ones. So, the Rabbis said, "Prophecy rests only upon the wise, the brave and the rich" (Ned. 38a; Shab. 92a). By the word "wise" they undoubtedly refer to all the perfections. By "rich" they designate the moral perfection of contentment, for they call the contented man rich, their definition of the word "rich" being, "Who is rich? He who is contented with his lot" (Ab. 4:1), that is one who is satisfied with what fortune brings him, and who does not grieve on account of things which he does not possess. Likewise, "brave" stands for a moral perfection; that is, one who is brave guides his faculties in accordance with intelligence and reason. . . . The rabbis say, "Who is brave? He who subdues his passions" (*ibid.*, 4:1).

It is not, however, an indispensable requirement that a prophet should possess all the moral virtues, and be entirely free from every defect, for we find that Scripture testifies in reference to Solomon, who was a prophet, that "the lord appeared to Solomon in Gideon," although we know that he had the moral defect of lust, which is plainly evident from the fact that he took many wives, a vice springing from the disposition of passion which resided in his soul. It plainly says, "Did not Solomon sin by these things?" (Nehemiah 13:26). Even David, a prophet according to the words, "To me spoke the rock of Israel" (II Sam. 23:3)—we find guilty of cruelty,

306

and although he exercised it only against the heathens and in the destruction of unbelievers, being merciful towards Israel, it is explicitly stated in Chronicles that God, considering him unworthy, did not permit him to build the Temple, as it was not fitting in His eyes because of the many people David caused to be killed. So, God said to him, "Thou shalt not build a house to my name, because much blood hast thou shed?" (I Chr. 22:8). We find also that Elijah gave vent to his anger, and also he did so against unbelievers, against whom his wrath blazed up, the Sages declared that God took him from the world, saying to him, "He who has so much zeal as thou hast is not fit to guide men, for thou wilt destroy them" (San. 113a). Likewise we find that Samuel feared Saul, and that Jacob was afraid to meet Esau. These and similar characteristics were so many partitions between the prophets (peace be unto them!) and God. . . .

Thou must not be surprised to learn, however, that a few moral imperfections lessen the degree of prophetic inspiration; in fact, we find that some moral vices cause prophecy entirely to be withdrawn. Thus, for instance, wrath may do this, as our Rabbis say, "If a prophet becomes enraged, the spirit of prophecy departs from him!" (Pes. 66b). They adduce proof for this from the case of Elisha, from whom when he became enraged, prophecy departed, until his wrath had subsided, at which he exclaimed, "And now bring me a musician!" (II K. 3:15).

Grief and anxiety may also cause cessation of prophecy, as in the case of the patriarch Jacob who, during the days when he mourned for Joseph, was deprived of the Holy Spirit, until he received the news that his son lived, whereupon Scripture says, "The spirit of Jacob, their father, revived" (Gen. 45:27), which the Targum renders, "And the spirit of prophecy descended upon their father, Jacob." The Sages, moreover, say, "The spirit of prophecy rests not upon the idle, nor upon the sad, but upon the joyous" (Sab. 30b).

When Moses our Teacher discovered that there remained no partitions between himself and God which he had not removed, and when he had attained perfection by acquiring every possible moral and mental virtue, he sought to comprehend God in His true reality, since there seemed no longer to be any hindrance thereto. He therefore implored God, "Show me, I beseech Thee, Thy glory" (Ex. 33:18). But God informed him that this was impossible, since he was a human being, was still influenced by matter. So God's answer was,

"For no man can see me and live" (*ibid.*, 33:20). Thus there remained between Moses and his comprehension of the true essence of God one transparent obstruction, which was his human intellect still resident in matter.

God, however, was gracious in imparting to him, after his request, more knowledge of the divine than he had previously possessed, informing him that the goal [he sought] was impossible of attainment because he was a human being. The true comprehension of God Moses designates by the term, "beholding the divine face," for when one sees another face to face his features become imprinted upon the mind, so that one will not confuse him whom he has seen with others; whereas if he sees only his back, he may possibly recognize him again, but will more probably be in doubt, and confuse him with others. Likewise, the true comprehension of God is a conception of the reality of His existence fixed in the mind [of the knower] which, as concerns this existence is a conception not shared by any other being; so that there is firmly implanted in the mind of the knower a knowledge of God's existence absolutely distinct from the knowledge the mind has of any other being [that exists]. It is impossible, however, for mortal man to attain this high degree of comprehension, though Moses [peace be unto him] almost, but not quite, reached it, which thought is expressed by the words, "Thou shalt see my back parts" (Ex. 33:23). . . .

So, since the Sages [peace be unto them] knew that these two classes of vices, that is, the mental and the moral, separated man from God, and that according to them the ranks of the prophets varied, they (the Rabbis) said to some of their own number, with whose wisdom and morality they were acquainted, "It is fitting that the spirit of God should rest upon them, as it did upon Moses, our Teacher" (Suk. 28a; B.B. 134a). Do not, however, mistake the intention of the comparison. They did, indeed, compare them with Moses, for they were far [God forbid] from giving them equal rank. In the same way they speak of others, characterizing them as being "like Joshua."

Eight Chapters, 7

PROPHETS BEFORE MOSES

There were prophets before Moses, as the patriarchs Shem, Eber, Noah, Methuselah, and Enoch, but of these none said to any portion of mankind that God sent them to them and commanded them to convey to them a certain message or to prohibit or to command a certain thing. Such a thing is not related in Scripture, or in authentic tradition. . . . Men like Abraham who received a large measure of prophetic inspiration, called their fellow-men together and led them by training and instruction to the truth which they had perceived. Thus Abraham taught and showed by philosophical argument that there is one God, that He has created everything that exists beside Him, and that neither the constellations nor anything in the air ought to be worshipped: He trained his fellow-men in this belief, and won their attention by pleasant words as well as by acts of kindness. Abraham did not tell the people that God sent him to them with the command concerning certain things which should or should not be done. Even when it was commanded that he, his sons, and his servants should be circumcised, he fulfilled that commandment, but he did not address his fellow-men prophetically on this subject. . . . Also Isaac, Jacob, Levi, Kohath, and Amram influenced their fellow-men in the same way. Our Sages when speaking of prophets before Moses, used expressions like the following: The *bet-din* (court of justice) of Eber, the *bet-din* of Methuselah, and in the school of Methuselah; although all these were prophets, yet they taught their fellow-men in the manner of preachers, teachers, and pedagogues, but did not use such phrases as the following: "And God said to me, Speak to certain people so and so." This was the state if prophecy before Moses.

Guide, II, 39

DEGREES OF PROPHETS

Maimonides distinguished eleven degrees of prophecy, the first two being only preparatory steps, not constituting one who possesses them a prophet:

The first degree of prophecy consists in the divine assistance which is given to a person, and induces and encourages him to do something good and grand, e.g., to deliver a congregation of good men from the hands of evil-doers, to save one noble person, or to bring happiness to a large number of people; he finds himself the cause that moves and urges him to this deed. This degree of divine influence is called "the spirit of the Lord," and of the person who is under that influence we say that the spirit of the Lord came upon him, clothed him, or rested upon him, or the Lord was with him, and the like. All the judges of Israel possessed this degree, for the following general statement is made concerning them: "The Lord raised up judges for them; and the Lord was with the judge, and He saved them" (Judges 2:18). . . . This faculty was always possessed by Moses from the time he had attained the age of manhood. . . . David likewise was filled with this spirit when he was anointed with the oil of anointing.

The second degree is this: A person feels as if something came upon him, and as if he had received a new power that encourages him to speak. He treats of science, or composes hymns, exhorts his fellow-men, discusses political and theological problems; all this he does while he is awake and in the full possession of his senses. Such person is said to speak by the holy spirit. David composed the Psalms, and Solomon the Book of Proverbs, Ecclesiastes, and the Song of Solomon by this spirit; also Daniel, Job, Chronicles, and the rest of the Hagiographa were written in this holy spirit; therefore they are called *ketubim* [writings, or written], i.e., written by men inspired by the holy spirit. Our Sages mention this expressly concerning the Book of Esther. . . . This class includes the seventy elders of whom it is said, "And it came to pass when the spirit rested upon them, that they prophesied and did not cease" (Nu. 11:25). . . . You must know that Balaam likewise belonged to this class when he was good. . . . They belonged to the class of men that spoke inspired by the *ruah ha-kodesh*, "the holy spirit." Also in the order of the holy writings, no distinction is made between the books of Proverbs, Ecclesiastes, Daniel, Psalms, Ruth, and Esther; they are all written by divine inspiration. The authors of all these books are called prophets in the more general sense of the term.

The third class is the lowest [class of actual prophets, i.e.] of those who introduce their speech by the phrase, "And the word of the Lord came unto me," or similar phrase. The prophet sees an allegory in a dream . . . and in the prophetic dream itself the allegory is interpreted. Such are most of the allegories of Zechariah.

The prophet hears in a prophetic dream something clearly and distinctly, but does not see the speaker. This was the case with Samuel in the beginning of his prophetic mission.

A person addresses the prophet in a dream, as was the case in the prophecies of Ezekiel. Comp. "And the man spake unto me, Son of man," etc. (Ezek. 40:4).

An angel speaks to him in a dream; this applies to most of the prophets; e.g., "And an angel of God said to me in a dream of night" (Gen. 31:11).

In a prophetic dream it appears to the prophet as if God spoke to him. Thus Isaiah says, "And I saw the Lord, and I heard the voice of the Lord, saying, Whom shall I send, and who will go for us?" (Is. 6:8).

Something presents itself to the prophet in a prophetic vision; he sees allegorical figures, such as were seen by Abraham in the vision "between the pieces" (Gen. 15:9, 10); for it was in a vision by daytime as is distinctly stated.

The prophet hears words in a prophetic vision; as e.g., is said in reference to Abraham, "And, behold, the word came to him, saying, This shall not be thine heir" (*ibid.*, 15:4).

The prophet sees a man that speaks to him in a prophetic vision; e.g., Abraham in the plain of Mamre (*ibid.*, 18:1), and Joshua in Jericho (Josh. 5:13).

He sees an angel that speaks to him in a vision, as was the case when Abraham was addressed by an angel at the sacrifice of Isaac (Gen. 22:11). This I hold to be—if we except Moses—the highest degree a prophet can attain according to Scripture.

Guide, II, 45

PROPHECY IS LIKE A LIGHTNING FLASH

At times the truth shines so brilliantly that we perceive it as clear as day. Our nature and habit then draw a veil over our perception, and we return to a darkness almost as dense as before. We are like those who, though beholding frequent flashes of lightning still find themselves in the thickest darkness of the night. On some the lightning flashes in rapid succession, and they seem to be in continuous light, and their night is as clear as the day. This was the degree of prophetic excellence attained by (Moses) the greatest of prophets, to whom God said, "But as for thee, stand thou here by Me" (Deut. 5:28), and of whom it is written "the skin of his face shone," etc. (Ex. 34:29). [Some perceive the prophetic flash at long intervals; this is the degree of most prophets.] By others only once during the whole night is a flash of lightning perceived. This is the case with those of whom we are informed, "They prophesied, and did not prophesy again" (Nu. 11:25). There are some to whom the flashes of lightning appear with varying intervals; others are in condition of men, whose darkness is illumined not by lightning, but by some kind of crystal or similar stone, or other substances that possess the property of shining during the night; and to them even this small amount of light is not continuous, but now it shines and now it vanishes, as if it were "the flame of the rotating sword."

Guide, Introduction

THE LANGUAGE OF THE PROPHETS

Maimonides contrasts the allegorical method of the Prophets with the superficial or literal sense of the Bible which distorts its inner meaning and significance. The Prophets, he says, had developed a diction, or picture-language, of their own.

If we hear a person speaking whose language we do not understand, we undoubtedly know that he speaks, but do not know what his words mean; it may even happen that we hear some words which mean one thing in the tongue of the speaker and exactly the reverse in our language, and taking the words in the sense which they have in our language, we imagine that the speaker employs them in that sense. . . . The same things to the ordinary reader of the Prophets; some of the words he does not understand at all, like those to whom the prophet says (Is. 29:11), "the vision of all has become unto you as the words of a book that is sealed;" in other passages he finds the opposite or the reverse of what the prophet meant. . . . Besides, it must be borne in mind that every prophet has his own peculiar diction, which is, as it were, his own language, and it is in that language that the prophecy addressed to him is communicated to those who understand it.

Guide, II, 29

Maimonides follows up this general observation with illustrations of the highly poetic form in which various prophets had described the fall of Sennacherib, the destruction of the Babylonian empire, the ruin of the Edomites, and the defeat, exile, and restoration of the kingdom of Israel. He continues:

I do not think that any person is so foolish and blind, and so much in favor of the literal sense of figurative and rhetorical phrases as to assume that at the fall of the Babylonian kingdom a change took place in the nature of the stars of heaven, or in the light of the sun and moon, or that the earth moved away from its center. For all this is merely the description of a country that has been defeated; the inhabitants undoubtedly find all life dark, and all sweet things bitter, the whole earth appears too narrow for them, and the heavens are changed in their eyes.

He [Isaiah] speaks in a similar manner when he describes the poverty and humiliation of the people of Israel, their captivity and their defeat, the continuous misfortunes caused by the wicked Sennacherib when he ruled over all the fortified places of Judah, or the loss of the entire land of Israel, when it came into the possession of Sennacherib. . . . At the end of the same prophecy, when Isaiah describes how God will punish Sennacherib, destroy his mighty empire, and reduce him to disgrace, he uses the following figure (24:23): "Then the moon shall be confounded, and the sun ashamed, when the Lord of hosts shall reign," etc. The prophet then pictures the peace of the children of Israel after the death of Sennacherib, the fertility and the cultivation of their land, and the increasing power of their kingdom through Hezekiah. He employs here the figure of the light of the sun and the moon. . . . Moreover, the light of the moon shall be as the light of the sun, and the light of the sun shall be sevenfold, as the light of seven days, in the day that the Lord bindeth up the breaches of his people, and healeth the stroke of their wound (Is. 30:19, 26); that is to say, when God will raise them up again after they had fallen through the wicked Sennacherib.

Ibid.

The metaphor and hyperbole are deeply rooted in Judaism. The Sages of the Talmud long before Maimonides called attention to its use by the Prophets.

It is undoubtedly clear and evident that most prophecies are given in images, for this is the characteristic of the imaginative faculty, the organ of prophecy. We find it also necessary to say a few words on the figures, hyperboles, and exaggerations that occur in Scripture. They would create strange ideas if we were to take them literally without noticing the exaggeration which they contain, or if we were to understand them in accordance with the original meaning of the terms, ignoring the facts that these are used figuratively. Our Sages say distinctly Scripture uses hyperbolic or exaggerated language; and quote as an instance, "cities walled and fortified, rising up to heaven" (Deut. 1:28). As a hyperbole our Sages quote, "For the bird of heaven carries the voice" (Ecc. 10:20); in the same sense it is said, "Whose height is like that of cedar trees" (Amos 2:9). . . . As regards the Scriptural statement about the length of man's life in those days, I say only the persons named lived so long, whilst other people enjoyed the ordinary length of life. The men named were exceptions, either in consequence of different causes, as e.g., their food or mode of living, or by way of miracle, which admits of no analogy. . . .

You must explain passages not quoted by me by those which I have quoted. Employ your reason and you will be able to discern what is said allegorically, figuratively, or hyperbolically, and what is meant literally, exactly according to the original meaning of the words. You will then understand all prophecies, learn and retain rational principles of faith, pleasing in the eyes of God who is most pleased with truth; your mind and heart will not be so perplexed as to believe or accept as law what is untrue or improbable, whilst the Law is perfectly true when properly understood. Thus, Scripture says, "Thy testimonies are righteous forever" (Ps. 119:144); and "I, the Lord, speak righteousness" (Is. 45:19). If you adopt this method, you will not imagine the existence of things which God has not created, or accept principles which might lead to atheism, or to a corruption of your notions of God so as to ascribe to Him corporeality, attributes or emotions . . . nor will you believe that the words of the prophets are false, for the cause of this disease is ignorance of what we have explained. These things belong likewise to the mysteries of the Law.

Ibid.

18. IDOLATRY AND SUPERSTITION

Since time immemorial wayward Israel never rested quite happily in the God of Sinai. Sacred shrines and pillars of foreign deities had often threatened to obscure the Jewish pure God-idea. Idolatry was the price the people paid for their fraternization with the pagan tribes round about them. The Prophets thundered mightily against the heathen practices, and the Bible may be said to be in part Jehovah's perpetual struggle against the "false gods." In a striking passage in The Guide for the Perplexed *(I, 36), Maimonides makes the remarkable observation: "You must know that the idolaters when worshipping idols do not believe that there is no God beside them; and no idolaters ever did assume that any image made of metal, stone, or wood has created the heavens and the earth, and still governs them. Idolatry is founded on the idea that a particular form represents the agent between God and His creatures." In his great Code, Maimonides treats his readers to a highly interesting survey of the rise and origin of idolatry, its manner of worship, and how it dominated and corrupted the innate religious sense of the world:*

IN THE DAYS of Enosh, the people fell into gross error, and the counsel of the wise men of the generation became foolish. Enosh himself was among those who erred. Their error was as follows: "Since God," they said, "created these stars and spheres to guide the world, set them on high and allotted unto them honor, and since they are ministers who minister before Him, they deserve to be praised and glorified, and honor should be rendered them; and it is the will of God, blessed be He, that men should aggrandize and honor those whom He aggrandized and honored—just as a king desires that respect should be shown to the officers who stand before

Him, and thus honor is shown to the king." When this idea arose in their minds, they began to erect temples to the stars, offered up sacrifices to them, praised and glorified them in speech, and prostrated themselves before them—their purpose, according to their perverse notions, being to obtain the Creator's favor. This was the root of idolatry, and this was what the idolaters, who knew its fundamentals, said. They did not however maintain that there was no God except the particular star [which was the object of their worship].

Idolatry, 1

FALSE PRIESTS AND PROPHETS

In course of time, there arose among men false prophets who asserted that God had commanded and expressly told them, "Worship that particular star, or worship all the stars. Offer up to it such and such sacrifices. Pour out to it such and such libations. Erect a temple to it. Make a figure of it, to which all the people—the women, children, and the rest of the folk—shall bow down." The false prophet pointed out to them the figure which he had invented out of his own mind, and asserted that it is the figure of that particular star, which had been shown him in his prophetic vision. And then, they began to make figures in temples under the trees, on the mountain-tops and the hills. There they would assemble, bow down to the figures, and tell all the people that this particular figure conferred benefits and inflicted injuries, and that it was proper to worship and fear it. Their priests would say to them, "Through this worship, shall ye increase and prosper. Do this, and do not do that." Other imposters then sprang up, who declared that the star, celestial sphere or angel, had communed with them, and said to them "Worship me in such and such fashion," had taught them a definite ritual and said to them "Do this, and do not do that." So gradually the custom spread throughout the world of worshipping figures with various modes of worship, such as offering up sacrifices to them, and bowing down to them. As time passed, the honored and revered name of God was forgotten by mankind, vanished from their lips and hearts, and was no longer known to them. All the common people and the women and children knew only the figure of wood and stone, and the temple edifice in which they had, from their childhood, been trained to prostrate themselves to the figure, worship it and swear by its name. Even their wise men, such as priests and men of similar standing, also

316

fancied that there was no other god but the stars and spheres, for whose sake and in whose similitude these figures had been made. But the Creator of the Universe was known to none, and recognized by none, save a few solitary individuals, such as Enosh, Methuselah, Noah, Shem, and Eber. The world moved on in this fashion, till that Pillar of the World, the Patriarch Abraham, was born.

Idolatry, 1

THE TORAH PRECEPT REGARDING IDOLATRY

The essential principle in the precepts concerning idolatry is that we are not to worship anything created—neither angel, sphere, star, none of the four elements, nor whatever has been formed from them. Even if the worshipper is aware that the Eternal is God, and worships the created thing in the sense in which Enosh and his contemporaries did, he is an idolater. It is against this that the Torah warns us when it says "And lest thou lift up thine eyes unto heaven and seest the sun . . . which the Lord thy God hath allotted unto all the peoples" (Deut. 4:19). This means that when your mind rose and you observe that the world is guided by these spheres and that God placed them in the world, as beings that live, endure permanently, and do not disintegrate, like all other things, you may say that it is proper to bow down to these spheres and worship them. Concerning this tendency, God commanded and said, "Take heed lest your heart be deceived" (Deut. 11:16); that is to say, do not be led astray by the fancies of your mind, to worship these beings as intermediaries between yourselves and the Creator.

Many volumes have been composed by idolaters on idolatry, dealing with its essential principles, rites, and rules. The Holy One, blessed be He, has enjoined us not to read these books, nor to meditate on idol-worship, nor upon anything appertaining to it. It is forbidden to gaze upon the picture of an idolatrous figure, as it is said "Turn ye not unto idols" (Lev. 19:4). In this connection it is further said "And that thou inquirest not after their gods, saying 'How do these nations serve'" (Deut. 12:30). That means that you shall not inquire in regard to an idol, as to the mode of its worship, even if you are not worshipping it. For this would cause you to turn after it and do as the idolaters do, as the text continues "Even so will I do likewise" (Deut. 12:30). . . .

Idolatry, 2

317

The precept relating to idolatry is equal in importance to all other precepts put together, as it is said, "And when ye shall err and not observe all these commandments" (Nu. 15:22). This text has traditionally been interpreted as alluding to idolatry; hence the inference that acceptance of idolatry is tantamount to repudiating the whole Torah, the prophets and everything that they were commanded, from Adam to the end of time, as it is said "From the day that the Lord gave commandment and onward, throughout your generation" (Nu. 15:23). And whoever denies idolatry confesses his faith in the whole Torah, in all the prophets and all that the prophets were commanded, from Adam to the end of time. And this is the fundamental principle of all the commandments.

Ibid.

IDOLATRY: SIN, SINNER, AND PUNISHMENT

An Israelite who worships an idol is regarded as an idolater in all respects and not as an Israelite who committed a transgression, the penalty for which is death by stoning. A pervert to idolatry is regarded as having renounced the whole of the Torah. So too, the infidels in Israel are in no wise to be regarded as Israelites; as is said, "None that go unto her will return, neither will they attain the paths of life" (Prov. 2:19). Infidels are those who in respect to the follies of which we have spoken, go after the fancies of their hearts, till at last they become transgressors of the fundamental precepts of the Torah, in a spirit of defiance and arrogance, asserting that there is nothing wrong in what they do. It is forbidden to hold converse with them or give them any reply, as it is said, "And come not nigh the door of her house" (Prov. 5:8). The mind of the infidel tends toward idolatry.

Idolatry, 2

THE NAZARENES AND THE MOHAMMEDANS

For the first time during his brief residence in Palestine, Maimonides lived in a country under Christian domination, and what he saw—religious processions with the holy images of Jesus and Mary before which the people kneeled and prayed, made on him a painful impression. He therefore classed the Christian in the category of idol worshippers who did not subscribe to the Unity of God. In his great Code he writes:

The Nazarenes are idolaters. The first day of the week is their festival. Hence it is forbidden in Palestine to have commercial intercourse with them on the fifth and sixth day; and obviously on the first day itself, this is everywhere forbidden. A similar rule applies to all their feasts.

Idolatry, 9
Mishnah Commentary

When, on the other hand, he was asked whether the laws against idolatry applied to the Mohammedans, his reply was:

The Ishmaelites [Mohammedans] are not considered pagan in any sense. No trace of paganism is left in their speech and in their hearts. They confess the Unity of God in its strict and unconditional meaning. People say that their houses of worship are pagan and contain pagan symbols which were revered by their ancestors. Even if they still bow to them, their hearts are directed toward God. They may be deluded and in error in various matters, but concerning monotheism they are not at all mistaken.

Responsum, 369, ed. Freimann

KIDDUSH AND HILLUL HASHEM

Sanctification and Desecration of the Name are terms applying to the highest positive and negative precepts of Jewish religious ethics, derived from Lev.22:32. Throughout Jewish history martyrdom in the cause of religion is called "sanctification of God's name." In course of time, the term denoted every act of humanity and generosity calculated to bring credit to the Jewish name. The contrary, Hillul Hashem, denotes sins for which the Day of Atonement does not atone.

All the members of the house of Israel are commanded to sanctify the great Name of God, as it is said "But I will be hallowed among the children of Israel" (Lev. 22:32). They are furthermore cautioned not to profane it, as it is said "Neither shall ye profane my holy name" (Lev. 22:32). How are these precepts to be applied? Should an idolater arise and coerce an Israelite to violate any one of the commandments mentioned in the Torah under the threat that otherwise he would put him to death, an Israelite is to commit the transgression rather than suffer death; for concerning the commandments

319

it is said "which, if a man do them, he shall live by them" (Lev. 18:5): "Live by them, and not die by them." And if he suffered death rather than commit a transgression, he himself is to blame for his death.

Fundamental Principles of the Torah, 5

This rule applies to all the commandments except the prohibition of idolatry, unchastity, and murder. With regard to these: if an Israelite should be told "transgress one of them or else you will be put to death," he should suffer death rather than transgress. The above distinction holds good if the idolater's motive is personal advantage; for example, if he forces an Israelite to build him a house or cook for him on the Sabbath, or forces a Jewess to cohabit with him, and so on; but if his purpose is to compel the Israelite to violate the ordinances of his religion, then if this thing took place privately and ten fellow-Israelites were not present, he should commit the transgression rather than suffer death. But if the attempt to coerce the Israelite to transgress was made in the presence of ten Israelites, he should suffer death and not transgress, even if it was only one of the remaining commandments that the idolater wished him to violate.

Ibid.

Sanctifying the Name

Martyrdom of death applies to any of the commandments involving idolatry, incest, and bloodshed whether coerced to commit publicly, in the presence of ten Israelites, or privately.

He [God] has commanded us that we are to sanctify His Name. This [injunction] finds expression in His words, "But I will be hallowed among the children of Israel" (Lev. 22:32). The purpose of this commandment is that we are in duty bound to proclaim this [our] true faith in the world, and that [in doing so] we are to disregard all fear of injury from any source. Even where one uses force against us, seeking to constrain us [to a denial of Him], we are not to heed him, but we are rather to submit to death, and we are not so much as to mislead him into supposing that we have denied Him even while in our hearts we continue to affirm our faith in Him, praised be He.

This is the commandment concerning the Sanctification of the

Name in the observance whereof the children of Israel are commanded as a body; that is to say, [we are to] surrender ourselves to die by the hand of the one who would force us for the love of Him, praised be He, and for [our] faith in His unity, even as Hananiah, Mishael, and Azariah did in the time of the wicked Nebuchadnezzar when he commanded [everyone] to worship the [golden] image, (Daniel 3:1), and when all the masses, the Israelites included, prostrated themselves before it so that there was none there to sanctify the name of Heaven, all being in terror, the disgrace whereof devolved upon all Israel, in that this commandment was lost [i.e., left unhallowed] in their midst.

Now it is only in connection with circumstances similar to those prevailing on that great and celebrated occasion, when the whole world was terrorized that this commandment was ordained, that by such [sanctification of His Name] His Unity is to be proclaimed. The Lord has testified through Isaiah in order that Israel might not be completely disgraced on such an occasion, and to the end that when the young men of those trying times saw such [conduct] death could hold no longer any terrors for them, and they should then give up their lives and proclaim the Faith, sanctifying the Name publicly, even as He had assured [us] when He said, "Jacob shall not now be ashamed, neither shall his face now wax pale when he seeth his children, the work of My hands in the midst of him that they sanctify My name" (Is. 29:22-23).

Sefer ha-Mitzvot, Com. 9

All the foregoing applies to a time free from religious persecution. But at a period when there is such persecution, such as when a wicked king arises like Nebuchadnezzar and his confederates, and issues decrees against Israel, with the purpose of abolishing their religion or one of the precepts, then it is the Israelite's duty to suffer death and not violate any one, even of the remaining commandments, whether the coercion takes place in the presence of ten Israelites or in the presence of idolaters.

Fundamental Principles of the Torah, 5

TRANSGRESSION UNDER DURESS

When one is enjoined to transgress rather than be slain and suffers death rather than transgress, he is to blame for his death. When one is enjoined to die rather than transgress and suffers death so as not to transgress, he sanctifies the name of God. If he does so in the presence of ten Israelites, he sanctifies the name of God publicly, like Daniel Hananiah, Mishael, and Azariah, Rabbi Akiba and his colleagues. These are the martyrs, than whom none ranks higher. Concerning them it is said, "but for Thy sake we are killed all day long; we are accounted as sheep for the slaughter" (Ps. 44:23). And to whom also the text refers, "Gather my saints together unto Me, those that have made a covenant with Me by sacrifice" (Ps. 50:5).

When one is enjoined to suffer death rather than transgress, and commits a transgression and so escapes death, he has profaned the name of God. If the transgression is committed in the presence of ten Israelites, he has profaned the Name of God in public, failed to observe an affirmative precept—to sanctify the name of God—and violated a negative precept—not to profane His name. Still, as the transgression was committed under duress, he is not punished with stripes and, needless to add, he is not sentenced by a court to be put to death, even if, under duress, he committed murder. For the penalty of death and stripes is only inflicted on one who transgresses of his own free will, in the presence of witnesses and after due warning.

If heathens said to a group of Jewish women "Surrender one of your number to us, that we may defile her, or else we will defile you all," they should all suffer defilement rather than surrender to them a single person in Israel. So, too, if heathens said to Israelites, "Surrender one of your number to us, that we may put him to death, otherwise, we will put all of you to death," they should all suffer death rather than surrender a single Israelite to them. But if they specified an individual, saying, "Surrender that particular person to us, or else we will put all of you to death," they may give him up, provided that he was guilty of a capital crime like Sheba, son of Bichri [who rebelled against David]. But this rule is not told them in advance. If the individual specified has not incurred capital punishment, they should all suffer death rather than surrender a single Israelite to them.

Fundamental Principles of the Torah, 5

PRINCIPLE OF NON-LIABILITY

The principle of non-liability in the case of duress also applies to sickness. If one is dangerously sick, and the physicians assert that he can be cured by the application of a remedy which involves violation of a precept of the Torah, the remedy should be applied. Where life is in danger, anything forbidden in the Torah may be used as a curative agent, except the practice of idolatry, unchastity, or murder. Even to save life, these offenses must not be committed. If a patient transgressed the prohibition and recovered, the Court sentences him to the punishment prescribed for the offense.

Ibid.

Whence is the rule derived that even when life is in danger, none of those three offenses may be committed? From the text, "And thou shalt love the Lord, they God, with all thy heart, with all thy soul, and with all thy might" (Deut. 6:5). This means that love for God has to be manifested even at the cost of life. As to taking the life of an Israelite to cure another individual or to rescue a person from one who threatens violence, reason indicates that one human life ought not to be destroyed to save another human life. Offenses against chastity are analogous to the destruction of human life; for it is said, "As when a man rises against his neighbor, and slayeth him, even so is this matter" (Deut. 22:26).

Ibid.

The rule that forbidden things may only be employed as remedies whereas danger to life applies only to their use in the ordinary way in which food is enjoyed, as for instance, if a patient is prescribed a diet of "abominable" and crawling creatures (Lev. 11:29, 41, 43), or of leavened bread during Passover, or of any food on the Day of Atonement. But where forbidden things are to be used not in the ordinary way in which they are enjoyed, as for example, to apply on Passover a plaster or poultice made of leaven, or one made of fruit of the first three years produce of a tree at any time, or to drink a potion in which forbidden food is mingled with a bitter ingredient, so that the palate is not gratified—in all these cases the use of forbidden food is permitted even where there is no danger to life.

Ibid.

If one transgresses any of the commandments laid down in the Torah, of his own will and not under the stress of compulsion, but wantonly and in a spirit of provocation, he profanes the Name of God. . . . On the other hand, whoever abstains from a transgression or fulfils a precept, not from any personal motive, not induced thereto by fear and apprehension or by the desire for honor, but solely for the sake of the Creator, blessed be He, as Joseph did when he resisted his master's wife, sanctifies the Name of God.

Ibid.

PROFANATION BY UNSEEMLY CONDUCT

There are other things that are a profanation of the Name of God. When a man, great in the knowledge of the Torah and reputed for his piety does things which cause people to talk about him, even if the acts are not express violations, he profanes the Name of God. As, for example, if such a person makes a purchase and does not pay promptly, provided that he has means and the creditors ask for payment and he puts them off; or if he indulges immoderately in jesting, eating or drinking, when he is staying with ignorant people or living among them; or if his mode of addressing people is not gentle, or he does not receive people affably, but is quarrelsome and irascible. The greater a man is the more scrupulous should he be in all such things, and do more than the strict letter of the law requires. And if a man has been scrupulous in his conduct, gentle in his conversation, pleasant towards his fellow-creatures, affable in manner when receiving them, not retorting, even when affronted, but showing courtesy to all, even to those who treat him with disdain, conducting his commercial affairs with integrity, not readily accepting the hospitality of the ignorant nor frequenting their company, not seen at all times, but devoting himself to the study of the Torah, wrapped in Talith and crowned with phylacteries, and doing more than his duty in all things, avoiding, however, extremes and exaggerations—such a man has sanctified God, and concerning him, Scripture saith, "And he said unto me, 'Thou art my servant, O Israel, in whom I will be glorified'" (Is. 49:3).

Fundamental Principles of the Torah, 5

SUPERSTITIOUS BELIEFS AND PRACTICES

All through Bible times, and deep in the Middle Ages, magic in its various forms and expressions, had a powerful attraction for the masses of the Jewish people. In Deuteronomy (18:10-11) we have an almost exhaustive list of the superstitious beliefs and practices current among the people. They were not necessarily Jewish in origin, for the Bible brands them as "the abomina-

tions of those nations," but their influence upon the early Israelites was long and baneful. The Prophets frowned on them and denounced them in no uncertain terms, but they flourished just the same.

Moses Maimonides, the consistent and indomitable rationalist that he was, had not only exposed the senseless folly and absurdity of idolatry but held up to scorn and denunciation the various magical practices which he regarded as an offshoot of idolatry. He was particularly severe on Jews who joined in the heathen superstitious beliefs and practices because of the contradiction they implied to the pure monotheistic faith. He nevertheless permitted a spell to be whispered over a patient stung by a snake or a scorpion even on the Sabbath which, although it was magic and perfectly useless, yet might have the effect of easing the distraught wounded person's mind.

Israelites may not resort to divination like the gentiles, as it is said, "neither shall ye practice divination" (Lev. 19:26). What is divination? The following are examples. To say: "Since my piece of bread dropped out of my mouth or my staff fell from my hand, I shall not go today to such a place, for if I go, my business will not be successfully accomplished"; or, "since a fox ran past me in the night, I shall not today go outside of the door of my house, for if I do, a cheat will accost me"; or when people hear a bird twittering and say; "it will happen thus and not thus"—"it is good to do this, and bad to do that"; or when people say: "Kill this cock because it crowed in the evening"; "kill this hen because it crowed like the cock"; or if one sets for himself a sign and says, "If a certain thing happens to me, I will follow this course of action; if it does not happen, I will not do so"—as Eleazar, Abraham's servant did—these and all things similar are forbidden. Whoever does anything as a result of any of these happenings is punished with stripes.

Idolatry, 11

To say: "This dwelling which I have built has turned out lucky for me; this woman that I married was a blessing to me; from the moment that I bought this beast, I became rich"; or to ask a child, "What verse art thou learning," and if the child recites a verse from the Blessings, to rejoice and say: "that is a lucky sign"—all these and similar things are permitted. For, as the person did not adjust his activities in accordance with them nor refrained from doing aught because of them, but only regarded them as signs of what had already happened, such acceptance is permitted.

Ibid.

COMMUNION WITH THE SPIRIT WORLD

One who practices communion with ghosts or familiar spirits of his own free will and presumptuously, incurs the penalty of excision. And if witnesses were present and a warning had been previously given, he is put to death by stoning. If the offense had been committed unwittingly, he brings the appointed sin-offering. How is communing with ghosts practised? The practitioner stands up, offers a certain kind of incense, holds in his hand a myrtle twig, and waves it. He pronounces softly certain words known to the practitioner of this art, till the one who consults him fancies that someone is conversing with him, and answering his questions in words that sound as if they came from beneath the ground in exceedingly low tones almost inaudible to the ear and only apprehended by the mind. Or he takes a dead man's skull, burns incense to it and uses arts of divination till one hears a sound as if a voice, exceedingly low, came from under his armpit and replied to him—all acts of such nature constitute communion with ghosts. Whoever does any of these things is put to death by stoning.

Ibid., 6

ASTROLOGY

"The belief in astrology," wrote Alexander Marx, "so generally prevalent during the Middle Ages was fully shared by the Jews. We find its traces in the Talmud and Midrash," and he might have included the Bible, where hobre shamayim (Is.47:13) is generally translated "astrology." "The people," Alexander Marx continues, "were fully convinced of the fundamental truth of the power of the celestial bodies to influence human destiny, while thinking persons early realized the difficulty of reconciling these theories with the principles of the Jewish faith."

Moses Maimonides was one of the very few outstanding Jewish authorities who not only dared raise his voice against this almost universally held belief but even branded it as a superstition akin to idolatry. He denounced astrology as a fallacy and delusion in his famous letter to Yemen, he inveighed sharply against it in his equally celebrated epistle to the Provençal Jews who inquired of him on the subject, and the question was never raised but that he denounced it as a deception that was subversive of the faith and teachings of Judaism. He assured his correspondents that he did not take the matter lightly, but had studied it thoroughly and came to the conclusion that astrology was an irrational illusion of fools who mistake vanity for wisdom and superstition for knowledge. In the following excerpt, Maimonides points to the halakic element pertaining to the "observer of times."

What is an "observer of times"? The term applies to those who assign seasons declaring that astrologically a particular day is favorable, while another day is unfavorable; that a certain day is propitious for the execution of a specific work and a certain year or month is unfavorable for a specific thing.

Ibid., 11

It is forbidden to be an "observer of times" even if he committed no overt act but only uttered the lies which fools imagine are words of truth, words of the wise. And whoever is influenced in his actions by astrology and arranges his work or journey to take place at the time fixed by the astrologers, is punished with stripes, as it is said, "Ye shall not observe times" (Lev. 19:26). So too, a conjurer who deceives the eyes and pretends to the beholder to be doing something extraordinary which in reality he does not do, is included in the category of "observer of times" and is punished with stripes.

Ibid.

NECROMANCY

The ancient art of calling up the dead for divinatory purposes was well-known in biblical and talmudic times. Though forbidden by the Law of Moses, Saul resorted to this means to consult with his deceased mentor, Samuel, through the medium of the famous witch of Endor. Talmudic strictures were hardly more effectual, for Rab, one of the leading authorities, among others, questioned the dead. However, judging from the comparatively few references, this mode of divination played only a minor role in Jewish magic, due to the consistently condemnatory judgment of the leaders of Jewish thought, and the deeply ingrained sentiment of mingled fear and respect and affection for the dead." (Joshua Trachtenberg in Jewish Magic and Superstition.)

What is a necromancer? One who starves himself and goes and spends the night in a cemetery in order that the dead shall appear to him in a dream and instruct him on matters about which he enquires. Others again put on special robes, utter certain words, offer a special incense and sleep alone, so that a particular dead person shall appear to them in a dream and converse with them. Whoever does anything, in order that the dead shall come and instruct him, is punished with stripes, as it is said, "There shall not be found among you . . . a necromancer" (Deut. 18:11).

It is forbidden to consult one who professes to have a ghost or a familiar spirit, as it is said, "there shall not be found among you one who . . . consulteth a ghost or a familiar spirit" (Deut. 18:11). Hence, it is learnt that while one who professes to have a familiar spirit is punished with death by stoning, whoever consults such people violates a prohibition and is punished with stripes for contumacy. If he regulates his activities according to their instructions, he is punished with stripes according to scriptural statute.

Ibid.

These practices are all false and deceptive, and were means employed by the ancient idolaters to deceive the peoples of various countries and induce them to become their followers. It is not proper for Israelites who are highly intelligent to suffer themselves to be deluded by such inanities or imagine that there is anything in them, as it is said "For there is no enchantment with Jacob, neither is there any divination with Israel" (Num. 23:23); and further, "For these nations that thou art to dispossess hearken unto soothsayers and unto diviners; but as for thee, the Lord, thy God, hath not suffered thee so to do" (Deut. 18:14). Whoever believes in these and similar things and, in his heart, holds them to be true and scientific and only forbidden by the Torah, is nothing but a fool, deficient in understanding, who belongs to the same class with women and children whose intellects are immature. Sensible people, however, who possess sound mental faculties, know by clear proofs that all these practices which the Torah prohibited have no scientific basis but are chimerical and inane; and that only those deficient in knowledge are attracted by these follies and, for their sake, leave the ways of truth. The Torah, therefore, in forbidding these follies, exhorts us, "Thou shalt be wholehearted with the Lord, thy God" (Deut. 18:13).

Ibid.

19. GOVERNMENT

*Maimonides maintains the authority of the State to be supreme in all matters
pertaining to the happiness and well-being of its citizens. The State is the
guardian and protector of the social order and of the rights and privileges of
the individual man. In Maimonides' view the function of the State is to
regulate the moral and ethical order of society, to prevent crime, restrain
injustice, and establish good relations among men. It is Maimonides' opinion
that such infractions of the law as theft, robbery, murder, and even false
weights and measures, are not only wrongs committed against the individual
person but are of concern to the State. It is therefore for the common good
and welfare of the social order that the State should have the right to punish
crime, prevent injustice, and suppress violence in its midst. "They are feeble-
minded," says Maimonides, "who contend that the abolition of all penalties
would be an act of mercy toward men; on the contrary, it would be perfect
cruelty toward them and injury to the social order."*

PRIVILEGES AND LIMITATIONS OF KINGS

*In Kings and Wars Maimonides sets forth the privileges and limitations
of kings, their power and abuse of their royal prerogatives. In the words
of Dr. Abraham M. Hershman (Yale Judaica Series, vol. III, pp. XII-XIII),
"He [Maimonides] stresses, however, the duty of the king to make himself
worthy of the exalted position he occupies, to prove 'loyal to the royal' in
him. In order that he may live up to the responsibilities the office involves,
he is bidden to carry a copy of the scroll of the Law about him."*

He [God] has commanded us that we are to appoint a king over
ourselves, who will bring together our whole nation and act as our

leader. This [injunction] finds expression in His words, blessed be He, "Thou shalt in any wise set a king over thee" (Deut. 17:15). . . . In the words of the Siphre, [this teaches us that] his awe shall be over thee. Further, we are to be altogether in awe before [the king's] glory, greatness, renown, and pre-eminence in the highest degree—so much that he should rank with us as greater than any of the prophets of his generation. Thus in explanation [of this commandment the Sages have said: "A king precedes a prophet" (Hor. 13a)].

As long as the king's command is such as not to conflict with the commandment of the Torah, we are obliged to obey him therein, and it is proper and permissible for the king to slay him who deliberately transgresses his words. . . . The life of him who rebels against the [authority of the] king set up in accordance with the Torah is at [the mercy] of the king.

Sefer ha-Mitzvot, Com. 173

The first king of a dynasty cannot be set up save by the court of seventy [-one] elders and a prophet, as was the case with Joshua, who was appointed by Moses, our teacher, and his court, and was the case with Saul and David, who were appointed by Samuel the Ramathite and his court.

No king is appointed from a congregation of Proselytes, even after the lapse of many generations, unless his mother is a Jewess by descent, as it is said: "Thou mayest not put a foreigner over thee who is not thy brother" (Deut. 17:15). This rule applies not only to the office of king but also to any other office. . . .

No woman is eligible to head the State, for it is said *king* (*ibid.*), that is, not a queen. So, too, whatever the office to which appointment is made, only a man is qualified to hold it.

The following may not be set up as king or High Priest: a butcher, a barber, a bathhouse keeper, or a tanner, not because they are legally disqualified, but because their occupations are despised and the people will always have a low opinion of [those who were engaged in] them. Therefore one who was engaged only one day in any of these occupations is ineligible.

Kings, 1

KINGSHIP IS HEREDITARY

. . . As soon as he [the king] is anointed, he acquires the office for himself and his children forever. The right thereto is transmitted as a legacy, as it is said "To the end that he may prolong his days in his kingdom, he and his children in the midst of Israel" (Deut. 17:20). If he left a son who is a minor, the kingdom is held for him till he grows up, as Jehoiada acted in the case of Joash. Whoever is first in the order of inheritance is first in the order of succession to the kingship. The older son takes precedence of the younger one.

But not only the office of king but every position of appointive office held by the father descends to his son and son's son in perpetuity, provided that the son is entitled to fill the vacancy by reason of wisdom and piety.

As soon as David was anointed king, he acquired the crown of royalty, which became hereditary in his male line forever, as it is written: "Thy throne shall be established forever" (II Sam. 7:16). But he acquired it only for the deserving ones [among his descendants], as it is written "if thy children keep my covenant" (Ps. 132: 12). But although he acquired it only for the deserving (among his children), the kingdom will not be cut off from the seed of David forever. . . .

If the prophet appoints a king from any tribe of Israel [other than that of Judah] and that king walks in the way of the Law and the commandments and fights the battles of the Lord, he is deemed a legitimate king, and all the rules set forth with regard to the king apply to him, even though the kingship belongs primarily to David and therefore one of his descendants should be the ruling monarch. For Ahijah the Shilonite appointed Jereboam king and said to him: "And it shall be, if thou wilt hearken to all that I command thee. . . . I will build thee a sure house, as I built for David" (I Kings 11:38).

Ibid.

The king is to be accorded great honor. The attitude of his subjects toward him should be one of awe and reverence, as it is said: "Thou shalt in anywise set him king over thee" (Deut. 17:15), implying that his awe should be over you. No commoner may ride on his horse, sit on his throne, make use of his sceptre or crown, or any of his general utensils. At his death these objects are burned in his honor. Nor is anyone but a king to make use of his men-servants, maidservants, or attendants. . . .

It is forbidden to see the king when he is naked, or when his hair is being cut, or when he is taking a bath, or when he dries himself [after his bath]. He may not perform *halizah*. . . . This is an act of humiliation. Even if he is willing to submit to the humiliation, no heed is paid to him, for in the case of a king, if he forgoes the honor due him, it is not remitted. Since he cannot perform *halizah* he cannot contract a levirate marriage.

The king has his hair trimmed every day, pays due regard to his personal appearance, adorns himself with beautiful clothes—as it is written: "Thine eyes shall see the king in his beauty" (Is. 33:17)—sits on his throne in his palace, sets his crown on his head. All the people come before him when he is disposed to see them, they stand in his presence, and bow down to the ground. Even the prophet stands in the presence of the king and bows down to the ground, as it is written: "Behold Nathan the prophet. . . ."

The High Priest, however, comes before the king only when he is disposed to do it; he does not stand in his presence, but the king stands before him, as it is said: "And he shall stand before Eleazar the priest" (Nu. 27:21). Nevertheless, it is the duty of the High Priest to give honor to the king, to ask him to be seated, to rise before him when the latter comes to see him. . . .

So, too, it is incumbent upon the king to give honor to students of the Torah. When the members of the Sanhedrin and Sages of Israel visit him, he shall rise before them and sit them at his side. . . .

Just as Scripture accords great honor to the king and bids all pay him honor, so it bids him cultivate a humble and lowly spirit. He must not exercise his authority in a supercilious manner. . . . He should deal graciously and compassionately with the small and the great, conduct their affairs in their best interests, be wary of the honor of even the lowliest. When he addresses the public collectively, he shall use gentle language, as did David when he said: "Hear me, my brethren, and my people" (I Chr. 28:2). . . . At all times his conduct should be marked by a spirit of great humility. . . . He should put up with the cumbrances, burdens, grumblings, and anger of the people as a nursing father puts up with a sucking child. The

Bible styles the king "shepherd," [as it is written] "to be shepherd over Jacob His People" (Ps. 78:71).

Ibid., 2

As soon as the king ascends the throne, he must write a scroll of the Law for himself, in addition to the one which his ancestors have left him. . . . If his father left him no scroll, he must write two copies; one, the writing of which is obligatory upon every Jew, he shall place in his treasure-house, and the other is to be with him all the time. . . . When he goes forth to war it shall be with him; when he returns [from war], it shall be with him; when he sits in judgment, it shall be with him; when he sits down to eat, it shall be with him, as it is said: "And it shall be with him, and he shall read therein all the days of his life" (Deut. 17:19).

The king is forbidden to drink to the point of intoxication, as it is written: "It is not for kings to drink wine" (Prov. 31:4). He shall be occupied day and night with the study of the Law and the need of Israel, as it is said: "And it shall be with him, and he shall read therein all the days of his life" (Deut. 17:19).

Whoever disobeys the royal decree because he is engaged in the performance of a religious commandment, even it be a light commandment, is not liable, because (when there is a conflict) between the edict of the Master (God) and the edict of the servant (the king), the former takes precedence of the latter. It goes without saying that if the king issues an order annulling a religious precept, no heed is paid to it.

Ibid., 3

It is within the power of the king to levy taxes upon the people for his own needs or for war purposes. He fixes the custom duties, and it is forbidden to evade them. He may issue a decree that whoever dodges them shall be punished either by confiscation of his property or by death. . . .

His sole aim and thought should be to uplift the true religion, to fill the world with righteousness, to break the arm of the wicked, and to fight the battles of the Lord. The prime reason for appointing a king was that he execute judgment and wage war, as it is written: "And that our king may judge us, and go out before us, and fight our battles" (I Sam. 8:20).

Ibid., 4

PRIMARY AND OPTIONAL WARS

The primary war which the king wages is a war for a religious cause. Which may be denominated a war for a religious cause? It includes the war against the seven nations, that against Amalek, and a war to deliver Israel from the enemy attacking him. Thereafter he may engage in an optional war, that is, a war against neighboring nations to extend the borders of Israel and to enhance his greatness and prestige.

For a war waged for a religious cause, the king need not obtain the sanction of the court. He may at any time go forth of his own accord and compel the people to go with him. But in case of an optional war, he may not lead forth the people save by a decision of the court of seventy-one.

He may break through [private property] to make a road for himself, and none may protest against it. No limit can be prescribed for the king's road; he expropriates as much as is needed. He does not have to make detours because someone's vineyard or field [is in his way]. He takes the straight route and attacks the enemy.

All provinces conquered by the king at the decision of the court are deemed a national conquest and become in all respects an integral part of the Land of Israel conquered by Joshua, provided that they are annexed after the whole of Palestine, the boundaries of which are specified in the Bible, has been reconquered.

Ibid., 5

He who fights [a primary war, i.e., for a religious cause] with all his heart, without fear, with the sole intention of sanctifying the Name, is assured that no harm will befall him. He will build for himself a lasting house in Israel, acquiring it for himself and his children forever, and will prove worthy of life in the World-to-Come, as it is written: "For the Lord will certainly make my lord a sure house, because my lord fighteth the battles of the Lord; and evil is not found in thee. . . . Yet the soul of my lord shall be bound in the bundle of life with the Lord thy God" (I Sam. 25:28, 29).

Ibid., 7

LEADERS AND MEN

It has already been fully explained that man is naturally a social being, that by virtue of his nature he seeks to form communities;

man is therefore different from other living beings that are not compelled to combine into communities. He is, as you know, the highest form in the creation, and he therefore includes the largest number of constituent elements; this is the reason why the human race contains such a great variety of individuals, that we cannot discover two persons exactly alike in any moral quality, or in external appearance. The cause of this is the variety in man's temperament and in accident dependent on his form; for with every physical form there are connected certain special accidents different from those which are connected with the substance. Such a variety among the individuals of a class does not exist in any other class of living beings; for the variety in any other species is limited; only man forms an exception; two persons may be so different from each other in every respect that they appear to belong to two different classes. Whilst one person is so cruel that he kills his youngest child in his anger, another is too delicate and faint-hearted to kill even a fly or worm. The same is the case with most of the accidents. This great variety and the necessity of social life are essential elements in man's nature.

But the well-being of society demands that there should be a leader able to regulate the actions of man; he must complete every shortcoming, remove every excess and prescribe for the conduct of all, so that the natural variety should be counterbalanced by the uniformity of legislation, and the order of society be well established. I therefore maintain that the Law, though not a product of Nature, is nevertheless not entirely foreign to Nature. It being the will of God that our race should exist and be permanently established, He in His wisdom gave it such properties that man can acquire the capacity of ruling others. Some persons are therefore inspired with theories of legislation, such as prophets and lawgivers; others possess the power of enforcing the dictates of the former, and of compelling people to obey them, and to act accordingly. Such are kings, who accept the code of lawgivers and [rulers] who pretend to be prophets, and accept, either entirely or partly, the teaching of the prophets. They accept one part while rejecting another part, either because this course appears to them more convenient, or out of ambition, because it might lead people to believe that the rulers themselves had been prophetically inspired with these laws, and did not copy them from others. For when we like a certain perfection we find pleasure in it, and wish to possess it, we sometimes desire to make others believe that we possess that virtue, although we are fully aware that we do not possess it. Thus people e.g., adorn themselves with the poems of others, and publish them as their own productions. It also occurs in the works of wise men on the various branches of science that an ambitious, lazy person sees an opinion expressed by another person, appropriates it and boasts that he himself originated it.

Guide, II, 40

20. JUDGES, COURTS, AND JUSTICE

How many regular tribunals are to be set up in Israel? How many members is each to comprise? First there is established a Supreme Court holding session in the sanctuary. This is styled "the Great Sanhedrin" and consists of seventy-one elders. . . . The one who excels in wisdom is appointed head of the tribunal. He is the presiding officer of the college and is always designated by the Sages as *Nasi*. He occupies the place of Moses, our teacher. The most distinguished of the seventy is next in rank. He is seated to the right of the Nasi and is known as *Ab Bet Din*. . . .

Sanhedrin, 1

In addition [to the Great Sanhedrin], two other tribunals, each numbering twenty-three members, are set up [in Jerusalem], one sitting at the entrance of the Temple Court, and the other at the entrance of the Temple Mount.

Moreover, in each town with a population of one hundred and twenty and upward there is set up a small Sanhedrin, meeting at the gate of the town, as it is said: "And establish justice in the gate" (Amos 5:15). How many are to make up the small Sanhedrin? Twenty-Three. The most learned among them is presiding judge. . . . If a town has a population of less than one hundred and twenty, a court-of-three is set up there. There can be no tribunal of less than three members, for there must be a majority and a minority in case a difference of opinion arises on a question of law.

Although there can be no court less than three, according to bib-

lical law even one man may try a case, as it is said: In righteousness
shalt thou judge thy neighbor (Lev. 19:15). On the authority of
the Scribes, however, there must be three to try a case. If two try a
case, their decision is not valid.

Ibid.

No city, even if its population reaches into the thousands, can
qualify for a Sanhedrin unless it has two great scholars—one competent to teach the whole Torah and to decide questions within its
entire domain, and the other who understands [the whole Torah]
and is able to discuss learnedly [all legal questions].

Ibid.

Only those are eligible to serve as members of the Sanhedrin—
whether the Great or a Small—who are wise men and understanding,
that is, who are experts in the Torah and versed in many other
branches of learning; who possess some knowledge of the general
sciences, such as medicine, mathematics, [the calculation of] cycles
and constellations; and are somewhat acquainted with astrology, the
arts of diviners, soothsayers, sorcerers, the superstitious practices of
idolaters, and similar matters, so that they be competent to deal with
cases requiring such knowledge.

Neither a very aged man nor a eunuch is appointed to any Sanhedrin, since these are apt to be wanting in tenderness; nor is one
who is childless, because a member of the Sanhedrin must be a person
who is sympathetic.

The king of Israel is not given a seat on the Sanhedrin, because
it is forbidden to differ with him or to rebel against his word. But
the High Priest may be given a seat if he is fit for the office by reason
of scholarship.

Elsewhere it is said "Men of valor" (Ex. 18:21), that is, men
strong in the performance of the commandments, and strict with
themselves, men who control their passions, whose character is above
reproach, aye, whose youth is of unblemished repute. The phrase
"men of valor" implies also stout-heartedness to rescue the oppressed
from the hand of the oppressor, as it is said: "But Moses stood up and
helped them" (Ex. 2:17). And just as Moses, our teacher, was
humble, so every judge should be humble. "Such as fear God" (Ex.
18:21)—this is to be understood literally; "hating gain" (*Ibid.*),
that is, they are not anxious about their own money and do not strive

to accumulate wealth, for he that hastens after riches, want shall come upon him; "men of truth" (*Ibid.*), that is, they pursue righteousness spontaneously and of their own accord; they love the truth, hate violence, and flee anything that savors of unrighteousness.

Ibid.

Just as the members of the court must be free from all suspicion with respect to conduct, so must they be free from all physical defects. Every conceivable effort should be made to the end that all the members of that tribunal be of mature age, imposing stature, good appearance, that they be able to express their views in clear and well-chosen words, and be conversant with most of the spoken languages, in order that the Sanhedrin may dispense with the services of an interpreter.

In the case of the court-of-three, all the above mentioned requirements are not insisted upon. Nevertheless it is essential that every one of the members thereof possess the following seven qualifications: wisdom, humility, fear of God, disdain of gain, love of truth, love of his fellow men, and a good reputation.

Ibid., 2

OBEYING THE GREAT COURT

He [God] has commanded us that we are to hearken to the Great Court and to do whatever [the judges thereof] command [us] concerning [things] forbidden, and [things] permissible, there being no difference in this between [a decision] which they have arrived at by reasoning, or a decision [they] have derived from an application of the analogies by which the Torah is interpreted, or a decision which they have agreed on as constituting a prohibition of the Torah, or any matter whatsoever which in their opinion is fair, and strengthens [the authority] of the Torah: in all these [cases] we are obligated to hearken, obey, and abide by the words [of the Great Court]—we must not depart from them.

Sefer ha-Mitzvot, Com. 174

Although the kings of the House of David may not be given seats on the Sanhedrin, they judge others and are judged in a suit against them. But the kings of Israel may neither judge nor be judged, because they do not submit to the discipline of the Torah. [To sit in judgment on them] might lead to untowered consequences.

Sanhedrin, 2

It is stated by the Rabbis that the Great Sanhedrin used to send messengers throughout the Land of Israel to examine [candidates] for the office of judge. Whoever was found to be wise, sin-fearing, humble and contrite, of unblemished character, and enjoying the esteem of his fellow-men was installed as local judge. From the local court, he was promoted to the court situated at the entrance of the Temple Mount; thence to the court situated at the entrance of the Court; thence to the Supreme Court.

One who is recognized by the public as well qualified, or has obtained authorization from the court may judge alone. In some respects, however, he cannot be said to constitute a court. And though he had the right to act as sole judge, the Rabbis enjoin upon him the duty of associating others with himself. They said: "Judge not alone, for none may judge alone save One" (Ab. 4:8).

Ibid.

The Divine Presence dwells in the midst of any competent Jewish tribunal. Therefore it behooves the judges to sit in court enwrapped [in fringed robes] in a state of fear and reverence and in a serious frame of mind. They are forbidden to behave frivolously, to jest, or to engage in idle talk. They should concentrate their minds on matters of Torah and wisdom.

Ibid., 3

Said the Rabbis: "Say not, 'So-and-so is a handsome man, I will make him judge; So-and-so is a man of valor, I will make him judge; So-and-so is related to me, I will make him judge; So-and-so is a linguist, I will make him judge." If you do it, he will acquit the guilty and condemn the innocent, not because he is wicked, but because he is lacking in knowledge. Therefore Scripture says: "Ye shall not respect persons in judgment."

Moreover, the injunction "Thou shalt not make with Me gods of silver or gods of gold" (Ex. 20:20) has been interpreted by the Sages to mean: gods who came into being through the influence of silver or gold, that is, a judge who owes his appointment to his wealth only.

Ibid.

It is forbidden to rise before a judge who procured the office he holds by paying for it. The Rabbis bid us slight and despise him, regard the judicial robe in which he is enwrapped as packsaddle of an ass.

It was the habit of the early Sages to shun appointment to the position of judge. They exerted their utmost endeavors to avoid sitting in judgment unless they were convinced that there were no others so fit for the office as they, and that were they to persist in their refusal, the cause of justice would suffer. Even then they would not act in the capacity of judges until the people and the elders brought pressure upon them to do so.

"Thou shalt take no gift" (Ex. 23:8). The purport of this prohibition is not to caution the judge against accepting a gift with the intention of perverting justice. Its purpose is to warn him not to accept a bribe even if he proposes to acquit the innocent and condemn the guilty. He who does it transgresses this negative command. To him too is addressed the admonition "Cursed be he that taketh a bribe" (Deut. 27:25). He is bound to return the bribe if the giver demands it.

Ibid.

The giver of a bribe as well as the receiver, contravenes a negative command, as it is said: "Not put a stumbling block before the blind" (Lev. 19:14).

Ibid.

A judge who borrows things from others is ineligible to try a suit in which the man he borrows from is involved. This applies only to a judge who has nothing to lend in return. If, however, he is in possession of things to lend to others, he is qualified, for the man from whom he borrows may borrow things from him.

He is also forbidden to treat the people with disrespect, though they be ignorant. He should not force his way through the holy people [to get to his seat], for though they be uninformed and lowly, they are the children of Abraham, Isaac, and Jacob, of the host of God, brought forth out of Egypt with great power and with a mighty hand. He should bear patiently the cumbrance and burden of the community, as did Moses, our teacher, concerning whom it is said: "as a nursing father carrieth the sucking child" (Nu. 11:12).

341

It is also said: "And I charged your judges" (Deut. 1:16). This is an exhortation to the judge to bear patiently with the congregation.

Ibid., 25

Just as the judge is bidden to observe this command, so is the congregation bidden to accord respectful treatment to the judge, as it is said: "And I commanded you" (Deut. 1:18). This is an exhortation to the congregation to regard the judge with a feeling of reverence. The judge therefore must not make himself contemptible or indulge in frivolity.

Ibid.

If the court has many cases on the docket, the case of an orphan is tried before that of a widow, as it is said, "Judge the fatherless, plead for the widow" (Isa. 1:17), the case of a widow comes before that of a scholar, a scholar's before an illiterate's, the suit of a woman before that of a man, for the humiliation is greater in the case of a woman.

Ibid., 21

At all times a judge should think of himself as if a sword was suspended over his head and Gehenna gaping under him. He should know whom he is judging and before Whom he is judging, and Who will call him to account if he deviates from the line of truth, as it is written: "God standeth in the congregation of God, in the midst of the judges" (Prov. 22:23). A judge who, even for a single hour renders absolutely true judgment is as though he had [helped to] set the world in order and cause the Divine Prescence to dwell in Israel, as it is written "God standeth in the congregation of God" (Ps. 82:1).

Ibid.

If a man takes payment for acting as judge, his decisions are null. This ruling obtains only if it is evident that the payment represents compensation for judicial services. But if he has an occupation in which he is engaged and two men come before him with a lawsuit, and he says to them, "Either procure me one who will attend to my work until I shall have adjudicated your case or remunerate me for loss of time," he is permitted to do so, provided that it is obvious that the payment is for loss of time only and no more and that the fee he receives is contributed equally by both parties to the suit and is given him in the presence of both. Under these circumstances he is permitted to accept payment.

Ibid., 23

A man is forbidden to act as judge for a friend . . . even though the latter is not his most intimate friend. Nor is he to act as judge for one whom he dislikes, although he is not his enemy, seeking his harm. It is essential that both parties to the suit should be alike in his estimation and affection. The judge who does not know either litigant and the life he leads is in the best conceivable position to render a righteous judgment.

Two scholars who dislike each other are forbidden to sit together in judgment, for this might lead to the rendering of a perverted judgment. Prompted by hostility each will be inclined to refute the arguments of the other.

At all times while the litigants are before you, regard them as guilty, on the presumption that there is no truth in the statements made by either of them, and be guided by what appears to you from the general drift of the arguments to be true. But when they have departed from your presence regard them both as innocent, since they have acquiesced in the sentence passed by you, and judge each of them by the scale of merit.

Ibid.

The Great Sanhedrin, in contradistinction to the lesser judicial bodies designated by that name exercised supreme civil and religious authority. In addition to its many other functions, it arranged the calendar and prepared correct copies of the Torah. It was presided over by the actual president who bore the title Nasi, and the second, or vice-president, who was the Ab Bet Din (father of the court).

The Great Sanhedrin of Jerusalem is the root of the Oral Law. The members thereof are the pillars of instruction; out of them go forth statutes and judgments to all Israel. Scripture bids us repose confidence in them, as it is said, "According to the Law which they shall teach thee" (Deut. 17:11).

Rebels, 1

So long as the Supreme Court was in existence, there were no controversies in Israel. . . . After the Supreme Court ceased to exist, disputes multiplied in Israel; one declaring "unclean," giving a reason for his ruling; another declaring "clean," giving a reason for his ruling; one forbidding, the other permitting.

Ibid.

If the Supreme Court instituted a decree, enacted an ordinance, or introduced a custom which was universally accepted in Israel, and a later Supreme Court wishes to rescind the measure, to abolish the ordinance, decree or custom, it is not empowered to do so unless it is superior to the former both in point of wisdom and in point of numbers. If it is superior in wisdom but not in numbers, or in numbers but not in wisdom, it is denied the right to abrogate the measure adopted by its predecessor, even if the reason which prompted the latter to enact the decree or ordinance has lost all force.

Ibid., 2

But how is it possible for any Supreme Court to exceed another in number, seeing that each Supreme Court consists of seventy-one members? We include in the number the wise men of the age who agree to and accept without demur the decision of the [contemporaneous] Supreme Court.

Ibid.

The last ruling applies only to prohibited measures, which like many other measures do not have as their purpose the safeguarding of the Torah. But decrees and prohibitions designed by the court to serve as a protective fence to the Law, if they have been universally accepted in Israel, no later Supreme Court, even if it be superior to the former, is empowered to abrogate or permit.

Ibid.

However, the court, even if it be inferior [to the former] is authorized to dispense for a time even with these measures. For these decrees are not to be invested with greater stringency than the commands of the Torah itself, which any court has a right to suspend as an emergency measure. . . . So, too, if in order to bring back the multitude to religion and save them from general religious laxity, the court deems it necessary to set aside temporarily a positive or a negative command, it may do so, taking into account the need of the hour. Even as a physician will amputate the hand or the foot of a patient in order to save his life, so the court may advocate, when an emergency arises, the temporary disregard of some of the commandments, that the commandments as a whole may be preserved. This is in keeping with what the early sages said: Desecrate on his account one Sabbath that he be able to observe many Sabbaths (Yoma 85b).

Ibid.

Before instituting a decree or enacting an ordinance or introducing a custom which it deems necessary, the court should calmly deliberate [the matter] and make sure that the majority of the community can live up to it. At no time is a decree to be imposed upon the public which the majority thereof cannot endure.

If the court has issued a decree in the belief that the majority of the community could endure it, and after the enactment thereof the people made light of it and it was not accepted by the majority, the decree is void and the court is denied the right to coerce the people to abide by it.

If after a decree had been promulgated, the court was of opinion that it was universally accepted by Israel and nothing was done about it for years, and after the lapse of a long period a latter court investigates the doings of Israel and finds that the decree is not generally accepted, the latter court, even if it be inferior to the former in wisdom and number, is authorized to abrogate it.

Ibid.

The court does not impose the penalty of death on mere conjecture but on the conclusive testimony of witnesses. Even if the witnesses saw him [the assailant] chasing the other, gave him warning, and then lost sight of him, or they followed him into a ruin and found the victim writhing [in death agony], while the sword dripping with blood was in the hands of the slayer, the court does not condemn the accused to death, since the witnesses did not see him at the time of the slaying.

Sanhedrin, 20

Forty years before the destruction of the Second Temple the right of Israel to try capital cases ceased. Though the sanctuary still existed, the

Sanhedrin was exiled and no longer held sessions in the place assigned to it in the sanctuary.

I believe a day will come when all sages and scholars will reach an agreement to appoint a member of one of the academies as head, an event which will take place in Palestine. This man will establish an academy. Being ordained, he will ordain others as he sees fit. Otherwise the restoration of the Great Court of Law will never be possible. We have however the divine promise that it will be re-established, as it is said: "And I will restore thy judges as at the first and thy counsellors as at the beginning; afterwards thou shalt be called 'the city of righteousness, the faithful city' " (Is. 1:26). This will surely be before the advent of the Messianic Age.

Mishnah Commentary

The court is forbidden to spare a murderer. It should not say, "This man is already slain; what good will it do to execute the other?" and thus prove lax in the duty of putting the murderer to death. For Scripture says: "And thine eyes shall not pity him, but thou shalt put away the blood of the innocent from Israel" (Deut. 19:13). . . . Likewise in cases that do not involve action in tort, no compassion is to be shown to one who is poor. Say not: "This man is poor, his opponent rich. Since I and the rich man are under obligation to support him, I will give judgment in his favor and he will be able to maintain himself honorably." Therefore the Torah admonishes: "Neither shalt thou favor a poor man in his cause" (Ex. 23:3), and it is said: "Thou shalt not respect the person of the poor" (Lev. 19:15).

Sanhedrin, 20

It is forbidden to show respect to a great man [at a trial]. For instance, if two litigants come before you for trial, one of whom is a great scholar, and the other is an ordinary man, do not greet the great man first, showing him friendliness and esteem. The outcome of such partiality will be that the other will find it impossible to marshal his arguments. The judge should therefore maintain an attitude of neutrality until the verdict is reached, as it is written: Nor favor the person of the mighty (*Ibid.*). Said the Rabbis, "Say not, 'This man is rich, this one is well connected. How can I put him to shame and see him humiliated?' "

Ibid.

When two litigants come before you, one of whom is a worthy person, and the other wicked, do not say, "Since this one is wicked, the presumption is that he is lying and the other is truthful, I will therefore turn the verdict against the wicked."

Ibid.

It happened once that a judge was crossing a river on a small fishing boat, when a man stretched forth his hand and helped him to get ashore. That man had a lawsuit, but the judge said to him, "I am disqualified from acting as judge in your suit." It also happened that a man once removed a bird's feather from a judge's mantle; another man once covered a spittle from a judge. In each of these instances, the judge said, "I am barred from trying your case." . . . There is still another incident of a tenant farmer who on Fridays used to bring to the owner figs from the garden he was cultivating. On one occasion, however, he brought the figs on Thursday, because he had a lawsuit. The judge, however, said, "I am barred from acting as judge in your case," for though the figs were his, since the tenant brought them ahead of time, he was ineligible to try the case.

Ibid., 23

It is forbidden to lead the community in a domineering and arrogant manner. One should exercise one's authority in a spirit of humility and not arrogance. The man at the head of the congregation who arouses excessive fear in the hearts of the members thereof for any but a religious purpose will be punished. It will not be given to him to have a son who will be a scholar.

Ibid., 25

As soon as a man is appointed leader of the community, he is forbidden to do [menial] labor in the presence of three men, lest he loses their respect.

Ibid.

Whoever submits a suit for adjudication to heathen judges in their courts, even if the judgment rendered by them is in consonance with

Jewish law, is a wicked man. It is as though he reviled, blasphemed, and rebelled against the law of Moses, our teacher.

Ibid., 26

THE LAW OF EVIDENCE

It is the duty of him who is in possession of evidence to testify in court whether the evidence will lead to condemnation or vindication. . . . In monetary matters, this duty devolves upon him only if he is asked to give evidence.

If the man in possession of evidence is a great scholar, and the members of the tribunal are inferior to him in wisdom, seeing that it is beneath his dignity to appear before them as witness, he need not testify. The positive command to pay respect to Torah [and its exponents] takes precedence over the negative command. This applies only in monetary cases, but in case of a prohibition the infraction of which his testimony would avert, or in cases involving either capital or corporal punishment, it is his duty to appear in court and testify. . . . Whenever there is a profanation of the Name [of God] the honor due to a teacher is disregarded.

The High Priest is under no obligation to act as witness save in a suit involving the king of Israel, in which case he repairs to the Supreme Court and testifies. In all other suits, he is exempt from giving evidence.

The witnesses are also made to undergo a cross-examination bearing upon aspects of the evidence which are not pivotal to the testimony and do not affect its validity. This is styled *bedikot* [cross-examination]. The more numerous the bedikot, the more praiseworthy is the judge. . . .

Evidence, 1

In capital cases it is required that the witnesses should see the culprit simultaneously, while he is committing the offense. They must testify at the same time and in the same court. This is not so in civil cases. . . .

Ibid., 4

Neither in civil nor in capital cases is a legal decision given on the evidence of one witness, as it is said: "One witness shall not rise up against a man for any iniquity, or for any sin (Deut. 19:15). By tradition it has been learned that "he rises up" (against a man) in a suit involving an oath.

Ibid., 5

In case of an epileptic, during a fit he is ineligible; in the interval [between fits], he is eligible, whether the paroxysm occurs periodically or at regular intervals, provided that he is not mentally disordered all the time, for there are epileptics who are always confused in mind. The question of the admissibility of epileptics requires careful consideration.

Ibid., 9

The blind, although they recognize voices and thus identify persons, are ineligible by biblical law, as it is said: "He being a witness, whether he hath seen" (Lev. 5:1), only one who can see may give evidence. The blind in one eye is eligible as witness.

Ibid.

Transgressors are ineligible as witnesses by biblical law, for it is said, "Put not thy hand with the wicked to be an unrighteous witness" (Ex. 23:1). The traditional interpretation of this injunction is: "Accept not the wicked as a witness. . . ."

Who is a transgressor? Whoever violates a negative command carrying with it the penalty of flogging is a transgressor and is therefore ineligible. . . . It goes without saying that whoever has incurred the sentence of death by the court is ineligible, as it is said: "that he is wicked deserving of death" (Nu. 35:31).

Ibid., 10

So too, in case of a loan on interest, both lender and borrower are disqualified. If the interest was direct, they are ineligible by biblical law; if indirect, they are ineligible by the authority of the Rabbis. So too, whoever is guilty of what according to the Rabbis is robbery is barred by rabbinical authority from giving evidence. To cite a case in point: those who coerce a sale, that is, seize land or chattel against the desire of the owner, although they pay for it, are disqualified by rabbinical law.

So too, tax farmers in general are ineligible. The presumption is that they exact [from the community] a sum in excess of that allowed them by the government, and appropriate the surplus. Tax collectors in general are eligible; if, however, it is discovered that they have collected even once, more than what they are entitled to, they are disqualified.

So, too, pigeon fowlers in populous areas are ineligible, because the presumption is that they decoy pigeons that belong to others without paying for them.

A dice player is disqualified [as witness] if he has no other occupation. In view of the fact that he contributes nothing to welfare of society, the presumption is that he makes his living out of dice playing, which is a form of robbery. . . . Likewise the ineligibility is extended . . . to those who indulge in the racing of cattle, beasts of chase, or birds, stipulating that the owner of the one that passes or overcomes the other shall get both, or any similar agreement made with regard to this sport, provided that the person under consideration has no other occupation. All these are disqualified on rabbinical authority.

Ibid.

Whoever has no knowledge of the Scripture, the Mishnah, and right conduct, has the status of a (potential) sinner and is, by rabbinical authority, ineligible as witness. The presumption is that a person on such low level will commit most of the transgressions that assail him.

Ibid., 11

Therefore an *am ha'arez* is not invited as witness, nor is his testimony accepted. If, however, he is known to be a person engaged in religious acts and the practice of benevolence and leads a righteous life, so that "right conduct" may be ascribed to him, his testimony is accepted, even though he is ignorant, i.e., is devoid of knowledge of the Scriptures and the Mishnah.

It follows therefore that every scholar is to be deemed eligible, unless he is found to be ineligible, and that every ignorant person is to be regarded as ineligible, unless it is known that he walks in the way of the righteous.

Likewise the self-abased are disqualified on the authority of the Rabbis. These comprise men who walk in the street eating in the sight of the public, and those who walk about naked in the street while they are engaged in a repugnant occupation, and those who do similar things indicative of a lack of sense of shame. They are on a level with dogs and will not hesitate to give false evidence. Included in this class are those who publicly accept charity from heathen when it is possible for them to accept it privately. They thus demean themselves and have no compunction in doing it. All these are disqualified by rabbinical law. . . .

As to informers, epicureans, and apostates, the Rabbis did not deem it necessary to include them among the ineligibles, because they enumerated only the wicked among the Israelites. But these rebellious disbelievers are on a lower level than heathens. . . .

Ibid.

Women are disqualified as witnesses by biblical law, as it is said, "At the mouth of two witnesses" (Deut. 19:15). The text employs the masculine, not the feminine gender.

Ibid., 9

By Scriptural authority kinsmen are ineligible to act as witnesses, as it is said, "The fathers shall not be put to death for the children, neither shall the children be put to death for the father" (Deut. 24:16). It is learned by tradition that included in this command is the exhortation not to condemn fathers to death on the testimony of their sons, nor sons on the testimony of their fathers. This applies also to other relatives. By biblical law only paternal relatives are disqualified, to wit: father, son and son's son; brothers by the same father; sons of brothers [by the same father]; uncles and brothers' son. By rabbinical authority, even maternal relatives and relatives by marriage are ineligible to testify concerning one another.

Ibid., 13

21. THOSE WHO FORFEIT LIFE ETERNAL

THE FOLLOWING have no portion in the World-to-Come, but are cut off and perish, and for their wickedness and sinfulness are condemned for ever and ever. Heretics and Epicureans; those who deny the Torah, the resurrection of the dead or the coming of the Redeemer; apostates; those who cause a multitude to sin, and those who secede from the ways of the community; any one who commits transgressions like Jehoiakim, in high-handed fashion and openly; informers; those who terrorize a community, not for a religious purpose; murderers and slanderers, and one who obliterates the physical mark of his Jewish origin.

Repentance, 3

HERETICS

Five Classes are termed Heretics; he who says that there is no God and the world has no ruler; he who says that there is a ruling power but that it is vested in two or more persons; he who says that there is one ruler, but that he is a body and has form; he who denies that He alone is the First Cause and Rock of the Universe; likewise, he who renders worship to any one besides Him, to serve as a mediator between the human being and the Lord of the Universe. Whoever belongs to any of these five classes is termed a heretic.

Repentance, 3

EPICUREANS

Three classes are called Epicureans: he who denies the reality of prophecy and maintains that there is no knowledge which emanates from the Creator and directly reaches the human mind; he who denies the prophecy of Moses, our teacher; and he who asserts that the Creator has no cognizance of the deeds of the children of men. Each of these classes consists of Epicureans. Three classes are deniers of the Torah; he who says that the Torah is not of divine origin—even if he says of one verse, or of a single word, that Moses said it, of himself—is a denier of the Torah; likewise, he who denies its interpretations, that is, the Oral Law, and repudiates its reporters, as Zadok and Boethus did; he who says that the Creator changed one commandment for another, and that this Torah, although of divine origin, is now obsolete, as the Nazarenes and Moslems assert. Everyone belonging to any of these classes is a denier of the Torah.

Repentance, 3

DEGREES OF APOSTASY

There are two classes of apostates—an apostate with respect to the violation of a single precept, and an apostate with respect to the whole Torah. The former is a person who has determined to violate a certain precept, commits the transgression habitually and has become notorious for it. Even if it is one of the lighter sins, as, for instance, if a person wears a garment "of diverse sorts" (a mixture of wool and flax) (Deut. 22:11) or "rounds the corner of his head" (Lev. 19:27), doing so habitually, so that it appears that the precept is regarded by him as no longer binding, he is an apostate in regard to that particular observance, provided that he acted in a provocative spirit. An apostate with respect to the whole Torah is one, for example, who at a time of religious persecution becomes converted to the idolators' religion, clings to them, saying, "What advantage is it to me to adhere to the people of Israel, who are of low estate and persecuted. Better for me to join these nations who are powerful." A person who acts thus is apostate in respect to the whole Torah.

Repentance, 3

Those who cause the multitude to sin, include one who induces others to sin, whether in a great matter, like Jeroboam, Zadok and Boethus, or in a light matter, if he only induces them to nullify the observance of an affirmative precept; and any one who coerces others to sin, like Manasseh who put Israelites to death and so forced the people into idolatry; or deceives others and leads them astray.

Ibid.

One who separates himself from the Community, even if he does not commit a transgression but only holds aloof from the congregation of Israel, does not fulfil religious precepts in common with his people, shows himself indifferent when they are in distress, does not observe their fasts, but goes his own way, as if he were one of the Gentiles and did not belong to the Jewish people—such a person has no portion in the world to come. He, who, like Jehoiakim, commits transgressions arrogantly, whether these are light or grave offenses, has no portion in the world to come. Such a one is called a shameless transgressor, because he exhibits effrontery and shamelessness and is unabashed by the words of the Torah.

Ibid.

LESSER OFFENSES

There are transgressions less grave than those mentioned, concerning which, however, the Sages said that whoever habitually commits them will have no portion in the world to come. One should therefore avoid and beware of such transgressors. They are those who give another a nickname, call another by his nickname, put him to shame in public, seek honor by another person's humiliation, contemn scholars or one's teachers, treat the festivals with contempt, desecrate things sacred. When it is said that one who commits any of these sins has no part in the world to come, the statement is to be understood as only applying to the sinner who dies impenitent. But if he repented of his wickedness and expired while still penitent, he is of those who will have a portion in the world to come; for there is nothing that stands in the way of repentance. Even if a person, throughout his life, denied the essential principle of religion and repented at the end, he will have a portion in the world to come; as it is said "Peace, peace to him that is far off and to him that is near, saith the Lord, and I will heal him" (Is. 57:19). All wicked persons, transgressors, apostates and the like, who come back penitent, whether openly or secretly, are accepted, as it is said, "Return, ye backsliding children" (Jer. 3:22). Even if one is still a backslider—since he only returns in secret and not openly—he is accepted if he repents.

Repentance, 3

INFORMERS

There are two classes of informers: one who delivers a coreligionist into the power of a heathen, who will put him to death or assault him; and one who delivers the property of a coreligionist to a heathen or to a despot, who is like a heathen. Both classes of informers have no portion in the world to come.

Belonging to the group, are five offenses of such a nature that he who comimts them will always be addicted to them and will find it hard to break away from them. Hence, a person should be on his guard lest he become habituated to them, seeing that they are all pernicious habits. They are as follows: Tale-bearing, Evil Speech, Choleric Temper, Evil Thoughts; keeping company with a wicked person, for thus one learns his ways which become impressed on the heart.

As for those who deviate from the practices of the congregation—that is, men who cast off the restraints of the commandments, and did not join their fellow-Jews in the performance of the precepts . . . but felt free to do as they pleased—for those no mourning is observed. In the event of their death, their brethren and other relatives don white garments, and wrap themselves in white garments, eat, drink, and rejoice, because the enemies of the Lord have perished.

Repentance, 3

SUICIDES

For one who has committed suicide, no funeral rites are performed, no mourning is observed, no lamentation is made; but the relatives stand in line [to be comforted], the Mourner's Benediction is recited, and all that is intended as matter of honor for the living is done.

Who is to be regarded as suicide? Not he who climbing up to a roof fell and died, but one who said: "Look! I am climbing to the top of the roof." If he has been ascending it, agitated by anger or fear, and then fell and died, the presumption is that he committed suicide. But if he is found strangled or hanging from a tree, or slain, or fallen upon his sword, his status is that of any other person who died. His obsequies are attended to and none of the last rites are denied him.

Repentance, 3

TALE-BEARERS, SCANDAL-MONGERS, AND FLATTERERS

Who is a tale-bearer? One who carries reports, and goes about from one person to another and says "So-and-so said this;" "Such and such a statement have I heard about so-and-so." Even if what he says and repeats may be true, the tale-bearer ruins the world. There is a still graver offense that comes within this prohibition, namely, the evil tongue. This means talking disparagingly of anyone, even though what one says is true; but he who utters falsehood is called a slanderer. A person with an evil tongue is one who, sitting in company, says "That person did such a thing;" "So-and-so's ancestors were so-and-so;" "I have heard this about him;" and then proceeds to talk scandal. Of such a person Scripture says "May the Lord cut off all smooth lips, the tongue that speaketh proud things" (Ps. 12:4).

Ethical Conduct (Deot), 7

The sages say "There are three offenses for which one is punished in this world and forfeits his portion in the world to come. These are idolatry, incest, and murder; but the evil tongue is equal to all three put together." The sages further said "To indulge in evil speech is like a denial of the fundamental principle of religion," as it is said "Who said our tongue will we make mighty; our lips are with us; who is Lord over us?" (Ps. 12:5). The sages also said "The evil tongue slays three persons; the utterer of the evil, the listener, the one spoken about; and the listener will be punished worse than the speaker."

Ibid.

There are modes of speech that may be styled "dust of the evil tongue." Such are remarks like the following: "Who would have thought of so-and-so that he would be as he is now." Or "be silent about so-and-so. I do not wish to tell what happened, etc." To speak in a person's favor in the presence of his enemies, savors of the evil tongue. For it will provoke them to speak of him disparagingly. Referring to this, Solomon said "He that blesseth his friend with a loud voice, rising early in the morning, it shall be counted a curse unto him" (Prov. 27:14). For out of what has been said to his good proceedeth evil. Such too is the case of one who indulges in evil speech jokingly and frivolously, and not out of hatred. And so, Solomon in his wisdom, says "As one who mockingly casteth firebrands, arrows and death, and saith, am I not jesting?" (Prov. 26:18). Equally reprehensible is one who indulges in evil speech deceitfully, that is, speaks as it were in all innocence, as if unaware that what he says is an evil utterance, and when a protest is made, replies, "I do not

know that this is evil speech, or that such is the conduct of so-
and-so."

Ibid.

Whether one indulges in evil speech about a person in his presence,
or in his absence, or makes statements which, if repeated, would tend
to hurt him physically or injure him financially, distress or alarm him
—all this is evil speech. If a statement of this character had been
made in the presence of three persons, the subject matter is regarded
as public and generally known, and if one of the three repeats it, he
is not guilty of evil speech, provided he had no intention to give the
story wide currency.

All such persons are scandal-mongers in whose neighborhood it is
forbidden to reside; and still more is it forbidden to cultivate their
society and listen to them. The sentence passed upon our forefathers
in the wilderness was confirmed, only because they were guilty of the
sin of the evil tongue.

Ibid.

He who takes revenge, violates a prohibition, as it is said "Thou
shalt not take vengeance" (Lev. 19:18). What is "taking vengeance?"
The following is a case. A neighbor says to me, "Lend me your axe."
He replies "I will not lend it to you." The next day, the latter needs
a similar favor from the neighbor and says to him "Lend me your
axe," and receives the reply "I will not lend it to you, for you did
not lend me your axe when I asked it of you." Any one who acts in
this way is "taking vengeance." But when he comes to borrow aught,
one should give what is asked cheerfully, and not repay discourtesy
with discourtesy. And so in similar cases. Thus David, expressing his
excellent sentiments, said "If I have requited him that did evil unto
me, or despoiled mine adversary" (Ps. 7:5).

Ibid.

So too, one who bears a grudge against a fellow-Israelite violates
a prohibition as it is said, "Nor bear a grudge against the children
of thy people" (Lev. 19:18). What is "bearing a grudge?" A said to
B, "Let this house to me, or let me borrow this ox." B refuses. After
a time B comes to A to borrow or hire something. A replies "Here it
is. I lend it to you. I am not like you. I will not treat you as you

treated me." One who acts thus, transgresses the commandment "Thou shalt not bear a grudge." For as long as one nurses a grievance and keeps it in mind, one may come to take vengeance. The Torah, accordingly, emphatically warns us not to bear a grudge, so that the impression of the wrong shall be quite obliterated and be no longer remembered. This is the right principle. It alone makes civilized life and social intercourse possible.

Ibid.

If one observes that a person committed a sin or walks in a way that is not good, it is a duty to bring the erring man back to the right path and point out to him that he is wronging himself by his evil course, as it is said "Thou shalt surely rebuke thy neighbor" (Lev. 19:17). He who rebukes another, whether for offenses against the rebuker himself or for sins against God, should administer the rebuke in private, speak to the offender gently and tenderly, and point out that he is only speaking for the wrongdoer's own good, to secure for him life in the World-to-Come. If the latter accepts the rebuke, well and good. If not, he should be rebuked a second, and a third time. And so one is bound to continue the admonitions, till the sinner assaults the admonisher and says to him "I refuse to listen." Whoever is in a position to prevent wrongdoing and does not do so, is responsible for the iniquity of all the wrongdoers whom he might have checked.

Ibid., 6

It is forbidden to accustom oneself to smooth speech and flatteries. One must not say one thing and mean another. Inward and outward self should correspond; only what we have in mind, should we utter with the mouth. We must deceive no one, not even an idolater. A man, for example, must not sell to an idolater flesh from a beast that has died naturally, as if it were meat of an animal ritually slaughtered. Nor should one sell a shoe, the leather of which came from the hide of a beast that met with a natural death, allowing it to be believed that the leather had come from the hide of a ritually slaughtered animal. One must not urge another to join one at a meal, when one is aware that the invitation will not be accepted. Nor should one press upon another any marks of friendship which one knows will be declined. So too, casks of wine, which must be opened for sale, should not be broached in such a way as to deceive a guest and make him

believe that they have been opened in his honor, and so forth. Even
a single word of flattery or deception is forbidden. A person should
always cherish truthful speech, an upright spirit and a pure heart
free from all forwardness and perversity.

Ibid., 2

TERRORISTS

The terrorists of a community, not for the sake of God, are those who
rule a congregation arbitrarily so that all fear and are afraid of them
—their aim, like that of the heathen kings, being to advance their
own glory and interests but not to promote the glory of God.

Repentance, 3

One should not cherish large desires—hurrying to get rich—nor
be melancholy and idle, but should be contented, engage a little in
secular occupation, and devote oneself to the study of the Torah, and
rejoice in the little one has as his portion. One should not be quarrelsome, jealous, or sensual; nor run after honor. Thus our wise men said,
"Envy, lust and ambition take a man from the world" (Ethics of
the Fathers, 4:8). In fine, in every class of dispositions, a man should
choose the mean so that all one's dispositions shall occupy the exact
middle between the extremes. This is what Solomon expressed in the
text "Balance the course of thy steps, so that all thy ways may be
right" (Prov. 4:26).

Ethical Conduct (Deot), 2

It is forbidden to lead the community in a domineering and arrogant manner. One should exercise one's authority in a spirit of humility. The man at the head of the congregation who arouses excessive fear in the hearts of the members thereof for any but a religious
purpose will be punished. It will not be given to him to have a son
who will be a scholar. . . . He is also forbidden to treat the people
with disrespect though they may be ignorant. He should not force
his way through the holy people [to get to his seat], for though they
may be uninformed and lowly, they are the children of Abraham,
Isaac, and Jacob, of the hosts of God, brought forth out of Egypt
with great power and a mighty hand. He should bear patiently the
encumbrance and burden of the community, as did Moses, our
teacher, concerning whom it is said: as a nursing father carrieth
the suckling child (Nu. 11:12).

Sanhedrin, 25

REBUKING THE SINNER

Chastisement may lead to repentance, but it must be gentle, not offensive or embarrassing.

He has commanded us that we are to rebuke the sinner or him who is disposed to sin, hindering him therein by words of chastisement. It is not proper for one to say, "Since I am not the one who is to sin, let him sin who will; what concern have I with him or with his God?" [Such an attitude] is repugnant to [the principles of] the Torah. On the contrary, we are commanded not to sin as well as not to permit any one of our compatriots to rebel [against the word of God]; and if he persists in his rebelliousness we are under obligation to rebuke him, causing him to repent, so that even though no witness be present to testify against him [we are to apprise him of liability for violation of the Law]. This [injunction] finds expression in His, praised be He, "Thou shalt surely rebuke thy neighbor, [and not bear sin because of him]" (Lev. 19:17).

Embraced in this commandment is [the obligation] that if one of us be offended by the other, he is to rebuke [the offender], so that we are to bear no one any grudge in our heart, and entertain no evil design towards him, being rather commanded to rebuke him with words so that no trace [of ill-feeling] against him shall be left in us. In the words of the Siphra: "Whence do we derive [the maxim] that even if he rebuked [the offender] twice or three times he remains under the obligation to rebuke him again [and again]? Scripture therefore says, 'Thou shalt surely rebuke [thy neighbor]'—even a thousand times. One might think that in rebuking [the offender] you may cause him shame, Scripture therefore says, 'And thou shalt not bear sin because of him'" (*ibid.*, Siphra).

The Sages have already explained that the obligation involved in this commandment rests upon every person [to this extent], that even an inferior person is under obligation to rebuke a man of high rank. If [the person rebuked] curses or insults him he is nevertheless not to desist from rebuking him up to the point of suffering blows— as those who received the Traditions of the Torah have explained, namely, that (one is to rebuke his neighbor) to the point of suffering blows (Arak. 16b).

Sefer ha-Mitzvot, Com. 205

22. TRADE, LABOR, AND CHARITY

While Maimonides was not an economist he was acutely aware of the trade and occupational life of the people about him. A goodly portion—one third —of his great Code is taken up with the practical day-to-day life of the Jews of his time. Here only a few illustrations of Maimonides' social and economic thinking can be given, but any one interested in the subject must be referred to Prof. Salo W. Baron's instructive and illuminating study, "The Economic Views of Maimonides" in Essays on Maimonides *(Columbia University Press, 1941).*

I F ONE SELLS commodities by measure or by weight or by number and has made even the slightest error, the difference must always be returned because the law of overreaching applies only to errors in money value, while in errors of quantity the difference must be returned.

Sales, 15

It is forbidden to deceive people in buying and selling or to deceive them by creating a false impression. A heathen and an Israelite are to be treated alike in this respect.

Ibid., 18

One is forbidden to sell to another real or movable property the title of which is disputed and upon which litigation is pending unless he informs the buyer about it, because though the vendor is responsible, nevertheless no one wants to pay money and then have to go to court to answer claims lodged against him.

Ibid., 19

Oral deception is more heinous than monetary fraud, because restoration is possible in the latter while no restoration is possible in the former, and the latter concerns one's money while the former affects his person. The verse "And thou shalt fear thy God" (Lev. 25:17), is appended to the commandment against oral deception because it is a matter of the heart. Hence it may be inferred that in all matters of the heart Scripture says: "And thou shalt fear thy God" and whosoever cries out to the Lord because of distress caused by oral deception is answered immediately, as it is said: "For I am the Lord" (Lev. 25:17).

Ibid., 14

USURY

Both the Bible and talmudic law speaks out strongly against the charge of interest on money loans made to coreligionists. It not only prohibits such increments as illegitimate but forbids every subtle evasion of the law. Indeed, Maimonides, reflecting the attitude of the Rabbis, includes under the term of usurious gain every courtesy shown by the debtor to the creditor, such as greeting him first, visiting him in his home, or teaching him Bible or Talmud if he was not wont to do so before.

Why is [interest] called *nesek?* Because he who takes it bites his fellow, causes him pain, and eats his flesh. Just as it is forbidden to lend money on interest, so it is forbidden to borrow on interest. . . . If robbers and lenders on usury make an offer of restitution, it is not to be accepted from them. . . . Only the principal is recoverable, and not the usury, on a writing which contains usury. . . . He who borrows and lends on usury in privacy is deemed as though he denied the Lord, the God of Israel, and the Exodus from Egypt.

Creditor and Debtor, 4

He who borrows something from his fellow must not be quick to greet him first if he was not accustomed to do so before the loan was made, needless to say, must not flatter him with words of praise or pay him visits frequently at his house. For it is written *interest of any word* (Deut. 23:20), that is, even words are forbidden. Similarly, the borrower is forbidden, while the loan remains unpaid, to teach the lender Scripture or Gemara if he was not accustomed to do so before the loan was made, for it is written *interest of any word.*

It is forbidden to purchase the produce of an orchard before it ripens, because when the vendor sells for less, say for 10 denar, produce which will be worth more, say 20 denar, when it is ripe, the difference is due to the advancing of the money.

Ibid., 5

No agreement may be made with respect to produce before the market price has been published; but once the market price has been published, such an agreement may be made. . . . No agreement may be made on the basis of the market price in small towns, because the market price there is not a stable one, but only on the basis of the market price in the principal towns of the region. . . . Once the market price has been established, it is permissible to make an agreement to deliver at a high rate, if such should prevail at the time of delivery.

Ibid., 9

SLAVES

"Living in a world in which slaves supplied a part of agricultural and industrial labor and the bulk of domestic employment, Maimonides regarded slavery as a natural, though 'accursed,' state, inflicted upon the individual through God's will. He certainly saw no reason to depart from the well-established attitude of the biblical and talmudic legislation . . . Nevertheless, Maimonides treats slaves juridically as human beings rather than as chattels . . . the point, however, is that both piety and wisdom dictate that a Jew should be compassionate and charitable to his slave, not to impose upon him too severe a yoke nor oppress him, but that he should let him share in his own food and treat him with dignity and humanity . . . because cruelty and haughtiness are to be found among the Gentiles only . . ." (S. W. Baron)

The Hebrew slave mentioned in Scripture refers to an Israelite whom the court sold into servitude against his will or to one who sells himself voluntarily into servitude.

Slaves, 1

It is forbidden to work any Hebrew slave with rigor. What constitutes work with rigor? It is work which has no fixed limits and unnecessary work which is done only with the purpose of keeping the slave occupied. Hence the Sages say that the master should not tell the Hebrew slave, "Hoe under the vines until I arrive," because he does not give him a time limit; rather should he say to him, "Hoe until such such-and-such a time or up to such-and-such a place."

Ibid.

It is forbidden for an Israelite who buys any Hebrew slave to make him do menial tasks which are assigned to slaves only, such as to make him carry his clothes after him to the bathhouse or take off his shoes, for it is said: "Thou shalt not make him to serve as a bondservant" (Lev. 25:39). He must treat him as a hired man, as it is said: "As a hired servant and as a settler, he shall be with thee" (Lev. 25:40).

The Hebrew bondman, however, may cut the master's hair, wash his garment, and bake his dough. But the master should not make him an attendant at a public bath or a public barber or a public baker.

If that was his trade before he was sold, he may follow it. He should not be taught a new trade, however, but be allowed to work at the same trade he plied before.

This applied only to a Hebrew bondman, who feels humiliated because he was sold into servitude. It is permitted, however, to make an Israelite who was not sold do the work of a slave inasmuch as he does that work of his own volition.

The master is obligated to support the wife of his Hebrew slave, the one married to him but not the one that is only betrothed to him, or the one who is waiting to be married to him because she is his brother's childless widow. . . . The master is likewise obliged to support his slave's sons and daughters.

Ibid., 3

If a slave flees from a foreign land to the land of Israel he is not restored to slavery. . . . If the master refuses to free him the court releases him from his servitude and he may depart.

Ibid., 8

If a slave declares his wish to go to the Land of Israel his master is compelled either to go with him or to sell him to one who will take him thither. If the master wishes to go to a foreign land he cannot take his slave with him unless he consents.

The master must treat his Hebrew male and female slaves as equals in regard to food, drink, clothing, and shelter, as it is said: "Because he is well with thee" (Deut. 15:16); i.e., you should not eat white bread and the slave black bread, you drink old wine and he new wine, you sleep on down feathers and he on straw; you reside in the city and he in the country, or you reside in the country and he dwell in the city, for it is further said: "He shall go out from thee" (Lev. 25:41). Hence the Sages have said: "He who buys a Hebrew bondman it is as if he had bought a master for himself." One must treat his Hebrew slave as a brother, as it is said: "And over your brethren the children of Israel" (Lev. 25:46).

Ibid., 1

. . . The master should not disgrace them by hand or by word, because scriptural law has delivered them only unto slavery and not unto disgrace. Nor should he heap upon the slave oral abuse and anger, but should rather speak to him softly and listen to his claims. So it is also explained in the good paths of Job, in which he prided himself: "If I did despise the cause of my manservant, or of my maidservant, when they contended with me. . . ." (Job 31:13).

Cruelty and effrontery are not frequent except with heathen who worship idols. The children of our father Abraham, however, i.e., the Israelites, upon whom the Holy One, blessed be He, bestowed the favor of the Law and laid upon them statutes and judgments, are merciful people who have mercy upon all. . . . Furthermore, whoever has compassion will receive compassion, as it is said: "And He will show thee mercy, and have compassion upon thee, and multiply thee" (Deut. 13:18).

Ibid., 9

NEIGHBORLINESS

The residents of a city can compel one another to help build the wall, the gates and the bolt for the city, to help build a synagogue, and to help buy scrolls of the Law, Prophets, and Hagiographa so that any one who wishes to read them may do so.

Neighbors, 6

When they collect from the residents of the city funds for the building of the wall they collect according to the proximity of the house to the wall: the closer one lives to the wall the more he must give.

If a man has lived in a city twelve months, or if he has bought a house of residence there, he shares with the inhabitants of the city in all the things necessary for the repair of the wall and the gates, the hire of the horsemen that guard the land, and all similar matters that pertain to the guarding of the city.

All the inhabitants of the city, even orphans, are taxed for all the things necessary for the guarding of the city, but not the scholars, because scholars do not need protection; their learning is their protection. For the repair of the open places, however, even scholars are taxed. If all the people go out and themselves repair these scholars should not go out with them because it is not proper for a scholar to lower himself in the presence of the common people.

Spice merchants who travel from town to town cannot be hindered by residents of a town from plying their trade, because it is an enactment of Ezra to allow them to travel in order that perfume may be readily available to the daughters of Israel.

Carcasses, graves, and tanneries must be kept fifty cubits from the town.

A tannery may be set up only on the east side of the town because the east wind is mild and reduces the unpleasantness of the odors produced by the tanning of the hides.

Ibid.

CHARITY

Charity is one of the most precious jewels in Israel's system of social ethics. "The Israelites," reads a well-known passage in the Talmud (Yeb.79a), "are distingiushed for their charity, modesty, and benevolence." In the spirit of Judaism, the poor and distressed stand under God's special care and He answers their cry first. "Thou shalt open thine hand wide unto thy brother, to thy poor and thy needy in thy land" (Deut.15:11).

But in the Jewish conception, zedakah *is a comprehensive term, and it covers more than mere almsgiving; it is a human obligation which man owes to his fellow-men. "More than the householder does for the needy, the needy does for the householder," say the Rabbis (Lev.R.24:8).*

"Zedakah calls for more than mere almsgiving, because in its exercise there must be kindness, tenderness, not to shame the poor or put him to disgrace. Sacred unto the Lord is the human dignity and personality of the recipient of charity, and they must not be hurt or lowered. Moreover, of

greater merit than giving to the poor, is to help him to become self-supporting (Sab.63a).

LENDING TO THE POOR

He [God] has commanded us that we are to lend [money] to the poor man so as to alleviate his poverty and afford him generous support, this being the highest and most obligatory mode of [administering] charity in fulfilment of the commandment pertaining thereto; for he who has been reduced to begging and debasing himself openly at the hands of people does not suffer from the straits of poverty as he who, desiring secretly to be aided, would not openly confess his poverty or debase himself because of it. The obligatory character of this commandment finds expression in His words, praised be He, "If thou lend money to any of my people [even to the poor with thee]."

Sefer ha-Mitzvot, Com. 197

In his great Code, section Matnot Aniyim *(10:7–13),* Maimonides *expounds the Jewish conception of the ethics of charity:*

We are in duty bound to be more heedful with regard to the discharge of the commandment relating to charity than with all the other precepts of the Torah, for benevolence is the characteristic of the righteous descendants of the seed of Abraham, our father, of whom it is said, "For I know him to the end that he command his children and his household after him that they may keep the way of the Lord, to do *zeddakah*" (Gen. 18:19). The throne of Israel cannot be firmly established nor will the true faith be permanently secured by any other means than *zeddakah,* as it is said, "In Zeddakah shalt thou be established" (Is. 54:14), and "Zion shall be redeemed with justice, and they that return of her with *zeddakah*" (*Ibid.* 1:27)

A man is never impoverished by almsgiving, nor will any evil befall him because of it, as it is said, "The work of *zeddakah* shall be peace" (Is. 32:17). I have never known a community that did not arrange for a *kuppah shel zeddakah,* a charity chest. Who displays mercy shall have mercy displayed toward him, as it is said, "And show thee mercy and have compassion upon thee, and multiply thee" (Deut. 13:18). Whoever hardens his heart and is merciless to the poor may justly be suspected of his pure Israelite descent, because hard-heartedness is only found among the gentiles, as it is said, "They are cruel and have no compassion" (Jer. 6:23), whereas all Israelites and those that ally themselves unto them are like brothers, as it is said, "Ye are children of the Lord, your God" (Deut. 14:1). If not to their fellow-Jews to whom, then, shall the poor of Israel turn? Shall they turn to the nations of the earth who hate them and rejoice in their misfortune?

Matnot Aniyim, 10

Maimonides was not contented with merely laying down the law of zeddakah *but was concerned that it be carried out in the least offensive and embarrassing manner.*

Whoever gives charity to the poor with bad grace and downcast looks, though he bestow a thousand gold pieces, all the merit of his action is lost. He must give with good grace, gladly, cheerfully, and with an abundance of sympathy for the poor in his plight. It is the kind word, the gentle reception and sympathetic attitude that help and encourage the poor and needy more than the giving of a coin. . . . Woe to the person who shames the poor man! Be to him like a parent whether in compassion or in kindly words. "Happy is he that considereth the poor" (Ps. 41:2), and the Rabbis point out that the word used is *"considereth,* not *giveth.*

Ibid.

KINDNESS, RIGHTEOUSNESS, AND JUDGMENT

Maimonides gives the fine distinction between hesed, *"kindness,"* Zeddakah, *"righteousness," and* mishpat, *"judgment," in both their biblical and talmudic connotations:*

In our Commentary on the Sayings of the Fathers (chap. V, 7) we have explained the expression *hesed* as denoting an excess of moral quality. It is especially used of extraordinary kindness. Loving-kindness is practiced in two ways: first we show kindness to those who have no claim whatever upon us; second, we are kind to those to whom it is due in a greater measure than is due to them. In the inspired writings, the term *hesed* occurs mostly in the sense of showing kindness to those who have no claim to it whatever. For this reason the term *hesed* is employed to express the good bestowed upon us by God; "I will mention the loving-kindness of the Lord" (Is. 63:7). On this account, the very act of the creation is an act of God's loving-kindness. "I have said the Universe is built up in loving-kind-ness" (Ps. 89:3); i.e., the building up of the Universe is an act of loving-kindness. . . .

The term *zeddakah* is derived from *zeddek,* "righteousness"; it de-notes the act of giving every one his due, and of showing kindness to every being according as it deserves. In Scripture, however, the expression *zeddakah* is not used in the first sense and does not apply to the payment of what we owe to others. When we therefore give the hired laborer his wages, or pay a debt, we do not perform an act of *zeddakah.* But we do perform an act of *zeddakah* when we ful-fill those duties towards our fellow-men which our moral conscience imposes upon us; e.g., when we heal the wounds of the sufferer. Thus Scripture says, in reference to the returning of the pledge [to the poor debtor]: "And it shall be *zeddakah* [righteousness] unto thee" (Deut. 24:13). When we walk in the way of virtue we act right-eously towards our intellectual faculty, and pay what is due unto it; and because every virtue is thus *zeddakah,* Scripture applies the term to the virtue of faith in God. Comp. "And he believed in the Lord and He accounted it unto him as righteousness" (Gen. 15:6). . . .

The noun *mishpat,* "judgment," denotes the act of deciding upon a certain action in accordance with justice which may demand either mercy or punishment.

Guide, III, 53

EIGHT DEGREES OF ALMSGIVING

Based largely on the teaching of the Rabbis on almsgiving which, in their opinion, is of the highest value when given in secret and in a way that will help the poor become self-supporting, Maimonides expounded his famous "Eight Degrees of Almsgiving." It is worth remarking that the Bible uses the dignified term terumah, *"uplifting," for giving to a holy cause, which best describes the Jewish and Maimonides' conception of charity:*

There are eight degrees in the giving of charity, one higher than the other. The highest degree, than which there is nothing higher, is to take hold of a Jew who has been crushed and to give him a gift or a loan, or to enter into partnership with him, or to find work for him, and thus put him on his feet that he will not be dependent on his fellow-men. Concerning this it is said (Lev. 25:35): "Then shalt thou *uphold* him." *Uphold* him, so that he should not fall and become a dependent.

Lower in degree to this is the one who gives charity, *zedakah*, to the poor, but does not know to whom he gives it, nor does the poor man know from whom he received it. This is an unselfish meritorious act comparable to what was done in the Chamber of the Secret in the Temple where the charitable would deposit [alms] secretly and the poor of better family would help themselves secretly. Related to this degree is the giving to the [public] alms-chest. One should not give to the alms-chest unless he knows that the officer in charge is reliable, wise, and a capable administrator, like Hananiah ben Tradion, for example. [This martyr, (d. about 135), was very scrupulous with charity funds].

Lower in degree to this is when the giver knows to whom he gives, but the poor does not know from whom he receives. An example of this are the great scholars [of talmudic times] who used to go about in secret and leave their money at the door of the poor. This is proper practice, particularly meritorious when the officers in charge of charity are not administering properly.

Lower in degree to this is when the poor knows from whom he receives, but the giver does not know to whom he gives. An example of this are the great scholars who used to tie up their money in [the corner of] their cloaks and throw them back over their shoulders. The poor would then come and take it without being put to shame.

Lower in degree to this is when one gives even before he is asked.

Lower in degree to this is when one gives after he has been asked.

Lower in degree to this is when one gives less than he should, but graciously.

Lower in degree to this is when one gives grudgingly.

The great scholars used to give a coin to the poor before every prayer and then they would pray, for it is said in the Bible (Ps. 17: 15): "As for me, I shall behold Thy face in 'righteousness' [that is, through 'charity']."

Matnot Aniyim, 10 (trans. by Jacob R. Marcus,
The Jew in the Medieval World)

23. ISRAEL AND PALESTINE

Maimonides loved Jews with a deep and abiding love. He grieved in their sorrows and looked forward hopefully to their triumph. Israel suffered grievously, but their suffering was not due to any fault of their own but to their position in the world as a people of God. He had faith in Israel, faith in their survival and their ultimate redemption. He pleaded for the unity of Israel in face of their oppressors and warned against the disastrous consequences of internal discord and dissension.

IT IS INCUMBENT on every one to love each individual Israelite as himself, as it is said, "Thou shalt love thy neighbor as thyself" (Lev. 19:18). Hence a person ought to speak in praise of his neighbor and be careful of his neighbor's property as he is careful of his own property and solicitous about his own honor. Whoever glorifies himself by humiliating another person, will have no portion in the world to come.

Ethical Conduct (Deot), 6

Whoever entertains in his heart hatred of any Israelite, transgresses a prohibition, as it is said, "Thou shalt not hate thy neighbor in thy heart" (Lev. 19:17). The violation of this precept is however not punishable with stripes, as no overt act is involved. The Torah in this text only warned against hatred in the heart. But any one who smites or reviles his neighbor, although he is not permitted to do so, is not infringing the precept, "Thou shalt not hate thy brother."

Ibid.

THE UNITY OF ISRAEL

The house of Israel that bears the name of Jacob and upholds the religion of Moses our teacher, must be one united community. Nothing whatsoever should create dissension. You are wise and understanding people and you must know how serious are the consequences of discord and to what misfortunes it leads.

Responsum, 111, ed. Freimann

The antagonism of the nations toward us is due to our unique position as a people of faith. This is why their kings oppress us and visit upon us hatred and hostility. But the Creator endowed us with confidence, so that whenever the fury of persecution arises against Israel, it will surely be endured. The power of the kings presses down upon us and they exercise a hard rule over us; they persecute and torment us with oppressive decrees, but they cannot destroy us or wipe out our name.

Do you not know, brethren, that in the time of the wicked Nebuchadnezzar Israel was forced to worship foreign gods, and only Daniel, Hananiah, Mishael, and Azariah were rescued? But in the end this king and his authority were destroyed and truth was restored. The same happened in the time of the Second Temple, when the wicked dynasty of Seleucus came into power and persecuted Israel in order to destroy its religion. The Syrians forced Israel to desecrate the Sabbath and the covenant of circumcision and publicly to renounce belief in God. This oppression lasted fifty-two years, and then God annihilated both the government and the religion of the enemy.

God promised us through the prophets that we shall never perish and never cease to be a nation of faith. Our life is correlated with the existence of the Lord, as it is said, "For I, the Lord, change not, therefore ye, O sons of Jacob, are not consumed." And Moses, our Teacher, said in the Torah: "And yet, for all that, when they are in the land of their enemies, I will not reject them, neither will I abhor them, to destroy them and to break My covenant with them; for I am the Lord their God."

Therefore, brethren, be strong and of good courage. If persecutions arise, let them not disconcert you. Let not the mighty hand of the enemy and the weakness of our nation frighten you. These events are but trial and proof of your faith and your love. By holding firm to the law of truth in times like these, you prove that you belong to those of Jacob's seed who fear God and who are named "the remnant whom the Lord shall call."

From The Epistle to the Jews of Yemen

THE KARAITES

Maimonides' tolerance and love of peace matched fully his love and devotion to Torah. Although a zealous upholder and, indeed, a pillar of the rabbinic tradition, he did his utmost to establish friendly relations with the Karaites who opposed it. When he was asked how the Rabbanites should conduct themselves toward the followers of Anan who did not abide by the Oral Law as expounded by the Rabbis, his reply was:

In the matter of the Karaites who reside in Cairo, Alexandria, Damascus, and in other places in Arabia and the Holy Land, (my opinion is) that they should be treated with respect, honor, kindness and humility as long as they keep within the bounds of decency and do not scoff at the scholars and slander the authorities of the Mishnah and the Talmud. They may be associated with, enter their homes, circumcise their children, bury their dead, and comfort their mourners. The Talmud enjoins us to observe a friendly demeanor toward the heathens and idolators, visit their homes and support their poor, how much more so toward those who descend from the seed of Jacob and acknowledge the Unity of God.

Graetz (Hebrew), vol. IV, p. 352

OTHER RELIGIONS

While both Christianity and Mohammedandism coerced followers of other faiths to accept their respective religions, Maimonides legislated equal rights for the "righteous heathen" who observed the seven Noahidic laws, the basic principles of morality. These seven injunctions are against idolatry, blasphemy, homicide, incest, robbery, dismembering live animals, and anarchy. Under no circumstance would Judaism permit Jews to coerce others into acceptance of their faith:

Moses, our teacher, bequeathed the Law and commandments to Israel, as it is said, "An inheritance of the congregation of Jacob" (Deut. 33:4), and to those of other nations who are willing to be converted (to Judaism) as it is said: "One law and one ordinance

373

shall be both for you, and for the resident alien" (Nu. 15:16). But no coercion to accept the Law and commandments is practiced on those who are unwilling to do so. . . . Moreover, Moses, our teacher, was commanded by God to compel all human beings to accept the commandments enjoined upon the descendants of Noah. . . . He who does accept them is styled a resident alien. . . .

Kings, 8

A heathen who accepts the commandments and observes them scrupulously is a "righteous heathen," and will have a portion in the world to come, provided that he accepts them and performs them because the Holy One, blessed be He, commanded them in the Law and made known through Moses, our teacher, that the observance thereof had been enjoined upon the descendants of Noah even before the Law was given. But if his observance thereof is based upon a reasoned conclusion, he is not deemed a resident alien, or one of the pious of the Gentiles, but one of their wise men.

Ibid.

PROSELYTES

Judaism regards with particular affection the proselyte (Ger) who joins Israel's monotheistic faith with no ulterior motive in view and assigns to him full and equal rights with native-born Jews. In the letter quoted below, Maimonides is roused to anger by the lack of tact and tolerance of a scholar toward a proselyte.

To love the proselyte who comes to take refuge beneath the wings of the *Shekinah* is the fulfilment of two affirmative precepts. First because he is included among neighbors [whom we are commanded to love (Lev. 19:18)]. And secondly, because he is a stranger, and the Torah said "Love ye therefore the stranger" (Deut. 10:19). God charged [us] concerning the love of the stranger, even as He charged us concerning love of Himself, as it is said "Thou shalt love the Lord thy God" (Deut. 6:15). The Holy One, blessed be He, loves strangers, as it is said "And He loveth the stranger" (Deut. 1018).

Ethical Conduct (Deot), 6

When your teacher called you a fool for denying that Moslems were idolators he sinned grievously, and it is fitting that he ask your pardon, although he be your master. Then let him fast and weep and pray; perhaps he will find forgiveness. Was he intoxicated that he forgot the thirty-three passages in which the Law admonishes concerning "strangers?" For even if he had been in the right and you in error, it was his duty to be gentle; how much more when the truth is with you and he was in error! And when he was discussing whether a Moslem is an idolator, he should have been more cautious not to lose his temper with a proselyte of righteousness and put him to shame, for our Sages have said, "He who gives way to anger shall be esteemed in thine eyes as an idolator." And how great is the duty which the law imposes on us with regard to proselytes. Our parents we are commanded to honor and fear; to the Prophets we are ordered to hearken. A man may honor, fear and obey without loving. But in the case of 'strangers' we are bidden to love with the whole force of our heart's affection. And he called you 'fool!' Astounding! A man who left father and mother, forsook his birthplace, his country and its power, and attached himself to this lowly, despised, and enslaved race; who recognizes the truth and righteousness of this people's Law, and cast the things of this world from his heart—shall such a one be called fool? God forbid! Not witless but wise has God called your name, you disciple of our Father Abraham, who also left his father and his kindred and inclined Godwards. And He who blessed Abraham will bless you, and will make you worthy to behold all the consolations destined for Israel; and in all the good that God shall do unto us He will do good unto you, for the Lord hath promised good unto Israel. . . .

From Franz Kobler, *A Treasury of Jewish Letters*, vol. I, p. 196.

In answer to a query by Obadiah the Proselyte whether he, being a convert to Judaism may join in all the prayers recited by Jews, Maimonides wrote:

Thus says Moses the son of Rabbi Maimon, one of the exiles from Jerusalem, who lived in Spain.

I received the question of the master Obadiah, the wise and learned proselyte, may the Lord reward him for his work, may a perfect recompense be bestowed upon him by the Lord of Israel, under whose wings he has sought cover.

You ask me if you, too, are allowed to say in the blessings and prayers you offer alone or in the congregation: "Our God" and "God of *our* Fathers," "Thou hast sanctified *us* through Thy commandments," "Thou has separated *us*," "Thou hast chosen *us*," "Thou hast inherited *us*," "Thou who hast brought *us* out of the land of Egypt," "Thou who hast worked miracles for our fathers," and more of this kind.

Yes, you may say all this in the described order and not change it in the least. In the same way as every Jew by birth says his blessing and prayer you, too, shall bless and pray alike, whether you are alone or pray in the congregation. The reason for this is, that Abraham, our father, taught the people, opened their minds, and revealed to them the truth, faith and the unity of God; he rejected the idols and abolished their adoration; he brought many children under the wings of the Divine Presence; he gave them counsel and advice, and ordered his sons and the members of his household after him to keep the ways of the Lord forever, as it is written, "For I have known him to the end that he may command his children and his household after him, that he may keep the way of the Lord, to do righteousness and justice." Ever since then whoever adopts Judaism and confesses the unity of the Divine Name, as it is prescribed in the Torah, is counted among the disciples of Abraham, our father, peace be with him. These men are Abraham's household, and he it is who converted them to righteousness.

In the same way as he converted his contemporaries through his words and teaching, he converts future generations through the testament he left to his children and household after him. Thus, Abraham, our father, his pious posterity who kept his ways, is the father of his disciples and of all proselytes who adopt Judaism.

Therefore you shall pray, "Our God" and "God of our fathers," because Abraham, peace be with him, is *your* father. And you shall pray, "Thou who hast taken for his own our fathers, for the land has been given to Abraham," as it is said, "Arise, walk through the land in the length of it and in the breadth of it, for I will give it unto thee." As to the words, "Thou who hast brought us out of the land of Egypt," or "Thou who hast done miracles for our fathers"—these you may change, if you will, and say, "Thou who hast brought Israel out of the land of Egypt," and "Thou who hast done miracles for Israel." If, however, you do not change them, it is no transgression, because since you have come under the wings of the Divine Presence and confessed the Lord, no difference exists between you and us, and all miracles done to us have been done, as it were, to us and to you. Thus it is said in the book of Isaiah, "Neither let the son of the stranger, that hath joined himself to the Lord, speak, saying, 'The Lord hath utterly separated me from his people.'" There is no difference between you and us. You shall certainly say the blessing, "Who hast chosen us," "Who hast given us," "Who hast taken us for Thine own" and "Who has separated us": For the Creator, may He be extolled, has indeed chosen you and separated you from the nations and given you the Torah. For the Torah has been given to us *and* to the proselytes, as it is written, "One ordinance shall be both for you of the congregation, and also for the stranger that sojourneth with you, an ordinance forever in your generations; as you are so shall be the stranger before the Lord." Know that our fathers, when they came out of Egypt, were mostly idolators; they had mingled with the pagans in Egypt and imitated their way of life, until the Holy One, may He be blessed, sent Moses our Teacher, the master of all prophets, who separated us from the nations and brought us under the wings of the Divine Presence, us and all proselytes, and gave to all of us one law.

Do not consider your origin as inferior. While we are the descendants of Abraham, Isaac and Jacob, you derive from Him through whose word the world was created. As it is said by Isaiah: "One shall say, I am the Lord's, and another shall call himself by the name of Jacob."

Ibid., pp. 194-96

Treatment of Proselytes

Jewish law surrounds the neophyte with exceeding tenderness. It cautions against offending him, speaking to him harshly, or reminding him of his antecedents. It makes an injury to a proselyte tantamount to an injury to God (Hag.5a). Maimonides but reflects the spirit and injunction of the Rabbis of the Talmud when he speaks out with unmeasured severity against defrauding or over-teaching a convert to Judaism.

Whoever defrauds a proselyte, whether in matters of money or by spoken words, transgresses three negative injunctions, as it is said: "And a stranger shalt thou not wrong" (Ex. 22:20), which refers to verbal overreaching; "neither shalt thou oppress him" (*Ibid.*), which refers to monetary overreaching. Hence we learn that he who overreaches a proselyte [by words] transgresses three negative injunctions, as it is said: "And the stranger shalt thou not wrong" (Ex. 22:20), which refers to verbal overreaching; "neither shalt thou oppress him" (*ibid.*), which refers to monetary overreaching. Hence we learn that he who overreaches a proselyte [by words] transgresses three negative injunctions, to wit: "And ye shall not wrong one another" (Lev. 25:17); ye shall not wrong one another" (Lev. 25:14); "And a stranger shalt thou not wrong" (Ex. 22:20).

Sales, 14

Thus if a man is a penitent one must not say to him, "Remember your former deeds." If he is a son of proselytes one must not say to him, "Remember the deeds of your fathers." If he is a proselyte and comes to study the Law one must not say to him, "Shall the mouth that ate unclean and forbidden food come and study the Law, which was uttered by the mouth of the Lord?" If he is afflicted with sickness and suffering or if he had buried his children one must not say to him, as his companions said to Job: "Is not thy fear of God thy confidence, and thy hope the integrity of thy ways? Remember, I pray thee whoever perished being innocent?" (Job 4:6-7).

Thus also if one has overreached a proselyte in matters of money he transgresses the following three negative injunctions: "Ye shall not wrong one another" (Lev. 25:14); "And ye shall not wrong one another" (Lev. 25:17); "neither shalt thou oppress him" (Ex. 22:20).

But why is one, when deceiving a proselyte, guilty of transgressing the negative injunctions referring to oral deception, even if he has committed a fraud in money matters, and vice versa? Because Scripture has expressed both by the unqualified term of wrongdoing; and in the negative injunction against deceiving a proselyte there is explicit reference to the two kinds of deception, i.e., "shalt thou not wrong and neither shalt thou oppress."

Ibid.

THE RIGHTEOUS OF NATIONS

As to your question about the nations, know that the Lord desires the heart, and that the intention of the heart is the measure of all things. That is why our sages say, 'The pious men among the Gentiles have a share in the World-to-Come,' namely, if they have acquired what can be acquired of the knowledge of God, and if they ennoble their souls with worthy qualities. There is no doubt that every man who ennobles his soul with excellent morals and wisdom based on the faith in God, certainly belongs to the men of the World-to-Come. That is why our sages said, 'Even a non-Jew who studied the Torah of our master Moses resembles the High Priest. What is essential is nothing else than that one tries to elevate his soul towards God through the Torah. Thus said David, "I put The Lord always before me; because He is on my right hand I do not waver (Ps. 16:8)." And Moses is praised for this reason: 'This man was very humble' because this is the height of perfection. Our sages said also, "Be exceedingly humble (Ab. 4, 4)." . . . And the philosophers declared that it is very difficult to find a man who is completely perfect in morality and wisdom. He in whom this perfection is found is called a Saint, and surely such a man is on the steps which lead to the higher world. . . . Besides, there is no doubt that the patriarchs as well as Noah and Adam, who obviously did not observe the Torah, by no means became denizens of Gehinnom. On the contrary: as they achieved what pertains to the ennoblement of man they are raised aloft. All this cannot be secured by fasting, praying and lamentation if knowledge and true faith are absent, because in such behavior God can be near to the mouth but far from the heart. The basis of all things is [knowledge] that nothing is eternal save God alone. . . .

> Letter to Hasdai Halevi, written about
> the last quarter of the twelfth century.

THE OBLIGATION TO LIVE IN PALESTINE

Although Maimonides' visit in Palestine was brief—the country was unsafe, the Jews few and poor, and for its lack of intellectual comradeship there was little attraction for him to remain there—his ties to the Holy Land were strong and deep. Although himself choosing to live in exile, he felt that only in Palestine could Faith and People arise to new life.

At all times one should live in Palestine even in a place the majority of whose population is heathen, and not live outside Palestine even in a place the majority of whose population is Jewish; for he who leaves Palestine is as though he would serve idolatry, as it is written: "For they have driven me out this day that I should not cleave unto the inheritance of the Lord, saying: Go, serve other gods" (I Sam. 26:19).

379

In (predicting) punishment, the prophet says: "Neither shall they enter into the land of Israel" (Ez. 13:0).

Kings, 5

The Rabbis said that the sins of him who lives in Palestine are forgiven, as it is written: "And the inhabitants shall not say, 'I am sick'; the people that dwell therein shall be forgiven their iniquity" (Isa. 33:24). Even if one walks four cubits, one is assured of life in the world to come. So too, one who is buried there will obtain atonement; it is as though the place (where one lies) were an altar which effects atonement, as it is said: "And the land doth make expiation for His people" (Deut. 32:43). In (forcasting) punishment, (the prophet) says: "And thou thyself shalt die in an unclean land" (Amos. 7:17). There is no comparison between one whom Palestine receives while he is living and one whom it receives after his death; nevertheless the greatest of our wise men brought their dead there. Think of Jacob, our father, and of Joseph, the righteous!

Ibid.

It is forbidden to emigrate from Palestine and go abroad, unless one goes to study the Law, or to marry a wife, or to rescue property from heathens and then returns to Palestine. So, too, one may leave on business. But to make one's home abroad, unless there is a famine in Palestine so severe that a denar's worth of wheat is selling at two denar. This holds good only if money is available and food is high. But if food is cheap and money is scarce and one is unable to earn it and has no savings, one may go to any place where one can make a living. But though one is permitted to emigrate, if one does, the act is not in conformity with the law of saintliness. Remember Mahlon and Chilion! They were the two great men of their generation. They left Palestine at a time of great distress; nevertheless, they incurred thereby the penalty of extinction.

The greatest of our sages used to kiss [the rocks] on the borders of Palestine. They used to kiss the stones of the land and rolled themselves in its dust, as it is written: "For Thy servants take pleasure in her stones, and love her dust" (Ps. 102:15).

Ibid.

Customs Observed in Memory of Destruction of Jerusalem

When the Temple was destroyed, the Sages of the time ruled that a Jew should not build a painted and wainscoted house, but daub it with clay, wash it with lime, and leave about the entrance a square cubit's spot unwashed. The Sages likewise ordained: Whoever sets his table for a feast should let something be missing on it, and should leave one place empty without the service plate that otherwise would have been put there. When a woman orders ornaments of silver or gold, she should omit one of the details so that it should not appear perfect. When a man takes a wife, he should strew hearth-ashes on his head. All this one should do in remembrance of Jerusalem. As it is said: "If I forget thee, O Jerusalem, let my right hand forget her cunning. Let my tongue cleave to the roof of my mouth if I remember thee not; if I set not Jerusalem above my chiefest joy" (Ps. 137:5-6).

Fasting (Taanit), 5

24. HEALTH AND HYGIENE

Self-conquest and self-control are not only moral but also physical virtues. Food is necessary to maintain one's physical health, but it may become injurious to one's well-being when taken unwisely and in unnecessary quantities.

SINCE, by keeping the body in health and vigor one walks in the ways of God,—it being impossible during sickness to have any understanding or knowledge of the Creator—it is a man's duty to avoid whatever is injurious to the body, and cultivate habits conducive to health and vigor. These are as follows: One should not take food except when one is hungry; nor drink unless one is thirsty. One should not neglect the calls of nature for a single moment, but respond to them immediately.

Ethical Conduct (Deot), 4

DIET

Food should not be taken to repletion; during a meal, about one-third less should be eaten than the quantity that would give a feeling of satiety, and only a little water should be drunk—and that mixed with wine. After the process of digestion has commenced, water may be taken as needed. But even after food has been digested, it should not be drunk copiously. Before eating, careful attention should be paid to the functions of excretion. No meal should be taken without previously walking till the body begins to get warm, or engaging in manual labour, or tiring oneself with other activities. In short, strenuous exercise should be taken every day in the morning, till the body is in a glow. Then, there should be an interval of rest till one has recovered composure. The meal may then be taken. If the exercise is followed by a bath of warm water, so much the better. In this case too, there should be an interval of repose before the meal.

The day and night consists of twenty-four hours. It is sufficient to sleep for a third of that period, namely eight hours. And these hours should be in the latter part of the night; that is to say, the period from retirement to dawn should be eight hours so that one will arise from his bed before dawn.

One should not sleep face downwards, nor on one's back, but lying on the side; at the beginning, on the left side, and at the close of one's rest, on the right side. One should not go to sleep immediately after a meal, but only when three or four hours have elapsed. One should not sleep during the day.

Laxative foods, such as grapes, figs, mulberries, pears, watermelon, the various kinds of cucumbers or gherkins, should be taken before the meal. These, however, should not be mixed with the main dish that constitutes the meal. An interval should elapse till these have passed out of the stomach before the meal is taken. Immediately after, foods that tone up the digestive organs should be eaten, such as pomegranates, quinces, apples, and small pears; but even these fruits must not be indulged in too freely.

In the summertime, cold food should be consumed; one should be sparing with condiments; vinegar should be used. During the winter, warm foods should be eaten; condiments should be liberally used with a little mustard and assafoetide. A similar plan should be followed in cold and warm countries. The diet in every district should be chosen to suit the climate.

Some foods are very injurious and ought never to be eaten. For example, large salted stale fish; salted stale cheese; truffles and mushrooms; stale salted meat; *must* (fresh wine taken from the wine press); cooked food kept so long that it has lost its savour; any food that is malodorous or very bitter—all these are like deadly poison to the body. There are other kinds of food that are injurious but not to the same extent as those just mentioned. A little of them at a time may therefore be taken, but only at intervals of several days. One should not accustom oneself to make a meal of them or to eat them regularly with the meal. Examples of this class are large fish; cheese;

milk, twenty-four hours after milking; the meat of big steers and big goats; beans, lentils, peas; barley bread; unleavened bread; cabbage; leeks, onions, garlic; mustard, and radish. All these are bad foods. They should be eaten very sparingly and only during winter. In the summer, they should not be eaten at all. Neither in summer nor in winter should beans or lentils be eaten as a separate dish. Gourds may be eaten in summer.

One should always be abstemious in regard to fruits which grow on trees. These should not be eaten freely, even when dried, and, needless to add, when they are fresh. Before they are quite ripe, they are like daggers to the body. So too locust (St. John's bread) is always bad. All sour fruits are bad and should be eaten sparingly, and only during summer or in hot climates. But figs, grapes, and almonds are always good to eat—whether fresh or dried and may be eaten as much as one needs; but they should not be eaten constantly, even though they are best of the tree-fruits.

Ethical Conduct (Deot), 4

GENERAL RULES OF HEALTH

At every period of life, it should be one's care to secure free action of the bowels, approximating to a relaxed condition. It is a leading principle in medicine that if there is constipation or if the bowls move with difficulty, grave disorders result. How is a slight costive condition to be remedied? If the patient is a youth, he should eat, every morning, salty foods well cooked and seasoned with olive oil, fish brine and salt, without bread. Or he should drink the liquid of boiled spinach or St. John's bread, mixed with olive oil, fish brine and salt. An old man should drink, in the morning, honey diluted with warm water, and wait about four hours before taking his breakfast. This regimen should be observed for one day, or, if necessary, for three or four successive days till the bowels move freely.

Honey and wine are bad for young children, but good for the aged, particularly in the winter. The quantity taken in the summer should be two-thirds of that consumed in the winter.

Another great principle of hygiene, physicians say, is as follows: As long as a person takes active exercise, works hard, does not overeat and keeps his bowels open, he will be free from disease and will increase in vigor, even though the food he eats is coarse.

Ethical Conduct (Deot), 4

But if one leads a sedentary life and does not take exercise, neglects the calls of nature, or is constipated—even if he eats wholesome food and takes care of himself in accordance with medical rules—he will, throughout his life, be subject to aches and pains and his strength will fail him. Overeating is like a deadly poison to any constitution and is the principal cause of all diseases. Most maladies that afflict mankind result from bad food or are due to the patient filling his stomach with an excess of food that may even have been wholesome. Thus Solomon, in his wisdom, said, "He who keeps his mouth and tongue, keeps his soul from trouble" (Prov. 21:23)—which text can be applied to the individual who guards his mouth from bad food and overeating, and keeps his tongue from all speech except that which is necessary to obtain his needs.

Ibid.

The correct procedure in bathing is to take a bath once a week. One should not step into the bath directly after a meal nor when hungry, but only after digestion has begun. The entire body should be bathed in water that is warm but not scalding. The head alone may be washed with water hot enough to scald the body. The body should then be washed in tepid water, then in lukewarm water, and so on, gradually reducing the temperature, till the water finally used is quite cold. Water, either lukewarm or cold, should not be poured upon the head. In the rainy season cold baths should not be taken. Nor should one rinse the body before it has perspired and become supple. Nor should one stay too long in the bath, but as soon as one perspires and the body has become supple, one should complete the ablutions and leave.

Ibid.

When one who has come out of the bath, [he] should put on his clothes and cover his head in the outer chamber, so as to avoid catching cold. Even in summer, this precaution should be taken. After leaving the bath, a person should wait a while till he has recovered his composure, and his body is rested and cool. Then a meal may be taken. A little sleep after taking the bath and before the meal is excellent. Cold water should not be drunk after bathing and certainly not while taking the bath. If after the bath, one feels thirsty and cannot resist the desire to drink, the water should be mixed with wine or honey and then it may be drunk. During the winter anointing the body with oil, after the final ablution, is beneficial.

Ibid.

One should not accustom oneself to being frequently bled. Recourse to this procedure should only be had in case of special needs. One should not be bled in summer or winter, and only to a slight extent in the month of Nissan and Tishri. After the age of fifty, this treatment should be entirely discontinued. A person should not be bled and take a bath on the same day or set out on a journey on the same day; nor should one be bled on the day when he has returned from a journey. On the day when one is bled, less food and drink should be taken than usual. On that day he should rest and avoid exertion and violent physical exercise, and not take in sport.

All useful rules here recommended are suitable to those who enjoy good health. But a person who is generally ailing or suffers from a local disorder, or has for several years been addicted to an evil habit, needs special treatment, according to the nature of his sickness—as is expounded in medical literature. "Change of mode of living is the beginning of sickness" (Ket. 110b).

Ibid.

Whosoever indulges in sexual dissipation becomes prematurely aged; his strength fails; his eyes become dim; a foul odor proceeds from his mouth and armpits; the hair of his head, eye-brows and eye-lashes drop out; the hair of his beard, armpits and legs grow abnormally; his teeth fall out; and besides these, he becomes subject to numerous other diseases. Medical authorities have stated that for each one who dies of other maladies, a thousand are the victims of sexual excess. A man should, therefore, be careful in this regard if he wishes to lead a happy life. He should only cohabit when he finds himself in good health and vigor, experiences involuntary erections which persist after he has diverted his mind to other things, is conscious of a heaviness from the loins downwards as if the spermatic cords were being drawn and his flesh is hot. Such a condition calls for cohabitation which then is conducive to health. One should not cohabit when sated with food, nor when one is hungry, but only after a meal has been digested. Before and after coition, attention should be paid to the excretory functions.

Ibid.

Whoever lives in accordance with the directions I have set forth, has my assurance that he will never be sick till he grows old and dies; he will not be in need of a physician, and will enjoy normal health as long as he lives—unless his constitution be congenitally defective, or he has acquired bad habits from his early childhood, or if the world should be visited by pestilence or drought.

Ibid.

No disciple of the wise may live in a city that is unprovided with the following ten officials and institutions, namely: A physician, a surgeon, a bath-house, a lavatory, a source of water supply such as a stream or a spring, a synagogue, a school teacher, a scribe, a treasurer of charity funds for the poor, a court that has authority to punish with stripes and imprisonment.

Ibid.

Maimonides, a leading exponent of a new approach to philosophic thinking was also the author of novel ideas—novel for his time—on the subject of personal hygiene. In the book, Regimen Sanitatis, *he discusses the subjects of hygiene, dietetics, psychotherapy, the interrelation between mind and body, and first-aid remedies when a competent physician is not immediately available.*

A man should aim to maintain physical health and vigor, in order that his soul may be upright, in a condition to know God. For it is impossible for one to understand sciences and meditate upon them, when he is hungry or sick, or when any of his limbs is aching. . . . Whoever throughout his life follows this course will be continually serving God, even while engaged in business and even during cohabitation, because his purpose in all that he does will be to satisfy his needs, so as to have a sound body with which to serve God. Even when he sleeps and seeks repose, to calm his mind and rest his body, so as not to fall sick and be incapacitated from serving God, his sleep is service of the Almighty. In this sense, our wise men charged us, "Let all thy deeds be for the sake of God" (Ethics of the Fathers, 2:17).

And Solomon, in his wisdom, said, "In all thy ways know Him, and he will make thy paths straight" (Prov. 3:6).

Ethical Conduct (Deot), 3

MENTAL DISCIPLINE

It is well known to our master—may God grant him a long life—that emotions of the soul affect the body and produce great, significant and wide-ranging changes in the state of health. Physicians therefore advise that the emotions of the soul be watched, regularly examined, and kept well balanced. The physician should see to it that the sick and healthy alike be of cheerful disposition; emotions that cause upset and disorders should be smoothed out. This is essential for the cure of every patient, and especially for the care of mental cases like hypochondria, depressed and melancholy persons. Likewise, in the case of a patient who is afflicted by hallucinations or nervous anxiety in matters that should not cause distress, or by lack of cheerfulness in matters that usually cause joy, the physician should apply no treatment before he removes the irritating condition.

The physician should not consider the treatment of upset emotions a medical skill. It is rather a problem of practical philosophy and religious ethics. Philosophers who have written books on many branches of science have also dealt in numerous works with the training of character, with spiritual education, and with the matters of acquiring virtues. They show the ways by which to remove characterfaults so that the disposition to wrong action may disappear.

We find emotional affections of great intensity only in persons who have no notion of philosophical principles, of religious ethics, and of ethical teachings in general. Such persons are unbalanced, timid and unenergetic. Distress and misfortune aggravate their trouble so that they scream and cry and strike their cheeks and chest; some persons are so completely unnerved by misfortune that they die suddenly or after a short time as a result of it. And, likewise, if persons of this kind meet with good luck, they become overexcited. Those lacking psychical balance exaggerate the importance of the lucky circumstance to such an extent that they die in excess of joy, as a result of the sudden reaction of the mind to an extraneous element, as Galen has stated.

Those, however, who are trained in philosophy and in religious and general ethics gain strength thereby. Their souls are only slightly exposed to extraneous influences. The more mental training man has, the less affected he will be by luck or misfortune. He will not get excited over a very fortunate event and will not exaggerate its value. Likewise, if one meets disaster, he will not be disturbed and aggrieved, but will bear it valiantly. This discourse does not intend to demonstrate the truth of this thesis. Much has already been written on it at various times and among civilized nations that cultivate the sciences. Your servant only desired to set forth a few simple remarks on mental discipline and on the usefulness of ethical literature and the teachings of the wise. They teach how to strengthen the soul that it may regard the truth as true and the false as false. Then the emotions will calm down, and the nervous anxiety disappear; the disposition will be cheerful, regardless of the situation in which a person may find himself.

From *Rules of Health,* written about 1198
and dedicated to Sultan Al-Malik Alfadal

A LIMB OF THE SOUL

While in Judaism the care of one's physical well-being is regarded as a religious duty, Maimonides would not have us forget that the body is but a limb of the soul which should be the object of one's deepest concern.

It is the duty of man to subordinate all the faculties of his soul to his reason. He must keep his mind's eye fixed constantly upon one goal, namely the attainment of the knowledge of God (may He be blessed), as far as it is possible for mortal man to know Him. Consequently one must so adjust all his actions, his whole conduct, and even his very words, that they lead to this goal, in order that none of his deeds be aimless, and thus retard the attainment of that end. So, his only design in eating, cohabiting, sleeping, waking, moving about, and resting, should be the preservation of his bodily health, while, in turn, the reason for the latter is that the soul and its agencies may be in a sound and perfect condition, so that he may readily acquire wisdom, and gain moral and intellectual virtues, all to the end that man may reach the highest goal of his endeavors.

Accordingly, man will not direct his attention merely to obtain bodily enjoyment, choosing of food and drink and the other things of life only the agreeable, but he will seek out the most useful, being indifferent whether it be agreeable or not. There are, indeed, times when the agreeable may be used from a curative point of view, as, for instance, when one suffers from loss of appetite, it may be stirred up by highly seasoned delicacies and agreeable palatable food. Similarly, one who suffers from melancholia may rid himself of it by listening to singing and all kinds of instrumental music, by strolling through beautiful gardens and splendid buildings, by gazing upon beautiful pictures, and other things that enliven the mind, and dissipate gloomy moods. The purpose of all this is to restore the healthful condition of the body, but the real object in maintaining the body in good health, is to acquire wisdom. Likewise, in the pursuit of wealth, the main design in its acquisition should be to expend it for noble purposes and to employ it for the maintenance of the body and the preservation of life, so that its owner may obtain a knowledge of God, in so far as that is vouchsafed unto man.

From this point of view the study of medicine has a very great influence upon the acquisition of the virtues and of the knowledge of God, as well as upon the attainment of true spiritual happiness. Therefore, its study and acquisition are pre-eminently important religious activities, and must not be ranked in the same class with the art of weaving, or the science of architecture, for by it one learns to weigh one's deeds, and thereby human activities are rendered true virtue. The man who insists upon indulging in savory, sweet-smelling and palatable food—although it be injurious, and possibly may lead to serious illness or sudden death—ought, in my opinion, to be classed with the beasts. His conduct is not that of a man in so far as he is a being endowed with understanding, but it is rather the action of a man in so far as he is a member of the animal kingdom, and so "he is like the beasts who perish." Man acts like a human being only when he eats that which is wholesome, at times avoiding the agreeable, and partaking of the disagreeable in his search for the beneficial. Such conduct is in accordance with the dictates of reason, and by these acts man is distinguished from all other beings. Similarly, if a man satisfy his sexual passion whenever he has the desire, regardless of good or ill effect, he acts as a brute, and not as a man. . . . The real duty of man is, that in adopting whatever measures he may for his well-being and the preservation of his existence in good health, he should do so with the object of maintaining a perfect condition of the instruments of the soul, which are the limbs of the body, so that his soul may be unhampered, and he may busy himself in acquiring the moral and mental virtues.

Eight Chapters, 5

COUNSEL OF PERFECTION

Body and soul must be kept clean and fresh, for both are equally responsible for man's welfare. Moderation in food, as in all other physical pleasures, is Maimonides' counsel of perfection.

It is the object of the perfect Law to make man reject, despise, and reduce his desires as much as is in his power. He should only give way to them when absolutely necessary. It is well known that it is intemperance in eating, drinking, and sexual intercourse that people mostly rave and indulge in; and these very things counteract the ulterior perfection of man, impede at the same time the development of his first perfection, and generally disturb the social order of the country and the economy of the family. For by following entirely the guidance of lust in the manner of fools, man loses his intellectual energy, injures his body, and perishes before his natural time; sighs and cares multiply; there is an increase of envy, hatred and warfare for the purpose of taking what another possesses. The cause of all this is the circumstance that the ignorant consider physical enjoyment as an object to be sought for its own sake.

Cleanliness in dress and body by washing and removing sweat and dirt is included among the various objects of the Law, but only if connected with purity of action, and with a heart free from low principles and bad habits. It would be extremely bad for man to content himself with a purity obtained by washing and cleanliness in dress, and to be at the same time voluptuous and unrestrained in food and lust. These are described by Isaiah (66:17), that is to say they purify and sanctify themselves outwardly as much as is exposed to the sight of the people, and when they are alone in their chambers and the inner part of their houses, they continue their rebelliousness and disobedience and indulge in partaking of forbidden food. . . . They appear outwardly clean, but their heart is bent upon their desires and bodily enjoyments, and this is contrary to the spirit of the Law. For the chief object of the Law is to [teach man to] diminish his desires, and to cleanse his outer appearance after he had purified his heart. Those who wash their bodies and cleanse their garments while

391

they remain dirty by bad actions and principles, are described by Solomon as "a generation that are pure in their own eyes, and yet are not washed from their filthiness" (Prov. 30:12-13).

Guide, III, 33

Maimonides advocates the moderate life. Austerity and hedonism are equally censured by him. Neither of them contributes to man's bodily or spiritual welfare.

Possibly a person may say: "Since envy, cupidity and ambition are evil qualities to cultivate and lead to a man's ruin, I will avoid them to the uttermost, and seek their contraries." A person following this principle, will not eat meat, nor drink wine, nor marry nor dwell in a decent home, nor wear comely apparel, but will clothe himself in sackcloth and coarse wool like the idolaters' priests. This too, is the wrong way, not to be followed. Whoever persists in such a course is termed a sinner. . . . The Sages accordingly enjoined us that we should only refrain from that which the Torah has expressly withdrawn from our use. And no one should, by vows and oaths, inhibit to himself the use of things permitted. "Do not the prohibitions of the Torah," say our Sages, "suffice thee, that thou addest others for thyself?" In this condemnation, those are included, who make a practice of fasting; they too are not walking in the right way; our wise men prohibited self-mortification by fasting. And concerning this and similar excesses Solomon exhorts us, "Be not over-righteous, nor excessively wise. Wherefore shouldst thou be desolate?" (Eccles. 7:16).

Ethical Conduct (Deot), 3

PSYCHOLOGICAL ABNORMALITIES

In parts of Hilkot Deot *and* Eight Chapters *Maimonides deals with mental or psychological abnormalities. The soul, like the body, he says, may suffer from sickness, in which former case he advises consulting a mental specialist (Rofe ha-Nefesh) who will prescribe the necessary treatment. With Aristotle, he says that actions are good only when they follow the Golden Mean, or Middle Course between two extremes. He also discusses the subject of heredity and environment as factors in human behavior.*

Every human being is characterized by numerous moral dispositions which differ from each other and are exceedingly divergent. One man is choleric, always irascible; another sedate, never angry;

or, if he should become angry, is only slightly and very rarely so. One man is haughty to excess; another humble in the extreme. One is a sensualist whose lusts are never sufficiently gratified; another is so pure in soul that he does not even long for the few things that our physical nature needs. One is so greedy that all the money in the world would not satisfy him, as it is said, "He who loveth silver shall not be satisfied with silver" (Eccles. 5:9). Another so curbs his desires that he is contented with very little, even with that which is insufficient, and does not bestir himself to obtain that which he really needs. One will suffer extreme hunger for the sake of saving, and does not spend the smallest coin without a pang, while another deliberately and wantonly squanders all his property. In the same way, men differ in other traits. There are, for example, the hilarious and the melancholy, the stingy and the generous, the cruel and the merciful, the timid and the stout-hearted, and so forth.

Ethical Conduct (Deot), 1

THE SICK SOUL

The ancients maintain that the soul, like the body, is subject to good health and illness. The soul's healthful state is due to its condition, and that of its faculties, by which it constantly does what is right, and performs what is proper, while the illness of the soul is occasioned by its condition, and that of its faculties, which results in its constantly doing wrong and performing actions that are improper. . . . Now, just as those, who are physically ill, imagine that, on account of their vitiated tastes the sweet is bitter and the bitter is sweet . . . so those whose souls are ill, that is, the wicked and the morally perversed, imagine that the bad is good, and that the good is bad. The wicked man, moreover, continually longs for excesses which are really pernicious, but which, on account of the illness of his soul, he considers to be good.

[Now], just as when people unacquainted with the science of medicine, realize that they are sick, and consult a physician, who tells them what they must do, forbidding them to partake of that which they imagine beneficial, and prescribing for them things which are unpleasant and bitter, in order that their bodies may become healthy and that they again may choose the good and spurn the bad, so those whose souls become ill should consult the Sages, the moral physicians who will advise them against those evils which they [the morally ill] think are good, so that they may be healed. But if he who is morally sick be not aware of his illness, imagining that he is well, or, being aware of it, does not seek a remedy, his end will be similar to that of one, who, suffering from bodily ailment, yet continuing to indulge himself, neglects to be cured, and who in consequence surely meets an untimely death.

Eight Chapters, 3-4

THE GOLDEN MEAN

Between any moral disposition and its extreme opposite, there are intermediate dispositions more or less removed from each other. Of all the various dispositions, some belong to one from the beginning of his existence and correspond to his physical constitution. Others are such that a particular individual's nature is favorably predisposed to them and prone to acquire them more rapidly than other traits. Others again are not innate, but have either been learnt from others, or are self-originated, as the result of an idea that has entered the mind or, having heard that a certain disposition is good for him and should be cultivated by him, one trained himself in it till it became part of his nature.

Ethical Conduct (Deot), 1

The right way is the mean in each group of dispositions common to humanity; namely, the disposition which is equally distant from the two extremes in its class, not being nearer to the one than to the other. Hence, our ancient Sages exhorted us that a person should always evaluate his dispositions and so adjust them that they shall be at the mean between the extremes, and this will secure his physical health. Thus a man should not be choleric, easily moved to anger, nor be like the dead without feeling; but should aim at the happy medium; be angry only for a grave cause that rightly calls for indignation, so that the like shall not be done again. He will only desire that which the body absolutely needs and cannot do without, as it is said, "The righteous eats to satisfy himself" (Prov. 13:25). He will only labor at his occupation to obtain what is necessary for his sustenance, as it is said, "A little that a righteous man hath is better than the riches of many wicked" (Ps. 37:16). He will not be tight-fisted nor yet a spendthrift, but will bestow charity according to his means and give suitable loan to whoever needs it. He will be neither frivolous and giving to jesting, nor mournful and melancholy, but will rejoice all his days tranquilly and cheerfully. And so will he comport himself with regard to all his other dispositions. This is the way of the wise. Whoever observes on his dispositions and the mean is termed wise.

Ibid.

Whoever is particularly scrupulous and deviates somewhat from the exact mean in disposition, in one direction or the other, is called a saint. For example, if one avoids haughtiness to the utmost extent and is exceedingly humble, he is termed a saint, and this is the standard of saintliness. If one only departs from haughtiness as far as the mean, and is humble, he is called wise—and this is the standard of wisdom. And so with all other dispositions. The ancient saints trained their dispositions away from the exact mean towards the extremes; in regard to one disposition in one direction; in regard to another in the opposite direction. This was supererogation. We are bidden to walk in the middle paths which are the right and proper ways, as it is said, "and thou shalt walk in His ways" (Deut. 28:9).

How shall a man train himself in these dispositions, so that they become ingrained? Let him practise again and again the actions prompted by those dispositions which are the mean between the extremes, and repeat them continually till they become easy and are no longer irksome to him, and so the corresponding dispositions will become a fixed part of his character. . . . Whosoever walks in this way secures for himself happiness and blessing, as the text says, "In order that the Lord might bring upon Abraham that which He spoke concerning him" (Gen. 18:19).

To those who are sick in body, the bitter tastes as if it were sweet, and the sweet as if it were bitter. Among sick folk, some long and yearn for things unfit for food, such as earth and charcoal, and have an aversion to wholesome foods, like bread and meat—the perversity depending on the severity of the illness. Similarly, human beings whose souls are sick and love evil dispositions, and hate the way that is good and are too indolent to walk therein, and find it exceedingly irksome because of their sickness. And so Isaiah says of such people, "O, they that say of evil that it is good, and of good that it is evil, that turn darkness into light and light into darkness, who take bitter for sweet and sweet for bitter" (Is. 5:20). And of such it is also said, "Who forsake the paths of integrity to walk in the ways of darkness" (Prov. 2:13). What is the corrective for those who are sick in soul? They should go to the wise who are physicians of the soul and they will heal their maladies by instructing them in the dispositions which they should acquire till they are restored to the right path. Of those who realize that their dispositions are bad and nevertheless do not resort to the wise to be cured, Solomon says, "Wisdom and discipline, fools despise" (Prov. 1:7).

Ibid.

THE METHOD OF CURE

What is the method of effecting their cure? If one is irascible, he is directed so to govern himself that even if he is assaulted or reviled, he should not feel affronted. And in this course he is to persevere for a long time till the choleric temperament has been eradicated. If one is arrogant, he should accustom himself to endure much contumely, sit below everyone and wear old and ragged garments that bring the wearer into contempt, and so forth, till arrogance is eradicated from his heart and he has regained the middle path, which is the right way. And when he has returned to this path, he should walk in it the rest of his days. On similar lines, he should treat all his dispositions. If, in any of them, he is at one extreme, he should move to the opposite extreme, and keep to it for a long time till he has regained the right path which is the normal mean in every class of dispositions.

There are some dispositions in regard to which it is forbidden merely to keep to the middle path. They must be shunned to the extreme. Such a disposition is pride. The right way in this regard is not to be merely meek, but to be humble-minded and lowly of spirit to the utmost. And therefore was it said of Moses that he was "exceedingly meek" (Num. 12:3), not merely that he was "meek." Hence, our Sages exhorted us, "Be exceedingly, exceedingly lowly of spirit" (Ethics of the Fathers 4:4). They also said that anyone who permits his heart to swell with haughtiness has denied the essential principle of our religion, as it is said, "And thy heart will be proud, and thou wilt forget the Lord, thy God" (Deut. 8:14). Again they have said, "Under a ban be he who is proud, even in the smallest degree." Anger, too, is an exceedingly bad passion, and one should avoid it to the last extreme. One should train oneself not to be angry even for something that would justify anger. . . . The ancient Sages said, "He who is angry—it is the same as if he worshipped idols." They also said, "One who yields to anger—if he is a sage, his wisdom departs from him; if he is a prophet, his prophetic gift departs from him" (Pes. 63). Those of an irate disposition—their life is not worth living. The sages, therefore, charged us that anger should be avoided to such a degree that one should train oneself to be unmoved even by things that naturally would provoke anger; and this is the good way. The practice of the righteous is to suffer contumely and not inflict it; to hear themselves reproached, not retort; to be impelled in what they do in love, and to rejoice in suffering. Of them Scripture saith, "And they that love Him are like the going forth of the sun in his strength" (Judges 5:31).

One should always cultivate the habit of silence, and only converse on topics of wisdom or on matters of moment to one's existence. Of Rav, disciple of our sainted teacher [R. Judah, the Prince] it was said that throughout his life he never indulged in idle conversation, of which most people's talk consists. And even of our material needs, we should not speak much. In this connection, our wise men charged, "He who multiplies words causes sin" (Ethics of the Fathers, 1:17). They further said, "I have found naught of better service to the body than silence" (Ibid). So too, in discussing Torah and Wisdom, a man's words should be few but full of meaning.

"A fence to wisdom is silence" (Ethics of the Fathers, 3:17). Hence, a man should not be hasty to reply, nor talk much. He should teach his pupils gently and calmly, not shouting, and avoiding prolixity. Solomon said, "The words of the wise, spoken quietly, are heard" (Eccl. 9:17).

Ibid., 2

25. THE MESSIAH AND THE MESSIANIC ERA

The conception and the personality of the Messiah are so heavily freighted with all sorts of bizarre hopes and beliefs, extravagant myths and fancies born largely of the desperate fate of the Jews that it became increasingly difficult to know what Judaism really teaches on the subject. Between the mystic visionaries who had almost deified the Messiah and ascribed to him supernatural powers and the Jewish philosopher who took a more rational view of his origin and activity there is a wide and bewildering gap.

Moses Maimonides, who made the belief in the advent of the Messiah an article of the Jewish faith, takes his stand with Samuel the Babylonian, of the third century who was the author of the remarkable declaration, "The Messianic Era differs from the present in nothing except that Israel will throw off the yoke of the nations and regain its political independence" (Ber. 34b). The Messiah, says Maimonides, will be a mortal human being who will die and will be succeeded by his son who will reign after him. He will excel in wisdom and learning and the fear of God. The world will continue in its usual course; there will be rich and poor, strong and weak, no change in the order of nature or man, except that, freed from oppression, the Jews will be able to devote themselves more completely to the service of God and knowledge of the Torah.

Maimonides entered upon a full discussion of the Messiah and the Messianic Kingdom in his correspondence and throughout his works, notably his Mishnah Commentary *and the* Mishneh Torah, *with some minor references in the* Guide.

THE ROLE OF THE MESSIAH

King Messiah will arise and restore the kingdom of David to its former state and original sovereignty. He will rebuild the sanctuary and gather the dispersed of Israel. All the ancient laws will be reinstated in his days: sacrifices will again be offered; the Sabbatical and Jubilee years will again be observed in accordance with the commandments set forth in the Law.

He who does not believe in the restoration or does not look forward to the coming of the Messiah denies not only the teachings of the Prophets but also those of the Law of Moses, our teacher, for Scripture affirms the rehabilitation of Israel, as it is said: "Then the Lord thy God will turn thy captivity, and have compassion upon thee, and will return and gather thee . . . if any of thine that are dispersed be in the uttermost parts of heaven . . . and the Lord thy God will bring thee unto the land which thy fathers possessed" (Deut. 30:3, 4, 5). These words stated in Scripture include all that the Prophets said. . . . The prophecy in that section bears upon the two Messiahs: the first, namely, David, who saved Israel from the hand of their enemies; and the later Messiah, a descendant of David, who will achieve the final salvation.

Kings, 11

Hence, all Israelites, their Prophets and Sages, longed for the advent of Messianic times, that they might have relief from the wicked tyranny that does not permit them properly to occupy themselves with the study of the Torah and the observance of the commandments; that they might have ease, devote themselves to getting wisdom, and thus attain to life in the World to Come. Because the King who will arise from the seed of David will possess more wisdom than Solomon and will be a great Prophet, approaching Moses, our teacher, he will teach the whole of the Jewish people and instruct them in the way of God; and all nations will come to hear him, as it is said, "and at the end of days it shall come to pass that the mount of the Lord's house shall be established as the top of the mountains" (Micah 4:1, Is. 2:2). The ultimate and perfect reward, the final bliss which will suffer neither interruption nor diminution is the life in the World-to-Come. The Messianic Era, on the other hand, will be realized in this world; which will continue in its normal course except that independent sovereignty will be restored to Israel. The ancient Sages already said, "The only difference between the present and the Messianic Era is that political oppression will then cease."

Repentance, 9

If there arise a king from the House of David who meditates on the Torah, occupies himself with the commandments, as did his ancestor David, observes the precepts prescribed in the Written and the Oral Law, prevails upon Israel to walk in the way of the Torah and to repair its breaches, and fights the battles of the Lord, it may be assumed that he is the Messiah. If he does things and succeeds, rebuilds the sanctuary on its site, and gathers the dispersed of Israel, he is beyond all doubt the Messiah. He will prepare the whole world to serve the Lord with one accord, as it is written: "For then will I turn to the peoples a pure language, that they may call upon the name of the Lord to serve Him with one consent" (Zeph. 3:9).

Kings, 11

ELIJAH IS THE FORERUNNER OF MESSIAH

Some of our Sages say that the coming of Elijah will precede the advent of the Messiah. But no one is in a position to know the details of this and similar things until they have come to pass. They are not publicly stated by the Prophets. Nor have the Rabbis any tradition with regard to these matters. They are guided solely by what the Scripture texts seem to imply. Hence there is a divergence of opinions on the subject. But be that as it may, neither the exact sequence of these events nor the details thereof constitute religious dogmas. No one should ever occupy himself with the legendary themes nor spend much time on midrashic statements bearing on this and like subjects. He should not deem them of prime importance, since they lead neither to the fear of God nor to the love of Him. Nor should one calculate the end. Said the Rabbis: "Blasted be those who reckon out the end" (San. 97b). One should wait [for his coming] and accept in principle this article of faith, as we have stated before.

Kings, 12

Do not think that King Messiah will have to perform signs and wonders, bring anything new into being, revive the dead or do similar things. It is not so. Rabbi Akiba was a great Sage, a teacher of the Mishnah, yet he was also the armor-bearer of Ben Kozba. He affirmed that the latter was King Messiah; he and all the wise men of his generation shared this belief until Ben Kozba was slain in [his] iniquity, when it became known that he was not [the Messiah]. Yet the Rabbis had not asked him for a sign or token.

Ibid., 11

Let no one think that in the days of the Messiah any of the laws of nature will be set aside, or any innovations be introduced into creation. The world will follow its normal course. The words of Isaiah: And the wolf shall dwell with the lamb, and the leopard shall lie down with the kid (Is. 11:6) are to be understood figuratively, meaning that Israel will live securely among the wicked of the heathens who are likened to wolves and leopards. . . . They will all accept the true religion, and will neither plunder nor destroy, and together with Israel earn a comfortable living in a legitimate way.

Said the Rabbis: "The sole difference between the present and the Messianic days is deliverance from servitude to foreign powers" (San. 91b).

Ibid., 12

The Sages and Prophets did not long for the days of the Messiah that Israel might exercise dominion over the world, or rule over the heathens or be exalted by the nations, or that it might eat and drink and rejoice. Their aspiration was that Israel be free to devote itself to the Law and its wisdom, with no one to oppress or disturb it, and thus be worthy of the life of the world to come.

In that era will be neither famine nor war, neither jealousy nor strife. Blessings will be abundant, comforts within the reach of all. The one preoccupation of the whole world will be to know the Lord. Hence Israelites will be very wise; they will know the things that are now concealed, and will attain an understanding of their Creator to the utmost capacity of the human mind, as it is written: For the earth shall be full of the knowledge of the Lord as the waters cover the sea (Is. 11:9).

Ibid.

RESURRECTION, IMMORTALITY, AND LIFE HEREAFTER

Man's craving for life has given rise to the belief in continued existence after death. This oldest and most persistent of beliefs is sustained by the Prophets, supported by the synagogue liturgy, and expresses the deepest hope and longing of millions of men since the beginning of time.

But while Immortality has been universally agreed upon as one of the cardinal principles of the Jewish faith, the belief in Resurrection, or the union of the soul and body after death, has been a heatedly discussed subject among Jewish philosophers. Moses Maimonides involved himself in no end of difficulties when, in his Mishnah *Commentary, he considers the resurrection of the dead as an unalterable article of faith, while ignoring it completely in his great Code. He includes, however, Resurrection among the twenty-four items by the denial of which one forfeits the World-to-Come, leaving the world in a quandary as to what his view on the subject really is.*

The belief in Resurrection had taken too deep root in the Jewish consciousness to be left in doubt by the greatest of Jewish teachers, so that to clarify his thoughts on the subject and to hurl back the charge that he was really skeptical on what was considered a basic creed of Judaism, he wrote his Ma'amar Tehiyat ha-Metim, *or "Treatise on Resurrection." Explaining his position, Maimonides writes:*

The resurrection of the dead is a cardinal point of our religion universally acknowledged by our people, incorporated in our prayers, (composed by wise and inspired men), and to which the Talmud frequently reverts—is capable of no other interpretation than the literal. It would therefore be unJewish to disbelieve that the soul will be reunited with the body, for there has been no dissenting voice raised against it among our nation. The resurrection of the dead, or the reunion of the soul with the body, is mentioned in Daniel (12:2) couched in such words that it is impossible to render them otherwise than according to the very letter: "And many of them that sleep in the dust of the earth shall awake, some to everlasting life, and some to reproach and everlasting abhorrence."

The expression of our Sages allow free scope to the assumption that the bodies restored to life will eat, drink, and generate and die after a prolonged existence, as at the time of the Messiah, but that the life which is not destined to end is that in which the spirit will not be confined in the bodily tenements. This truth is obvious to the mind of every intelligent person, I mean that in the World-to-Come we must be incorporeal as angelic beings. The body ministers to the soul and is directed in all its operations, wherefore has nature supplied it with the means of its own preservation by endowing it with diverse organs, with those of nutrition as the mouth, the stomach, the liver and intestines, with those of procreation, and with the others which complete the corporeal construction, such as the senses, the arteries, the ligaments, the bones, etc., whereby the living being is enabled to go in quest of his food, [and] of whatever is calculated to benefit him [and flee from its opposites]. . . .

It thence follows that when that object is no longer to be attained, the existence of the body is rendered useless. And so it would be indeed after our decease in the World-to-Come when as our Rabbis teach, "neither eating nor drinking nor any of the functions by which the animal economy is carried on will be needed." For to suppose the existence of a body in such a state would be tantamount to saying that the actions of the most Wise are like those of the heathen, who fashioned their idols with eyes that cannot see, with ears that cannot hear, and nose that cannot smell. Aye, we would harbor an irreverent thought if we deemed it possible that He should give us limbs unnecessarily. . . .

What may, in all likelihood, have led men to misjudge us, is the fact, that while we dilate on the dogma of immortality, offering appropriate illustrations from Scriptural and rabbinical authorities, we are, on the contrary, very brief when alluding to resurrection, and content ourselves with the mere assertion that it is an essential creed of our religion. . . . It [resurrection] must be apprehended by our own senses, or credited because related by reliable witnesses. Therefore we expatiate on our future experience in order that the intellect may obviously discover how immortality is a direct consequence of the soul, but are brief, touching the resurrection of the dead, because it demands no explanation at our hands. It is faith and not reason that can persuade us that it will occur, just as we have learned with certainty that other miracles have been performed in our behalf. But as it does not appertain to the natural, no proof can be advanced in support thereof. How, then, could it be expected that we should have discussed it at length? Are we to devote our time in commenting on the legends and tales which were written about that looked-for event? It may suit others to do so, but not ourselves who have invariably avoided launching into polemics. Verily, could we condense the whole Talmud in a single chapter, we would not use two. Hence it is vain to ask of us to introduce in our works all which has been said in parables by our predecessors. A repetition of them would be to no purpose.

When we accurately peruse the Bible, we discover that it abounds in passages that gainsay the resurrection of the dead. For instance,

"Shall a man die and live again?" (Job 14:14). "As the cloud is consumed and vanishes away, so he that goeth down to the grave shall come up no more" (*Ibid.*, 7:19); "Before I go whence I shall not return" (*Ibid.*, 10:21); besides other numerous sentences in the same book. So also did King Hezekiah exclaim: "They that go down into the pit cannot hope for thy truth; but the living, the living, they shall praise Thee" (Isa. 38:18-19), thus demonstrating that "they who go down into the pit" are forever dead. In the same spirit can only be understood the following speech of the wise woman of Tekoah: "For we must needs die and become as water spilled on the ground which cannot be gathered up again" (II Sam. 14:14). So we find likewise: "Shall the dead arise and praise Thee" (Ps. 30:10); "For we remember that they were but flesh, a wind that passeth and cometh not again" (*Ibid.*, 78:12). . . . So it has happened that those contradictions with which Holy Writ is fraught touching resurrection gave rise to a great deal of controversy. Some have altogether doubted the veracity of the dogma, and others who faithfully believe in it were compelled to strain the sense of the verses above quoted.

In solving the query, we would remark that the inspired writings are simply the exponent of the laws which nature has ordained. . . . The decomposition of material substances will be slow, but, nevertheless, so certain that in the lapse of time not one part will be distinguished from the other; but that man into whom God Himself breathed a heavenly spirit which must needs survive the consumption of his body. Such is the gist of the passages above quoted, which coincides with the decision of those who have deeply searched into this momentous topic. Moreover, the sacred pages afford a palpable demonstration of our argument by placing the soul or the spirit in juxtaposition of the body as we read in Ecclesiastes: "The dust shall return to the earth as it was, but the spirit shall return unto God who gave it." So that humanly speaking, the question of Job, "Whether a man that dieth can live again" is not any more startling than that of Moses when he wrathfully exclaimed, "Shall we draw water for you out of this rock?" both the occurrences being naturally beyond the range of possibility. Still through a miracle the water did issue out of the rock, so will also the dead revive by the same marvellous agency. In like manner, there exists no difference between Jeremiah's inquiry, "Whether an Ethiopean can ever change his swarthy skin."

And the ejaculation of the Psalmist, "Will the dead arise and praise Thee" (30:10). Yet in a miraculous manner did once a purely healthy hand assume a snowy white color. . . . Hence we maintain that whenever biblical expressions are in opposition to the dogma of Resurrection, they simply describe natural causes and effects and do not by any means subvert a creed universally accepted because the Almighty can at His will, infuse new life into dead bodies. . . . However, there may be some who agree that a resurrection will take place, but deny the reunion of body and soul, inasmuch as the occurrence is inconceivable to the human mind. But, then, they must needs for the same reason reject all miracles chronicled in Holy Writ by which they would place themselves beyond the pale of Judaism. For whosoever believes that God has created the world out of nothing must concede the possibility of miracles, and surely no one can style himself a follower of Abraham and Moses who doubts that verity. Resting upon the solidity of this argument we have numbered the resurrection of the dead among the essential creeds of our religion.

Ma'amar Tehiyat ha-Metim

THE WORLD-TO-COME

Maimonides was no less severely attacked for his views on immortality and the World-to-Come than he was for his explanation of resurrection. Maimonides had ample support from the Bible and the Talmud to sustain his views, but the longing of the people was greater for the actual literal fulfilment of their craving for life and the delights of heaven than for their philosophical interpretation. As against the prevailing view, Maimonides taught a doctrine of immortality which was the fusion of the purified soul with the original spirit, and a World-to-Come that was denuded of the joys and pleasures of the senses which, credulously, were associated with it. He writes:

The good reserved for the righteous is life in the world to come, —a life which is immortal, a good without evil. Thus it is written in the Torah "that it may be well with thee and that thou mayest prolong thy days" (Deut. 22:7); the traditional interpretation of which is as follows: "that it may be well with thee," in a world altogether good; "that thou mayest prolong thy days," in a world unending, that is, the World-to-Come. The reward of the righteous is that they will attain this bliss and abide in this state of happiness; the punishment of the wicked is that they will not attain this life but will be

405

cut off and die. He who does not attain this life will be dead, in the sense that he will never live again but will be cut off in his wickedness and perish like the brute beast.

Repentance, 8

In the World-to-Come, there is nothing corporeal, and no material substance; there are only souls of the righteous without bodies,—like the ministering angels. And since in that world there are no bodies, there is neither eating there, nor drinking, nor aught that human beings need on earth. None of the conditions occur there which are incident to physical bodies in this world, such as sitting, standing, sleep, death, grief, merriment, etc. So the ancient Sages said, "In the life hereafter, there is no eating, no drinking, no connubial intercourse, but the righteous sit with their crowns on their heads and enjoy the radiance of the Shechinah" (Ber. 17a). This passage clearly indicates that as there is no eating or drinking there is no physical body hereafter. The phrase "the righteous sit"—is allegorical and means that the souls of the righteous exist there without labor or fatigue. The phrase "their crowns on their heads" refers to the knowledge that they have acquired, and for the sake of which they have attained life in the World-to-Come. Thus is their crown, in the same sense as where Solomon says "with the crown wherewith his mother hath crowned him" (Song of Songs 3:11). And just as in the text "Everlasting joy shall be upon their heads" (Is. 35:10), joy is not to be understood as a material substance that actually rests on the head, so "The Crown," of which the Sages here speak, is not to be taken literally but refers to knowledge. And what is the meaning of the Sages' statement: "they enjoy the radiance of the Shechinah?" It means that the righteous attain to a knowledge and realization of the truth concerning God to which they had not attained while they were in the murky and lowly body.

Ibid.

THE WORLD-TO-COME IS NOT A SENSUAL PARADISE

Possibly you may esteem this boon [of life hereafter] lightly, and imagine that the only reward for fulfilling religious precepts and walking consistently in the ways of truth is to enjoy good food and drink; to have intercourse with "beautiful forms"; to wear fine linen and brocade; to dwell in palaces of ivory; to be served on gold and silver plate and enjoy similar things, as indeed those foolish and silly Arabs, who lead dissolute lives, imagine. The wise and intelligent know, however, that all these pleasures are exaggerated and inane, and there is no profit in them. They are regarded by us as a great boon because we are beings with physical bodies and material frames which have need of all these things. The soul only desires and longs for them because they are necessary to the body, and enable it to attain its needs and maintain its health; and when the body ceases to exist, all these things become null and void. As to the blissful state of the soul in the World-to-Come, there is no way on earth in which we can comprehend or know it. For in this earthly existence we only have knowledge of physical pleasure; and it is for this that we long. But the bliss of the life hereafter is exceedingly great, and can only metaphorically be compared with earthly enjoyments. In reality, however, there is no comparison between the bliss of the soul in the life hereafter and the gratification afforded to the body on earth by food and drink. That spiritual bliss is unsearchable and beyond compare. So David said, "How great is Thy goodness which Thou hast laid up for them that fear Thee" (Ps. 31:19).

Ibid.

THE WORLD-TO-COME EXISTS NOW

The reason why the Sages styled it "The World-to-Come" is not because it is not now in existence and will only come into being when this world shall have passed away. That is not so. The World-to-Come now exists, as it is said, "which Thou hast treasured up for them that fear Thee, which Thou hast wrought for them that trust in Thee before the children of men" (Ps. 31:19-20). It is called the world to come only because human beings will enter into it at a time subsequent to the life of the present world in which we now exist with body and soul—and this existence comes first.

Ibid.

The severest retribution beyond which punishment can no further go, is that the soul shall be cut off and not attain the life hereafter, as it is said, "That soul shall be utterly cut off; his iniquity shall be upon him" (Nu. 15:31). This destruction it is to which the prophets metaphorically apply these terms "the Pit of destruction," "Abaddon," "Tophet," "Leech": and all other expressions which connote cessation

407

and destruction are applied to it, because it is a ruin that is irreparable and a loss which is irrecoverable.

How David yearned and longed for the life in the world to come, as it is said, "Had I not believed to see the goodness of the Lord in the land of the living" . . . (Ps. 27:13). The ancient sages taught us that a clear comprehension of the bliss in the life hereafter is unattainable to any man. None but God knows its grandeur, beauty and power. All the boons which the prophets prophesied to Israel only refer to material things that Israel will enjoy in the days of King Messiah, when sovereignty will be restored to Israel. But as for the bliss in the world to come, nought can be compared with, or likened to it. And the prophets did not depict it, so as not to depreciate it by their imaginary picture. Thus Isaiah said, "Eye hath not seen beside Thee, O God, what He prepareth for him that waiteth for Him" (Is. 64:3); that is, the bliss which neither the eye of the prophet nor any one else but God hath seen, He hath prepared for the man who waits for Him. The sages say, "All the prophets only prophesied concerning the days of the Messiah, but the world to come no eye hath seen but Thine, O God."

Ibid.

IN THE LIFE-TO-COME

It is known that the reward for the fulfilment of the commandments and the good to which we will attain if we have kept the way of the Lord, as prescribed in the Law is life in the World-to-Come, as it is said, "That it may be well with thee, and that thou mayest prolong thy days" (Deut. 22:7), while the retribution exacted from the wicked who had abandoned the way of righteousness prescribed in the Torah is excision, as it is said, "that soul shall be utterly cut off; his iniquity shall be upon him" (Nu. 15:31). What, then, is the meaning of the statement found everywhere in the Torah that "if ye obey it will happen to you thus; if you do not obey, it will be otherwise"; and all these happenings will take place in this world, such as war and peace; sovereignty and subjection; residence in the Promised Land, and exile; prosperity in one's activities and failure, and all the other things predicted in the words of the Covenant (Lev. 26. Deut. 28).

All those promises were [once] truly [fulfilled] and will again be so. When we fulfill all the commandments of the Torah, all the good things of this world will come to us. When, however, we transgress the precepts, the evils that are written in the Torah will befall us. But nevertheless, the good things are not the final reward for the fulfilment of the commandments, nor are those evils the last penalty exacted from one who transgresses all the commandments. These matters are to be understood as follows: the Holy One, blessed be He, gave us this Law—a tree of life. Whoever fulfills that is written therein and knows it with a complete and correct knowledge will attain thereby life in the World-to-Come. According to the greatness of his deeds and abundance of his knowledge will be the measure in which he will attain that life.

He has further promised us in the Torah, that, if we observe its behests joyously and cheerfully, and continually meditate on its wisdom, He will remove from us the obstacles that hinder us in its observance, such as sickness, war, famine, and other calamities; and will bestow upon us all the material benefits which will strengthen our ability to fulfill the Law, such as plenty, peace, abundance of silver and gold. Thus we will not be engaged all our days, in providing for our bodily needs, but will have leisure to study wisdom and fulfill the commandment, and thus attain life in the World-to-Come. Hence, after the assurance of material benefit, it is said in the Torah, "And it shall be righteousness unto us, if we observe to do all this commandment before the Lord, our God, as He hath commanded us" (Deut. 6:25). So too, He taught us in the Torah that if we deliberately forsake it and occupy ourselves with temporal follies as the text says, "But Jeshurun waxed fat and kicked" (Deut. 32:15)—the true judge will deprive the forsakers of all those material benefits which only served to encourage them to be recalcitrant, and will send upon them all the calamities that will prevent their attaining life hereafter, so that they will perish in their wickedness. This is expressed in the Torah by the text: "Because thou didst not serve the Lord, thy God, with joyfulness and with gladness of heart, by reason of the abundance of all things, therefore shalt thou serve thine enemy whom the Lord shall send against thee" (Deut. 28:47-48).

Hence, all those benedictions and maledictions are to be explained as follows: If you have served God with joy and observed His way, He will bestow upon you those blessings and avert from you those curses, so that you will have leisure to become wise in the Torah and occupy yourselves therewith, and thus attain life hereafter, and then it will be well with you in the world which is entirely blissful and you will enjoy length of days in an existence which is everlasting. So you will enjoy both worlds—a happy life on earth leading to the life in the World-to-Come. For if wisdom is not acquired and good deeds are not performed here, there will be nought meriting a recompense hereafter, as it is said, "for there is no work, nor device, nor knowledge nor wisdom in the grave" (Eccl. 9:10).

But if you have forsaken the Lord and have erred in eating, drinking, fornication, and similar things, He will bring upon you all those curses and withhold from you all those blessings till your days will end in confusion and terror, and you will have neither the free mind nor the healthy body requisite for the fulfilment of the commandments so that you will suffer perdition in the life hereafter and will thus have lost both worlds—for when one is troubled here on earth with diseases, war, or famine, he does not occupy himself with the acquisition of wisdom or the performance of religious precepts by which life hereafter is gained.

Repentance, 9

26. THE PURPOSE OF LIFE

Man is a composite of body and soul, of flesh and spirit. He has not emerged perfect from the hand of his Creator, but he has been endowed with the capacity of striving after and attaining perfection. This he can do by directing his thoughts on the formation of correct ideas, the acquisition of true knowledge, and the union of his mind with the Divine Intellect.

MAN'S SHORTCOMINGS and sins are all due to the substance of the body and not to its form; while his merits are exclusively due to his form. Thus, the knowledge of God, the formation of ideas, the mastery of desire and passion, the distinction between that which is to be chosen and that which is to be rejected, all these man owes to his form; but eating, drinking, sexual intercourse, excessive lust, passion, and all vices, have their origin in the substance of the body. Now it was clear that this was the case—it was impossible, according to the wisdom of God, that substance should exist without form, or any of the forms of the bodies without substance, and it was necessary that the very noble form of man, which is the image and likeness of God, as has been shown by us, should be joined to the substance of dust and darkness, the source of all defect and loss. For these reasons the Creator gave to the form of man power, rule and dominion over the substance—the form can subdue the substance, refuse the fulfillment of its desires, and reduce them, as far as possible, to just and proper measure.

The station of man varies according to the exercise of this power. Some persons constantly strive to choose that which is noble, and so seek perpetuation in accordance with the direction of their noble part—their form; their thoughts are engaged in the formation of ideas, the acquisition of true knowledge about everything, and the union with the divine intellect which flows down upon them, and which is the source of man's form. Whenever they are led to the wants of the body to that which is low and avowedly disgraceful, they are grieved at their position, they are ashamed and confounded at their situation. They try with all their might to diminish this disgrace, and to guard against it in every possible way. They feel like a person whom the king in his anger ordered to remove refuse from one place to another in order to put him to shame; that person tries as much as possible to hide himself during the time of his disgrace; . . . he perhaps removes a small quantity a short distance in such manner that his hands and garments remain clean, and he himself be unnoticed by his fellow-men. Such would be the conduct of a free man, whilst a slave would find pleasure in such work—he would not consider it a great burden, and throw himself into the refuse, smear his face and his hands, carry the refuse openly, laughing and singing.

This is exactly the difference in the conduct of different men. Some consider, as just said, all wants of the body as a shame, disgrace, and defect to which they are compelled to attend; this is chiefly the case with the sense of touch, which is a disgrace to us, according to Aristotle, and which is the cause of our desire for eating, drinking, and sensuality. Intelligent persons must, as much as possible, reduce these wants, guard against them, feel grieved when satisfying them, abstain from speaking of them, discussing them, and attending to them in company with others. Men must have control over all these desires, reduce them as much as possible, and only retain of them as much as is indispensable. His aim must be the aim of man as man, viz., the formation of ideas, and nothing else. . . . This is man's task and purpose. Others, however, that are separated from God form the multitude of fools, and do just the opposite. They neglect all thought and all reflection on ideas, and consider as their task the cultivation of the sense of touch—that sense which is the greatest disgrace; they only think and reason about eating and love. The whole book of the Proverbs of Solomon treats of this subject, and exhorts to abstain from lust and intemperance. . . . When a man possesses a good sound body that does not overpower him, nor disturb the equilibrium in him, he possesses a divine gift. In short, a good constitution facilitates the rule of the soul over the body, but it is not impossible to conquer a bad constitution by training. For this reason King Solomon wrote the moral lessons; also all the commandments and exhortations in the Pentateuch aim at conquering the desires of the body.

Guide, III, 8

THE USES OF WISDOM

Maimonides analyses the word hakmah *(wisdom) and finds that it stands in the Bible for any number of things. At its highest it connotes intellectual wisdom and perfection in the knowledge of God and instruction in His Law, but it also implies subtlety and cunning planning for evil. Our author distils from* hakmah *the wisdom of and training in correct reasoning for the perfect understanding of the Divine Law.*

The term *hakmah* ("wisdom") in Hebrew is used of four different things; (1) It denotes the knowledge of those truths which lead to the knowledge of God. Comp. "But where shall wisdom be found?" (Job 28:12); "If thou seekest her like silver" (Prov. 2:4). The word occurs frequently in this sense. (2) The expression *hakmah* denotes also knowledge of any workmanship. Comp. "And every wise-hearted among you shall come and make all that the Lord hath commanded" (Ex. 35:10); "And all the women that were wise-hearted did spin" (*Ibid.*, 25). (3) It is also used of the acquisition of moral principles. Comp. "And teach his elders wisdom" (Ps. 105:22); "With the ancient is wisdom" (Ps. 105:22); "With the ancients is wisdom" (Job 12:12); for it is chiefly the disposition for acquiring moral principles that is developed by old age alone. (4) It implies, lastly, the notion of cunning and subtlety; comp. "Come on let us deal wisely with them" (Ex. 1, 10). In the same sense the term is used in the following passages: "And fetched thence a wise woman" (II Sam. 14:2); "They are wise to do evil" (Jer. 4:22). It is possible that the Hebrew *hakmah* ("wisdom") expresses the idea of cunning and planning, which may serve in one case as a means of acquiring intellectual perfection, or good moral principles; but may in another case produce skill in workmanship, or even be employed in establishing bad opinions and principles. The attribute *hakam* ("wise") is therefore given to a person that possesses great intellectual faculties, or good moral principles, or skill in art; but also to persons cunning in evil deeds and principles.

According to this explanation, a person that has a true knowledge of the whole Law is called wise in a double sense; he is wise because the Law instructs him in the highest truths and, secondly, because it teaches him good morals. But as the truths contained in the Law are taught by way of tradition, not by a philosophical method, the knowledge of the Law, and the acquisition of true wisdom, are treated in the books of the Prophets and in the words of our Sages as two different things; real wisdom demonstrates by proof those truths which Scripture teaches us by way of tradition. It is to this kind of wisdom, which proves the truth of the Law, that Scripture refers when it extols wisdom, and speaks of the high value of this perfection, and of the consequent paucity of men capable of acquiring it in sayings like these: "Not many are wise" (Job 32:9); "But where shall wisdom be found?" (Ibid., 28:12). In the writings of our Sages we notice likewise many passages in which distinction is made between knowledge of the Law and wisdom. They say of Moses, our teacher, that he was Father in the knowledge of the Law, in wisdom and in prophecy. When Scripture says of Solomon "And he was wiser than all men" (I Kings 5:2), our Sages add, "but not greater than Moses"; and the phrase, "than all men," is explained to mean, "than all men of his generation"; for this reason [only] "Haman, Chalcol, and Darda, the sons of Mahol," the renowned wise men of that time are named.

Our Sages further say, that man has first to render account concerning his knowledge of the Law, then concerning the acquisition of wisdom, and at last concerning the lessons derived by logical conclusions from the Law, i.e., the lessons concerning his actions. This is also the right order: we must first learn the truths by tradition, after this we must be taught how to prove them, and then investigate the actions that help to improve man's ways. The idea that man will have to render account concerning these three things in the order described, is expressed by our Sages in the following passage: "When man comes to the trial, he is first asked, 'Hast thou fixed certain seasons for the study of the Law? Hast thou been engaged in the acquisition of wisdom? Hast thou derived from one thing another thing?'" (Sab. 31a). This proves that our Sages distinguished between the knowledge of the Law on the one hand, and wisdom on the other, as the means of proving the lessons taught in the Law by correct reasoning.

Guide, III, 54

THE THREE WHO DIED BY A KISS: A LEGEND

The midrashic legend of the three who died by a kiss symbolized for Maimonides the perfect life which, concentrated on the thought and love of God, is spared the fear and anguish of death. The Hebrew wording applied for the death of Moses, Aaron, and Miriam was elaborated by post-biblical legend for which their demise was a favorite theme. They glided out of life, as it were, without regret or remonstrance, God having kissed their souls out of them. (See Louis Ginzberg, The Legends of the Jews, *vol. III).*

The philosophers have already explained how the bodily forces of man in his youth prevent the development of moral principles. In a greater measure this is the case as regards the purity of thought which man attains through the perfection of those ideas that lead him to an intense love of God. Man can by no means attain this so long as his bodily humors are hot. The more the forces of his body are weakened, and the fire of passion quenched, in the same measure does man's intellect increase in strength and life; his knowledge becomes purer, and he is happy with this knowledge. When this perfect man is stricken in age and is near death, his knowledge mightily increases, his joy in that knowledge rises greater, and his love for the object of his knowledge more intense, and it is in this great delight that the soul separates from the body.

To this state our Sages referred, when in reference to the death of Moses, Aaron, and Miriam, they said that death was in these three cases nothing but a kiss. They say thus: "We learn from the words, 'And Moses, the servant of the Lord died there in the land of Moab by the mouth of the Lord'" (Deut. 34:5), that his death was a kiss. The same expression is used with Aaron: "And Aaron, the priest, went up into Mount Hor . . . by the mouth of the Lord, and died there" (Nu. 33:38). Our Sages said that the same was the case with Miriam; but the phrase "by the mouth of the Lord" is not employed, because it was not considered appropriate to use these words in the description of her death as she was a female. The meaning of this saying is that these three died in the midst of the pleasure derived from the knowledge of God and their great love for Him. When our Sages figuratively call the knowledge of God united with intense love for Him a kiss they follow the well-known poetical diction, "Let him kiss me with the kisses of his mouth" (Song I:2).

This kind of death, which in truth is deliverance from death, has been ascribed by our Sages to none but to Moses, Aaron, and Miriam. The other prophets and pious men are beneath that degree; but their knowledge of God is strengthened when death approaches. Of them Scripture says, "Thy righteousness shall go before thee; the glory of the Lord shall be thy reward" (Isa. 58:8). The intellect of these men remains then constantly in the same condition, since the obstacle is removed that at times has intervened between the intellect and the object of its action; it continues forever in that great delight, which is not like bodily pleasure.

Guide, III, 51

THE FOUR GOALS OF LIFE

Here, at the conclusion of his book, in almost tender and beseeching words, Maimonides addresses the reader on the goal and meaning of life. The whole drama of man's longings and ambitions—material possessions and acquisitions, the perfections of health, wisdom, and character—passes before him. The author neither derides nor belittles them. He knows man's need and hunger for them. But they are not the ultimate, durable satisfactions of life man should strain and labor for. Man has written his need of God, his hunger for the Infinite, high above the things he unwisely glories and takes pride in. "But let him that glorieth, glory in this, that he understandeth and knoweth Me," said the Prophet Jeremiah.

The ancient and modern philosophers have shown that man can acquire four kinds of perfection. The first kind, the lowest, in acquisition of which people spend their days, is perfection as regards property; the possession of money, garments, furniture, servants, land, and the like; the possession of the title of a great king belongs to this class. There is no close connection between this possession and its possessor; it is a perfect imaginary relation. When on account of the great advantage a person derives from these possessions, he says, "This is my house, this is my servant, this is my money, and these are my hosts and armies." For when he examines himself, he will find that all these things are external, and their qualities are entirely independent of the possessor. When, therefore, that relation ceases, he that has been a great king may one morning find that there is no difference between him and the lowest person, and yet no change has taken place in the things which were ascribed to him. The philosophers have shown that he whose sole aim in all his exertions and endeavors is the possession of this kind of perfection, only seeks perfectly imaginary

416

and transient things; and even if these remain his property all his lifetime, they do not give him any perfection.

The second kind is more closely related to man's body than the first. It includes the perfection of the shape, constitution, and form of man's body; the utmost evenness of temperament, and the proper order and strength of his limbs. This kind of perfection must likewise be excluded from forming our chief aim; because it is a perfection of the body, and man does not possess it as man, but as a living being; he has this property besides in common with the lowest animal; and even if a person possesses the greatest possible strength, he could not be as strong as a mule, much less can he be as strong as a lion or an elephant. . . . The soul derives no profit whatever from this kind of perfection.

The third kind of perfection is more closely connected with man himself than the second perfection. It includes moral perfection; the highest degree of excellency in man's character. Most of the precepts aim at producing this perfection; but even this kind is only a preparation for another perfection, and is not sought for its own sake. For all moral principles concern the relation of man to his neighbor; the perfection of man's moral principles is, as it were, given to man for the benefit of mankind. Imagine a person being alone, and having no connection whatever with any other person, all his good moral principles are at rest, they are not required, and give man no perfection whatever. These principles are only necessary and useful when man comes in contact with others.

The fourth kind of perfection is the true perfection of man; the possession of the highest intellectual faculties; the possession of such notions which lead to true metaphysical opinions as regards God. With this perfection man has obtained his final object; it gives him true human perfection; it remains to him alone; it gives him immortality, and on its account he is called man. Examine the first three kinds of perfection, you will find that, if you possess them, they are not your property, but the property of others, although, according to the ordinary view, they belong to you and to others. But the last kind of perfection is exclusively yours; no one else owns any part of it. . . . Your aim must therefore be to attain this [fourth] perfection that is exclusively yours, and you ought not to continue to work and weary yourself for that which belongs to others, whilst neglecting your soul till it has lost entirely its original purity through the dominion of the bodily powers over it. The same idea is expressed in the beginning of those poems, which allegorically represent the state of our soul. "My mother's children were angry with me; they made me the keeper of the vineyard; but mine own vineyard have I not kept" (Songs I:6). Also the following passage refers to the same subject, "Lest thou give thine honor unto others, and thy years unto the cruel" (Prov. 5:9).

The Prophets have likewise explained unto us these things, and have expressed the same opinion on them as the philosophers. They say distinctly that perfection in property, in health, or in character is not a perfection worthy to be sought as a cause of pride and glory to us; that the knowledge of God, i.e., true wisdom is the only perfection which we should seek and in which we should glorify ourselves. Jeremiah referring to these four kinds of perfection, says: "Thus saith the Lord: Let not the wise man glory in his wisdom, neither let the mighty man glory in his might, let not the rich man glory in his riches; but let him that glorieth glory in this, that he understandeth and knoweth me" (Jer. 9:22, 23). See how the Prophet arranged them according to their estimation in the eyes of the multitude. The rich man occupies the first rank; next is the mighty man; and then the wise man, that is, the man of good moral principles: for in the eyes of the multitude who are addressed in these words, he is likewise a great man. This is the reason why the three classes are enumerated in this order.

Our Sages have likewise derived from this passage the abovementioned lessons, and stated the same theory that has been explained, viz., that the simple term hakmah as a rule denotes the highest aim of man, the knowledge of God; that those properties which man acquires, makes his peculiar treasure, and considers as his perfection, in reality do not include any perfection; and that the religious acts prescribed in the Law, viz., the various kinds of worship and the moral principles which benefit all people in their social intercourse with each other, do not constitute the ultimate aim of man, nor can they be compared to it, for they are but preparations leading to it. Hear the opinion of our Sages on this subject in their own words. The passage occurs in Bereshit Rabba, and runs thus, "In one place Scripture says, 'And all things that are desirable (hafezim) are not to be compared to her' (Prov. 8:11); and in another place, 'And all things that thou desirest (hafazeha) are not to be compared unto her' "

(*Ibid.* 3:15). By "things that are desirable" the performance of Divine precepts and good deeds is to be understood, whilst "things that thou desirest" refers to precious stones and pearls. Both—things that are desirable and things that thou desirest—cannot be compared to wisdom, but "in this let him that glorieth glory, that he understandeth and knoweth me." Consider how concise this saying is, and how perfect its author; how nothing is here omitted of all that we have put forth after lengthy explanations and preliminary remarks.

Having stated the sublime ideas contained in that Scriptural passage, and quoted the explanation of our Sages, we will now complete what the remainder of that passage teaches us. The Prophet does not content himself with explaining that the knowledge of God is the highest kind of perfection; for if this only had been his intention, he would have said, "But in this let him who glorieth glory, that he understandeth and knoweth me," and would have stopped there; or he would have said, "that he understandeth and knoweth me that I am One," or, "that I have not any likeness," or, "that there is none like me," or a similar phrase. He says, however, that man can only glory in the knowledge of God and in the knowledge of His ways and attributes, which are His actions, as we have shown (Part I:54) in expounding the passage, "Show me now Thy ways" (Ex. 33:13). We are thus told in this passage that the Divine acts which ought to be known, and ought to serve as a guide for our actions, are *hesed* "loving-kindness," *mishpat*, "judgment," and *zedakah*, "righteousness."

Another very important lesson is taught by the additional phrase, "in the earth." It implies a fundamental principle of the Law; it rejects the theory of those who boldly assert that God's providence does not extend below the sphere of the moon, and that the earth with its contents is abandoned, that "the Lord hath forsaken the earth" (Ez. 8:12). It teaches, as has been taught by the greatest of all wise men in the words, "The earth is the Lord's" (Ex. 9:29), that His Providence extends to the earth in accordance with its nature, in the same manner as it controls the heavens in accordance with their nature. This is expressed in the words, "That I am the Lord which exercise loving-kindness, judgment, and righteousness in the earth." The Prophet thus, in conclusion, says, "For in these things I delight, saith the Lord," i.e., my object [in saying this] is that you shall practice loving-kindness, judgment, and righteousness in the earth. In a similar manner we have shown (Part I, 54) that the object of the enumeration of God's thirteen attributes is the lesson that we should acquire similar attributes and act accordingly. The object of the above passage is therefore to declare, that the perfection, in which man can truly glory, is attained by him when he has acquired —as far as this is possible for man—the knowledge of God, the knowledge of His Providence, and of the manner in which it influences His creatures in their production and continued existence. Having acquired this knowledge he will then be determined always to seek loving-kindness, judgment, and righteousness, and thus to imitate the ways of God. We have explained this many times in this treatise.

This is all I thought proper to discuss in this treatise, and which I considered useful for men like you [Joseph Ibn Aknin]. I hope that, by the help of God, you will, after due reflection, comprehend all the things which I have treated here. May He grant us and all Israel with us to attain what He promised us, "Then the eyes of the blind shall be opened, and the ears of the deaf shall be unstopped" (Isa. 35:5); "The people that walked in darkness have seen a great light; they that dwell in the shadow of death, upon them hath the light shined" (*Ibid.* 9:1).

God is near to all who call Him if they call Him in truth and turn to Him. He is found by every one who seeks Him, if he always goes towards Him, and never goes astray. Amen.

Guide, III, 54

APPENDIX

Maimonides' Ethical Testament

Scholars are divided on the authenticity of Maimonides' testamentary letter to his son. Dr. Steinschneider, who first accepted the document as genuine, had afterwards recanted. Graetz found the instrument too diffuse and moralising to measure up to the philosopher's known higher style of writing. What, however, set most critics against the authenticity of the Testament, is the fact that it is addressed to the writer's children, while Maimonides is known to have had only one child, his son, Abraham, his other child, a daughter, having died in her infancy.

Yet, plausible as the arguments may seem to be, they are not in themselves sufficiently conclusive to dismiss the letter out of hand as spurious or in-authentic. Indeed, there is everything in the document to militate against any such assumption. The spirit of Maimonides as philosopher, theologian, and moral and ethical teacher is represented in its almost every line and para-graph. His robust faith in God; his plea for justice, truth and righteousness; his exhortation to seek out the lowly and the downcast and not abash them by reason of one's gifts; his admonition not to become entangled in quarrels and arguments (mahlokot) but practice forbearance in which is "true strength and real victory;" his insistence upon the sanctity of one's word and verbal promise more binding than legal contracts or witnessed deeds, and, lastly, the philosophical reflections of the "Letter" on such matters as Free Will, the Golden Mean, etc.—how Maimonedean these things sound, not tarnished by cheap imitation of other hands! The "Letter" is indeed a human document of the highest value, containing all the elements of Maimonides' spiritual personality. It is addressed, of course, to his "children," by which are meant his son Abraham and his offspring, for the religious and secular guidance of their lives.

421

Maimonides' Ethical Testament, which Steinschneider derived from the Bodleian MS. and published, was translated into English by Israel Abrahams and included in his Hebrew Ethical Wills *(The Jewish Publication Society of America, Philadelphia, 1926).*

I will bless the Lord, who hath given me counsel, and hath led me in the right way. I will make mention of His mercies, according to all that He hath bestowed upon me. He hath chastened me sore, but hath not given me over unto death. He held me by my right hand, and in the shadow of His hand He hid me. From the burdens of fortune's wheel He delivered me, and saved me from life's vicissitudes. In the melting pot of time He tried me, and from the blackness of youth He made me white. From its perverseness He kept me aloof, and from the conflict of passion He hath given me rest. He rebuked the serpent which enticed me, and gave me to taste the sweet. From the dust He raised me, and with princes He hath made me sit. My days have taught me, experience hath made me wise, time hath been my reproof. Thus far hath the Lord blessed and preserved me, granting unto me wisdom beyond my fellows, and enabling me to distinguish between good and evil. My end is in His hand, and He hath made me conscious of it, though I know not how long, nor how short-lived am I! Therefore hath His love stirred me to admonish the children whom He hath graciously bestowed on me, that they may observe the way of the Lord. I would teach them what He hath taught me, bequeath to them the heritage which He gave me, ere He call me away, and His Glory shall gather me in!

Hear me, my children! Blessed be ye of the Lord, who made heaven and earth, with blessing of heaven above, blessings of the deep that croucheth under, blessings of the breasts and of the womb! Be strong and show yourselves men! Fear the Lord, the God of your father, the God of Abraham, Isaac, and Jacob; and serve Him with a perfect heart, from fear and from love. For fear restrains from sin, and love stimulates to virtue. Know that He will bring all to judgement, for what is open and for what is hidden, for good and for evil. He who leads a good life finds good even in this world; for they that see him glorify him and those who know him declare him blessed. And when the tale of his years is full, and he departs from the children of men, he will rejoice in the worthiness of his work and will find comfort. No fear of death will distress him, for he will not be anxious concerning punishment; he will await the good reward, to see the bliss treasured up for them that fear the Lord, and his house will be established for ever. But if a man corrupt his way and pursue evil, evil shall pursue and overtake him and in turn corrupt his conduct farther. They that see him will despise and condemn him in his life-time; and in his death "his flesh grieveth for him, and his soul mourneth over him." For "he departeth in darkness and with darkness is his name covered;" yea, "he shall lean upon his house, but it shall not stand!"

I entreat you to recognize the excellency of light over darkness. Reject ye death and evil, choose ye life and good, for the free choice is given unto you! Accustom yourselves to habitual goodness, for habit and character are closely interwoven, habit becoming as it were second nature. Again, the perfection of the body is an antecedent to the perfection of the soul, for health is the key that unlocks the inner chamber. When I bid you to care for your bodily and moral welfare, my purpose is to open for you the gates of heaven! Conduct yourselves with gravity and decency; avoid association with the wanton; sit not in the streets, sport not with the young, for the fruit thereof is evil. Be found rather in the company of the great and learned, but behave modestly in their presence, occupying the lower seats. Incline your head, and open the ears of your heart to listen and to understand their words, and what they praise and blame; weigh their opinions and thus will ye be set in the right way. Guard your tongue from wearying them, measure your words with judgement, for the more your words the more your errors. Be not supercilious or conceited when with them; be not ashamed to ask explanations, but do so at the right moment and in fitting terms. Ponder well over every word before you utter it, for you cannot recall it afterwards.

Love wisdom, seek her as silver, search for her as for hidden treasures. Be found on the threshhold of the wise, those that learn and those that teach. There obtain your recreation; there take delight in hearing discourse of science and morals, as well as the new thoughts and ingenious arguments of the students. Emulate those who seek knowledge, despise those who have no intellectual curiosity. Whether you ask a question or answer one, speak without haste or obscurity, softly and without stammering. Use refined phrases, let your utterance be clear, tranquil, and apt to the point. Behave as one who wishes to learn and to discover the truth, not as one whose aim is to dispute and win a wordy victory. Attend there in a receptive frame of mind, determined to profit by your attendance; then will study be pleasant and facile. But if you allow your heart to wander hither and thither, you will fail in the main purpose of your attendance, for you will learn nothing, and the heavy confinement will wear out your body. When ye leave the college, realize what you are taking home; grave it on your brain, bind it to your heart! Learn in your youth, when ye eat what others provide; while your mind is still free, and unencumbered with cares; ere the memory lose its vigor. For the time will come when ye will wish to learn but will be unable. And, even if ye do not entirely fail, ye will labor much to little effect; for your mind will lag behind your lips, and when it does keep pace, the memory will not hold fast what the mind attains.

Behold, my counsel is committed into your hand, you may profit much from the study of it to confirm truth, to settle the mind, and to remove doubt. When you find in the Law or the Prophets, or the books of the Sages, a deep text or an obscure saying, which you cannot understand nor can penetrate into its secret; which appears subversive of the corner-stones of the Torah or altogether absurd; do not budge from your faith, let not your mind be confounded. Stand fast in your stronghold, and attribute the fault to yourselves, for it is not a vain thing, and if it be vain, it is because of your lack of understanding. Place it "in a corner" and do not abominate the whole of your faith because you are incompetent to solve a single problem of philosophy. "God understandeth the way thereof, and knoweth its place."

Love truth and righteousness, and cleave to them. Prosperity so obtained is built on a sure rock. Hate falsehood and injustice, lust not after their dainties, for such happiness is built on sand. To one who so acts apply the Scriptural words: "Say unto them that daub a wall with whited plaster, that it shall fall."

Therefore, let truth and righteousness, by which ye may seem to lose, be more lovely in your sight than falsehood and unrighteousness, by which ye may seem to gain. For thus said the Wise Man in his admonition: "Buy the truth, and sell it not." Know that truth and righteousness are adornments of the soul and givers of strength and durability to the body. I have found no remedy for weakness of heart comparable to an infusion of truth and righteousness. Nor could the company of friends, the deep shelter of Ashteroth Karnayim, javelin or coat of mail, give me the same sense of security as the helmet of truth and the shield of righteousness!

So shall it come to pass in the day when I bequeath unto you the possessions which the Creator has preciously bestowed on me, I will hand on to you the honesty of purpose by which God has enabled me to possess this store, for with my staff I crossed over to gain my daily bread and its drink offering, and lo! the Lord has blessed me thus far. Faithfulness has introduced me into places where my kinsmen could not admit me, and has dowered me with more than my fathers had to leave unto me. It has given me authority over men greater and better than I, and I have prospered myself and have been a source of profit to others. Therefore take heed therein, even toward one whose good the Law does not enjoin us to seek. Stand by your words, let not a legal contract or witnessed deed be more binding than your verbal promise, whether publicly or privately given. Disdain reservations and subterfuges, tricks, sharp practices, and evasions. Woe to him that builds his house thereon! For if one getteth riches and not by right, "in the midst of his days he shall leave them and at his end he shall be a fool." Live in sincerity, integrity, innocence! Touch not that which is not yours, be it a small matter or great. Taste not that which is not clearly and decisively your own. Flee from doubtful possessions, treat them as the property of others. Remember that the tasting of the doubtful leads to indifference as to the certain; the little to the great, the inadvertent to the designed, till one becomes a hardened cheat, liar, thief and bandit, from whom men turn hastily away. "The buyer from him will not rejoice, nor the seller mourn." He shall be ashamed in his life and confounded in his death. All this have I seen and laid it to my heart. "He that conceives chaff shall bring forth stubble," but "he that sows according to righteousness shall reap according to mercy." Let your moral life be your pride of lineage, and your loyalty to truth your sufficient wealth, for there is no pedigree noble as virtue, no heritage equal to honor.

Bring near those who are far off, bow to the lowly, and show the light of your countenance to the downcast. Be pitiful to the poor and to the sorrow-stricken. See to it that they share your joys! Help them in your feasts, according to the good hand of the Lord upon you. But beware lest they be put to the blush by reason of your gifts. Never cease to do good to all whom it is in your power to serve, and be on your guard against working ill to any man whatsoever.

Contemn idleness and loathe ease, for these corrupt the body, and lead to all manner of penury and perversity, in pocket and in conversation. They are the ladder to Satan and his servitors. Such is the fruit of pernicious sloth, whereas "in all labour there is profit."

Make not your souls abominable by dissension, which wastes body and soul and substance. And what else remains? I have seen the white become black, the high of station brought low, families smitten sore, princes humiliated from their position, great cities ruined, assemblies dispersed, the pious destroyed, men of faith perish, and the honorable held in light esteem, —all because of contention. Prophets have prophesied, sages have spoken wise words, philosophers have probed, all have dilated on the evils of faction without exhausting the subject. Therefore hate dissension and flee from it; keep aloof from its lovers, its supporters, its admirers. If your own flesh and blood be among the lovers of strife, make yourselves as strangers unto them—ignore your kinship, lest ye be consumed in all their sin. Glory in forbearance, for that is real strength and true victory. If ye seek revenge, perchance ye will not attain it, and your heart will be sick with hope deferred; and ye may add shame to your disgrace, like one who rolleth a stone which returns unto himself. And if ye do attain the sought-for revenge, behold ye have sinned against the Lord! For, realize what the result must be to yourselves! Hatred, a vindictive heart, confusion of mind, sleeplessness, interruption of your work, the exposure of your faults and failings, degeneration in look and speech, destruction of the soul, a devouring jealousy, disturbance of family peace, and in the end remorse!

Therefore, recognize the worth of forbearance. Sanctify yourselves and be ye holy in the eyes of your enemies. They will relent of their animosity, and your soul will be great in their eyes. They will repent and will better their heart, if they be indeed men of heart. If they are hopelessly base, they will be pained that ye are not as despicable as themselves, in that ye do not as they do, and ye will reign over them with the crown of virtue. Behave, then, with humility for it is the ladder to the topmost heights; if ye possess that quality, forbearance itself will not be necessary. There is no ornament so comely as meekness. The Master of the Prophets, Moses, was not so distinguished in Scripture for any of his qualities as for his virtue of humility. Keep a curb on your mouth, a bridle on your tongue. God bestowed the faculty of speech on man, because He loved man above all other creatures; a faculty desirable for understanding and lauding God and declaring His wonders; a gift fitted to help man meditate in His Law, learning and teaching, an instrument by which man might promote peace among human kind. It would be ungrateful to turn good into evil, to utter indecent or lying words and to slander—this is indeed an iniquity to be punished by the Judge!

But make matter subject to mind, the body to the soul, for this subjection is your freedom, here and hereafter! Therefore, as to the body, "further not its evil device," for to minister to its cravings is to increase its demands, until it yearns for the unattainable, and in the end the divine element perishes with it. But if the spirit rule, and the body is dominated and humbled, man will seek nothing beyond the necessary; he will be satisfied with the little and will disdain superfluities; he will be contented in life and comforted in death!

Eat, then, that ye may live, and lay a ban on excess. Do not imagine that abundance of food and drink strengthens the body and expands the mind as though you were dealing with a sack which is filled by what is put therein. The contrary is true. By taking the little food which is easily digested by the natural heat, a man's vigor and health increase, his mind becomes clear and calm. But if he eat more than enough, overtaxing his digestion, his food "is a vile thing, it shall not be accepted." His body is emaciated, his intellect dulled, his purse emptied. Overeating is, in fact, the cause of many maladies. Work before ye eat, rest after ye have eaten. Feed not ravenously, like people afflicted with bulimy; fill not your mouths gulp after gulp without breathing space.

Hate injurious viands as you would hate a foe who seeks to slay you. Eat not in the public ways, do not incessantly nibble like mice, take your meals at fixed hours in your homes. Avoid frequent feastings with young men. The breeding of a man, whether for good or ill, is discerned by his manner at a public banquet. Many a time have I returned to my house hungry and thirsty, because I was aghast at the shame of some of the other guests. Beware of wine, which destroys the strong and degrades the honored. How excellent in my eyes is the ordinance of Jonadab unto his children, yet will I not lay the same command on you; for I have not accustomed you to complete abstinence from wine from your earliest years. But break the strength of the wine with water, and drink it as food not as a pastime. Not without purpose was the shame of Noah written; the record was preserved to point a moral.

Expenditure is divisible into four categories: Profit, Loss, Aversion, Honor. Profit, is the expenditure on the bestowal of loving-kindness, the interest of which ye enjoy while the capital remains. Loss, is expenditure on gambling by which a man loses his money, his dignity, his time. If he win he weaves a spider's web; it is a trespass, certainly he is guilty! Aversion, is the designation of expenditure on food. Honor, is the expenditure on wearing apparel, on which one should spend what he can afford. But eat less than your means allow, enough to keep you alive; loathe gambling, keep aloof from gamblers. Stretch your means beyond their capacity to sow in charity, and reap according to mercy!

Enjoy life in the society of your friends and the wife of your young manhood. Remember the warnings of Scripture against unchastity. "She hath cast down many wounded, yea a mighty host are her slain." Imagine that ye had been in Noah's ark, and be comforted. Never excite desire, and when in the course of nature it comes upon you, satisfy it in the manner ordained by moral rule, to raise up offspring, and perpetuate the human race. Though it is not meet that ye should be dominated by your wives or reveal to them secrets placed in your keeping, you must honor your wives, for they are your honor. "All glorious is the King's daughter within the palace." Serve those who love you, and those near unto you, with your person and your substance, according to the good hand of the Lord upon you. But take heed lest ye serve them with your soul, for that is the divine portion!

CHRONOLOGY OF THE LIFE AND WORKS
OF MOSES MAIMONIDES

1135	Born to his father Rabbi Maimon, an eminent member of the Cordova court and a scion of a distinguished family, on March 30—14th of Nissan—1135.
1148	Given the choice of exile or conversion in course of a fanatical Almohade persecution, the Maimon family chose the migratory life. Undaunted, young Moses continued his studies in rabbinic literature and the sciences.
1151	The Maimon family had a brief respite in Port Almeira, but were forced to retire shortly after when the Almohades captured the place.
1148–58	The ten fruitful years of the youthful scholar. He composed *Ma'amar ha-Ibbur*, a treatise on the Jewish calendar, *Millot ha-Higayon*, a book on Logic, wrote commentaries to several "Orders" (*sedarim*) of the Babylonian Talmud, and began working on the *Mishnah Commentary*, the first of his three masterpieces.
1160	Weary of their nomadic life, the Maimon family passed over into Fez, Morocco, likewise under the fanatical Almohade rule. David, Moses' younger brother, managed the family business in precious stones while Moses continued his researches in Jewish and general scholarship.
1160	When the Jews of Morocco were persecuted and threatened with the alternative of death or conversion, Maimonides (son of Maimon) wrote his famous *Ma'amar Kiddush ha-Shem* ("Epistle on the Sanctification of the Name of God"), or

Iggeret ha-Shemad ("Epistle Concerning Apostasy"), in which he stated his position on sham-apostasy under duress.

1165   Almohade fanatical persecution tightened against the Jews of Morocco, and Maimonides, feeling himself no longer safe in Fez, left with his family for the Holy Land. Their voyage was perilous, but they landed safely at Acco, and visited the holy places in Hebron and Jerusalem.

1166   Conditions in the Holy Land were not conducive to making his home there, so with his father, brother, and sister, he left for Egypt, settling first in Alexandria, and after some time making his home in Fostat, old capital of the country.

1168   Maimonides finished and published his first major work, the *Mishnah Commentary* which, besides explaining and interpreting the Mishnah, he provided it with an extensive Introduction in which he discusses important theological and philosophical problems.

1169   Maimonides had no sooner completed the *Mishnah Commentary* than he began working on his *Mishneh Torah*, or *Yad ha-Hazakah,* Code of Jewish Jurisprudence. He began this work by first establishing the *Taryag,* or the six hundred and thirteen mitzvot—two hundred and forty-eight positive and three hundred and sixty-five negative precepts of the Torah. He wrote the book in the Arabic language and it was published under the title *Sefer ha-Mitzvot,* the "Book of Commandments."

1172   Twelve years after his "Epistle Concerning Apostasy," Maimonides wrote his celebrated *Iggeret Teman,* "Letter to Yemen," occasioned by the persecution of the Jews of Yemen, on the Red Sea, in which he held out consolation to the sufferers and demolished the claims to messiahship of an overly misguided enthusiastic individual.

1173–74   Maimonides suffers the loss of his father, and shortly after his brother David, the principal supporter of the family, went down in a shipwreck in the Indian Ocean together with the family fortune in precious stones he carried with him. Maimonides laments over his severe reverses in a letter to Rabbi Japhet ben Eliahu in Acco, Palestine.

1174   Dynastic changes in Egypt. Last of the Fatimid dynasty died, and Saladin, already Grand Vizier, became the supreme master of Egypt and her widening empire.

1174   Compelled by his brother's death to become the supporter of the family, Maimonides takes up the practice of medicine. Is patronized by Saladin's Grand Vizier Alfadhel, who later appointed him as physician to the Sultan's court.

1174   Maimonides is recognized as head of the Jewish community of Egypt and, indeed, as authoritative head of the Jews in the Moslem world. Plays a leading role in all communal matters, represents the Jews at the Court, is active in the ransom of captives, works for the pacification of Jewish dissident religious groups, and conducts a heavy correspondence with rabbis and communities in Moslem and Christian countries.

1180   Maimonides completes the *Mishneh Torah*, Code of Jewish Jurisprudence, the most brilliant performance in Rabbinic literature. It is the only one of his major works which he wrote in the Hebrew language. The work is arranged in fourteen books, the first, *Sefer ha-Madda*, "Book of Knowledge," dealing with a variety of subjects—problems of metaphysics, philosophy, ethics, and health. Its reception varied, meeting with unbounded enthusiasm on the part of some scholars and severe censure at the hands of other rabbis, particularly Samuel bar Ali of Baghdad who engaged the author in a long and bitter controversy.

1183   Maimonides marries his second wife, a sister of the secretary to Saladin's Court.

1186   She bears him two children, a daughter who died in her infancy, and a son, Abraham, who became his father's greatest joy and happiness. He resembled his father in many respects, but lacked his intellectual stature.

1190   Maimonides completes his philosophical work *Dalalat al-Harin, Moreh Nebukim* in Hebrew, the *Guide for the Perplexed*, which he dedicated to his favorite pupil, Joseph Ibn Aknin. The Hebrew translation, which was done by Samuel Ibn Tibbon under the author's supervision, came too late for Maimonides to see it, as it arrived shortly after he died. A less satisfactory Hebrew translation of the Guide was the work of Judah Alharizi. Not long after its appearance, the book was translated into Latin and circulated all over Christian Europe. The *Guide* was read and quoted copiously by many of the leading scholastic churchmen in Europe. The book is to this day one of the most important and widely-read medieval philosophical works. It saw many editions and translations into most of the cultured languages of the world. Like *Mishneh Torah*, the Guide is also one of the most hotly contested works of Maimonides.

1190–1204   The last fourteen years of Maimonides' life were devoted almost exclusively to the science and practice of medicine. He was as prolific in his medical writings as he was in his philosophical and theological works. Ten books, covering almost every phase of the theory and practice of medicine, are the products of the concluding period of his life. He edited the "Aphorisms" (*Pirke Moshe* in Hebrew) of Hippocrates and Galen, wrote a treatise "Health Regulations" for his royal master, and composed monographs and full-sized books on poisons, hemorrhoids, and sex-hygiene.

1204   Maimonides died on December 13 (the 20th of Tebet), and was buried according to his wish in Tiberias, Palestine, mourned by all, Jews and Moslems.

SELECTED BIBLIOGRAPHY

The Maimonides literature is rich in volume and content, and it is written in almost all European languages. It is particularly well represented in the German language in which the most devoted scientific work was done. Needless to say that the *Rambam* figures extensively in the language in which his greatest work in rabbinic literature was produced. Indeed, outside the Bible and the Talmud, Maimonides is the most written-about author in Jewish literature. In the following bibliography it was aimed to give the nonprofessional Jewish student an opportunity to continue his interest in the subject through the books and language most easily accessible to him.

TRANSLATIONS

BERNARD, HERMAN HEDWIG. *The Main Principles of the Creed of the Jews.* London, 1832.

CHAVEL, CHARLES B. *The Book of Divine Commandments (Sefer ha-Mitzvoth).* Soncino Press. London, 1940.

COHEN, BOAZ. *Moses Maimonides' Letter to Yemen.* American Academy for Jewish Research. New York, 1952.

EFROS, ISRAEL. *Millotha-Higgayon,* English and Hebrew (Maimonides' Treatise on Logic). American Academy for Jewish Research, Proceedings, vol. 8. 1937–1938.

FRIEDLÄNDER, M. *The Guide of the Perplexed.* London, 1881.

GLAZER, SIMON. *Mishneh Torah Yod ha-Hazakah.* vol. 1. Maimonides Publication Co. New York, 1927.

HYAMSON, MOSES. *The Mishneh Torah by Maimonides.* New York, 1937.

GORFINKLE, JOSEPH I. *The Eight Chapters by Maimonides on Ethics.* Columbia University Press. New York, 1912.

MORAIS, S. *A Discourse on the Resurrection of the Dead.* The Jewish Messenger, vol. VI, 1859.

PEPPERCORN, JAMES W. *Laws of the Hebrews from the Mishneh Torah.* London, 1840.

RABIN, CHAIM. Maimonides. *The Guide of the Perplexed,* with an introduction by Julius Guttmann. East and West Library, London, 1952.

YALE JUDAICA SERIES. *The Code of Maimonides.* Yale University Press.

ANTHOLOGIES

COHEN, A. *The Teachings of Maimonides.* London, 1927.

GLATZER, NAHUM N. *In Time and Eternity.* Schocken Books, New York.

———. *Maimonides Said.* The Jewish Book Club. New York, 1942.

SPERO, SHUBERT. *The Faith of a Jew.* Jewish Pocket Books. New York, 1949.

BIOGRAPHIES

BOKSER, BEN ZION. *The Legacy of Maimonides.* Philosophical Library. New York, 1950.

MÜNZ, ISAK. *Maimonides (The Rambam).* Translated by Henry T. Schnittkind. Winchell-Thomas Co. Boston, 1935.

YELLIN, DAVID, and ABRAHAM, ISRAEL. *Maimonides.* Jewish Publication Society of America. Philadelphia, 1946.

ZEITLIN, SOLOMON. *Maimonides, a Biography.* Bloch Publishing Co. New York, 1955.

STUDIES AND ARTICLES

AHAD HA-AM (ASHER GINZBERG). "The Supremacy of Reason." *Essays, Letters, Memoirs.* Translated by Leon Simon. East and West Library. London, 1946.

BARON, SALO W. "The Historical Outlook of Maimonides." Proceedings of the American Academy for Jewish Research, vo.. VI.

———. "Economic Views of Maimonides." *Essays on Maimonides,* Columbia University Press. New York, 1941.

BLUMENFIELD, SAMUEL M. "Towards a Study of Maimonides the Educator." *Hebrew Union College Annual,* vol. 23.

EPSTEIN, I. "Ethical Trends of His (Maimonides') Halachah." *Moses Maimonides 1135–1204.* The Soncino Press. London, 1935.

FELDMAN, W. M. "Maimonides as a Physician and Scientist" (Ibid.).

FEDERBUSH, SIMON, editor, *Maimonides* (in Hebrew and English). World Jewish Congress. New York, 1956.

FRIEDENWALD, HARRY. *The Jews and Medicine,* vol. I. The Johns Hopkins Press. Baltimore, 1944.

FRIEDLAENDER, ISRAEL. "Moses Maimonides." *Past and Present*. Ark Publishing Co. Cincinnati, 1919.

————. "Maimonides as an Exegete" (Ibid.).

————. "Maimonides as a Master of Style" (Ibid.).

GEIGER, ABRAHAM, *Judaism and Its History*. Bloch Publishing Co., N.Y., 1911.

GOLDMAN, SOLOMON. *The Jew and the Universe*. Harper Brothers. New York, 1936.

GRAETZ, H. *History of the Jews*, vol. III. Jewish Publication Society of America, Philadelphia.

HERZOG, ISAAC. "Maimonides as Halachist." *Maimonides*. Soncino Press.

HUSIK, ISAAC. *History of Medieval Jewish Philosophy*. The Macmillan Company. New York, 1918.

JEWISH ENCYCLOPEDIA. Vol. IX.

KAGAN, R. *Jewish Medicine*. Medico-Historical Press. Boston, 1952.

LEWIS, H. S. "Maimonides." *Aspects of the Hebrew Genius*. London, 1910.

MANN, JACOB. *The Jews in Egypt and in Palestine under the Fatimid Caliphs*. Oxford University Press. 1920.

MARX, ALEXANDER. *Essays in Jewish Biography*. The Jewish Publication Society of America, 1947.

MEYERHOF, MAX, in *Essays on Maimonides*. Columbia University Press, 1941.

MINKIN, JACOB S. "Guide for the Perplexed," *The Great Jewish Books*. Horizon Press, Inc. 1952.

————. "Essays on Moses Maimonides" in *Congress Weekly*, December 20, 27, 1954; April 4, June 20, 1955.

ROTH, LEON. *The Guide for the Perplexed*. Hutchinson University Library. London, 1948.

————. *Spinoza, Descartes, and Maimonides*. Oxford, 1942.

————. *The Legacy of Israel*. Oxford, 1927.

SINGER, CHARLES, and SINGER, DOROTHEA WALEY. "The Jewish Factor in Medieval Thought." *The Legacy of Israel*.

WAXMAN, MEYER. *A History of Jewish Literature*, vol. I. Bloch Publishing Co. New York, 1930.

WECHSLER, ISRAEL. "Maimonides the Physician." *The Menorah Journal*, 1936.

WOLFSON, HARRY. Maimonides and Halevi. *Jewish Quarterly Review* (New Series), vol. 1911–1912.

NOTES

1

1. *The Making of the Modern Jew*, Bobbs-Merrill Company, 1933, p. 38.

2. *Man's Own Show: Civilization*, Harper Brothers, 1931, p. 645.

3. Henry Malter, *Saadia Gaon*, Jewish Publication Society of America, 1921, p. 27.

4. *History and Destiny of the Jews*, The Viking Press, 1933, p. 248.

5. *Past and Present*, Ark Publishing Co., 1919, p. 165.

6. *Maimonides* (J.P.S.), 1946, p. 43.

7. Maimon's Letter of Consolation was translated into English in *The Jewish Quarterly Review* (Old Series) in 1890, and in a considerably abridged form in *A Treasury of Jewish Letters*, I, 167–77.

8. *Kobez* II. English Yellin-Abrahams, *Maimonides*, and Franz Kobler, *A Treasury of Jewish Letters*.

9. Nu. 20:12.

10. I K. 19:10.

11. According to a talmudic legend, Isaiah suffered martyrdom at the hands of Manasseh, his son-in-law and king of Judah because he called Israel "a people of unclean lips" (Is. 6:15). See L. Ginzberg, *The Legends of the Jews*, IV, 374.

12. *Ibid.*, Ginzberg, VI, 188.

13. Although Ahab was held up as a warning to sinners, he is also described as displaying noble traits of character (San. 102b). While he was an enthusiastic idolater, he paid great honor to students of the Law, for which reason he was permitted to reign for twenty-two successive years. When he repented, he is said to have undergone fasts and penances for a long time, praying to God for forgiveness.

14. Ginzberg, *Legends*, IV, 300.
15. Kohelet R. 7, 26.
16. S. Schechter, *Studies in Judaism*, First Series, 1911, p. 108.

2

1. *Mishneh Torah: Kings*, 5, 7.
2. *The Jews in Egypt and in Palestine under the Fatimid Caliphs*, Oxford University Press, vol. I.
3. *History of the Jews* (English), vol. III.
4. *Judaism and Its History*, Bloch Publishing Co., 1911.
5. *Kobez*, 163.
6. *Kobez* II. In the same letter Maimonides informs him of the death of his infant daughter.
7. Salo W. Baron, *The Jewish Community*, III, 181.
8. *Essays in Jewish Biography* (J.P.S.), 1947, p. 92.
9. *Kobez* II, and Graetz (Hebrew), IV, 338.
10. In his letter to Japhet, Maimonides broadly hints at informers against him.
11. George Foot Moor, *Judaism*, Harvard University Press, 1927, I, 157.
12. Git. 59a.; San. 36a.

3

1. In *Moses Maimonides, 1135–1204*, The Soncino Press, London, 1935.
1b. While Maimonides was undoubtedly influenced by Aristotle in his doctrine of the *Golden Mean*, which figures prominently as an important ethical principle in *Sefer ha-Madda*, the *Eight Chapters*, and the *Guide*, it is rather surprising that he failed to mention its parallel in rabbinic literature, stated unmistakenly in Tal. Jer., *Hagigah* 2:1. "The Torah," it is said there, "is likened unto two paths, one of fire and one of snow. Incline to one and you freeze, to the other and you burn; it is best, therefore, to walk in the middle." Comp. Krochmal, *Moreh Nebuke Hazman*, chap. 2.
2. Shab. 25b.
3. Deut. 30:15, 19.
4. Columbia University Press.
5. Deut. 4:6.
6. Shab. 30b.
7. Ket. 111b.
8. B.B. 74b.
9. Ber. 34b.

10. Ab. 1, 3.

11. Ps. 112:1.

12. Aboda Zara 19a.

13. Is. 26:19.

14. Ab. 4, 22.

15. *Kobez* II. Translated into English under, "A Discussion on the Resurrection of the Soul," by S. Morais, *The Jewish Messenger*, vol. VI, No. 11 (82–83), 1859.

16. Ber. 17a.

17. Is. 64:3.

18. Ber. 34b.

19. *Essays on Maimonides*, edited by Salo W. Baron, Columbia University Press.

20. See Joseph Sarachek, *Don Isaac Abravanel*, Bloch Publishing Co., 1938, p. 148.

21. *Studies in Judaism* (First Series), 1915, p. 164.

22. *Darke ha-Mishnah*, Warsaw, 1923.

23. Jer. 3:13.

24. Introduction, p. 40.

25. *Ibid.*, p. 39.

4

1. Jer. 35:2.

2. *Jewish Encyclopedia*, vol. X.

3. Jer. 31.

4. The "Letter," written in 1172, saw several translations into Hebrew, and because of its considerable length, appeared in a number of abridged English renditions. We follow the one done by Dr. Boaz Cohen, *Moses Maimonides' Epistle to Yemen*, American Academy for Jewish Research, New York, 1952.

5. Ber. R., 98, 3.

5

1. Edited by Rabbi Chaim Heller; translated by Rabbi Charles R. Chavel, The Soncino Press, London, 1940.

2. *History of the Jews* (English), III, 466.

3. *Ibid.*, p. 467.

4. *Past and Present* (above), p. 178.

5. In *Aspects of the Hebrew Genius*, edited by Leon Simon, London, 1910.

6. *Kobez* II. Friedlaender (above), p. 219.

7. *Ibid. A Treasury of Jewish Letters,* I, 215–16.
8. *Kobez* II. Translation from above, p. 199.
9. *Moses Maimonides,* The Soncino Press, London.
10. Yale Judaica Series, vol. VIII.
11. *Ibid.,* vol. II.
12. *Ibid.,* vol. IIII.
13. *Ibid.,* introduction, p. xxii ff.

6

1. Letter to Hasdai ha-Levi, *Kobez* II.
2. Slaves (Yale Judaica Series), V, 9, 8.
3. Gen. 18:19.
3a. *Matnot Aniyim* 10:2.
4. *Matnot Aniyim,* 10:4.
5. Hag. 5a.
6. *Ibid.*
7. Ps. 41:2.
8. Lev. R. 39, 1.
8a. *Matnot Aniyim,* 10.
9. *Guide* II, 40.
10. *Ibid.,* III, 54.
11. *Repentance,* 3.
12. *Theft,* IX, 7, 12.
13. Ket. 50a.
14. Introduction to *Mishneh Torah.*
15. *Jewish Encyclopedia,* I, 103.
16. *Essays in Biography.*
17. *Kobez* I, 140.
18. *Ibid.,* 154.
19. Graetz, *History of the Jews* (English), III, 476–77.
19a. *A Treasury of Jewish Letters.*
19b. *Ibid.*
20. *Essays on Maimonides,* Columbia University Press.
21. *Kobez* II; S. Morais, *The Jewish Messenger,* XX, No. 6, 1859.
22. Gustav Karpeles, *Jewish Literature* (J.P.S.), p. 165.
23. *Kobez* II; *"A Treasury,"* etc., vol. I.

7

1. *Judaism and Its History,* p. 353.
2. *The Legacy of Israel,* Oxford, 1927, pp. 272–73.

3. *Ibid.* In 1655 appeared Pocock's *Porta Mosis*, containing six sections of Maimonides' *Commentary on the Mishnah and Mishneh Torah.* John Selden, one of the most learned men of his time, had an extensive knowledge of biblical and rabbinic literature, and was a particular devotee of Maimonides.

4. *Moses Maimonides,* The Soncino Press, 1935.

5. *A Treasury of Jewish Letters,* I, 214–15.

6. *Essays, Letters, Memoirs of Ahad Ha-Am,* translated from the Hebrew by Leon Simon, East and West Library, Oxford, 1946.

7. *A History of Medieval Jewish Philosophy,* The Macmillan Company, 1918.

8. *Maimonides,* Introduction, East and West Library, London.

9. *The Guide for the Perplexed.* Hutchinson's University Library, London.

10. *Ibid.,* note 8.

11. "As a matter of fact," writes Dr. A. A. Roback *(Jewish Influence on Modern Thought),* "I should ascribe his curvature of the spine to congenital causes, for it is known that at least one of his daughters possessed the same defect in a slighter degree."

12. Above, note 6.

13. *Moses Maimonides,* The Soncino Press.

14. Introduction to the *Guide.*

14a. *Ibid.*

15. *Kobez,* translation, *A Treasury of Jewish Letters.*

16. Jacob S. Raisin, *The Haskalah Movement* (J.P.S.), 1913.

17. London, 1881.

18. Introduction to the *Guide.*

19. *Guide* I, 33.

20. *Ibid.*

21. A. Geiger. *Judaism and Its History.*

22. See "Attributes" in Part II.

23. *Guide* II, 15.

24. *Ibid.*

25. *Guide* II, 29.

26. Ab. 4:15.

27. *Eight Chapters,* 8.

28. *Moses Maimonides,* The Soncino Press.

29. Jer. 1:6.

30. *Guide* III, 31.

31. *The Legacy of Israel,* p. 358.

31a. Maimonides' professed contempt for history, which he characterized as "idle gossip" (end of *Abot,* 1), seems to be in flat contradiction to his acknowledged wide reading and intimate acquaintance with the cultural history and religious customs and practices of ancient civilizations, especially those of the Sabeans.

32. *Guide* III, 49.
33. *Ibid.*
34. *Ibid.*
35. *Ibid.*, 48; Ber. 25a.
36. Lev. R. 22:5.
37. *Guide* III, 32.
38. *Ibid.*
39. *Guide* III, 52.
40. *Ibid.*
41. Jer. 9:23.

8

1. *Kobez* I. Dr. Harry Friedenwald, *The Jews in Medicine*, The Johns Hopkins Press, I, 200.
2. Will Durant, *The Age of Faith*, Simon and Schuster, p. 246.
3. *Ibid.*, p. 247.
4. Deut. 4:15.
5. II Ch. 16:12.
6. Mish. Kid. IV, 14.
7. Pes. 13a.
8. San. 17b.
9. B.M. 85b.
10. *The Legacy of Islam*, Oxford, p. 193.
11. *The Menorah Journal*, 1936.
12. Maimonides also wrote a commentary on the *Aphorisms* of Hippocrates.
13. *The Jews and Medicine* (Friedenwald), vol. I.
14. *Bulletin of Cleveland Medical Library*, January, 1955.
15. *The Canadian Jewish Chronicle* (Montreal), April 12, 1935.
16. Dr. Kagan, *Jewish Medicine*, Boston, 1952.
17. *Moses Maimonides*, The Soncino Press.
18. Maimonides to the Rabbis of Lunel, circa 1199 or 1200.
19. Maimonides' letters to Ibn Tibbon (*Kobez* II) has seen several translations. We follow by permission Kober's rendition in "*A Treasury*," etc.
20. I Sam. 4:22.

INDEX